Surviving the Islamic State

Columbia Studies in Middle East Politics

Columbia Studies in Middle East Politics

MARC LYNCH, SERIES EDITOR

Columbia Studies in Middle East Politics presents academically rigorous, well-written, relevant, and accessible books on the rapidly transforming politics of the Middle East for an interested academic and policy audience.

Mayors in the Middle: Indirect Rule and Local Government in Occupied Palestine, Diana B. Greenwald

Smugglers and States: Negotiating the Maghreb at Its Margins, Max Gallien

The Suspended Disaster: Governing by Crisis in Bouteflika's Algeria, Thomas Serres

Syria Divided: Syria Divided: Patterns of Violence in a Complex Civil War, Ora Szekely

Shouting in a Cage: Political Life After Authoritarian Cooptation in North Africa, Sofia Fenner

Security Politics in the Gulf Monarchies: Continuity Amid Change, David B. Roberts

Classless Politics: Islamist Movements, the Left, and Authoritarian Legacies in Egypt, Hesham Sallam

Lumbering State, Restless Society: Egypt in the Modern Era, Nathan J. Brown, Shimaa Hatab, and Amr Adly

Friend or Foe: Militia Intelligence and Ethnic Violence in the Lebanese Civil War, Nils Hägerdal

Jordan and the Arab Uprisings: Regime Survival and Politics Beyond the State, Curtis Ryan

Local Politics in Jordan and Morocco: Strategies of Centralization and Decentralization, Janine A. Clark

Religious Statecraft: The Politics of Islam in Iran, Mohammad Ayatollahi Tabaar

Protection Amid Chaos: The Creation of Property Rights in Palestinian Refugee Camps, Nadya Hajj

From Resilience to Revolution: How Foreign Interventions Destabilize the Middle East, Sean L. Yom

Sectarian Politics in the Gulf: From the Iraq War to the Arab Uprisings, Frederic M. Wehrey

The Arab Uprisings Explained: New Contentious Politics in the Middle East, edited by Marc Lynch

Surviving the Islamic State

Contention, Cooperation, and Neutrality in Wartime Iraq

AUSTIN J. KNUPPE

Columbia
University
Press
New York

Columbia University Press
Publishers Since 1893
New York   Chichester, West Sussex
cup.columbia.edu

Copyright © 2024 Columbia University Press
All rights reserved

Library of Congress Cataloging-in-Publication Data
Names: Knuppe, Austin James, author.
Title: Surviving the Islamic State : contention, cooperation, and neutrality in wartime Iraq / Austin J. Knuppe.
Description: New York : Columbia University Press, [2024] | Series: Columbia Studies in Middle East Politics / Marc Lynch, series editor | Includes bibliographical references and index.
Identifiers: LCCN 2023056146 (print) | LCCN 2023056147 (ebook) | ISBN 9780231213868 (hardback) | ISBN 9780231213875 (trade paperback) | ISBN 9780231560078 (ebook)
Subjects: LCSH: Iraq—Politics and government—21st century. | Iraq—History—2003- | Islam and politics—Iraq. | Political violence—Iraq. | Survival—Iraq. | Government, Resistance to—Iraq. | Autonomy and independence movements. | Forced migration—Iraq. | Combatants and noncombatants (Islamic law) | Collaborationists—Iraq.
Classification: LCC JQ1849.A58 K58 2024 (print) | LCC JQ1849.A58 (ebook) | DDC 956.7044/3—dc23/eng/20240118
LC record available at https://lccn.loc.gov/2023056146
LC ebook record available at https://lccn.loc.gov/2023056147

Cover design: Elliott S. Cairns.
Cover image: Mosul riverside facade, March 2018.
   Courtesy of Ali Y. Al-Baroodi.

To my Iraqi friends in Canada, Germany, Iraq, Jordan, Lebanon, and the United States who made this project possible.

يُبَارِكُكَ الرَّبُّ وَيَحْرُسُكَ.
يُضِيءُ الرَّبُّ بِوَجْهِهِ عَلَيْكَ وَيَرْحَمُكَ.
يَلْتَفِتُ الرَّبُّ بِوَجْهِهِ إِلَيْكَ وَيَمْنَحُكَ سَلاماً.
العدد 6:24-26

Contents

List of Figures xi
List of Tables xv
Acknowledgments xvii
List of Abbreviations xxi
Note on Transliteration xxiii

1 How Do Ordinary People Survive War? 1

2 Survival Repertoires in Wartime 19

3 The Rise and Fall of the Islamic State, 2011–2017 47

4 Baghdad: Surviving War in the City of Peace 71

5 Fallujah, Ramadi, and Tikrit: Navigating Violence in the Sunni Triangle 106

6 Ninewa Plains, Sinjar, and Tal Afar: Resilience in the Land of Two Rivers 135

7 "We Have on This Land That Which Makes Life Worth Living" 162

Appendix A. Survey Methodology 181
Appendix B. Interview Methodology 201
Notes 205
Bibliography 243
Index 271

Figures

Figure 1.1. Map of Iraq. 8
Figure 2.1. Survival repertoires in wartime. 21
Figure 2.2. How do civilians survive insurgent control? 31
Figure 3.1. "Significant activity" events in Baghdad (January 2006–December 2009). 50
Figure 3.2. Civilian fatalities in Iraq (January 2003–December 2017). 52
Figure 3.3. Islamic State attacks by subdistrict (2016–2018). 65
Figure 4.1. Civilian fatalities in Baghdad Governorate (2014–2018). 76
Figure 4.2. IDP arrivals over time across Baghdad Governorate (2013–2018). 80
Figure 4.3. Network of IDP inflows across Baghdad Governorate (2014–2018). 81
Figure 4.4. Returnees by district over time across Baghdad Governorate (2014–2018). 82
Figure 4.5. Survey interviews occurred across twenty-seven Baghdad neighborhoods. 84
Figure 4.6. Respondent demographic characteristics. 85
Figure 4.7. Iraq national election results (2005–2018). 87
Figure 4.8. "How much confidence do you have in [group name] to improve the security situation in Iraq?" 88

Figure 4.9. "Do you prefer that future security cooperation between Iraq and [country] [become stronger/become weaker/stay the same]?" 89

Figure 4.10. Respondents were opposed or indifferent to foreign intervention by neighboring states. 91

Figure 4.11. Support for foreign intervention changes based on local violence conditions. 92

Figure 4.12. Support for intervention tactics changes based on intervener identity. 93

Figure 4.13. Support for the anti-IS coalition varies based on social identity and intervention tactics. 94

Figure 4.14. Respondents preferred that foreign intervention assist the Iraqi Army instead of the Kurdish Peshmerga. 96

Figure 4.15. Respondents in insecure neighborhoods preferred the support of foreign military trainers. 97

Figure 4.16. Major public protests in Baghdad (2011–2019). 101

Figure 4.17. "To what extent are you satisfied with the government's performance?" 102

Figure 4.18. "What are the most important challenges Iraq is facing today?" 103

Figure 4.19. "Do you prefer future security relations between and Iraq and the U.S. to [become stronger/become weaker/stay the same]?" 104

Figure 5.1. Map of the "Sunni Triangle." 108

Figure 5.2. Civilian fatalities in western Iraq (2014–2016). 112

Figure 5.3. Network of IDP flows from the Sunni Triangle (2014–2018). 114

Figure 5.4. IDP inflows by district across the Sunni Triangle (2014–2020). 115

Figure 5.5. Returnees by district across the Sunni Triangle (2014–2020). 119

Figure 6.1. Map of Ninewa Governorate and the Kurdistan Region. 139

Figure 6.2. Civilian fatalities in Ninewa Governorate (2014–2018). 142

Figure 6.3. IDP arrivals by district over time across Ninewa Governorate and the Kurdistan Region (2013–2018). 145

Figure 6.4. Network of IDP flows across Ninewa Governorate (2014–2018). 146

Figure 6.5. Returnees by district over time across Ninewa Governorate (2014–2018). 148
Figure A.1. How can researchers measure sensitive beliefs and attitudes using surveys in conflict zones? 182
Figure A.2. Distribution of questionnaire response similarity. 189
Figure A.3. Covariate balance for endorsement experiment. 194
Figure A.4. Sensitivity analysis for endorsement experiment. 195
Figure A.5. Treatment effects of each attribute level remain stable across five choice tasks. 199

Tables

Table 2.1.   Threat detection heuristics   27
Table 2.2.   Contentious repertoires   33
Table 2.3.   Neutral repertoires   38
Table 2.4.   Cooperative repertoires   42
Table 4.1.   Deadliest Islamic State attacks on Baghdad (2014–2017)   77
Table 5.1.   Anti-regime protests in western Iraq (2005–2018)   110
Table 5.2.   Sunni tribal resistance against the Islamic State (2011–2017)   124
Table 6.1.   Collaboration between Ninewa self-defense groups and the anti-IS coalition   152
Table A.1.   Question wording for the endorsement experiment (English)   183
Table A.2.   Conjoint experiment attributes   184
Table A.3.   Censored conjoint profiles   185
Table A.4.   Description of control variables in survey experiments   187
Table A.5.   Overview of multistage sampling design   188
Table A.6.   Enumerator characteristics   188
Table A.7.   Enumerator effects   189
Table A.8.   Description of incomplete interviews   190
Table A.9.   Support for security assistance by foreign intervener   191
Table A.10. Respondent sect and support for foreign intervention   192

Table A.11. District-level insecurity and support for foreign intervention 193
Table A.12. Covariate balance in endorsement experiment 194
Table A.13. Sensitivity analysis for endorsement experiment 195
Table A.14. How sensitive is conjoint analysis to sample size? 197
Table A.15. Foreign intervener randomization 198
Table A.16. Coalition member randomization 198
Table A.17. Intervention tactic randomization 198
Table A.18. Randomization in average marginal component effects by choice task 200
Table B.1. Descriptive statistics for key informant interviews 203

Acknowledgments

In a riff on the immortal words of New York Yankees legend Yogi Berra, academic research is "90 percent mental, and the other half is physical." While my name alone appears on the cover, this book is the result of professional and personal debts accrued over the past decade. At risk of leaving someone out, the following is my best attempt to acknowledge those who helped me complete this project.

The team at Columbia University Press, especially Caelyn Cobb, Marisa Lastres, and Monique Laban, provided a great environment for a first-time author to learn the ropes of academic publishing. Thanks to them and their staff for their help during the production process. Two anonymous reviewers offered incisive and helpful feedback during the publication process. As series editor, Marc Lynch provided a helpful sounding board from proposal to publication.

The University of Denver's Josef Korbel School of International Studies proved to be a great environment in which to host a manuscript review. A special debt of gratitude is due to Deborah Avant, Cullen Hendrix, Tiina Hyyppä, Oliver Kaplan, and Andrea Stanton for their sustained engagement with the manuscript. The Korbel Research Seminar also provided a welcome forum to discuss one of the book's empirical chapters. Special thanks to Audrey Elliott for serving as discussant, as well as Naaz Barma, Jack Donnelly, Lewis Griffith, and Tim Sisk for their comments.

Utah State University's Political Science Department has been a great place to begin my career. Damon Cann, Colin Flint, Greg Goelzhauser, Jeannie Johnson, Michael Lyons, John Pascarella, and Josh Ryan provided a warm welcome to Logan as I moved in the middle of the pandemic. Anna Pechenkina included me in her academic networks even before I joined the department, and has provided valuable feedback on various iterations of this project. Steve Sharp patiently read early drafts of several of the chapters and provided cogent feedback on both content and prose. Nicole Vouvalis and her team in the Office of Research provided vital assistance on an ethics review of the fieldwork. Zoe Denison, Kaitlin Holden, Hailey Parker, Jacob Sagers, Eden Ward, and Spencer Wing provided excellent research assistance at various stages of the project.

The John Sloan Dickey Center for International Understanding at Dartmouth College provided an environment that allowed me to transition from graduate student to assistant professor. I owe a special debt of gratitude for Jeff Friedman's mentorship, as well as Katy Powers for welcoming a fellow Buckeye to Hanover. My cohort mates, especially Kolby Hanson, Cullen Nutt, and Jen Spindel, proved to be not only smart colleagues, but wonderful people. An early draft of the Baghdad chapter received valuable feedback from the Dickey research seminar. Special thanks to Steve Brooks, Tom Candon, Charlie Glaser, Jenny Lind, Jay Lyall, Nick Miller, Daryl Press, Ben Valentino, and Bill Wohlforth for their comments and critiques.

Several friends and colleagues in Jordan, Lebanon, and Iraq—as well as in the Iraqi diaspora in Europe and North America—provided help with travel logistics, research, and Arabic language training. Thanks to Munqith Dagher, Rand Dagher, Arwa Dagher, and Omar Saleh at the Independent Institute and Administration Civil Society Studies for their help with the Baghdad survey and key informant interviews in Fallujah, Ramadi, Mosul, and Tikrit. Mariam Tadros and the rest of the Tearfund country office in Erbil were instrumental in arranging my first trip to the field. Additional thanks to Aram Habeeb for his insights and assistance with transcribing interviews and focus group discussions. In Columbus, Ohio, Ahmed al-Haek and the Iraqi Community Center of Central Ohio were important in helping me develop the first draft of the survey questionnaire. Lobna Ghabayen, Afnan Khateeb, Marite Lebaki, and Mostafa Ouajjani provided great Arabic language instruction along the way.

ACKNOWLEDGMENTS xix

The Ohio State University provided a great intellectual and personal support network during graduate school. Chris Gelpi was generous with his time and intellectual energy as he helped me refine my research question, argument, and analysis. Bear Braumoeller served as a mentor from the minute I accepted an offer to study at Ohio State in January 2012, and since then has taught me much about developing good research questions, writing well, and navigating the discipline as an emerging scholar. While he passed away shortly before this book was published, his memory provided the motivation to see the project to the finish line. William Minozzi was instrumental in shaping my interest in political methodology. More importantly, however, William took great care in checking in on me as a person. Bradley Holland provided detailed feedback on drafts of various chapters and served as a helpful sounding board for how to connect concepts and theory at the intersection of international relations and comparative politics. Karl Kaltenthaler graciously agreed to serve as an outside committee member. As the Middle East politics expert, Karl also helped me navigate fieldwork in the Middle East, including all the joys and frustrations of collecting data in conflict zones. A special thanks to Teri Murphy for providing valuable feedback on how to conduct conflict-sensitive research.

For all my complaints about graduate student life, very few are related to Ohio State. Numerous faculty members were generous with their time, ideas, and energy, including Larry Baum, Sarah Brooks, Skyler Cranmer, Rick Herrmann, Vlad Kogan, Marcus Kurtz, Erin Lin, Jennifer Mitzen, John Mueller, Michael Neblo, Irfan Nooruddin, Jan Pierskalla, Amanda Robinson, Randy Schweller, Alex Thompson, Daniel Verdier, Alex Wendt, and Tom Wood. Several friends provided a great support network, including Raphael Cunha, Marina Duque, Andy Goodhart, Adam Lauretig, Daniel Kent, Eleonora Mattiacci, Jason Morgan, Ruthie Pertsis, Dan Silverman, Greg Smith, Josh Wu, and Iku Yoshimoto. Special recognition goes to my fellow cohort members, including Jose Fortou, Reed Kurtz, Anna Meyerrose, Drew Rosenberg, and Avery White.

Outside of Ohio State, a host of friends and colleagues provided valuable feedback on various parts of the project. Special thanks belong to Manuel Almeida, Sonia Alonso, Nick Anderson, Bruce Berglund, Eli Berman, Steve Biddle, Graeme Blair, Hal Brands, Jay Buddhika, Matt Buehler, Sarah Bush, Matt Cancian, Jon Caverley, Luke Condra, Jesse Driscoll, Jeff Hass,

Doug Howard, Kristen Fabbe, Peter Feaver, Sharan Grewal, Will Inboden, Dan Jacobs, Renanah Miles Joyce, Josh Yousif Kalian, Mehran Kamrava, Josh Kertzer, Greg Kruczek, David Lake, Dave Lewis, Charles Lipson, Aila Matanock, Franky Matisek, Paul Miller, Mike Poznansky, Nuno Monteiro, Matthew Nanes, Gerd Nonneman, Tim Oliver, Bob Pape, Michael Reese, Mara Revkin, Justin Schon, Jake Shapiro, Travis Sharp, Matthias Staisch, Paul Staniland, Bob Trube, Austin Wright, Joel Westra, and Tom Wright. I would also like to acknowledge the generous financial support of the Charles Koch Foundation, the Mershon Center for International Security Studies, the Ohio State Decision Science Collaborative, the United States Institute of Peace, and Utah State University's College of Humanities and Social Sciences.

A final thanks goes to close friends and family. Joel Benedetti, Matt Hirdes, Nathaniel Fischer, Jonathan Fischer, and Steven Keil remind me on a regular basis that I am more valuable than my academic sinecure. As adopted parents and close family friends, Steve and Donna Wickersham have encouraged me at each step in my academic journey. My in-laws, Hugh and Sally Reid, have been a great support in all my academic pursuits since the time they entered my life in August 2007. My parents, Marty and Sue Knuppe, have encouraged me to pursue discernment, integrity, and wisdom. My four younger sisters—Catherine, Lauren, Shaylynn, and Victoria—serve as regular reminders to not take myself too seriously. Adding four new brothers-in-law to the mix added some much-needed humor. Thanks to Ben, Tyler, Joseph, and Jordan for joining the Knuppe clan. Lucas Wehner, my German "brother," has been a close friend since high school and has made Germany a second home for the Knuppe family.

My wife, Amy, and sons, Elliott and Ethan, have incurred the greatest debt in my academic journey. Amy has supported my career for the better part of a decade without complaint or objection. Her ability to balance her own career, our relationship, and motherhood is an inspiration. Elliott's birth in January 2017 came as a welcome distraction from academia and a reminder about what is truly important in life. Ethan's arrival on the precipice of the COVID-19 pandemic was another unexpected joy. Pursuing a life of the mind would not have been possible without them tending to my heart. I love you three.

Soli Deo gloria

Abbreviations

AAH	Asaʾib Ahl al-Haq (League of the Righteous)
AQI	al-Qaʿida in Iraq
CJTF-OIR	Combined Joint Task Force—Operation Inherent Resolve
COIN	counterinsurgency
CTS	Counter Terrorism Service (Jihaz Mukafahat al-Irhab)
HPE	Hêza Parastina Êzîdxanê (Êzîdxan Protection Force)
HPG	Hêzên Parastina Gel (People's Defense Forces)
IDP	internally displaced persons
IOM	International Organization for Migration (United Nations)
IS	Islamic State (ad-Dawlah al-Islamiyah; also known as Daʿesh)
ISF	Iraqi Security Forces (Quwwat al-Musallahah al-ʿIraqiyya)
JAM	Jaysh al-Mahdi (Mahdi Army)
JRTN	Jaysh Rijal at-Tariqa an-Naqshabandiyah (Army of the Men of the Naqshbandi Order)
KDP	Kurdistan Democratic Party (Partiya Demokrat a Kurdistanê)
KH	Kataʾib Hezbollah (Hezbollah Battalions [Iraq])
KRG	Kurdistan Regional Government (Hikûmetî Herêmî Kurdistan)
KRI	*Kurdistan Region of Iraq* (Herêmî Kurdistan)
MENA	Middle East and North Africa

OCHA	Office for the Coordination of Humanitarian Affairs (United Nations)
PKK	Partiya Karkerên Kurdistanê (Kurdistan Workers' Party)
PMF	Popular Mobilization Forces (al-Hashd ash-Shaʿbi)
SFHH	single female–headed households
SOFA	status of forces agreement
SOI	Sons of Iraq (Abnaʾ al-ʿIraq)
TMF	Tribal Mobilization Force (al-Hashd al-ʿAshaʾiri)
USIP	United States Institute of Peace
YBS	Yekîneyên Berxwedana Şengalê (Sinjar Resistance Units)
YPJ	Yekîneyên Parastina Jin (Women's Protection Unit)

Note on Transliteration

This book follows a modified version of the transliteration standards developed by the *International Journal of Middle East Studies*. In the interest of readability, I omit all diacritical marks with the exception of *ayn* (') and *hamza* ('). Exceptions include words taken from the Iraqi dialect, especially those with the suffix *-či*. For example, the Modern Standard Arabic term *aydiuluji* (ideological) is transliterated as *aydiuluchi*.

Arabic and Kurdish names for people, places, and institutions—as well as titles and technical terms—are transliterated without diacritical marks and are written as they are normally encountered in the English-language media. The definite article is omitted after the first mention of people, places, and institutions. For example, "Nouri al-Maliki" occurs for the first usage and is rendered "Maliki" thereafter. Anglicized plurals—as opposed to irregular plurals in Arabic or Kurdish—are formed by adding the singular *s*. For example, the plural of "sheikh" will be "sheikhs" instead of "shuyukh."

Surviving the Islamic State

1

How Do Ordinary People Survive War?

The war will end
The leaders will shake hands
The old woman will keep waiting
for her martyred son.
That girl will wait for her beloved husband
and those children will wait
for their heroic father.
I don't know who sold our homeland
but I know who paid the price.

—AUTHOR UNKNOWN

On June 4, 2014, the Islamic State (IS) extended its military offensive from Syria into northern Iraq, when approximately 1,500 insurgents attacked the regional capital of Mosul. In response, nearly 25,000 Iraqi soldiers and police officers fled their posts, abandoning weapons, ammunition, and other military equipment in their retreat.[1] Within seventy-two hours, IS captured government institutions and began providing public goods and services to Mosul residents. By week's end, the group controlled all of Mosul.

As IS ascended, Iraqis from different walks of life confronted existential decisions about how to survive the conflict. In response to the occupation of Mosul, over 500,000 Ninewa residents fled their homes for safe haven in Kirkuk and the Kurdistan Region of Iraq (KRI).[2] Others remained in their homes and tried to survive by hiding, laying low, or commuting. As the war progressed, however, most occupied residents had to come to terms with IS control.

In the eyes of the Islamic State, most Sunni Arabs—as well as some Shabak and Turkmen—could pass as "legitimate" Muslims. Some Sunnis disgusted by the sectarianism, corruption, and neglect of the Nouri al-Maliki government in Baghdad supported the creation of an Islamic state. "They were hopeful that Daʿesh will save them, provide security and jobs, and respect the citizens.... They wanted a savior and thought that Daʿesh will save them. They thought that Daʿesh will make the country settled and end bribes and bring a good government," explained a Sunni tribal leader in Mosul (respondent B18). An even smaller minority used IS's arrival as an opportunity to build status, pursue wealth, or settle past scores.

Shiʿa Iraqis—deemed "refusers" (*rafidun*) because of their deviation from Sunni doctrine—received little protection. As "People of the Book" (*Ahl al-Kitab*), Assyrian Christians were exempt from extreme violence, even as many women and girls faced the threat of forced marriage. Ethnoreligious minorities faced the most severe coercion—including ethnic cleansing, forced displacement, and sexual victimization—given their status as apostates (*murtadun*), devil worshippers (*ʿabdat al-Shaytan*), polytheists (*mushrikun*), and unbelievers (*kuffar*).[3]

For many Iraqis, the path of least resistance was passive acquiescence or weak cooperation. Others contended with IS control through various acts of "everyday resistance," active opposition, and even armed resistance. A reliable cellular or Internet connection created the opportunity for secretly informing to the anti-IS coalition. Those with a higher risk tolerance could use compact discs or graffiti to mark the locations of insurgents and weapons caches. "If they find a base, they define its location; they give its GPS to the air force and the aircrafts bomb them," recounted one militia recruit (respondent B14). Public opposition and armed resistance were less common. Those with connections to local elites who had guns or money could mobilize self-defense groups. As one Moslawi remarked, "At the time of Daʿesh, people could buy guns for forty or fifty thousand dinars [approximately thirty-five U.S. dollars]. Don't think that it was a real state where there aren't any uncontrolled weapons; on the contrary, there was a lot of corruption" (respondent B15).

When the anti-IS coalition reached Ninewa Governorate in October 2016, collaboration between local residents and coalition forces became more common. Even minority-run self-defense groups—from the Assyrian, Shabak, and Turkmen communities—integrated into a network of Shiʿa-dominated pro-government militias known as the Popular Mobilization Forces (al-Hashd ash-Shaʿbi). Other armed groups, such as a splinter faction of the Sinjar Resistance Units, distrusted the coalition and pursued autonomy from elites in Baghdad and Erbil.

What explains the wide variation in how ordinary Iraqis survived the IS occupation? When facing imminent danger, how do everyday people decide whether to stay in their homes or flee? For those who stay, what factors determine whether individuals cooperate or contend with insurgent control? Are neutrality or autonomy ever viable strategies for surviving insurgent violence? In short, how do ordinary people survive war when it arrives in their neighborhood?

The puzzle of wartime survival

There are as many ways to survive violence as there are those affected by it. Nevertheless, studying wartime survivors yields valuable lessons. In the case of Iraq, ordinary people responded differently to IS's consolidation of power. Many preemptively fled or were forcibly displaced from their homes. Among those who stayed, some chose to lay low or hide, while others tacitly cooperated or secretly resisted. Even Iraqis within the same ethnic or sectarian communities adopted different survival "repertoires," consisting of social practices, tools, organized routines, symbols, and rhetorical strategies for detecting and responding to violence.

Existing accounts of wartime survival either essentialize social identity or ignore it altogether by reducing survival to cost-benefit analysis. In the case of Iraq, conventional accounts emphasize the role of ethnic and sectarian divides in exacerbating conflict.[4] Shiʻa supported the government because it was controlled by fellow Shiʻa elites, Sunnis opposed the government because of political exclusion, and Kurds pursued autonomy given their secure oil wealth and geographic power base on the periphery of the state. Arguments that privilege coethnic affinity, however, fail to account for the different ways people *within the same identity group* detect and respond to threats. Just as Irish Catholics in New York City might share little in common with fellow believers in upstate New York, so, too, do cosmopolitan Sunnis in Baghdad feel little affinity for Sunnis in rural towns and villages in the western desert.[5]

Research on wartime survival also emphasizes the role of territorial control, perceptions of relative deprivation, and cost-benefit calculations.[6] Despite controlling upward of 40 percent of Iraq's territory at the height of its power (and ruling over nearly one in five residents), IS's totalitarian system of governance did not always incentivize civilian cooperation. Many Iraqis living under the group's control resisted or pursued autonomy. While a majority of non-Shiʻa felt some level of disenfranchisement from the central government, most people willingly collaborated with coalition forces during the anti-IS counteroffensive. Some Iraqis with wealth and influence fled to the diaspora, while others mobilized local self-defense groups. While opportunistic collaboration with IS was present in some Sunni communities, so, too, were principled and risky acts of defiance, disobedience, and armed resistance.

The different ways in which ordinary Iraqis survived IS motivates the book's central research question: *Why do survival repertoires vary among individuals in different communities over the course of a conflict?* Answering this question requires addressing three lines of inquiry. First, under what scope of conditions will individuals pursue cooperation, contention, and neutrality? Second, why do certain individuals opt for risk-averse repertoires such as hiding or laying low, while others pursue high-risk repertoires such as enlisting in a self-defense group? Third, what factors explain the consistency of survival repertoires in different communities over time. In other words, why do some individuals pursue the same repertoire throughout a conflict, while others modify or adopt new repertoires as conflict evolves? By answering these questions, this study provides a coherent framework for understanding how ordinary people detect and respond to wartime violence.

The argument in brief: Threat detection shapes survival repertoires

This book explores how ordinary people survive wartime violence. Focusing on areas of insurgent control rather than regime governance, it analyzes how individuals adopt survival repertoires to detect and respond to violence in their communities. Survival repertoires are based on intuitions informed by personal experience; they are creative, flexible, and often contradictory. As Roger Mac Ginty observes, repertoires express themselves in "inconsistent, opportunistic, and messy ways.... [Individuals] react, create, ignore, forget, don't give a damn, conform, rebel, and do more—often within the space of a day or an hour."[7] Most importantly, survival repertoires provide a means of coping with the inherent stress, uncertainty, and volatility of war.

This book argues that three basic heuristics—or decision-making shortcuts—influence how individuals evaluate insurgent control. First, individuals consider whether they share an identity trait (e.g., ethnicity or sect), worldview, or common in-group with insurgents. A shared in-group provides a shortcut as to whether insurgents are trustworthy, thereby signaling a lower likelihood of collective victimization. Second, individuals consider an insurgent group's reputation—drawing from personal experience and second-hand information—to form expectations about how the group will govern the community. Those who suffered from insurgent exploitation or victimization in the past will be more likely to resist insurgent control in the future. Finally, individuals consider coercive behavior, especially how insurgents identify and pursue targets. Coercive behavior informs how individuals think about the relative risk of suffering indiscriminate violence. As the risk of indiscriminate violence rises, so, too, does the likelihood of flight. Those who stay grapple with whether they can acclimate to or accommodate insurgent control without undermining access to basic needs or violating sacred values.

Most people will go to extraordinary lengths to stay in their homes amid extreme violence. They will acclimate to conflict by laying low, hiding, or adjusting their movement to avoid insurgent checkpoints. At some critical juncture, however, nearly everyone wrestles with the decision to remain or leave. More often than not, the motivation to flee emerges when one confronts a specific threat of violence or exploitation against a family member, friend, or neighbor. While many will remain internally displaced, those with enough resources and social connections might get the opportunity to resettle in a neighboring country. The most fortunate will find a new home in a diaspora community in western Europe or North America. Most who resettle in the diaspora will avoid the politics of their home country, while a select few might engage in various forms of diaspora activism. However, age, gender, and other demographic traits shape the opportunity to flee. Due to their physical limitations, children and the elderly face difficulties in escaping violence or accessing the resources needed for survival. Similarly, while girls and women face increased threats while on the move, they also have a higher likelihood of securing asylum, giving them access to education, employment, and marriage markets in the diaspora.

Those who remain—either by force or by choice—confront existential decisions about how they will respond to insurgent control. Heuristics inform whether they will pursue contention, neutrality, or cooperation. By their very nature, neutral repertoires such as hiding, laying low, or commuting, are short-lived. Eventually people run out of food, fuel, or medicine, driving desperation and competition among other community members. When survival dynamics in the neighborhood inevitably change, individuals revisit whether their current repertoires are serving their pressing needs.

Individuals decide whether to cooperate or contend based on whether they can accommodate insurgent control without undermining access to their basic needs or violating their sacred values. Basic needs represent the essential physiological, psychological, and social resources needed to survive, whereas sacred values are deeply held beliefs about what is good, right, and important in life. Those with a viable alternative for protection will pursue repertoires of contention, such as "everyday resistance," active opposition, and armed resistance. Those who are unable or unwilling to accommodate insurgent rule, but who lack viable alternatives for protection, are more likely to cooperate. The most vulnerable will passively acquiesce by complying with insurgents' demands. Those with a greater tolerance for risk—typically military-age males (between roughly the ages of sixteen and forty-five)—might collaborate with insurgent governance.

As the conflict evolves, individuals adapt and revise their survival repertoires. Decisions to flee or remain neutral precede repertoires of contention and cooperation. As government forces challenge insurgent control, so, too, do many local residents. Repertoires of active opposition and armed resistance will increase in frequency as individuals predict a likely shift in the local balance of power. When the status quo is in flux and individuals have outside options for protection, opportunistic forms of contention and cooperation are more common. As peacetime approaches, many will return to neutrality as they cautiously observe how government forces treat residents who remained in the community during the war. If government forces pose a renewed risk of exploitation or victimization, contention and cooperation reemerge as viable repertoires.

Empirical focus: Islamic State in Iraq

With the vast scope of IS's presence in Iraq and Syria, this book focuses on how ordinary men and women survived insurgent violence in Baghdad, the Sunni Triangle (including Anbar and Salah al-Din Governorates), and Ninewa Governorate (see figure 1.1). The analysis purposely excludes the KRI because it remained under the control of the Kurdish Regional Government, and because Kurdish participation in the anti-IS coalition remained consistent over the course of the conflict.[8]

Within these regions, the analysis focuses on three core criteria. First, this study seeks to understand why ordinary people adopt specific survival repertoires amid extreme violence. Most of the book's research subjects are civilians who did not participate in hostilities or belong to any state or non-state armed group.[9] A select few took up arms and violently resisted when their families or neighborhoods faced insurgent threats. While international humanitarian law draws a clear distinction between combatants and noncombatants, in practice, lines become blurred and roles interchangeable as local residents navigate wartime violence.

Second, this work examines survival within Iraqi communities that faced IS violence. Communities are comprised of individuals forming groups within a defined geographic area, engaging in frequent interactions across various domains. A community's geographic boundaries may include a collection of neighborhoods in a large city like Baghdad, or a village or town in rural areas of Anbar or Ninewa Governorates. Some communities faced contestation between government and insurgent forces, while others remained in the central government's control while confronting

FIGURE 1.1 Map of Iraq's eighteen governorates (*muhafazat*).

Source: "Iraq: National Reference Map (as of 28 Sep 2021)," Office for the Coordination of Humanitarian Affairs, United Nations, September 28, 2021, https://reliefweb.int/map/iraq/iraq-national-reference-map-28-sep-2021.

sporadic bouts of suicide terrorism. Analyzing variation in territorial control is appropriate for two reasons. First, contested communities are the very places where counterinsurgents choose to intervene, thereby increasing the likelihood that local residents will encounter a range of government and insurgent forces over time. As a result, survival decisions are more complex in contested communities because survival is based on how residents balance the relative identities, goals, and tactics of government and insurgent forces.

Third, this book explores violent and nonviolent forms of contention, neutrality, and cooperation. Most of the empirical analysis focuses on individuals who remained in their community, as opposed to those who fled. Everyday acts of cooperation, neutrality, and contention are the centerpiece, while less space is dedicated to exploring armed collective action. In Mosul, for example, some residents resisted IS control through graffiti, distribution of CDs, and other anti-IS media, while others covertly mobilized neighborhood self-defense groups and pro-government militias, which eventually merged with coalition forces (see chapter 7).

Alternative explanations for wartime survival

Past research on wartime survival highlights how threat perception shapes the ways in which ordinary people detect and respond to violence. "Civilians caught 'between two fires' must choose—on inadequate information and in a context of high uncertainty—which side to support, particularly when armed groups force residents to declare such choices," explains Elisabeth Jean Wood.[10] Despite the existential stakes of their decisions, civilians "are actors with agency whose ability to respond to the dangers of conflict derives from social cooperation."[11]

A broad consensus exists that threat perception emerges through an interaction of individual cognition and group socialization.[12] Marika Landau-Wells, for instance, argues that environmental stimuli affect how individuals classify different types of threats. Threat classification—"the idea that our brains rapidly distinguish between different types of threats and formulate responses accordingly with deliberate reflection"—motivates survival responses.[13] Anastasia Shesterinina emphasizes the social role of threat detection and response in the development of "collective threat framing" theory.[14] She observes that individuals anticipate threats by drawing on earlier conflict experiences and the social networks in which they are embedded. Evgeny Finkel describes the importance of heuristics in shaping how Jews across Poland's ghettos responded to the Nazi occupation.[15] Similarly, Aidan Milliff's study of ethnic politics in postwar India showcases how the manner in which individuals appraise their current circumstances affects the survival strategies they adopt during crises.[16]

However, disagreement remains about the relative influence of material and social variables in shaping survival decisions. One line of research emphasizes the role of rational action, including cost-benefit analysis. Rational choice explanations privilege the role of material variables, especially the balance of military capabilities and role of territorial control. Communities contested between government and insurgent forces create incentives for opportunistic collaboration and resistance.[17] The "loyalty-for-protection" bargain can also incentivize defection—especially when ethnic or sectarian cleavages exacerbate preexisting grievances.[18]

Government and insurgent forces also compete for public support by providing civilians protection in exchange for intelligence about their adversaries' goals and capabilities. In asymmetric conflicts—where disparities of power and authority characterize civilian-combatant relations—reliable intelligence and perceptions of legitimacy determine whether aid, development, and security fuel further competition or reduce violence.[19] However, local residents can also forego the short-term gains of instrumental collaboration in favor of alternative survival strategies. Individuals can opt out of the collaboration-resistance dilemma by fleeing the conflict or pursuing autonomy, neutrality, or nonalignment.[20] Shane Barter models survival decisions as a choice among "flight, support, and voice" based on a modification of Albert Hirschman's classic framework of "exit, voice, and loyalty."[21]

A contending line of research emphasizes the role of social identity, including ethnic and sectarian affinity. Social groups provide the primary context in which individuals collect, process, and exchange information about conflict developments. As such, threat perception is not only filtered through social identity, but is optimized for group belonging rather than information accuracy.[22] Most importantly, membership in a common in-group provides basic criteria for determining who to trust.[23]

Aside from social identity, local residents also perceive threats based on how combatants behave. How armed groups identify and pursue targets is the most important behavioral criteria shaping survival decisions. Indiscriminate targeting—even when deployed by in-group combatants—alienates local residents by increasing fear about potential damage or personal victimization.[24] In contrast, discriminate targeting (i.e., "selective violence") will decrease fear of victimization and bolster public support.[25]

Michael Callen and coauthors find that individuals exposed to wartime violence are more risk averse and place a premium on certainty. Other evidence points to victims of past trauma acting more altruistically, but also displaying higher risk acceptance and less patience.[26] The latter is especially true for young men, who often rely on a different set of coping mechanisms and social relationships to process trauma when compared to women in the same age cohort.

Current attempts to integrate material and social motivations into a coherent framework of wartime survival remain elusive. For example, how might local residents trade off support when rival organizations include coethnics? Many residents of Baghdad's Shiʿa-majority neighborhoods confronted the dilemma of whether to support the Shiʿa-dominant Iraqi Security Forces or local sectarian militias. When do the short-term gains of instrumental collaboration outweigh an individual's preexisting commitments to a common in-group? While some Shabak and Turkmen communities opportunistically collaborated with IS, they later suffered personal and collective blowback once their communities were liberated. Do the benefits of military intervention in support of one's in-group counteract aversion to foreign violations of local sovereignty? While many Sunnis resisted both the U.S. intervention in March 2003 and the presence of coalition forces, they later collaborated with the anti-IS coalition when insurgent control became unbearable.

This book reconciles competing findings from past research on foreign intervention, counterinsurgency warfare, and ethnic conflict by exploring how identity, behavior, and governance expectations shape wartime survival. It demonstrates how insurgents' identity and behavior reveal their motives and intentions, including whether they have the ability and interest to protect local communities. The result is a robust theory that can best explain the competing survival repertoires available to civilians navigating insurgent violence.

Contributions to research and practice

This study explores how insurgents' identity, reputation, and behavior affect the survival repertoires individuals adopt in order to survive violence. It joins a growing movement of scholars and practitioners committed to recognizing the agency of ordinary people during wartime.[27] The analysis foregrounds the voices of ordinary Iraqis in order to reflect on how the author's perspective as an external observer affects a broader understanding of Iraqi politics.

The book contributes to the research program on wartime survival in four ways. First, it offers original evidence from the field that challenges two widely held beliefs among scholars of civil war and insurgency: first, that territorial control motivates local support, and second, that civilians will resist foreign occupation based on a latent commitment to nationalism. Both perspectives are puzzling in light of evidence from wartime Iraq. With respect to territorial control, this study finds that even in communities under insurgent occupation, local residents chose to resist or remain autonomous from IS control. Violent resistance was present even among Sunni communities, the sole demographic who had the opportunity to actively collaborate with IS.

On the role of local resistance to foreign intervention, the analysis reveals that most Iraqis were remarkably pragmatic regarding who they allowed to violate their sovereignty. This revelation complicates not only who is considered a "foreign" combatant, but also how individuals construct and revise membership within their in-group in the face of evolving threats. While many Baghdad Shiʿa welcomed the mobilization of Iranian-backed militias, they later balked when the militias threatened their local autonomy. In Anbar, the fact that some Sunni residents felt the need to distinguish between cultural norms in Ramadi and Fallujah—communities less than an hour's drive from one another—highlights the importance of the "narcissism of minor differences" in shaping the adoption of survival repertoires. For social identity theorists, the book's core findings raise new questions about the elasticity of in-group favoritism in the absence of existential threats.

Second, the book's multi-method research design provides a model for understanding everyday life in conflict zones. To date, scholars have access to evidence of IS control in large urban centers like Raqqa and Mosul, but less evidence is available for how control varied at the level of local townships and villages. To provide a rural perspective on insurgent control, this study combines interviews, surveys, and quantitative datasets to demonstrate how Iraqis adapted their repertoires in the face of evolving threats. By combining observational and experimental data, the analysis explains not only how Iraqis formed their core beliefs and attitudes, but also what motivated their behavior.

Third, the study develops a new theoretical framework for understanding the scope of conditions under which specific repertoires emerge and evolve. Specifically, it offers a logic of repertoire selection and change that remains underdeveloped in the existing literature. It demonstrates how basic heuristics inform repertoire selection, emphasizing the role of local communities in shaping identity, narratives, and information flows among members. The framework also helps to explain how patterns of forced displacement affect the survival repertoires available to those who remain.

Finally, this book contributes to how scholars understand the legacy of Iraqi politics since the 2003 civil war. It highlights the ways in which a common set of grievances and security concerns united how ordinary Iraqis responded to al-Qaʿida violence during the U.S. intervention and IS violence after the U.S. departure. Narratives of collective victimhood under Saddam Hussein's regime shaped local responses to the U.S. occupation, including how Iraqis interacted with sectarian militias and insurgent groups. While many observers highlight the direct relationship between the 2003 U.S.-led intervention and the rise of IS, fewer note how the aftermath of the 1990–1991 Gulf War contributed to patterns of violence and contentious politics after the collapse of the Baʿthist regime.[28] The book showcases how path dependence shapes the survival decisions available to ordinary citizens many years after critical events occur.

Conflict-sensitive research: Methodology and practice

The data informing the book's analysis seek to give voice to ordinary Iraqis who were forced to make hard choices during times of intense danger and uncertainty. Some of the data came from preexisting sources, such as the United Nations' International Organization on Migration (IOM). Other data was collected in the field between 2017 and 2021.

Past work reinforces the necessity of a multi-method research design.[29] While quantitative analysis can reveal behavioral trends, understanding personal motivations requires local knowledge gleaned from the field. Accordingly, this study combines surveys, interviews, and quantitative datasets. Fieldwork data includes an original survey of six hundred Baghdad residents, as well as thirty interviews with IS survivors in northern and western Iraq. Analysis of quantitative datasets—ranging from forced displacements, violent events, and election results—generalizes findings from the field by demonstrating trends in displacement, violence, and electoral participation.[30]

Fieldwork in conflict-affected communities also presents ethical and logistical challenges. This work engages with practitioners in the fields of humanitarian assistance, economic development, and peace building who highlight the need for conflict-sensitive research methods. Conflict sensitivity involves not only ensuring the physical safety of local enumerators and research subjects, but also understanding how the context, format, and timing of human subjects research might unintentionally affect research subjects' emotional and psychological well-being.[31] Only by incorporating conflict sensitivity into one's fieldwork plan can researchers "conduct sound and rigorous research in the challenging contexts of conflict zones."[32] While training on conflict sensitivity has traditionally been restricted to the domain of practitioners, an increasing number of trainings and curricula are available for social scientists.[33]

Given the sensitive nature of this book's subject matter, extensive precautions were taken to protect researchers and human subjects. The Independent Institute for Administration and Civil Society Studies (IIACSS)—an Iraqi market research firm headquartered in Baghdad—enumerated the Baghdad survey in November 2017.[34] The survey team consisted of a project manager, three field supervisors, and ten enumerators. The author conducted training in Arabic with IIACSS personnel prior to enumeration. Each member of the survey team has past experience conducting face-to-face surveys in Baghdad.

Where possible, enumerators conducted interviews in their home neighborhoods. Female enumerators interviewed women, occasionally in the presence of other family members. On two occasions, local authorities detained IIACSS enumerators. All personnel were released unharmed the same day they were detained. To protect respondents' safety, enumerators did not ask directly about their sectarian identity or personal opinions about specific Iraqi politicians or military officials. Instead, enumerators privately recorded their best estimate of a respondent's sect based on their speech patterns, dress, and home decor (e.g., wall artwork of Ali or

Hussein). The geographic location of interviews was coded at the subdistrict level (ADM3) and GPS data was subsequently deleted.

Interviews in Anbar, Salah al-Din, Ninewa, and Erbil Governorates between 2017 and 2021 provide further evidence of survival repertoires during the IS occupation.[35] In Ninewa Governorate, the author interviewed Iraqi peace builders representing minority communities in Tal Afar, Sinjar, and the Ninewa Plains.[36] Interviewees were affiliated with Tearfund, a London-based nongovernmental organization that conducts peace building, economic development, and humanitarian assistance work across the Middle East and North Africa region. Tearfund provided a safe location in their regional office in Erbil to conduct interviews, including a local staff member who served as an interpreter for native Kurdish-speakers.

Interviews lasted between sixty and ninety minutes and were conducted in a mix of Modern Standard Arabic, Iraqi dialect, or Kurdish, depending on the interviewee's native language and educational background. Informed consent was verbally obtained prior to the start of the interview and interviewees were provided with paper documentation about the study's details. To respect interviewees' confidentiality, audio recordings were deleted after transcription. Notes relating to sensitive details of peace-building programs (e.g., opposition by a local political or religious leader) were also destroyed. While a gender balance enabled interviews with female peace builders, it also likely affected how interviewees discussed sensitive topics, especially sexual and gender-based violence.

Twenty additional key informant interviews were conducted among Iraqi survivors in Anbar and Salah al-Din Governorates. Unlike the Ninewa interviewee pool, members of local influential families and tribes, as well as enlistees in local paramilitaries and militias, were included. Due to the COVID-19 pandemic, the author hired IIACSS enumerators to conduct face-to-face interviews in locations across Fallujah, Mosul, Ramadi, and Tikrit. Similar to the Ninewa fieldwork, interviews lasted between sixty and ninety minutes and covered the same list of questions related to security, politics, and economic development before, during, and after the IS occupation. By including those who engaged in armed resistance, interviewees provided key insights into why the transition from unarmed to armed survival repertoires occurred.

Analysis of quantitative datasets generalizes findings from the field by exploring trends in forced displacement, patterns of violence, and electoral participation. Data from Iraq Body Count and the Empirical Studies of Conflict Project supplement data on combat operations, civilian casualties, and development projects. These data are essential for demonstrating individual behavior in the face of perceived threats. Data from the International Organization on Migration and the United States Institute of Peace's Conflict and Stabilization Monitoring Framework provide evidence on wider patterns of forced displacement. The IOM's Displacement Tracking Matrix provides quarterly observations of forced displacement and arrival figures for internally displaced persons at the subdistrict level. Election data provided by the Independent High Electoral Commission demonstrates how Iraqis resisted IS by voting in support of political parties competing for control of the central government.

Organization of the book

The book's exploration of wartime survival in Iraq unfolds over six chapters. Chapter 2 presents a theory of how ordinary people survive wartime violence. It explores the defining characteristics of complex conflicts as well as the blurred boundaries between combatants and civilians. It then describes how ordinary people detect and respond to threats. In particular, it outlines the core heuristics that inform survival repertoires and how community membership shape what information is most salient. Following that, it unpacks the concept of survival repertoires and explains how they are distinct from rational strategies such as cost-benefit calculations. Finally, it describes and provides examples of contention, neutrality, and cooperation, including the conditions under which each repertoire is likely to emerge.

Chapter 3 develops the analysis by describing the rise and fall of the Islamic State in Iraq over three acts. Act 1 explores the impact of the departure of U.S. forces in December 2011. Rather than conclusively defeating insurgents, the transition on the part of the United States to a population-centric counterinsurgency strategy in 2008 temporarily dampened a more fundamental conflict between insurgent groups, sectarian militias, and paramilitary organizations. Act 2 examines the "interwar" period between the 2011 Arab uprisings and beginning of IS's military offensive in June 2014. It focuses on the nascent rise of IS and Nouri al-Maliki's sectarian authoritarianism. It also offers a comprehensive picture of how IS governed its newly captured territory through a regimen of coercion, co-option, and persuasion. Act 3 analyzes the anti-IS offensive, including the formation, operations, and internal politics of the anti-IS coalition. It then provides a glimpse into how ordinary Iraqis navigated the twin threats of insecurity posed by coalition forces and IS insurgents.

The book's empirical investigation begins in chapter 4 with an exploration of how Baghdad residents survived the threat of IS terrorism. It begins by examining displacement data and concludes that ethnic cleansing and forced displacement homogenized and strengthened Shiʿa neighborhoods throughout the capital. While many Shiʿa neighborhoods began by actively resisting the U.S.-led intervention, they later collaborated with U.S. forces after confronting increased exploitation from neighborhood militias. The Abadi regime's inability—or unwillingness—to curb corruption, unemployment, and inflation produced a shift among Baghdad residents from support of the government to neutrality. The study's core claims are tested through a representative survey of six hundred Baghdad residents. Having been conducted near the end of the anti-IS campaign, the survey demonstrates how Iraqis shifted their repertoires from cooperation to neutrality after the insurgent threat subsided.

Next, chapter 5 examines how Sunnis in Fallujah, Ramadi, and Tikrit navigated IS control. Unlike those living in Baghdad, Sunnis balanced the threat posed by IS with the perceived danger of supporting the central government. Political exclusion forced many Sunni communities to pursue weak support and passive acquiescence as a means of protecting their survival. The chapter's empirical analysis comes from a series of key informant interviews among local residents. The interviews shed light on how Iraqis in the region perceived their own shift from contention to cooperation, and later, neutrality and autonomy. Interview evidence reveals that the systematic exclusion of the Sons of Iraq from Iraq's security apparatus not only fueled grievances among Sunnis toward the central government, but also weakened the ability of Sunni communities to protect themselves against the IS insurgency.

Chapter 6 shifts the focus to Iraq's northern Ninewa Governorate, where ethnoreligious minorities confronted a brutal IS occupation from June 2014 to December 2017. Flight proved the dominant strategy for most minorities across Ninewa, given their limited protection by coalition forces during a majority of the conflict. Those who remained pursued passive acquiescence and everyday resistance and later actively collaborated with coalition forces when the anti-IS counteroffensive arrived in their communities. Similar to Iraqis in Baghdad and Anbar, some minorities began exploring autonomy only after suffering from exploitation by coalition members, especially from local units of Peshmerga and the Popular Mobilization Forces. Empirical evidence for the chapter comes from key informant interviews with Iraqi peace builders during fieldwork in the KRI in 2019. Interviews with members of Ninewa's Assyrian Christian, Yazidi, and Kurdish communities provides evidence of how some Iraqis bargained with insurgents—through forced marriages, taxation, and other means of passive support—to shield their communities from further victimization.

Chapter 7 concludes by summarizing the book's core argument and highlighting its key findings. It then explores current economic, political, and social obstacles facing postwar Iraq before turning to a discussion of the book's broader implications for civilian protection, refugee resettlement, and post-conflict reconstruction. The study ends with a call for further contributions to the growing research program on civilian survival in wartime. More importantly, it serves as a poignant reminder of the remarkable resilience and hope expressed by those who endure life during conflict.

2
Survival Repertoires in Wartime

The dead are forgotten, unknown, and their bodies are swallowed by the fertile earth, but the ruins remain: the destroyed refinery that is now a playground of mangled steel chimneys and rusting tankers; the crippled and desolate villages; the municipal buildings and schools with their flattened roofs like concrete wafers—all stand witness to the horrors. The killers—bandits, insurgents, militias, soldiers would keep traveling, deploying new tactics, implementing new horrors under different names, but they all remain the same people—Iraqis.
—GHAITH ABDUL-AHAD, *A STRANGER IN YOUR OWN CITY*

What's worse is that people have been giving me a bad reputation. They're accusing me of committing crimes, but what they don't understand is that I'm the only justice in this country.... Because I'm made up of body parts of people from diverse backgrounds—ethnicities, tribes, races, and social classes.... I represent the impossible mix that never was achieved in the past. I'm the first true Iraqi citizen.
—"WHATSITSNAME" (ASHISMI) AHMED SAADAWI, *FRANKENSTEIN IN BAGHDAD*

When asked about the legacy of the 2011 Arab uprisings in Iraq, former prime minister Ayad Allawi quipped, "What spring is this? Spring is associated with green, renewal of life. We are having blood pouring everywhere in the region and destruction and dismemberment of countries, and chaos is happening."[1] Allawi's grim appraisal of the uprisings was not limited to Iraq. Despite public demands for "bread, freedom, and social justice" (*aysh, hurriya, ʾadala ijtimaʿiyya*), one of the darkest legacies of the Arab uprisings was a sixfold increase in civilian fatalities.[2] By 2021, conflicts throughout the region expelled over 9.4 million residents and internally displaced an additional 15.7 million.[3]

In the face of conflict, why do some individuals remain in their homes while others are forcibly displaced? Why do residents within the same community make different survival decisions despite facing similar insurgent threats? Past research examines wartime survival as collective action among members with a shared ethnic or sectarian identity. Ordinary people survive violence through an internal cost-benefit calculation of risks, defend those who belong to a common ethnic or sectarian in-group, and support armed groups that maintain territorial control.[4] Other work bridges the levels of analysis by exploring how personal survival decisions emerge through group socialization.[5]

This chapter contributes to the growing research program on wartime survival by theorizing how individuals adopt repertoires to survive violence in their communities. It focuses on how local residents survive *insurgent control* rather than regime governance. Survival repertoires consist of the *social practices, tools, organized routines, symbols, and rhetorical strategies that enable individuals to detect and respond to threats.* They are creative, flexible, and often contradictory, emerging from an individual's past experience, worldview, and interactions with government and insurgent forces. Repertoires represent how ordinary people rely on creativity, experimentation, and intuition—rather than utility optimization or cost-benefit calculations—to cope with the stress, uncertainty, and volatility of conflict environments.

Figure 2.1 outlines the three survival repertoires available to local residents who stay in their communities during war.

Survival repertoires emerge from a set of basic heuristics—or decision-making shortcuts—that enable individuals to quickly and efficiently

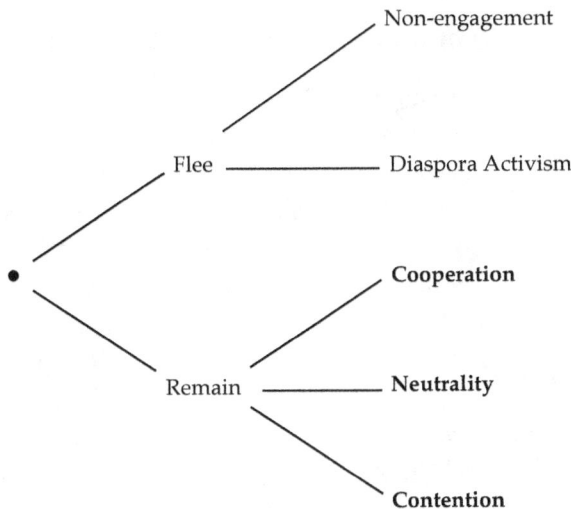

FIGURE 2.1 Survival repertoires in wartime.

Source: Author.

process information about the conflict. Community membership shapes how people interpret the conflict environment, providing a unifying social identity, common narrative, and sources of information for new developments. In this context, individuals reflect on their past experience and current circumstances. They wrestle with whether they can accommodate insurgent control without undermining access to basic needs or violating their sacred values. Crucially, age and gender also affect the availability and attractiveness of survival repertoires for community members facing similar threats.

The theoretical framework in this chapter unfolds in four steps. The next section explains how contemporary civil wars blur distinctions between civilians and combatants, as well as between wartime versus peacetime. The subsequent section explores how individuals draw on different heuristics to detect and respond to violence in their communities. The chapter then offers a framework of different survival repertoires, ranging from contention to cooperation, before concluding with a summary of the theory's core argument and empirical observations.

What threats do ordinary people confront in civil war?

The rise of increasingly fatal and protracted civil wars presents new threats to ordinary people.[6] In Syria, a 2011 popular protest movement to depose the Assad regime devolved into a conventional civil war, where regime and rebel forces—each backed by different foreign patrons—competed via direct military engagements along clear lines of control. In Libya and Yemen, in contrast, the uprisings produced armed contests between mutually brittle regimes and rebel forces vying for public support in the shadow of state collapse. Still other countries—including Iraq, Palestine, and Sudan—suffered from asymmetric or irregular conflicts, where the central government enjoys military superiority yet lacked sufficient public legitimacy to win local "hearts and minds."

Despite their unique contexts, contemporary civil wars across the Middle East and North Africa (MENA) share three attributes in common. First, social cleavages along ethnicity, sect, and class exacerbate conflict by fracturing state-society relations and incentivizing competition over scarce resources. Those on the losing side find themselves excluded from political representation, as well as the social networks necessary to find protection, employment, or other basic needs. As such, the stakes of the conflict are not simply a matter of controlling territory or resources, but also the very state institutions required to govern.

Second, contemporary civil wars involve overlapping coalitions, which in turn causes conflicts to spill across state borders.[7] The contagion of conflict allows transnational militant organizations—such as al-Qaʿida, and the Islamic State—to establish local franchises.[8] Other militant groups, like Hezbollah or Hamas, benefit from state sponsorship, while others operate as self-directed forces, such as Libyan mercenaries fighting in Mali, or Syrian Kurds fighting in northern Iraq. Worse yet, inter-coalition competition for power and influence prolongs and intensifies violence, putting local citizens in harm's way. The ongoing fragmentation of insurgent and rebel groups fighting the Assad regime in Syria provides a poignant case in point.

Third, contemporary civil wars feature proxy involvement from external states.[9] In Ethiopia's counterinsurgency against the Tigray People's Liberation Front, Iran, Turkey, and the United Arab Emirates provided security assistance to the Ethiopian government, whereas Qatar supported the insurgents through intermediaries in Somalia.[10] Similarly, Iranian and Russian patronage to Assad not only benefits the Syrian military and pro-government militias, but also the network of "ghosts" (*shabbiha*) who serve as street-level enforcers for the regime.[11]

Contemporary civil wars also inhibit civilians' ability to flee incoming violence, especially in urban settings. Residents of dense neighborhoods in cities like Baghdad, Beirut, or Damascus confront different risks than those living in the rural periphery.[12] For those desiring to flee, the arrival of external forces changes access to safe smuggling and migration routes.[13] In transit, individuals face the threat of collective victimization, as well as indiscriminate violence. Beyond the physical battlefield, mobile Internet, smartphones, and social media present new opportunities for individuals to obtain local information about violence in their neighborhoods. Such platforms also provide methods for regime and opposition forces to identify, surveil, and coerce local residents.[14]

The risks faced by ordinary people during wartime also differ based on key demographics, especially age, gender, and socioeconomic status. Age differences contribute to relative vulnerability, with children and the elderly requiring specific attention and protection. Children may rely on adult caregivers for protection and sustenance, with their survival heavily dependent on their family's ability to provide and navigate dangerous environments. The elderly, due to physical limitations, face difficulties in escaping violence or accessing essential resources. They may also depend on community support or assistance from younger family members. The likelihood that the young or old are available to successfully flee wartime violence depends as much on social networks as individual motivations and opportunities.

Gender differences also affect the type and severity of risks confronting local civilians. On the one hand, men are often expected to take on protective roles during wartime, prioritizing physical strength and combat skills, and making them more likely to engage in direct forms of collaboration or resistance. Men might voluntarily enlist in government forces or insurgent groups or be dragooned into combat through forced conscription.[15] In the Syrian conflict, for example, the forced recruitment of children into combat roles in support of the Assad regime and opposition groups, is especially prevalent in rural communities.

On the other hand, women face unique threats that require different survival repertoires. They often assume caregiving roles, safeguarding their families and communities through prioritizing and nurturing social networks that provide access to resources and protection. More severely, girls and women face a disproportionate risk of sexual and gender-based violence.[16] Even for those insulated from combatant victimization, increased stress, uncertainty, and vulnerability puts women at increased risk of intimate-partner violence.[17] Even as violence deescalates, stigma and ostracism related to perceived insurgent collaboration is also a risk, including accusations of exchanging sexual favors for physical protection.[18] However, war can also transform the nature of societal roles and gender expectations. "During conflicts, women experience substantial changes in their status and opportunities, sometimes taking on societal roles that were inaccessible prior to the outbreak of war. These experiences offer them a glimpse into a drastically altered society—one in which women have expanded rights and freedom," observes Jakana Thomas.[19]

Despite the unique threats confronting men and women, most people living in conflict zones are not helpless victims. They are neither at the mercy of brute determinism, nor atomized individualists unconstrained by their environment. Rather, individuals exercise *bounded rationality* over their decisions under conditions of rapid change, extreme stress, and evolving uncertainty. Even in the midst of fighting, few people in such environments pick up arms, participate in fighting, or claim membership in an armed group.[20] Some respond by fleeing the violence, while others stay in their homes. Among those who stay, some people lay low and hide, while others resist or cooperate with insurgent control.

International humanitarian law clearly distinguishes between "combatants" and "noncombatants," but contemporary conflicts reveal the flexible and interchangeable roles ordinary people must adopt in order to survive.[21] As one peace builder in Iraq conveyed, "Someone can participate in violence one day, rescue victims of violence the next, and have family members victimized by violence on the third day."[22] In order to grapple with the ambiguity of social roles during wartime, this book refers to research subjects as "local residents" or "citizens," instead of "civilians" or "noncombatants."

How do individuals detect and respond to threats in violent environments?

People survive conflict by drawing on an underlying set of heuristics, or cognitive shortcuts, that assist with making life-and-death decisions.[23] "A heuristic is a procedure for decision making under uncertainty. It ignores information to make decisions faster, more frugally, and/or more accurately than complex procedures," explain Gerd Gigerenzer and Wolfgang Gaissmaier.[24] Unlike a game of poker, where placing bets is risky but the underlying odds are known, conflict environments are volatile, uncertain, and complex. As a conflict evolves, exposure to high-stakes situations provides actionable feedback on which heuristics are most useful for avoiding danger.

Threat perception also emerges through the interaction of individual cognition and group socialization. Even those exposed to identical information about violent developments can choose different responses. The interaction of individual and group factors means that threat perception is inherently subjective—individuals belonging to the same ethnic or sectarian group during the same time period can differently assess insurgent threats based on variation in their prior beliefs, attitudes, and core values. As Roger Petersen observes, "people don't get pushed into rebellion because of their ideology ... they get pulled in because of their social networks."[25]

Contemporary models of threat perception build on landmark studies of bounded rationality,[26] risk literacy,[27] bias and heuristics,[28] and behavioral responses to acute stress, such as the "fight, flight, freeze, or fawn" instinct.[29] Structural factors interact with an individual's emotional state to shape how one appraises the threat environment.[30] Paul Slovic and coauthors identify an "affect heuristic," or an individual's propensity to appraise new events or information based on how those stimuli make them feel.[31] Similarly, Jennifer Lerner developed the "emotion-imbued choice model" to explain how emotional states affect cognitive appraisals.[32] Building on the role of emotions, Marika Landau-Wells emphasizes how different environmental stimuli affect the ways in which individuals classify threats into categories of physical harm, material loss, and moral contamination.[33]

While heuristics alleviate the cognitive burden of decision making, they also entail trade-offs between accuracy and speed. In volatile environments, individuals are especially "fast and frugal" with how they collect and assess information.[34] Moreover, motivated reasoning—a tendency to collect and process information in ways consistent with prior beliefs—also affects threat perception through the mechanisms of threat avoidance, identity maintenance, and the need for cognitive closure.[35] Using emotional reactions as a bellwether for risk is especially useful for individuals living in violent environments, because it fosters a sense of certainty and control over one's circumstances.[36] In wartime, trade-offs between accuracy and speed are especially important, because inaccurate threat detection or response can prove deadly.

Research on wartime survival also draws on threat perception to explain variation in survival decisions. Evgeny Finkel argues that heuristics, such as believing that personal experience is a useful predictor of future events, shaped how Jews across Poland's ghettos responded to information about the Nazi occupation.[37] Similarly, Aidan Milliff's study of ethnic politics in postwar India demonstrates how the manner in which individuals appraise their current circumstances affects the survival strategies they adopt during crises.[38] Anastasia Shesterinina emphasizes the social role of threat detection and response in the development of "collective threat framing" theory.[39] She argues that individuals anticipate threats by drawing on earlier conflict experiences and the social networks in which they are embedded. Marie Berry applies a similar framework to study how women in Rwanda and Bosnia-Herzegovina engaged in a range of survival activities, including forming women's organizations, running for political office, and advocating for women's rights and gender equality.[40] She finds that women's personal experience with violence created new opportunities for them to challenge traditional gender roles and take on new forms of community authority and influence. Berry's work provides a foundation on which to explore how gender differences affected survival decisions in the Iraq case.

Table 2.1 highlights the most salient heuristics for detecting and responding to threats while confronting insurgent violence. Three core criteria—social identity, reputation, and coercive behavior—inform how local residents evaluate insurgent control. Heuristics work in concert to inform the selection of survival repertoires. For example, sharing a common in-group provides a shortcut for whether insurgents are trustworthy,

TABLE 2.1 Threat detection heuristics

Heuristic	Key questions	Proposed mechanism
Social identity	Do I share an identity trait (e.g., ethnicity or sect) or worldview with insurgents?	Common in-group → higher social trust
Reputation	Have I encountered this insurgent group in the past? If not, what information do I trust about the group's past actions?	Personal experience → future expectations of insurgent behavior
Coercive behavior	How are insurgents behaving in my community? Can I acclimate to or accommodate insurgent control without threatening access to basic needs or violating sacred values? If not, what outside options do I have for protection?	Coercive behavior → risk of indiscriminate violence

thereby signaling that individuals will be less likely to be victimized by collective punishment or retaliation. Cooperation will be more likely than neutrality or contention because local residents expect to benefit from insurgent control by receiving physical protection, employment opportunities, or increased status.

A shared social identity or common in-group provides the first heuristic for evaluating insurgent control. The most common criteria for group membership include a shared ethnicity, race, sect, or economic class.[41] In conflicts marred by prewar social cleavages, a shared social identity provides a shortcut as to who is most likely to be trustworthy. As Jason Lyall, Yuki Shiraito, and Kosuke Imai explain, "coethnicity acts as a visible signpost that allows individuals to gauge the expected behavior of individuals, including the credibility of assurances (such as promises of anonymity when providing tips) and threats of retaliation."[42] Collective insecurity or perception of a shared threat exacerbate intergroup distinctions, generating a range of antagonistic attitudes and behaviors.[43] In polarized environments, individuals are more likely to attribute malign motives to out-group members, while drawing on situational factors to explain in-group behavior. As Christopher

Blattman observes, "Misconstrual means that when I look at my opponent, I attribute the wrongness of their views to their personal failings, such as enmity. I overlook their situation—they were scared, or poorly trained."[44]

Beyond providing for members' physical needs, social groups also meet psychological needs by providing a shared set of norms and values. Norms represent shared expectations about which beliefs, attitudes, and behaviors are appropriate and desirable.[45] Values refer to an individual's deeply held beliefs about what is good, right, and important in life.[46] Sacred values are particularly influential in shaping wartime judgments, especially when those values relate to what is holy, profane, or dignified in human behavior.[47] The defense of sacred values includes protecting vulnerable group members or risking one's personal safety for the sake of the group, as well as the pursuit of revenge, retaliation, or retribution.[48] Norms and values gain salience when they cohere with a group's collective memory—the pool of memories, knowledge, and information that is passed on from generation to generation. Narratives construct social identity by describing what it means to be a group member, as well as the purpose of the group in the wider world.[49] Collective memory simultaneously shapes what groups remember and who they venerate, as well as what they choose forget or marginalize (i.e., collective amnesia).[50]

Reputation is a second heuristic for evaluating insurgent control. Individuals gauge reputation based on personal experience and secondhand information they deem trustworthy. The human brain is wired to believe that past events are a useful predictor of future developments, especially when events are endowed with special significance or meaning. Past experience—filtered through the lens of social identity—informs the information available to individuals navigating present violence.[51] In anticipation of violence, individuals subconsciously ask themselves the following questions: "Have I encountered this group or situation before? If so, how did I respond and what was the result?" Experiences that left a vivid impression—either for good or ill—are more readily available in and more likely to influence how individuals appraise their current circumstances. The "representativeness heuristic" also provides tools for classifying the motives and intentions of government or insurgent forces based on their identity or reputation.[52] For example, if local police victimized community members in the past, residents will be less likely to inform on insurgent activity for the government in the future.[53] In the absence of personal experience, individuals rely on credible, second-hand information to gauge an insurgent group's reputation. Whether or not this second-hand information is accurate depends on the source's proximity to violence, as well as how information is distributed throughout the community.

Finally, heuristics inform how individuals appraise an insurgent group's coercive behavior. For those confronting wartime violence, two questions are most salient: "Can I acclimate to or accommodate insurgent control without sacrificing access to my basic needs or violating my sacred values? If not, do I have viable outside options for protection?" Foundational desires to protect access to basic needs—especially physical safety, economic opportunity, and personal significance—motivate these questions.[54] For residents worried about access to basic needs, insurgent rule can trigger loss aversion, making the fear of losing basic needs more salient than the opportunity to gain new resources or opportunities through insurgent cooperation. How residents perceive insurgent governance is also based on emotional states, including whether local rule generates emboldening emotions (e.g., anger, pride, joy) or dispiriting ones (e.g., fear, sadness, shame).[55] Those emboldened by insurgent rule will pursue survival repertoires distinct from those dispirited by it.

Conflict research supports the claim that local residents evaluate insurgent control based on how it shapes their daily lives.[56] In ethno-sectarian conflicts, local residents are especially sensitive to coercion employed by the out-group.[57] Insurgents who are perceived as occupiers—regardless of whether they are locals or foreigners—risk alienating citizens and activating latent nationalist sentiment.[58] In contrast, residents extend a "home team discount" to in-group insurgents who engage in civilian victimization, while penalizing government forces for committing similar crimes. In Afghanistan, Jason Lyall, Yang-Yang Zhou, and Kosuke Imai find that coalition violence decreased public support for ISAF security forces, whereas Taliban violence failed to trigger a similar decline in public support.[59] Luke Condra and Jacob Shapiro discovered an asymmetry with respect to self-reported incidents of indiscriminate violence. Insurgent violence increased in the aftermath of ISAF-attributed civilian casualties, but not after violence attributed to the Taliban.[60]

Survival repertoires: Contention, neutrality, and cooperation

Heuristics inform how individuals make life-and-death decisions when violence comes to their neighborhood. When confronting the prospect of insurgent control, individuals survive through creativity, intuition ("gut feelings"), and experimentation. In other words, survival reflects a set of *repertoires* instead of rational strategies. Survival repertoires consist of social practices, tools, organized routines, symbols, and rhetorical strategies, which enable individuals to navigate violent situations.[61] They are creative, flexible, and often contradictory, emerging from one's past experiences, personal worldview, and social context. As such, repertoires reflect a relational rather than individualist orientation toward survival.[62] In a relational framework, survival decisions emerge through social interactions between combatant and noncombatants situated in a particular context. As Lorenzo Bosi and Stefan Malthaner explain,

> Actors not only shift back and forth between violent and nonviolent forms of action, but also use them in various combinations. In other words, violence is not an entirely exceptional form of political action, but has to be examined in the context of other nonviolent and "routine" forms of political action. Thereby, the decision to use violent means or not is not only the result of available repertoires of action, but is shaped by the groups' goals and identity, orientation and, particularly, responds to changing environments and actions of their opponents and/or allies.[63]

Accounting for both the social and environmental context is key, because it limits the range of survival repertoires available to residents in a given community during a specific point in the conflict. Survival repertoires are multifaceted—individuals can combine various repertoires at the same time, especially when deployed in private.[64]

Figure 2.2 visualizes the survival repertoires available to ordinary people confronting insurgent violence, ranging from cooperation to contention. Cooperation reflects the degree to which an individual's actions benefit insurgents' goals, strategies, and capabilities. In contrast, contention frustrates, undermines, or directly opposes insurgent control. Neutrality represents the various ways in which individuals avoid taking sides between government and insurgent forces. While exceptional, neutrality also

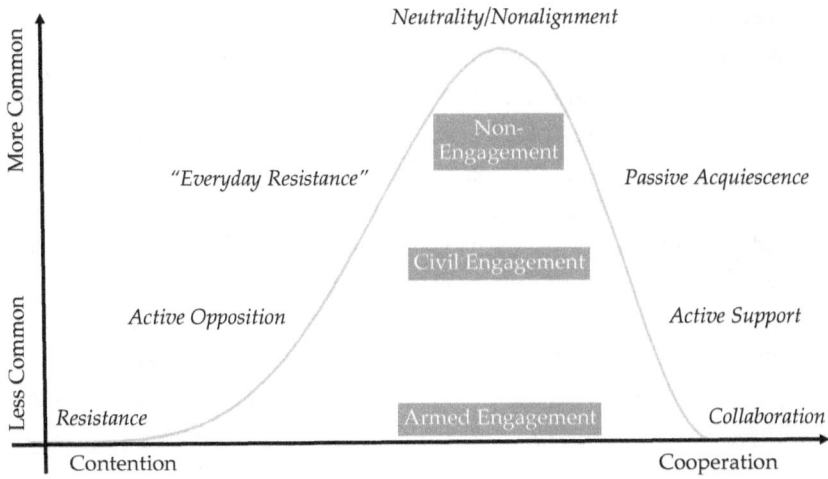

FIGURE 2.2 How do civilians survive insurgent control?

Source: Author.

includes autonomy, where individuals pursue independence from insurgent and government control through civil and armed tactics.[65] While it makes little sense to describe the "average" or "modal" repertoire, most people initially survive by hiding, laying low, or passively acquiescing to insurgent control. Given this reality, the distribution is left skewed, demonstrating that neutrality and passive acquiescence are more common than everyday resistance and armed contention.

Survival repertoires also vary based on their level of insurgent engagement. Engagement comprises action and inaction (e.g., speaking out versus staying silent), as well as public versus private actions (e.g., public protest versus confidential informing). Nonengagement—including hiding, laying low, avoidance, or evasion—is more common than direct engagement.[66] Similarly, civil engagement—such as providing food, shelter, money, or information to insurgents—is more common than violent engagement. During wartime, where potential costs include injury, death, or property destruction, one would expect individuals to pursue less risky repertoires when they have relatively more to lose, and more risky repertoires when they have already been injured, lost loved ones, or incurred damage to property or other material assets.[67]

Risk tolerance varies based on age and gender. Research suggests that young adults—especially men between the ages of sixteen and twenty-five—tend to exhibit higher levels of risk-taking behavior compared to other age cohorts.[68] Variation in risk tolerance can emerge from differences in developmental changes, peer influence, and cultural norms surrounding gender roles. Biological and sociocultural factors, including hormonal differences and societal expectations of masculinity, are also contributing factors.[69] In the context of wartime survival, one would expect to find greater variation in survival repertoires among younger demographics, with military-age males representing a majority of those individuals engaged in armed repertoires of collaboration and resistance.[70]

Survival also involves volition, or how much perceived agency individuals have over their decisions in times of crisis. Volition is crucial for understanding wartime survival, but difficult to observe because it involves exploring internal beliefs rather than evaluating external behaviors. It also entails, as Jeffrey Hass observes, respecting the tragic dimension of survival: "When agency is *compelled* by survival rather than volition and involves thinking the unthinkable, what agency is this, when we do what we would not otherwise do?"[71] A related challenge applies to understanding peoples' motivations, including how pragmatism and principle affect the adoption of specific repertoires. Whether individuals described their behaviors as forced or free is critical not only for understanding how people survive violence, but also how communities pursue justice, reconciliation, or retaliation after the war ends. This study examines questions of volition and agency, in detail, in the case studies on Baghdad, the Sunni Triangle, and Ninewa Governorate.

CONTENTION

Contention challenges insurgent control by harming, inhibiting, or undermining insurgents' goals, strategies, and capabilities. Contentious repertoires occur in public and private, including avoiding interactions with insurgents (i.e., nonengagement), as well as civil or armed resistance. It includes acts of commission (e.g., informing to government forces) as well as acts of omission (e.g., silence). Moreover, contention can be coerced, reluctant, or voluntary. In general, acts of "everyday resistance"—such as talking back, disobeying an order, violating curfew, or providing misleading information—are more common than direct resistance. Contention is also distinct from the absence of cooperation. Not all actions that undermine insurgent control necessarily benefit the government. In other words, not all forms of contention involve cooperation with government or coalition forces.

Table 2.2 categorizes contention based on the degree of insurgent engagement, as well as whether repertoires are civil or violent. "Everyday resistance," or the ways in which people's routine activities subtly

TABLE 2.2 Contentious repertoires

Repertoire	Description	Examples
"Everyday resistance"	Routine actions—including disobedience, defiance, dissent, and denial—that subtly undermine or challenge insurgent control	• Talking back or talking down to insurgents; refusing insurgent commands or orders • Quitting work or school • Violating enforced cultural norms or expectations • Feigned belief, cooperation, or obedience (e.g., *nifaq*)* • Spreading rumors, gossip, or innuendos • Playing banned music or sports; creating nonreligious artwork • Self-harm or suicide
Active opposition	Proactive, nonviolent actions (public and private) that undermine insurgent control	• Citizen journalism (posting insurgent activities to social media) • Public protests, demonstrations, or labor strikes • Theological debate or disagreement with IS clerics or fighters[†] • Spying or informing to pro-government militias, self-defense groups, or state security forces • Smuggling of goods, currency, or people in or out of the community
Armed resistance	Violent collective action aimed at harming insurgents or destroying their resources	• Sabotage or vandalism • Vigilantism • Mobilizing a community militia or neighborhood self-defense group • Enlisting in the army, police, or intelligence services of the incumbent regime

* *Nifaq* translates as "hypocrisy." *Munafiq* is a hypocrite or false Muslim (see Qurʿan 2:8–14).
† The term for this is ʿilm al-kalam or "the science of debate (discourse)."

undermine insurgents' power and authority in the community, is the most common form of contention among those living under insurgent control.[72] It includes disobedience, defiance, dissent, and denial, and it can take such forms as refusing to comply with insurgents' orders, directives, or authority, or complying in a manner that obfuscates or frustrates insurgents' interests or goals.[73] As Anna Johansson and Stellan Vinthagen observe, "everyday resistance is quiet, dispersed, disguised or otherwise seemingly invisible to elites, the state or mainstream society."[74] Everyday resistance can also be premeditated or spontaneous, such as a Moslawis' decision to play violin music from their apartment windows, or ride their bicycles in view of IS checkpoints.[75] Similarly, individuals can resist by feigning compliance or dishonestly collaborating with insurgents. Even individuals who lack reliable cell phone or Internet access can communicate with government forces, such as those Mosul residents who used compact discs to mark insurgent locations for coalition air strikes. Other examples include double entendre, satire, and wordplay tagged on public buildings, with phrases like "The Mythical State" (*ad-dawlah al-kurafiyya*) and "The Sex State" (*ad-dawlah al-jinsiyya*).[76]

Local residents can also contend with insurgent rule by engaging in various forms of active opposition.[77] Unlike everyday resistance, active opposition includes voluntary, organized, and public actions aimed at undermining insurgent control. Active opposition can be reluctant or voluntary, including direct or indirect forms of engagement, but it is always limited to civil action. Examples include organizing or participating in protests, riots, labor strikes, or online mobilization and social activism.[78] Unlike armed resistance, civil resistance is equally common among men and women living under insurgent rule. Isak Svensson and coauthors, for example, found that repertoires of civil resistance were equally likely among Sunni men and women living through IS control in Mosul.[79] In Syria, an elderly women displaced from rural Damascus gained notoriety throughout Daraa and Idlib for engaging in theological debates with IS clerics. Citing specific Qurʿanic verses popular with Islamists, she would conclude her arguments with "your caliphate is cursed (*dawlatocom malouna*)!"[80]

A similar example comes from post-conflict Sudan. During the protests against Sudanese president Omar al-Bashir held in the winter of 2018, citizens across major cities coordinated various acts of civil resistance. As Mai Hassan and Ahmed Kodouda write of the strategies of local protestors in

Khartoum, "Weekly 'schedules' of organized resistance were announced via Facebook, Twitter, and old-fashioned flyers. On some days, the SPA [Sudanese Professionals Association] asked civilians to attend a demonstration or protest. Other days were slated for 'individual initiatives'—low-level acts of resistance such as changing one's social-media profile picture or spray-painting anti-regime slogans on local streets."[81] Civil resistance can even verge on the absurd, as was the case during a 2020 public protest in Morocco, where local residents thwarted the police's ability to disperse the crowd by releasing dozens of feral cats with the flag of Western Sahara tied around their necks.[82]

Armed resistance is the riskiest form of contention. It can involve collaborating with rival armed actors (i.e., defection), or mobilizing a community militia or neighborhood self-defense group. However, public repertoires of armed resistance are quite rare. Only the most risk-acceptant individuals—especially military-age males—will opt to violently resist insurgent rule. Often, armed resistance is pursued in private, through sabotage, vandalism, and vigilantism. During the liberation of Mosul in summer 2017, for example, some local residents used the shifting balance of power to retaliate against IS insurgents and suspected collaborators (see chapter 6).[83] While rare in the Middle East context, examples of female-led armed resistance movements also exist, including the Women's Protection Units of the Syrian Democratic Forces in northeast Syria.

Under what conditions does contention emerge?

Local residents who benefit from government rule are the most likely to contend with insurgent control. Contention will be strongest and most viable among those residents who cannot acclimate to insurgent rule without sacrificing access to basic needs or violating sacred values. Acts of everyday resistance, in particular, will be most common among the subset of residents who are threatened by insurgent rule but who lack viable alternatives for protection. As insurgents consolidate control—typically through increasingly invasive strategies—grievance and resentments build, motivating the most risk-acceptant individuals to pursue civil and armed resistance.

Resisting foreign occupation represents a canonical example of contention by those who benefit from government protection.[84] Aversion to occupation—either by external militaries or foreign fighters—activates latent alienation, fear, and trauma, triggering various repertoires of resistance against the occupiers.[85] Highly invasive forms of occupation, in particular, trigger resistance by activating nationalist sentiment and fear of collective victimization.[86] During the Israeli invasion of southern Lebanon in 1982, popular support for the National Resistance Front enabled an opposing coalition of armed groups to undermine the Israeli offensive on West Beirut. Contention included providing misinformation to Israeli counterinsurgents, collaborating with armed groups like Hezbollah, and armed resistance against Israel's local proxy, the South Lebanon Army.[87]

Contention also emerges when ordinary people oppose insurgent control but lack viable alternatives for basic needs, especially physical protection. Similar to those displaced by conflict, the lack of viable alternatives might result from the absence of countervailing forces in the community, or because government forces or pro-government militias pose a similar threat to survival. In these scenarios, contention will be passive and less visible, such as private acts of disobedience, dissent, or denial. The lack of viable alternatives for protection, however, disincentivizes most people from pursuing civil or armed resistance.

The plight of Palestinian communities in the West Bank offers several salient examples. Given popular dissatisfaction with the Palestinian Authority since the failure of the 2000 Camp David Summit, and a staunch commitment to oppose further Israeli occupation, many local civilians pursued passive forms of noncooperation and civil disobedience. Public protests, riots, and acts of civilian disobedience against the PA security apparatus and the Israel Defense Forces are especially common among displaced populations in refugee camps in Nablus and Jenin. As one Palestinian refugee in the Balata camp outside Nablus explained, "We are all Palestinian and it doesn't matter how many times the Israelis raid the camp or how many of us they kill, we will fight back."[88]

Finally, opportunistic forms of contention are most common when insurgent control is in flux and local residents have an outside option for protection. Opportunistic contention is often spontaneous and flexible and can take the form of public acts of defiance or disobedience, as well as higher-risk forms of collective action. In most cases, opportunistic contention is preceded by neutrality or nonalignment, as people seek to leverage new opportunities for governance to secure privileged access to protection or material resources. During the 2007 "Anbar Awakening," for example, coalition forces forged an alliance of convenience with Sunni tribes in western Iraq. The coalition offered cash, guns, and training in exchange for armed resistance against al-Qaʿida.[89] While some tribal leaders resisted al-Qaʿida prior to the coalition's offer, the alliance between the coalition and Sunni tribes was critical in disrupting insurgent control in Anbar Governorate.

NEUTRALITY

Neutrality represents actions that neither advance nor undermine insurgent control. Such repertoires include "masking any allegiance to either side and seeking protection in non-combatant status,"[90] as well as "actively avoiding alignments, reducing civilian participation in the conflict, and demanding accountability through various armed and nonviolent mechanisms."[91] While neutrality can originate from principled or pragmatic motivations, neutral repertoires share in common a conscious decision to avoid alignment. Unlike contention or cooperation, however, it is unusual for individuals to be coerced into neutrality. Indeed, hiding or laying low is the most common initial response for those confronting escalating violence in their communities.

Table 2.3 describes how neutral repertoires vary with respect to engagement and risk. Most ordinary people remain neutral by avoiding initial contact with insurgents or government forces. Repertoires include hiding, laying low, or concealing property or other material resources from armed groups. "We did not leave the basement. We were lucky because we had men in the basement who knew how to handle welding machines. They put up an extra door; they put up additional levers that protected the door. We were already preparing. We understood that something terrible was coming," explained a Ukrainian survivor of the 2022 Bucha massacre.[92]

Hiding or laying low are temporary repertoires because food, cooking fuel, or medicine can only last so long. Once resources run out, most people are forced to stop hiding and risk encountering insurgents. Under such circumstances, commuting becomes a more effective repertoire for avoidance or evasion despite the increased personal risk. Individuals will regularly change locations, transit routes, or commute out of the community for medical care, school, or work. The risk of insurgent encounter increases

TABLE 2.3 Neutral repertoires

Repertoire	Description	Examples
Hiding	Avoiding contact with insurgents by staying in place	• Hiding or laying low in a home, school, or business • Concealing food, money, or other material resources
Commuting	Avoiding contact with insurgents by moving between locations	• Regularly changing locations or concealing movement • Commuting out of conflict-prone areas for school, medical care, or work • Changing transportation routes or evading checkpoints
Autonomy	Organized, public forms of collective action (civil and armed) aimed at achieving independence from insurgent or government control	• Declaring specific institutions or locations "off limits" to fighters (e.g., a school, hospital, or house of worship) • Armed secession or separatism

with the distance and timing of such movements; encounters with insurgents on the street or at checkpoints are seldom cost-free. "While neutrality is an option whenever the armed actor does not make demands and does not establish any rules, it is impossible when it actually does so," explains Ana Arjona.[93]

Autonomy is the riskiest neutral repertoire during wartime. "Autonomy" here refers to "independence in decision-making and the freedom from violence required to sustain it."[94] Unlike cooperation or contention, autonomy requires collective action. Most individuals who declare themselves separate from armed groups are incapable by themselves of defending against the violent repercussions of their perceived insubordination. As such, autonomy can involve civil or armed actions, but necessarily entails direct engagement with insurgents or government forces through negotiations, bargaining, or coercion.

Local institutions can even mitigate the effects of violence by altering fighters' incentives for victimizing civilians.[95] Jana Krause finds that vulnerable communities represented by effective leaders are able to prevent the escalation of violence through the development of social resilience.[96] Ashley Jackson observes a similar pattern in wartime Afghanistan, where customary authorities, private organizations, and prominent elites all developed creative strategies for bargaining with local Taliban.[97] For example, in Christopher Zürcher's research on civilian survival, Afghan villagers sustained neutrality by paying a tax to subsidize the Afghan Local Police, a network of pro-government militias, instead of mobilizing community members to fight for the Kabul government.[98]

Groups express autonomy through civil and armed repertoires. Civil autonomy can involve direct negotiations with armed actors about the political status of their community or assisting those affected by conflict independent of coordination with insurgent or government forces.[99] In her study of El Salvador's civil war, for example, Elisabeth Jean Wood describes how the Catholic Church's neutrality challenged the grievances motivating various factions of the conflict.[100] In Syria, volunteers trained as first responders and medical workers organized under an organization called the White Helmets (al-Hawdh al-bayda'). Also known as Syria Civil Defense (ad-Difaʿ al-Madani as-Suri), the White Helmets provide humanitarian assistance to victims in contested communities throughout the country. Despite their opposition to the Assad regime, the White Helmets intentionally pursued political neutrality, including by assisting wounded regime soldiers.

In other cases, community members pursue armed autonomy. Armed autonomy is particularly common when groups are seeking secession or separatism. Among Kurdish minorities in Turkey, Syria, Iraq, and Iran, the mobilization of self-defense groups is a particularly popular strategy.[101] Mobilizing community self-defense groups is also a common repertoire for civilians living in semiautonomous communities in southern Yemen, such as Aden and Hadhramaut.[102] In other cases, communities self-mobilize as a strategy of last resort in the face of existential threats. As Benny Morris notes, Palestinian villages used nonalignment as a strategy of political neutrality at the beginning of the 1948 Arab-Israeli War.[103] Moreover, for ethnoreligious minorities across the MENA region, community militias and self-defense groups serve as the last line of defense against predatory insurgents, rebels, and even government forces.

Under what conditions does neutrality emerge?

Hiding, laying low, or commuting are among the most common repertoires for citizens first encountering insurgent control. When conflict unexpectedly breaks out or escalates, the natural inclination is to lay low or avoid engagement with government or insurgent forces. The decision to hide, evade, or conceal will eventually give way to flight, everyday resistance, or passive acquiescence. Most people simply lack the resources or psychological stamina to remain hidden or constantly on the move. The ability to sustain neutrality over time, however, depends on one's relative insulation from wartime violence, as well as the opportunity to engage with insurgent and government forces. Higher-risk forms of neutrality, including armed autonomy, emerge when local residents can maintain access to basic needs and avoid direct contestation between the government and insurgents.

In contested communities, autonomy arises in two distinct scenarios. First, many people pursue autonomy out of necessity rather than choice. For those lacking the motivation or opportunity to flee, the combination of proximate threats and lack of viable alternatives incentivizes communities to pursue self-protection. When security alternatives are unavailable, community members will insulate themselves from direct insurgent engagement and mobilize self-defense groups or militias.

In the MENA region, armed autonomy is a particularly common strategy for minority groups. For Egypt's Coptic population, local churches have resorted to training "scouts" (*kashshafa*) within their congregations to vet and screen parishioners attending worship services.[104] As one volunteer scout explained, "The police alone cannot secure the church because they are outside the community, their lives aren't attached to this place. . . . The important advantage the scouts have is that they know the people who come to pray every day."[105] Druze communities across Syria similarly pursued autonomy in the face of simultaneous threats from the Assad regime and IS. Between 2018 and 2020, As-Suwayda residents mobilized community militias to fend off insurgent attacks while simultaneously engaging in anti-regime protests.[106]

Autonomy also emerges within communities who can protect access to basic needs in the face of competition between government and insurgent forces. By definition, such communities are insulated from the negative externalities of conflict and can therefore impose conditionality on their cooperation with armed groups. Communities may be insulated from proximate threats because they are located in an area that lacks strategic importance (e.g., an absence of natural resources, transit points, etc.), or because they have trusted local elites who can negotiate on their behalf. "Effective engagement with armed groups, negotiations over neutrality, and refusal to collaborate in attacks can only be achieved if community leaders can rely on broad support from their own community," explains Jana Krause.[107]

Community autonomy also occurred at the height of Iraq's civil war between 2003 and 2006. As the war escalated, a handful of neighborhoods within Baghdad's Karrada District remained insulated from political violence due to their socioeconomic status, ethnic heterogeneity, and relatively stable population. As Ami Carpenter explains, Shi'a militias were unable to penetrate Karrada because "residents rejected their attempts to recruit fighters and set up safe houses. . . . [The militias] sought community support for sectarian operations but 'people didn't allow them to get dominant there.'"[108] Karrada's internal social cohesion and relative insulation from political violence allowed residents to remain autonomous from the coalition, al-Qaʿida, and sectarian militias.

COOPERATION

Cooperation reflects the degree to which local residents identify with or provide material assistance to insurgents. It involves direct engagement with insurgents, as well as obedience or compliance absent direct interactions. Cooperation occurs at the individual and collective levels and includes public repertoires (e.g., providing labor) as well as privates ones (e.g., supplying money, food, or shelter). Similarly, cooperation involves proactive efforts (e.g., confidential informing) or intentional inaction (e.g., withholding information from government forces). Public cooperation entails greater personal risk, and as such, private repertoires are more common than public ones.

How individuals perceive their own sense of agency in the face of insurgent governance motivates different forms of cooperation. Whether cooperation is coerced, reluctant, or voluntary derives as much from self-perception as from insurgent behavior. As one Afghan translator recounted, "You think people have a choice to take sides. He's telling you that the Taliban does not allow there to be any 'civilians.' . . . Even if you do not fight with them, you must be on their side."[109] Such anecdotes reinforce Livia Schubiger's observation that individuals collaborate in order to "publicly convey their alignment with the stronger side to escape the victim category."[110]

As noted in table 2.4, cooperation occurs at various levels of engagement, including passive acquiescence, active support, and collaboration. Most people cope with insurgent governance by passively acquiescing in a manner that avoids direct or sustained engagement. Cooperation can be voluntary (e.g., the paying of taxes or tolls) or coerced (e.g., forced marriage), but seldom entails active support for insurgent rule. What separates those

TABLE 2.4 Cooperative repertoires

Repertoire	Description	Examples
Passive acquiescence	Compliance, obedience, and weak cooperation with insurgent control	• Adhering to mandatory norms, values, or cultural expressions (e.g., dress, diet, facial hair, etc.) • Allowing insurgent access to private property or resources • Tax, toll, or tithe paying (e.g., *zakat*)[*] • Arranged marriage between a local girl/woman and insurgent[†]
Active support	Semi- or fully voluntary cooperation with or support for insurgent control	• Public oath of allegiance or support (*bayʿah*)[‡] • Participating in schooling, courses, or events sponsored by insurgents • Attending public rallies, meetings, or demonstrations • Working for insurgent civil institutions (e.g., utilities provision) • Providing money, food, shelter, or private information to insurgents • Storing or transporting weapons, ammunition, or other military equipment
Collaboration	Actively assisting or advancing insurgents' interests and goals in the community	• Informing or spying on neighbors, friends, or relatives • Trafficking or smuggling humans, money, weapons, or other resources • Enlistment in an insurgent organization

[*] *Zakat* is an obligatory tithe (typically 2.5 percent of total income) required of all Muslims who can afford it.
[†] Arranged marriage is distinct from, but can include, sexual assault, trafficking, and rape.
[‡] A *bayʿah* is an oath of allegiance to a leader (see Qurʿan 48:18).

who cooperate from supporters or collaborators is the absence of civil or armed action against the state or its allies.

In the face of insurgent control, the best many residents can hope for is a set of effective coping skills.[111] Acquiescence, compliance, and obedience may not directly advance insurgents' authority or control, but neither do they inhibit insurgent operations in the community. Examples of reluctant compliance include allowing insurgents to access or use private property, attending compulsory religious services, or conforming to a shift in norms, values, or cultural expressions (e.g., dress). Examples include paying taxes, tolls, or tithes (*zakat*), or arranging a marriage between a fighter and community member. Coerced cooperation involves support for insurgents under conditions of extreme duress, especially the threat of physical punishment.

When insurgents govern effectively, they can also induce cooperation among the local population. For insurgents, local cooperation not only increases their group's military effectiveness (e.g., by identifying, isolating, and degrading defectors), but also bolsters public legitimacy. For local residents, the returns on passive acquiescence include preferential treatment, such as access to private goods like personal stipends or salaries, as well as a sense of social status. As Stathis Kalyvas notes, "Gaining control over an area brings collaboration, and losing control of an area brings much of that collaboration to an end."[112] In contested communities, a "combination of weak preferences and opportunism, both of which are subject to survival considerations," motivates local support.[113] The loyalty-for-protection bargain also incentivizes coethnic defection—when individuals join an opposing ethnic or sectarian group. Coethnic defection is not a simple matter of political opportunism. Rather, defection can be a way for individuals to protect themselves and their families, to pursue political or economic opportunities, or to express dissent or dissatisfaction with their in-group's leadership.[114]

Other people survive by actively supporting insurgent control. Active support can include publicly working for insurgent institutions—such as maintaining public utilities—or attending rallies, meetings, or demonstrations. It also includes transactional cooperation, where community members bargain, negotiate, or make deals with insurgents in order to receive special treatment.[115] During the Syrian Civil War, for example, some Sunni residents of Manbij arranged marriages between family members and IS insurgents as a strategy for avoiding further victimization.[116] A similar dynamic occurred during the IS assault on Yazidi villages in Sinjar, Iraq, in August 2014. During the attack on the village of Kocho, IS commander "Abu Hamza" (an epithet or *kunya*) bargained with the village *mukhtar* (village leader), Sheikh Ahmed Jasso, about which villagers would be allowed to leave, which would be allowed to convert, and which would face execution.[117] Cooperation can also take the form of spontaneous support, such as volunteering for specific jobs or tasks.[118] During the radicalization of Palestinian refugee camps in Jordan and Lebanon in the late 1960s, for example, many refugees supported the presence of militant organizations aligned with the Palestinian Liberation Organization given the lack of viable alternatives for safety and economic opportunities.[119]

Collaboration is the riskiest form of cooperation. Collaboration is proactive and voluntary support that advances or benefits insurgent control. "Collaboration may be entirely pragmatic and is consistent with a variety of motivations; it need not, though it may, involve allegiance to the occupier or support for its ultimate goals," explain Matthew Kocher, Adria Lawrence, and Nuno Monteiro.[120] One prominent example includes Jewish collaboration with Israeli nationalist forces during the 1948 Arab-Israeli War. Material support for and enlistment within irregular units like the Haganah, Irgun, and Stern Gang proved crucial to Jewish resistance to the British Mandate in Palestine.[121]

Under what conditions does cooperation emerge?

Cooperation with insurgents is most likely among local residents who have a long-standing grievance against the central government. In conflict-affected communities, the most common grievances include political or economic exclusion, as well as past victimization or exploitation by the state. Indeed, cooperation is most common among those who feel they can directly benefit from insurgent control. In other cases, individuals may not possess a viable outside option for protection, and are wagering that they can secure access to basic needs by bargaining or negotiating with insurgents. Consistent with Stathis Kalyvas's control-collaboration model, individuals will support insurgents who maintain control through selective violence and provide preferential treatment for local supporters. Preferential treatment might emerge due to a shared social identity, or because individuals make side payments through taxes, tolls, tithes, or arranged marriages.

In Yemen, the Southern Transition Council, a member of the broader Hirak movement, sustains local cooperation by demonstrating how support for southern secessionism tangibly benefits residents of cities such as Aden and Mukalla. In the aftermath of the 2011 Arab uprisings, for example, political entrepreneurs in southern Yemen "took the helm and redirected the movement towards separatism, diverting it away from general political aims and restricting their demands to separation alone. This was made possible largely thanks to their access to cash to finance activities and thus create a body of supporters."[122] Coethnic patronage allowed southern separatists to maintain autonomy from the incumbent regime in Sanaʿa, the Houthi insurgency, and local franchises of al-Qaʿida and IS.

Opportunistic or transactional cooperation will emerge among residents who have a credible outside option for protection. Consistent with past research on opportunism during wartime, local residents courting insurgents and government forces have the flexibility to hedge, double deal, or switch sides based on the local balance of power.[123] However, given the inherent risk of alienating previous allies, opportunistic cooperation is more likely to play out in the private rather than the public sphere. In the Israel Defense Forces' counterinsurgency campaign during the Second Intifada (2000–2005), Palestinians selectively cooperated with multiple opposition groups, such as Fatah, Hamas, and Islamic Jihad. Local cooperation was opportunistic and depended not only on whether residents lived in the West Bank or the Gaza Strip, but also the degree to which they suffered prior victimization by Israeli soldiers.[124]

Active collaboration is the rarest form of cooperation during wartime. As past research on radicalization notes, individuals are most likely to collaborate when they share a strong connection to a common social identity and perceive an external threat to their in-group's sacred values.[125] In order to act on a preexisting grievance or victimhood status, individuals must also perceive that they have agency over their decisions, and an opportunity to change their current circumstances through radical action.[126] In a study of 220 interviews with former IS recruits, Anne Speckhard and Molly Ellenberg uncovered a range of motivations for collaboration, including access to salaries or stipends, the desire to elevate social status, the need for a sense of community, and the opportunity to work toward a shared mission.[127]

Ordinary people survive wartime violence in different ways, even when they confront similar threats. Instead of operating as "passive, manipulated, or invisible actors,"[128] they survive through various social practices, organized routines, symbols, and rhetorical strategies, collectively known as survival repertoires. Individuals adopt specific repertoires by drawing on a set of heuristics formed by past experience and current conflict dynamics. Beyond the fundamental decision of whether to remain or flee the community, individuals consider what it would cost—materially and psychologically—to accommodate insurgent rule. While most people begin by hiding or laying low, as conflict endures residents confront difficult choices surrounding contention or cooperation. Acts of everyday resistance, as well as passive acquiescence, are most common. Those with a higher risk tolerance and a preference for governance under the status quo will pursue active resistance. Those who might privately benefit from insurgent rule are more likely to cooperate.

Survival repertoires are also a product of conflict processes, especially a community's collective experience with past violence. How do survival repertoires evolve as conflicts endure? The next chapter looks at Iraq's experience with protracted conflict after the 2003 U.S.-led intervention. It focuses, in particular, on the political and economic dynamics that led to the rise of the Islamic State after the departure of U.S. forces in December 2011.

3

The Rise and Fall of the Islamic State, 2011–2017

There is no doubt in our mind that limiting jihad to military efforts alone is foolish, especially in Iraq. Everybody is getting ready to benefit from the day the occupiers leave the country.
—FALLUJAH MEMORANDUM, DECEMBER–JANUARY 2010

You know, there were civilians in the house that was bombed last night.... I tried to stop it, I called the commander to say there were civilians, but they went ahead with the strike. The neighbours told me that most of the people got out but three died. Did I kill the civilians? Will God punish me for that?
—LIEUTENANT COLONEL MUNTADHER, BRIGADE COMMANDER, IRAQI COUNTER TERRORISM SERVICE

Ambiguity is endemic to civil wars; this turns their characterization into a quest for an ever-deeper 'real' nature, presumably hidden underneath misleading facades—an exercise akin to uncovering Russian dolls."[1] Many of the conversations I have had with Iraqis affected by wartime violence resonate with Stathis Kalyvas's description of the complex nature of civil war. One of the earliest conversations took place at an Arabic restaurant in Columbus, Ohio. One of my conversation partners was a Chaldean Christian who once worked as a police officer in Baghdad. "For all their problems," he explained, "at least the Baʿthists provided a stable paycheck and pension." A few other men around the table—Shiʿa who also lived and worked in Baghdad—demurred, stating that life was hard even for the employed thanks to eroding standards of living throughout the 1990s. Another young man—a teenager when U.S. forces arrived in Baghdad in April 2003—complained about the rampant corruption, unemployment, and sectarianism confronting friends and family members in his old neighborhood. "Maybe Iraq would have been better off had the U.S. never invaded in the first place," he quipped. Around the table I heard a few scoffs and saw a handful of sour looks, but no fierce objections.[2] Given what I knew about the brutality of Saddam's regime, the seeming consensus among group took me by surprise.[3]

Hearing from these men highlighted three lessons about how lived experience shapes conflict narratives. First, social identity informs how people reconstruct personal experiences of surviving wartime violence. Memories that reinforce the beliefs, values, or norms of one's home community are often the most salient, even among those insulated from conflict. Second, the experiences and identities most relevant to ordinary people are distinct from the categories most salient to foreign researchers. Concepts like "ethno-sectarian conflict" are ultimately useful fictions; they can muddy understanding as much as they illuminate it. Third, most people can cope with physical or economic insecurity if their community's social bonds remain intact. Conversely, increased safety or higher standards of living seldom improve livelihoods if social trust dissolves.

This chapter examines the rise and fall of the Islamic State in Iraq between 2011 and 2017. While it does not provide a comprehensive history of Iraq's post-Saddam conflicts, its goal is to demonstrate how the 2003 civil war and 2014 IS insurgency represent a single conflict punctuated by a brief interwar period. By identifying the continuity between the U.S.-led intervention and the rise of IS, it illuminates how ordinary Iraqis navigated their country's evolving civil conflict. More concretely, it focuses on the macro-level political and economic forces that shaped the range of survival repertoires available to ordinary Iraqis.

The narrative unfolds over three acts. Act 1 begins with the de-escalation of coalition forces after the U.S.-led "troop surge" of 2007–2008. Rather than conclusively defeating opposition forces, the surge temporarily dampened a more fundamental conflict between insurgent groups, sectarian militias, and paramilitary organizations. It then examines the negative, unintended consequences of the withdrawal of coalition forces in December 2011. Act 2 explores how preexisting Islamists groups—including al-Qaʿida in Iraq (AQI)—evolved into IS. It also analyzes IS's deployment of coercion, co-option, and persuasion to govern its newly captured territory. The chapter concludes with act 3, which provides an overview of the anti-IS coalition and the events that led to IS's defeat in December 2017. In the process, it describes how ordinary citizens survived violent encounters with coalition forces and IS insurgents.

Act 1: Elections, uprisings, and American departure (2010–2011)

The U.S.-led troop surge of 2007 and 2008 fundamentally transformed Iraq's civil war.[4] Prior to the surge, escalating violence and incompetent governance transformed the conflict from an anti-occupation insurgency into an ethno-sectarian civil war. The conflict also exacerbated the forced displacement that began in the final decade of Saddam's regime. After the introduction of twenty thousand new combat troops and a shift toward a "population-centric counterinsurgency strategy," insurgent-attributed violence decreased across Iraq. In Baghdad alone, coalition estimates of "significant activities" with insurgents decreased by 50 percent (see figure 3.1). As a result, the monthly rate of civilian fatalities in Iraq's most violent districts dropped.

Ultimately, the surge proved to be a military success but a political failure. Despite a decrease in political violence, coalition leaders were unable to facilitate political reconciliation among competing ethnic and sectarian groups. While the surge increased security for ordinary Iraqis, decreasing violence also relieved public pressure on the Maliki regime to pursue necessary political and economic reforms. Despite a rise in GDP between 2007 and 2009, corruption, inflation, and unemployment hampered economic growth. Worse yet, Maliki used the surge's tactical success to further consolidate control over the security apparatus. He also rewarded Shiʿa loyalists with promotions within the military and police, while purging competent Sunni commanders.[5] While the U.S. military insisted that Maliki incorporate the "Sons of Iraq" (Abnaʾ al-ʿIraq) militias into the

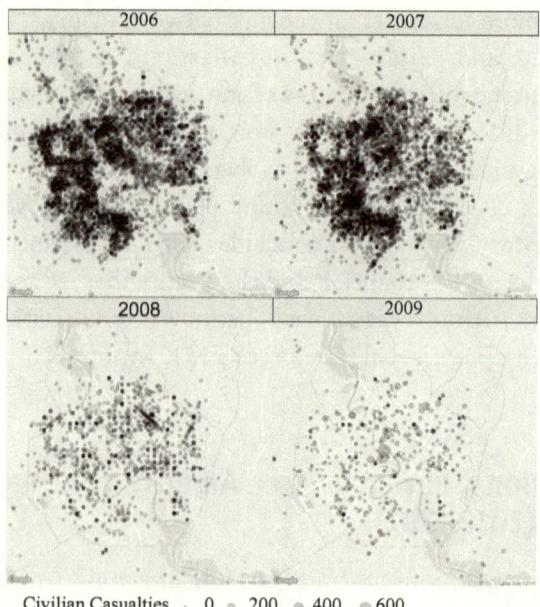

FIGURE 3.1 "Significant activity" events in Baghdad (January 2006–December 2009).

Source: "ESOC Iraq Civil War Dataset (Version 3)," Empirical Studies of Conflict, Princeton University, accessed November 3, 2023, https://esoc.princeton.edu/data/esoc-iraq-civil-war-dataset-version-3; map underlayment from Google Maps.

Ministry of Interior, Maliki and his supporters demobilized, imprisoned, or, on select occasions, killed tribal militiamen.[6] By 2011, political favoritism and coup-proofing crippled the Iraqi military beyond repair, despite a coalition investment of over $25 billion since March 2003.

NATIONAL ELECTIONS AND AMERICAN WITHDRAWAL

Iraqis approached their second parliamentary election in the post-Saddam period in March 2010. During the campaign, Maliki struggled to manage the internal balance of power within his Shiʿa coalition. In an effort to draw support from Maliki, the Islamic Supreme Council of Iraq and Sadrist parties formed a rival coalition—the National Iraqi Alliance—led by former prime minister Ibrahim al-Jaafari.[7] Despite finishing second to Ayad Allawi's Iraqi National Movement (Iraqiyya), Maliki's State of Law Coalition secured nearly one-quarter of the national vote, including eighty-nine seats in the Council of Representatives. While a second-place finish deprived Maliki of a victory against his Shiʿa rival, he was able to secure a second term after a nine-month battle marked by extra-constitutional measures and back-room deals.[8] One prominent example includes Maliki's repeated petitions to the Supreme Judicial Council requesting clarification for the constitutional definition of a "winning bloc."[9] However, Maliki's postelection maneuvering did not go unnoticed by voters. Among a random sample of Iraqis surveyed in March 2012, nearly 60 percent responded that the 2010 parliamentary elections were neither free nor fair.[10]

In forming his second cabinet, Maliki consolidated political power by excluding Shiʿa elites outside of the Daʿwa movement from key government positions. Despite giving token cabinet positions to members of the Islamic Supreme Council and Sadrists (e.g., in the Ministry of Construction and Housing), Maliki assumed the role of acting defense, interior, and national security minister.[11] Ironically enough, Maliki resurrected a series of Baʿthist-era laws that prohibited criticism of the central government. Throughout his second term, he used counterterrorism laws in conjunction with the security apparatus to victimize and imprison members of the Sunni opposition.[12]

The Arab uprisings arrived in the middle of Maliki's efforts to consolidate power. On February 25, 2011, "Day of Rage" protests (*yawm al-ghadab*) occurred throughout the country in response to Maliki's second term. The Arab uprisings' acceleration throughout the region demonstrated to many Iraqis the power of popular protest against the government's corruption, nepotism, and incompetence.[13] Most significantly, the uprisings provided an opportunity to protest the perceived fraud and inconsistencies of the 2010 parliamentary elections. On January 5, 2011, in his first public statement since returning from self-imposed exile in Iran, Muqtada al-Sadr had urged his followers to resist Iraq's foreign occupiers. Seeing an opportunity to gain political leverage over Maliki, Sadr organized a massive protest of more than one hundred thousand people on May 26, 2011. But despite sustained protests throughout the summer and fall of 2011, the uprisings failed to quell fear of renewed sectarian violence. As Marc Lynch notes, "the deep sectarian divides and the legacy of the all-too-recent horrific violence put sharp limits on how far the Iraqi population was willing to go in challenging the authorities."[14]

One unanticipated outcome of the Arab uprisings was increased pressure on Maliki to negotiate the withdrawal of U.S. combat troops. A key motivation was the negotiation of a Status of Forces Agreement (SOFA) between Baghdad and Washington, which guaranteed legal immunity to U.S. soldiers.[15] Opposition to the agreement was even higher among Shiʻa, especially among the Sadrists in parliament. Combined with opposition by the Allawi-led opposition, Maliki reached an agreement with the Obama administration to end the U.S. combat presence in Iraq by the end of 2011.

By December 18, 2011, a final convoy of 500 U.S. soldiers redeployed across Iraq's southern border with Kuwait, concluding eight years of foreign military occupation. Despite sustained state-building efforts, 200,000 Iraqi civilians were killed and upward of 4.7 million were displaced (see figure 3.2). Coalition casualties included 4,424 U.S. soldiers, 45,000 Iraqi Security Forces members, and 4,500 private contractors. An estimated

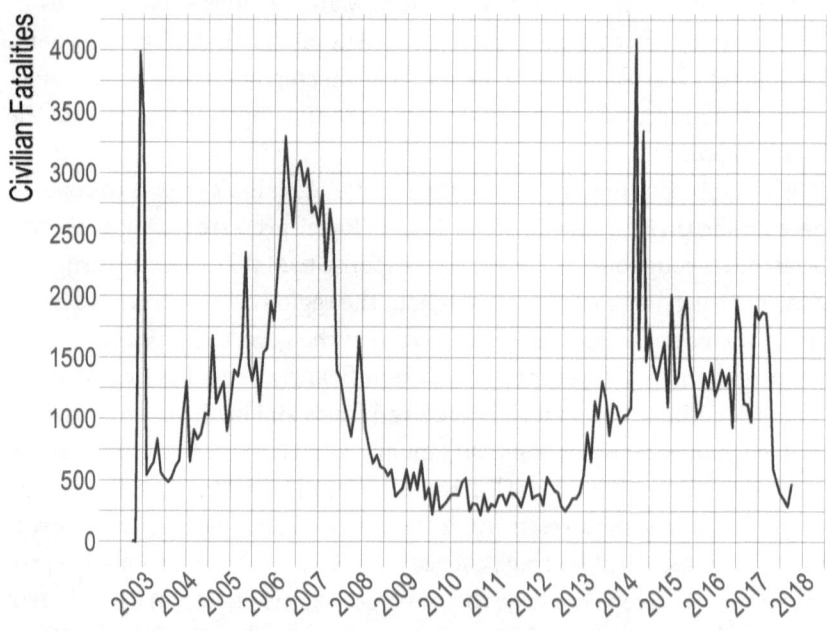

FIGURE 3.2 Civilian fatalities in Iraq (January 2003–December 2017).

Source: Iraq Body Count, https://www.iraqbodycount.org.

35,000 insurgents and militiamen were killed. The war's financial expenses, including past and anticipated costs, amounted to nearly $2 trillion.[16]

Even as security increased throughout Iraq, meeting basic needs became increasingly difficult. By 2011, one in four Iraqis under thirty were unemployed, and 40 percent of the population lacked reliable access to water, sanitation, electricity, education, and health care. "There isn't an Iraqi here who wants to enter and hasn't lost a brother or father, or received a threat," explained one refugee who resettled in Syria.[17] The percentage of those expressing a wish to return to their homes dropped from 45 percent in 2006 to 6 percent in 2012.[18]

Act 2: The interwar period and the Islamic State's rise (2012–2014)

Unanticipated by American and Iraqi leaders at the time, the departure of U.S. forces would unintentionally incubate a new generation of insurgents, militiamen, and paramilitaries. As early as June 2011, AQI was undergoing its transformation into the Islamic State. In July, then-leader Abu Bakr al-Baghdadi dispatched a small group of insurgents under the leadership of Abu Muhammad al-Golani to Syria in order to establish an al-Qaʿida affiliate to combat the Assad regime. While fallout between al-Qaʿida central command and IS would result in the creation of splinter Islamist groups aligned against Assad (e.g., Jabhat an-Nusrah), Baghdadi would consolidate control over IS from his base of operations in western Iraq.[19]

Three critical factors led IS to emerge as a formidable insurgency throughout Iraq and Syria. First, the Maliki government systemically excluded Sunnis from meaningful participation in national politics. Maliki's campaign of sectarian exclusion alienated a majority of Sunnis living outside of Baghdad. When Sunni communities protested this exclusion, Maliki used the Iraqi Army and Federal Police to harass, persecute, and victimize opposition leaders. In mid-December 2011, for example, the Iraqi Security Forces raided the home of Sunni vice president Tariq al-Hashemi based on accusations that he was leading a death squad. In response, Hashemi fled the country, was tried in absentia, and sentenced to death. During this same period, the government raided the home of Finance Minister Rafi al-Issawi and arrested his bodyguards. The following year, Ahmed al-Alwani—an influential Sunni member of parliament from Anbar who had publicly supported protests against the regime during the Arab uprisings—was also arrested. As a result, many Sunnis initially welcomed IS as an alternative source of governance because of marginalization (*mazlumiyya*) and victimization (*ihtiyal*) at the hands of the central government.

Relatedly, IS leveraged political and economic grievances among Sunnis in order to win local support. Between 2011 and 2013, several thousand Iraqis marched against the Maliki government in protests in Ramadi, Fallujah, Samarra, Mosul, and Kirkuk.[20] In an encore to the Arab uprisings, Sunnis and Kurds took to the streets again in 2013 to protest Maliki's creeping authoritarianism. The regime responded harshly to antigovernment protests. The most infamous example was the Iraqi Army's crackdown in Hawija in April 2013, killing 200 and injuring an additional 150 citizens.[21] In response to Maliki's repression, the speaker of the Iraqi parliament, Osama al-Najafi, called for the prime minister's resignation.

At the same time Sunni communities were confronting government repression, insurgents targeted local elites who could not be co-opted or persuaded to support IS. The most prominent victim of IS assassination was Sheikh Aifan Sadoun al-Issawi, a Sunni member of parliament, leader within the powerful Albu Issa tribe, and fierce critic of Islamist groups.[22] The pairing of government repression and insurgent victimization would also lead to the collapse of the Sons of Iraq as a viable resistance force against the IS occupation.

Third, IS relied on attrition (*nikaya*) and exhaustion (*ʿirhaq*) to secure an ideological and territorial advantage (*tamkin*) over government forces. Beginning in the summer of 2012, IS launched its "Breaking the Walls" campaign (*hamlat kasara al-jidran*), consisting of over two dozen suicide bombings and eight prison breaks, freeing hundreds of former al-Qaʿida fighters imprisoned in Kirkuk, Tikrit, Taji, and Abu Ghraib.[23] At the same time, insurgents launched the "Soldiers' Harvest" campaign (*hamlat hisad al-junud*) in an effort to recruit disaffected Baʿthist, ISF, and Sunni tribal fighters. The primary goal of each campaign was to reignite sectarian strife in an effort to drive Sunni support for IS. "These attacks were most likely strategically planned moves to prepare the battlefield for future operations. In particular, a number of these attacks appear to have been specially designed to not just inflict military damage, but also to spread psychological fear among the population," observes Daniel Milton.²⁴ In short, by taking advantage of local grievances and state fragility, insurgents were able to successfully deploy military coercion, economic inducements, and ideological persuasion to lay the foundations for Islamic State government in Iraq.

THE SUMMER 2014 OFFENSIVE

While IS began receiving international media attention in June 2014, their military offensive had begun eighteen months earlier. During this period, the exclusion and repression of Sunni communities, alongside the weakening of the ISF through coup-proofing, corruption, and nepotism, exposed many Iraqis to renewed levels of physical and economic insecurity.

In December 2013, insurgents capitalized on armed clashes between the Iraqi Army and Sunni tribes to launch an offensive on the provincial capital of Ramadi. In the following six months, IS would control nearly three-quarters of Anbar Governorate, including the cities of Fallujah, Al Qaʾim, Ar Rutba, and half of Ramadi. IS commanders coordinated combat operations with local tribes and community militias in order to create the perception of overwhelming force.²⁵ Throughout 2014, Sunni communities in Anbar, Diyala, and Salah al-Din witnessed levels of violence unseen since the height of the civil war.

It was the offensive on Mosul in June 2014, however, that marked IS's emergence as an existential threat to the Iraqi state. On June 4, 2014, approximately 1,500 IS insurgents under the command of Abu Abdulrahman al-Bilawi attacked Mosul's northwestern neighborhoods. In response, nearly 25,000 Iraqi soldiers fled their posts, abandoning weapons, ammunition, and other military equipment in their retreat.²⁶ As the remaining Iraqi Army and Federal Police forces launched an attempted counteroffensive, approximately 500,000 Moslawis fled their homes. Despite the government's brief counteroffensive, IS consolidated control over Mosul within six days.²⁷ In short order, IS began rebranding public institutions with the group's insignia, stamps, and signage.²⁸ As eyewitness and citizen journalist Omar Mohammad recounts, "In the first few days and weeks, there were three governance functions that the Islamic State seemed to really focus on. First, was the media department. . . . It was very important to Daʿesh that its media was functioning well. Second, was the Islamic State's police and *hisbah* [morality police]. . . . The third was finance and real estate. This was how the Islamic State controlled money and how the Islamic State controlled property and territories."[29]

By the end of June, IS control extended south into Salah al-Din and Diyala Governorates, bringing the group to within an hour's drive of Baghdad. The next week, on July 4, 2014, Baghdadi preached a Friday sermon (*khutbah*) from the pulpit (*minbar*) of Mosul's Grand Mosque of al-Nuri declaring himself caliph of a new Islamic state stretching from Aleppo, Syria, to Diyala, Iraq. By mid-August, insurgents had captured nearly 40 percent of Iraqi territory, with one in five Iraqis living under insurgent control.[30]

In the process, an estimated 9,000–10,000 Iraqis were killed and upward of 1.5 million displaced.[31] IS's ability to capture and control territory at lightning speed demonstrated the extent to which insurgent groups could not only fight like conventional militaries, but also control territory, provide basic governance, and deploy full-spectrum propaganda campaigns. More importantly, IS's rise proved a damning indictment of U.S. efforts to rebuild Iraq's government and security institutions after 2003.

IS's rise also demonstrated the dangerous, if unintended, consequences of Maliki's consolidation of power. Specifically, it showed the devastating effects that political favoritism and coup-proofing played in decimating the ISF's morale and combat effectiveness. It also revealed that the success of the Anbar Awakening had been the result of short-term interest alignment between the coalition and Sunni tribes, rather than a demonstration of grassroots support for the central government or unified resistance to foreign insurgents. It was an alliance of convenience (cemented through short-term bribes), rather than the "winning of hearts and minds," that led to AQI's temporary defeat.

GOVERNING THE CALIPHATE: COERCION, COOPTION, AND PERSUASION

After conquering territory, IS developed institutions and practices to regulate the behavior of citizens living under its control. The transition from insurgency to state building was fluid, as the group simultaneously operated as "an insurgent group, a state government, and a revolutionary movement."[32] IS governed through a "full spectrum, normative system of control within an all-encompassing propaganda state," consisting of coercion, co-option, and persuasion.³³ Thanks to insurgents serving as "accidental ethnographers," scholars now have access to dozens of private letters, public treatises, speeches, sermons, and other primary sources related to IS governing ideology and practice.³⁴

Civilian accounts of IS rule illustrate the comprehensive nature of IS "governance." One tribal leader in Tikrit explained the evolution of insurgent control in the following manner:

> In the beginning, Daʿesh did not harm anyone. They fooled the people by clearing the roads and removing all barriers that were put by the army, which had suffocated movement in the city. People felt at ease as if they broke free from prison. But after a while Daʿesh started putting pressure on people.... It was a gradual process. They first started dictating the dress code for women, then for men, they forbade smoking, then it was paying ransoms, sharing money, taking available properties for themselves on the justification that those properties were owned by military officers or those who are with Al-Maliki or work in the government. They confiscated state properties for themselves. They created problems that have side effects to this day.³⁵

Given the rapid speed at which insurgents captured territory, a critical factor for consolidating control was generating sufficient revenue to govern its sixteen provinces (*wilayat*) and hundreds of smaller townships (*qawati*). Toward that end, IS financed its growing bureaucracy and security apparatus through a "mix of taxation, confiscation, and donations," including "through smuggling oil and products originating in the Iraqi and Syrian oil sectors or through extorting entities in those sectors; through extortion and taxation of the local economy in the areas it controls; through looting war spoils, including the region's rare and valuable antiquities; and through black-market sales of stolen and looted goods."³⁶ At peak control, IS generated an annual income as high as $2.4 billion, making it the wealthiest militant organization in history.³⁷

The most significant revenue stream came from the sale of oil and natural gas. IS derived petro-carbon revenues not only from drilling, transporting, and smuggling oil and gas, but also from extorting or taxing firms operating in the energy sector. By the end of 2014, IS controlled more than 60 percent of the oil production in Syria and nearly 10 percent of Iraqi production. Insurgents also seized numerous natural gas fields throughout the region.[38] In concert, both energy sources provided the group with between $2 and $4 million in daily revenue, with an annual profit of over $750 million.[39] However, petro-carbon revenues steadily declined as coalition air strikes targeted energy infrastructure and transportation beginning in mid-2015.

IS also generated revenue through plunder (*fay'* or *ghanymah*), including the looting and sale of antiquities, currency, farmland, property, military equipment, and ammunition. During the summer 2014 offensive, it was common for IS insurgents to destroy archeological sites, plunder the artifacts, and sell them on the black market. The group also imposed taxes and tolls—between 20 to 50 percent—on antiquities excavated and smuggled out of its territories. At one point, the revenue generated through the control of antiquities reached more than $200 million, the second-highest aggregate revenue source after oil and gas.[40]

Finally, IS funded operations by collecting taxes, tolls, and tithes from local residents. To organize the collection of various rents, IS created three separate departments in charge of revenue collection: the Department of Zakat and Charities (Diwan al-Zakat wa al-Sadaqat), Department of Agriculture and Livestock (Diwan al-Zira'a), and the Department of Real Estate and Land Tax (Diwan al-Aqarat wa al-Kharaj). The latter coordinated with the civil police (*shurta*) to confiscate assets and real estate from Shi'a Arabs and Assyrian Christians, that were later redistributed or leased to IS loyalists. Experts estimate that IS insurgents generated more than $3 million per day by collecting different rents.[41]

Upon consolidating control, IS commanders would execute, imprison, or banish local elites in charge of preexisting institutions while retaining rank-and-file employees to ensure continuity of governance. For ordinary residents, insurgents offered protection and service provision in exchange for support in the form of oaths of obedience or loyalty (*bay'ah*), taxes and tithes, and labor.

As Michael Weiss and Hassan Hassan explain,

> Typically, when IS takes over a new town, the first facility it establishes is a so-called *Hudud* Square, to carry out Sharia punishments such as crucifixions, beheadings, lashings, and hand amputations. It then establishes a Sharia court, police force, and security operation station.

The work of Sharia police, known as *al-hisbah*, is not restricted to the implementation of the religious code, but also includes regulation of the marketplace. These police forces are more active in urban centers. IS divides regions into *wilayat*, or provinces, of which there are roughly sixteen in Iraq and Syria, and smaller *qawati*, or townships. One military commander, one or more security commanders, and a general emir are appointed for each township. They all answer to a *wali*, or governor.[42]

Beyond repression, IS used its revenue to deliver a litany of basic public goods and services. Service provision ranged from public utilities (electricity, water treatment, sewage, and trash collection), as well as education, health care, law enforcement, and security provision.

Toward that end, the group created a hierarchical yet decentralized bureaucracy consisting of dozens of departments and offices. As Will McCants and Aaron Zelin explain, "IS's systematizing, bureaucratizing, and formalizing its governance structures allow it to operate consistently and in parallel across its various *wilayat*."[43] The group's bureaucratic capacity stemmed from its ability to co-opt or repurpose preexisting government institutions rather than fundamentally transforming or replacing them. "Co-option is designed to smooth what is a disruptive period of transition and ensure its system of control is efficiently bureaucratized," explains Haroro Ingram.[44] By delegating power to provincial and township authorities, IS's central leadership was able to focus on grand strategy and broader political objectives. In practice, the leadership dedicated approximately 80 percent of the organization's personnel and resources toward military objectives, while reserving 20 percent for political and governance functions.

IS prioritized the distribution of goods and services based on their interpretation of Islamic law (*shariʿa*). "The nationalistic project will form a government in which all Iraqi factions will be represented regardless of any Islamic criteria. Therefore, Christians and Devil worshipers [a derogatory reference to Yazidis] and Shiʿa *rafidites* [refusers] will be represented," explains one of the group's earliest treatises. Sunni men received priority, then "People of the Book" (*Ahl al-Kitab*) (i.e., Christians) and "refusers" (*rafidun*) (i.e., Shiʿa), and then disbelievers (*kuffar*), apostates (*murtadun*), polytheists (*mushrikun*), and other nonbelievers.[45] As

People of the Book, Iraqi Christians had the option to convert to Islam, pay a tax (*jizyah*), or leave the community.

IS also developed an extensive security apparatus to enforce the rule of law. Institutions included a civil police force (*shurta*), Department of Religious Compliance (Diwan al-Hisbah), and Department of Judiciary and Grievances (Diwan al-Qada wa al-Madhalim). At the outset of their rule, IS police and courts (*mahakim*) built goodwill with local residents by cracking down on crime, including explicitly targeting thieves, murderers, drug dealers, and rapists.[46] The general lack of corruption and nepotism among the lower IS ranks contributed in large part to their charismatic legitimacy in the early days of the occupation.

As IS governance evolved, however, the coercive effects of the group's control became unbearable for Muslims and non-Muslims alike. IS's primary goal was to control all aspects of residents' lives, including their appearance, movement, behavior, and access to information. The merciless enforcement of religious and social norms demoralized the local population and served as a powerful deterrent for those considering disobedience, dissent, or resistance. The municipal police staffed security checkpoints, enforced traffic laws, and conducted investigations into criminal conduct. "Morality police" within the Department of Religious Compliance (Diwan al-Hisbah), in turn, enforced gender segregation, Islamic dress codes, religious observance (banning things like alcohol, cigarettes, and secular music), and compulsory attendance of Friday prayers.[47] In some respects, the group's tight control of information—including the banning of televisions, radios, and compact discs, as well as private Internet and cell phone access—was the most bearable aspect of their rule.[48]

IS enforced the law based on a tiered system of punishment rooted in specific interpretations of Qurʿanic passages and hadith. These included the *taʿzir* (punishment at the discretion of judges), *qisas* (retaliation or retributive justice), and *hudud* (corporal punishment for the crimes "fixed by God"). Specific punishments included public execution, beating, lashing, amputation, stoning, and crucifixion, among other practices. Residents convicted of apostasy (*irtidad*), including a failure or refusal to pay tithes, were at risk of corporal punishment or public execution (*alʾiʿdam*). Nonbelievers were not afforded the protections available to Christians. The sexual enslavement (*al-sabi*), trafficking, and rape of Yazidi women across Ninewa Governorate was particularly horrendous. Crimes against minority women and girls included human trafficking, rape, and sexual assault.[49]

IS would also co-opt local elites and residents to their cause. Strategies of co-option occurred in civil and armed contexts, including the recruitment of Sunni men to join the ranks of IS fighters. In exchange for an oath of loyalty (*bayʾah*), recruitments would receive training, arms, and ammunition, as well as a modest stipend or subsidy for food or fuel.[50] Recruits were required to pay a tax of 20 percent on all spoils of war acquired during military campaigns, including land, buildings, weapons, antiquities, and slaves.[51] On occasion, IS would also "deputize" tribal militias to fight as auxiliary forces in their home communities.[52] In addition to serving as a force multiplier on the battlefield, strategic allegiances with local tribes provided reliable information and tips, in addition to building trust with local elites who could be bought off.

IS was also effective at collecting and distributing charity to vulnerable residents. Local charity departments would provide gas canisters, redistribute surplus wheat from a successful harvest, and give cash handouts to needy citizens.[53] The Department of Religious Compliance also created a sponsorship (*kafala*) system that allowed sick residents to travel to the "lands of disbelief" (*bilad al-kufr*) for medicine or treatment in exchange for registering property (e.g., a car), which would be confiscated if they failed to return.[54] The Department of Real Estate and Land Tax (Diwan al-Aqarat wa al-Kharaj) also levied funds to invest in public infrastructure, as well as protective barriers around residents' houses and businesses.[55]

Beyond coercion and co-option, persuasion represented the most sophisticated dimension of IS control. IS created and refined a full-spectrum propaganda strategy—supported by a media department with several distinct agencies (Diwan al-Iʾlam al-Markazi)—for disseminating its Islamist ideology.[56] Advancing the goal of public outreach (*daʿwa*), as well as serving as "the new beacon that will light the path of the monotheists," IS's multiple propaganda arms were responsible for the daily distribution of content, including in print and online magazines published in Arabic, English, and multiple other languages, daily social media posts and videos on platforms like Twitter, Facebook, and Telegram, as well as printed billboards, signs, and posters in local communities.[57]

For residents living under IS control the propaganda efforts of the Daʿwa and Mosques Administration (Diwan al-Daʿwa wa-l-Masajid) and its

Department of Education (Diwan al-Talim) were equally significant. More than controlling or disseminating information, these departments worked in concert with the media agencies to shape the worldview of local residents, creating a new system of meaning for understanding life under the caliphate. The education department was responsible for recreating education curriculum for primary and secondary schools, while the Daʿwa and Mosques Administration provided adult education in the area of jobs training as well as Islamic theology and practice.

In sum, IS governed communities under its control through a deft combination of coercion, co-option, and persuasion. While many residents initially saw IS insurgents as a welcome relief to the abuses of the central government, the novelty of life under the caliphate soon diminished. As the anti-IS coalition gained momentum on the battlefield, Iraqis living under IS adapted their strategies for survival.

Act 3: The anti–Islamic State campaign (2014–2017)

While it would take until early September for Iraq's foreign allies to intervene, Baghdad's counteroffensive against IS began immediately after the fall of Mosul. What remained of the Iraqi Army, Federal Police, and Counter Terrorism Service fought alongside Kurdish Peshmerga and local pro-government militias to recapture territory.[58] To stem IS's advance toward Baghdad, government forces prioritized the protection of communities along Highways 1 and 2, the two main arteries connecting the periphery to the capital. Toward that end, a combination of Shiʿa militias and the Iraqi Army recaptured Muqdadiya on June 14.[59]

That same week in Najaf, Grand Ayatollah Sistani used his revered status among Iraqi Shiʿa to call for the mobilization of "citizens to defend the country, its people, the honor of its citizens, and its sacred places."[60] In response, over 150,000 Shiʿa volunteers mobilized into a network of pro-government militias called the Popular Mobilization Forces (PMF, or al-Hashd ash-Shaʿbi).[61] Two of the most powerful PMF groups—Asaʾib Ahl al-Haq and Kataʾib Hezbollah—were Iranian-backed militias with a history of violently resisting the U.S. occupation. Muqtada al-Sadr soon followed suit, remobilizing his Shiʿa militia into the Peace Companies (Sarayya al-Salam) and vowing to "shake the ground under the feet of ignorance and extremism."[62] Given the dire state of government security forces, Baghdad publicly recognized the PMF's legitimacy in the anti-IS coalition and deputized volunteers to take up arms. Despite this public recognition, most PMF units operated with considerable autonomy, remaining outside of the coalition's command-and-control structure. At the same time, internal rivalries among units loyal to Iran (Asaʾib Ahl al-Haq, Badr Organization, and Kataʾib Hezbollah), Sadr (Sarayya al-Salam), and Sistani (Abbas Division and Ali al-Akbar Brigade) would cripple the PMF's military effectiveness and relations with the civilian population throughout the war.

Outside of Iraq, the United States organized a seventy-four-state coalition to arm and assist local proxies aligned against IS in Iraq, Libya, and Syria. Under the mantle of Operation Inherent Resolve, the coalition sought to "degrade and ultimately destroy" the IS "parent tumor" by coordinating air strikes, special operations raids, and assistance to local security forces.[63] More surprisingly, it provided a forum for security cooperation among regional rivals, including Iran, Saudi Arabia, and Turkey. It also marked the first time U.S. and Russian forces coordinated security operations in the region since the 1991 Gulf War.

One of the coalition's first operations included a series of air strikes against IS insurgents in the villages of Sinjar and Zumar on August 2 and 3. The ethnic cleansing of Yazidi communities on Mount Sinjar, in particular, provided the clearest evidence of IS's willingness to wage genocide. Despite coalition air strikes, insurgents killed approximately 5,000 civilians, abducted between 6,000 and 8,000 women and children, and expelled over 200,000 local residents.[64]

Throughout the autumn of 2014, foreign coalition members advised, equipped, and assisted Iraqi Army, Federal Police, and Kurdish Peshmerga in their efforts to halt the IS advance. Coalition air strikes across Diyala, Ninewa, Kirkuk, and Salah al-Din prevented IS from capturing new territory, but were largely ineffective at dislodging insurgent control in consolidated areas. The deployment of nearly ten thousand coalition ground troops in October proved critical in bolstering the capabilities and combat effectiveness of Iraqi units.

By year's end, the anti-IS coalition liberated Hit, a strategic transit point in Salah al-Din, and began contesting IS control in Fallujah and Ramadi. More significantly, coalition airpower assisted the Peshmerga and Yazidi paramilitaries in liberating communities in Sinjar and Tal Afar. In the ensuing three weeks, Kurdish forces took control of territory surrounding Mount Sinjar. IS responded by returning to insurgent tactics—namely, ambushing coalition forces outside of urban centers, typically at night. Coalition forces also uncovered the first evidence of the attempted Yazidi genocide, including more than seventeen mass graves.[65]

TURNING THE TIDE: 2015–2016

Throughout 2015, the anti-IS campaign saw both setbacks and victories for coalition forces. The most significant setbacks occurred when IS consolidated control over Fallujah and Ramadi, two key urban centers in Anbar Governorate. While Fallujah came under IS control prior to the June 2014 offensive, Ramadi remained contested for the following ten months. When Ramadi finally fell to IS in May 2015, the insurgents' victory was strategically and symbolically important.[66] Figure 3.3 shows the distribution of IS attacks across Iraqi subdistricts between 2016 and 2018.

In neighboring Salah al-Din Governorate, insurgents and coalition forces competed for control over Tikrit over a nine-month period. While IS gained control of the regional capital during the summer of 2014, the anti-IS coalition launched the beginning of a successful counteroffensive in March 2015. Unlike in Anbar, coalition forces in Tikrit were forced to combat a series of IS-aligned militias, including ex-Baʻthists and Sunni Islamists.[67] By mid-April, a combination of Iraqi Army and PMF units routed the remaining contingent of IS insurgents from the city center. The liberation of Tikrit on April 17 marked the first major coalition victory outside of Baghdad.

IS's defeat in Tikrit demonstrated the PMF's combat effectiveness and battlefield resolve. Despite initial setbacks, PMF units soon learned to provide effective perimeter security, as well coordinate their operations alongside the Iraqi Army and Federal Police to clear urban neighborhoods. Iranian soldiers, such as the Quds Force commander Qasem Soleimani, also directed combat operations among the Tehran-supported PMF units (e.g., Badr Brigade and Kataʾib Hezbollah). To make matters more complicated, PMF units also engaged in extrajudicial killings and torture of captured insurgents, as well as retaliatory violence and looting against local Sunnis accused of collaborating with IS.[68]

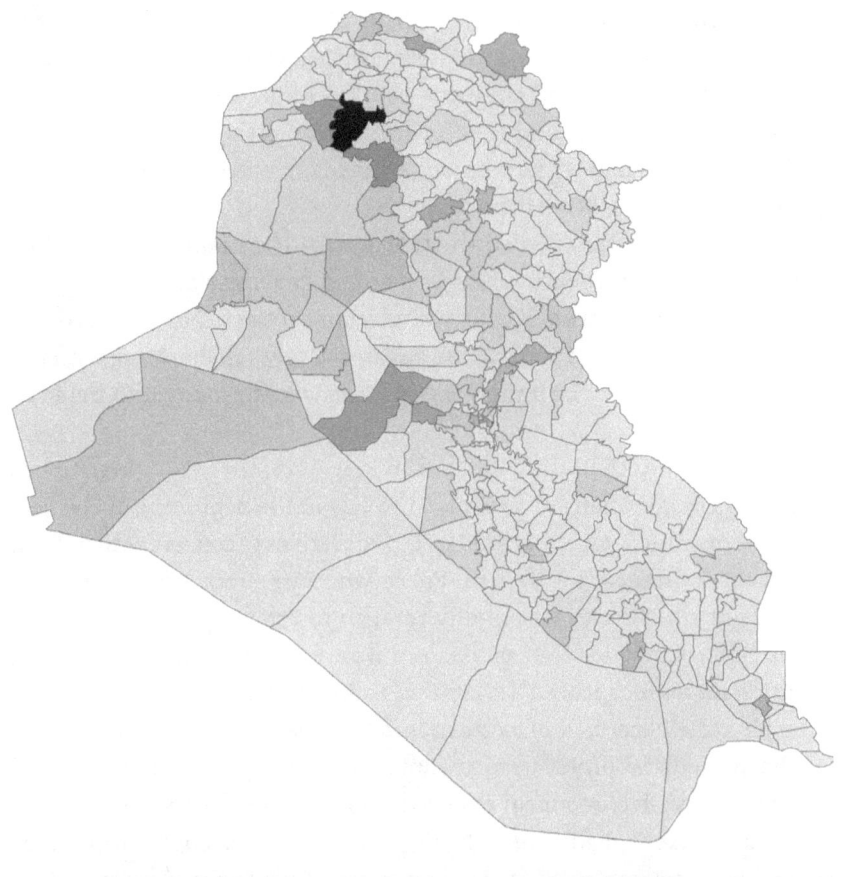

FIGURE 3.3 Islamic State attacks by subdistrict (2016–2018).

Source: Armed Conflict Location and Event Data Project, https://acleddata.com.

In northern Iraq, coalition forces made progress in liberating western Ninewa from IS control. In November, Peshmerga and Yazidi militias—with the support of coalition artillery and air strikes—liberated the town of Sinjar. Sinjar was an important victory for the coalition, as its capture eliminated a strategic waypoint along the main highway connecting Mosul to the Syrian border. However, soon after the victory, political discord emerged among the Kurdish units, leading to a breakdown in the coalition's internal cohesion. The conflict arose from disagreements concerning the postwar governance of Sinjar District, with loyalists of the Kurdistan Democratic Party in Erbil opposing the local fighters belonging to the People's Defense Forces and the Kurdistan Workers' Party.[69] Once again, Yazidis who returned to their homes after the liberation bore the consequences of inter-coalition disputes.

The anti-IS coalition turned the tide against the Islamic State in 2016. During this period, coalition forces liberated key areas of Anbar, Diyala, and Salah al-Din Governorates. In Anbar, many of the tribal militias originally affiliated with the Sons of Iraq began actively collaborating with the PMF. In some instances, Sunni tribal militias were formally integrated as PMF brigades.[70]

In response to the fall of Ramadi in May 2015, the Iraqi government launched a major offensive to retake the city at the beginning of the new year. The operation was supported by U.S. air strikes in concert with ground operations by Iraqi Army, Federal Police, and PMF units. After months of fierce fighting, the city was finally retaken in February 2016, marking a significant victory for the coalition in western Iraq. Four months later, coalition forces recaptured the cities of Fallujah and Hit. By the end of the summer, over 75 percent of western Iraq had been cleared of IS control.

The unpredictability of urban counterinsurgency affected the survival repertoires available to local residents. As coalition forces advanced on major cities like Ramadi and Fallujah, it became increasingly difficult for those who remained to either lay low or flee. During the five-week siege on Fallujah, for example, approximately fifty thousand local residents were trapped inside the city with little reliable access to food, water, or medical care.[71] An additional thirty thousand residents were able to flee before the coalition forces advanced.[72] Reports from inside Fallujah painted a grim picture, with civilians being used as human shields by insurgents and facing indiscriminate shelling by the Iraqi Army. During the siege, aid organizations also struggled to gain access to the city to provide assistance to beleaguered residents. According to a relief worker at the Danish Refugee Council, "The challenges faced are multiple. . . . From an insecure environment; access to Anbar, as the [government-controlled] Bzeibiz Bridge has been closed at various moments in the past; to a lack of sufficient coordination at various levels."[73] Often, coalition forces served as the sole reliable source for potable water, food, or cooking fuel.

By early 2017, IS control over key cities and towns in Anbar, Diyala, Ninewa, and Salah al-Din had been significantly reduced, and its ability to launch large-scale offensives had been weakened. Mosul stood as IS's final urban stronghold within Iraq.

LIBERATING MOSUL AND VICTORY OVER IS: OCTOBER 2016–DECEMBER 2017

The final phase of the anti-IS campaign involved the liberation of Ninewa Governorate. In autumn 2016, coalition forces advanced north from Salah al-Din and east from the Kurdistan Region, liberating rural communities located between Mosul and Kurdistan. By October, Assyrian and Shabak communities located along the Ninewa Plains—such as Bartalla and Qaraqosh—were clear of insurgent control.[74]

The ten-month battle to liberate Mosul proved the most decisive operation of the anti-IS campaign. Moving westward from the Ninewa Plains, Iraqi Army, Counter Terrorism Service, Federal Police, Kurdish Peshmerga, and PMF militias advanced on Mosul's neighborhoods east of the Tigris River. During the offensive, Prime Minister Abadi appealed to residents in eastern Mosul to shelter in place; about 550,000 people stayed in their homes, and only 160,000 left.[75] Combat operations involved intense street fighting and house-to-house combat by the CTS and Federal Police, supported by coalition artillery barrages and air strikes. Much like the operations to liberate Fallujah, Ramadi, and Tikrit, coalition commanders aimed to dampen sectarian tension and prevent retributive killings by insisting that Peshmerga and PMF units provide perimeter security, instead of fighting in urban neighborhoods. Coalition units that cleared urban areas—especially the CTS and Federal Police—suffered heavy casualties amounting to more than 40 percent of personnel and combat equipment.[76] By the end of the year, the coalition controlled approximately twenty neighborhoods in eastern Mosul, or 30 percent of the city's total population. One month later, at the end of January 2017, coalition forces liberated the majority of these areas.

The assault on western Mosul began in mid-February. Coalition forces advanced on the western banks of the Tigris from the southern periphery of the city. Western Mosul was more heavily fortified and populated than the eastern neighborhoods. While figures vary, coalition commanders estimated that five thousand insurgents remained in these parts of the city, with an additional twenty-five hundred fighting in an outer defensive ring. Insurgents defended territory through a combination of car bombs, suicide bombers, machine guns, and snipers, as well as improvised explosive drones and low-grade mustard gas. IS also rigged forward positions with explosives, so that when coalition artillery or airpower destroyed a building, shrapnel would kill or injure nearby civilians sheltering in place. At the Mosul airport, northwest of the city, IS used piles of debris, trenches, and sand berms to prevent coalition forces from using the airport as a command center. As one Iraqi Army colonel explained, "They [IS] have formidable fortifications. . . . They built a berm, with a deep trench behind it, and then built another berm, all laid with IEDs [improvised explosive devices]. In a whole day of fighting in this neighbourhood, we advanced no more than 150 metres."[77]

By early April progress to liberate western Mosul had stalled. As they moved closer to the densely populated neighborhoods in the five-square-mile subdistricts of the Old City, coalition forces began to see their progress slow. The Old City proved to be a difficult area to navigate. The narrow streets and tightly packed buildings made it easy for IS fighters to hide and launch surprise attacks. The al-Jumhuri Hospital, which IS used as a command-and-control center, also posed a significant challenge given the increased risk of civilian casualties. "Thousands of fighters—local and foreign—were trapped in a cluster of dense and circuitous streets and alleyways, with dwindling supplies of food and medicine and no water or electricity, bombed day and night by American drones and jet fighters. Caught in the siege were thousands of civilians. The few who escaped emerged emaciated, filthy and delirious from thirst and constant bombing," recounted Ghaith Abdul-Ahad.[78]

The fight to liberate Mosul's Old City would last five weeks. During the siege, IS fighters barricaded themselves within the Grand Mosque of al-Nuri, using local residents as human shields against coalition air strikes.[79] An estimated 9,000 to 11,000 civilians died, a third of them from coalition artillery and air strikes.[80] As Major General Sami al-Aradi later recalled, "I have been with the Iraqi Army for 40 years. I have participated in all of the battles of Iraq, but I've never seen anything like the battle for the Old City. We have been fighting for each meter. And when I say we have been fighting for each meter, I mean it literally."[81] As special operations forces approached the Grand Mosque on June 21, IS insurgents blew up the minaret, a twelfth-century monument known by locals as "the Hunchback" (al-Hadba'). One month later, on July 20, 2017, coalition forces finished clearing the mosque and surrounding neighborhoods of IS control. In the ten-month campaign to liberate Mosul, 9,000 civilians died and over 900,000 residents fled the city.[82] Over 1,300 coalition members were killed with an additional 6,800 wounded. UN data suggested that the rebuilding of Mosul alone would exceed $1 billion in the coming decade.[83]

In the aftermath of Mosul's liberation, coalition commanders were unable to prevent retaliatory violence against perceived IS collaborators. Accounts of civilian victimization, extrajudicial killings, arbitrary detention, and torture were common. As one Iraqi colonel explained, "We fight so hard, taking so many casualties, because we want to build new relations with people, and I lose men because of that. . . . And then comes some shitty unit that hasn't even seen fighting, and they start detaining people and destroying all the good work we've been doing."[84] Iraqi civilians were not immune to the temptations of revenge and retaliation. "Locals, keen to exact revenge on those they held responsible for the miseries of the last three years, started denouncing not only members of IS and their families, but any man of fighting age who came from the countryside, bore an injury, or simply looked suspicious. A schism between Mosul and its surrounding countryside had developed into animosity since most of the local senior leaders of IS came from the rural areas," observes Ghaith Abdul-Ahad.[85]

In the final months of 2017, the coalition extended its operations into rural communities throughout Anbar, Ninewa, and Salah al-Din. Fighting west from Mosul, coalition forces liberated Tal Afar in late August. Two months later, the same forces launched a major offensive to retake Hawija, which had been under IS control since June 2014. To the east in Kirkuk, Iraqi Army and Federal Police clashed with Kurdish Peshmerga, which had shielded the city from IS since the start of the insurgency. Inter-coalition clashes escalated after a controversial Kurdish independence referendum in September 2017, which had led to tensions between Baghdad and the Kurdistan Regional Government. By the end of the year, the coalition commenced operations to retake the western periphery of Anbar. The focus was on rural communities nestled along the Euphrates River, including Rawah and Al Qa'im. Both towns had been important IS strongholds and key transit points for foreign insurgents and supplies. By the end of the year, 95 percent of Anbar was under coalition control.

In a televised address to the nation on December 9, 2017, Prime Minister Haider al-Abadi formally announced Iraq's victory over IS. "We have accomplished a very difficult mission. Our heroes have reached the final strongholds of Daʿesh and purified it. The Iraqi flag flies high today over all Iraqi lands," the prime minister declared.[86] Reflecting on these events in his memoir, Abadi would later recount "The brave young men who gave their lives to serve their country. The families of the victims who sacrificed their loved ones and asked for nothing in return but hope. Hope for an end to the bloodshed. Hope for a brighter future for Iraq. The stories I heard from Iraqis on the frontlines of the conflict will stay with me for the rest of my life. We owe them everything."[87]

Victory over IS came at a steep price—in human lives and material costs. Between 2011 and 2018 somewhere in the range of 65,000–80,000 Iraqi civilians were killed as a result of IS violence; an additional 5 million were displaced from their homes.[88] Twenty-five thousand Arab and Kurdish coalition members were killed in combat, including more than 20,000 ISF and 2,500 Peshmerga.[89] The material costs—borne primarily by international coalition members—totaled over $15 billion by 2018.[90]

Even though the caliphate formally collapsed in December 2017, the Islamic State continued operating as an insurgent organization, carrying out sporadic attacks on civilians and coalition forces. The challenging terrain of the Hamrin Mountains—which stretch across Diyala, Salah al-Din, and Kirkuk Governorates—made it difficult to locate and target the remnants of IS.[91] Even in urban centers, such as Kirkuk, sporadic terrorism would reignite internal disagreements among Arab and Kurdish coalition members about who was responsible for securing the city.[92] Despite the liberation of Anbar in November 2017, IS also persisted in many rural districts along the Iraq-Syria border, establishing them as bases of operation for launching attacks across the country.[93]

How did Iraqis in Baghdad survive the IS insurgency? The next chapter explores how residents in the capital navigated sporadic bursts of suicide terrorism between 2014 and 2017. It focuses, in particular, on how Baghdad residents made survival tradeoffs in the face of insurgent violence, but without living under direct IS control.

4
Baghdad
Surviving War in the City of Peace

This city is amazing:
Her residents are always drunken.
Her stars are never sober.
She was bombed,
Trampled underfoot
Like a broken watch,
But she went on ticking,
As if she were just born,
From beneath the rubble broadcast,
On wings of broken light, a code for future generations.
Her heart keeps beating and beating, With solidarity,
With the sign of the broadcasting signal,
With all the strength and determination,
In all the words that are left to it:
This is Baghdad,
This is Baghdad,
This is Baghdad.

—SADIQ AL-SAIGH, "THIS IS BAGHDAD"

Twenty-four hours into the Islamic State occupation of Mosul, insurgents continued their offensive toward Baghdad. As Iraqi Security Forces retreated, insurgents traveled south along Highway 1, capturing Baiji, Tikrit, Samarra, and Balad, including a military base in Dhuluiya. By the end of June 2014, IS rule extended to within one hundred kilometers from the heart of the capital. Despite their conventional military success, IS members returned to unconventional tactics—especially suicide terrorism—as they approached rural communities encircling the capital, known as the "Baghdad Belt."

On June 11, 2014, a series of car bombs detonated in Tarmiya, a rural farming community within an hour's drive of Baghdad. The attacks targeted two Iraqi military officers as well as the home of a senior tribal leader in the Awakening (Sahwa) movement. That same morning, three suicide car bombs exploded in Shiʿa neighborhoods throughout Baghdad. In Kadhamiya District—home to a collection of Shiʿa shrines built in the eighth century—an IS-attributed attack killed or wounded nearly two dozen worshippers in Abdul Mohsen al-Kadhimi Square. Across the Tigris in Sadr City, three residents were killed in a crowded outdoor market in the al-Hayy neighborhood. Thirty Iraqis were later victims of a car bomb targeting a funeral procession circling Sadrain Square.

In response, the central government imposed a nighttime curfew, marking the first of its kind since the 2007 troop surge. The Maliki regime, however, did little to reassure the capital's war-weary residents. As one Sadr City resident remarked, "The army has proven to be a big failure. People have begun to depend on themselves because Daʿesh may enter Baghdad any minute."[1] Iraqis had good reason to be alarmed. The following morning, senior IS spokesman Abu Muhammad al-Adnani announced via YouTube, "Do not relent against your enemy.... The battle will rage in Baghdad and Karbala ... put on your belts and get ready."[2]

This chapter examines how Baghdad residents survived the Islamic State, focusing on the capital's Shiʿa-majority neighborhoods. Due to intercommunal violence and ethnic sorting, the Shiʿa became the dominant sectarian group in the capital by 2007. Moreover, Shiʿa residents adopted the widest array of survival repertoires compared to their Sunni and Christian neighbors. Most notably, Baghdad represents a case where contention took the form of violent collective action in the form of the Popular Mobilization Forces and their affiliated militias. Unlike self-defense groups in western and northern Iraq, however, the most powerful PMF units received foreign patronage from Iran, in addition to serving as the armed wings of influential political parties.

A multi-method research design provides evidence for Baghdad residents' beliefs, attitudes, and behaviors during the conflict. Observational data on internal displacement, election outcomes, and public protests provides behavioral evidence for flight, cooperation, and contention. An original survey of Baghdad residents complements secondary sources by providing direct evidence for respondents' motivations for selecting specific survival repertoires.[3] Experiments embedded within the survey gauge public attitudes on various anti-IS coalition members.

Several key findings emerge from the 2017 survey. First, most Baghdad residents remained in their homes, while internal displacement affected the inflow of Sunnis to communities throughout Baghdad Governorate. Internal displacement affected rural communities in the Baghdad Belt more than urban neighborhoods within the capital. For example, despite sharing fears about political exclusion and persecution by the ISF, Baghdad Sunnis in cosmopolitan neighborhoods shared little in common with Sunnis in rural communities outside of the capital. Second, Baghdad residents resisted IS through active and direct cooperation with coalition forces. As insurgent threats declined, Shiʿa residents prioritized neutrality, critical of the ineptitude of the central government, as well as Iran's perceived meddling in Iraqi politics. More importantly, opposition to the Abadi regime increased as proximate insurgent threats dissipated. As the anti-IS campaign advanced, the capital's Shiʿa majority revised their governance expectations vis-à-vis co-sectarian elites, such as Prime Minister Haider al-Abadi. At the same time, pro-government militias, such as Muqtada al-Sadr's Peace Companies, transitioned from resisting IS to seeking autonomy from fellow coalition members.

Suicide terrorism in the capital (2011–2017)

Unlike regions outside of the capital, Baghdad never fell under Islamic State control. Instead, IS launched sporadic suicide attacks against Shiʿa-majority neighborhoods throughout the city. Because Baghdad remained under government control throughout the war, local residents relied on a different set of survival repertoires than Sunni, Kurdish, and minority communities in western and northern Iraq.

Political disfunction, public protest, and economic stagnation plagued Baghdad after the departure of U.S. forces in December 2011. The rise of IS came at the same time as the demise of Nouri al-Maliki's political career. Despite maintaining the Daʿwa Party's support in the April 2014 parliamentary elections, Maliki's coalition, having won about a quarter of the national vote, fell short of a majority. Rising insurgent violence across Iraq would further sink Maliki's prospects of a third term. After nearly four months of political gridlock, Maliki formally resigned in mid-August 2014. Two weeks after the resignation, the Council of Representatives approved a new government formed by the new Daʿwa Party leader, Haider al-Abadi.

What best explains the demise of Maliki's political hegemony? Despite the electoral success of a pan-Shiʿa coalition in national elections in 2005 and 2009, Maliki gradually consolidated power among Daʿwa Party loyalists instead of distributing power among Daʿwa, the Islamic Supreme Council of Iraq (ISCI), and the Sadrists. "Using the powerful patronage available to him as chief executive, he pursued a policy of 'divide and rule' in dealing with other parties. He filled vacant positions in the military and administration with his loyalists and augmented the powers of his office and of networks related to him personally, thereby creating a kind of 'shadow state' within the government," explains Harith Hasan al-Qarawee.[4] During the January 2009 provincial election campaign, for example, Maliki would exclude from his coalition key allies within the ISCI and Sadrists movements. Even with the exclusion of rival Shiʿa parties, in the 2009 Baghdad provincial elections, the State of Law Coalition (Iʾtilaf Dawlat al-Qanun) secured 38 percent of the vote and just over half of the governorate's parliamentary seats. Outside of the coalition, Maliki increasingly excluded Sunni and Kurdish elites, even while formally recognizing consociational power sharing.[5]

Iraq's military, intelligence, and law enforcement were among the chief institutions to feel the effects of Maliki's centralization of power. Specifically, Maliki coup-proofed the Iraqi Army by "tying senior commanders and paramilitary units to him personally and thereby subverting the formal chain of command," a policy known as "ethnic stacking."[6] Toward that end, he promoted army officers based on political loyalty instead of merit, allowed loyalists to collect bribes, "fees," and kickbacks, and created parallel security forces and intra-government intelligence agencies to monitor political rivals (e.g., the *malikiyun*).[7] The Iraqi Special Operations

Forces—comprising the country's elite counterterrorism units—not only emerged as a parallel security force but would later play a pivotal role in defeating IS.

In addition to undermining military effectiveness and unit-level cohesion, Maliki's coup-proofing strategy also damaged civil-military relations. Iraqis across ethnic and sectarian divides began to perceive the security apparatus as little more than a sectarian institution. As social trust in the ISF decreased, so, too, did the government's ability to maintain public support. As a result, Iraq's military and police forces were unable to collect and evaluate local intelligence related to IS terrorism.

Between 2011 and 2013, IS consolidated control in neighboring Anbar, capturing territory less than sixty kilometers from the heart of the capital. Prison breaks in Taji and Abu Ghraib in July 2013 contributed over 1,000 new recruits to insurgent ranks. Throughout 2013, the capital would experience an escalation of political violence unseen since the peak of the civil war in 2006. Baghdad residents suffered from sporadic bouts of suicide terrorism, especially from car and truck bombs parked in crowded public areas. Between January 2012 and June 2014, Baghdad would experience 2,400 IS-affiliated attacks, including over 500 suicide car bombs; 7,500 Baghdad residents would be killed or injured (see figure 4.1).[8]

In the weeks following IS's successful occupation of Mosul in June 2014, insurgents extended their campaign south into the Sunni-majority governorates of Diyala and Salah al-Din. By mid-June, insurgents reached Adhim in Diyala Governorate, a cluster of small towns and villages approximately ninety kilometers north of Baghdad. Despite the success of the government's counteroffensive, Baghdad residents were never fully insulated from insurgent violence. The IS attacks that did penetrate Baghdad—consisting primarily of suicide car bombs (vehicle-borne improvised explosive devices)—occurred in Shiʻa neighborhoods, including commercial and residual areas as well as Shiʻa holy sites in Adhamiya, Kadhamiya, and Sadr City (see table 4.1).

The IS campaign of collective violence against the Shiʻa bolstered support for the coalition, attracting voluntary recruits to local PMF detachments. Over the course of the anti-IS campaign, popular support for the insurgents among Baghdad residents remained uniformly low, even as many Sunnis acquiesced to IS control in neighboring communities in Anbar and Salah al-Din. For example, a January 2016 poll found that 99 percent

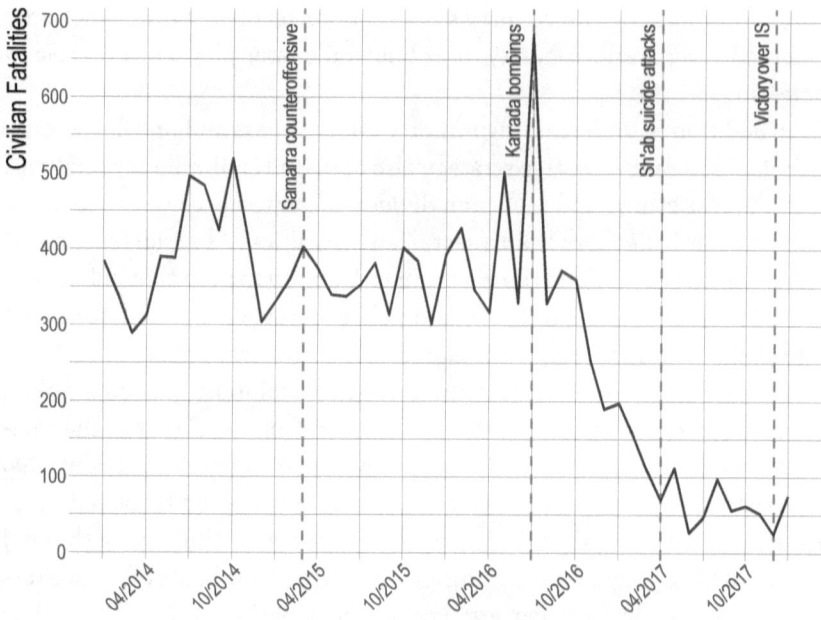

FIGURE 4.1 Civilian fatalities in Baghdad Governorate (2014–2018).

Source: Armed Conflict Location and Event Data Project, https://acleddata.com; Iraq Body Count, https://www.iraqbodycount.org.

of Shiʿa and 95 percent of Sunnis across several districts opposed the Islamic State.[9] Even in the city's Sunni-majority western neighborhoods, more than 90 percent of respondents viewed IS as an existential threat and supported international assistance to the Iraqi Army and Federal Police.

By the end of 2015, the anti-IS coalition began to turn the tide against the insurgency. A combination of Iraqi Army, Federal Police, and PMF units—protected by coalition airpower and artillery—liberated Ramadi (December 2015), Tikrit (April 2016), and Fallujah (June 2016). Despite the coalition's military success, Baghdad residents remained concerned about the state of domestic politics. On April 30, 2016, supporters of Muqtada al-Sadr stormed government buildings in Baghdad's Green Zone out of frustration at Abadi's inability to stem government corruption. Commenting on the protests from the Shiʿa holy city of Najaf, Sadr announced, "I'm waiting for the great popular uprising and the great revolution to stop the march of corrupted officials."[10] This period represents a transition of the

TABLE 4.1 Deadliest Islamic State attacks on Baghdad (2014–2017)

Date	District	Target	Casualties
2/6/2016	Karrada	Suicide bombings in Shaʿab neighborhood	383 killed, 200 wounded
5/11/2016	Sadr City, Kadhamiya	Suicide attacks on marketplace and police checkpoints	110 killed, 165 wounded
2/28/2016	Sadr City	Suicide attacks on Al-Maridi Market	82 killed, 125 wounded
8/13/2015	Sadr City	Suicide bombings in Jamila Market	68 killed, 152 wounded
1/2/2017	Sadr City	Three suicide attacks near hospitals	56 killed, 122 wounded
2/15–16/2017	Rashid	Suicide attack in Baya neighborhood	55 killed, 80 wounded
10/5–6/2013	Kadhamiya	Suicide attacks on Shiʿa pilgrims	54 killed, 85 wounded
9/9/2016	Rusafa	Suicide bombings at al-Nakheel Mall on Palestine Street	40 killed, 60 wounded
4/30/2016	Kadhamiya	Suicide truck bomb at Kadhamiya shrine	38 killed, 86 wounded
10/15/2016	Karrada	Suicide attack on market in Shaʿab neighborhood	38 killed, 40 wounded
12/25/2013	Karrada, Rashid	Three suicide attacks on Christian churches celebrating Christmas Mass	38 killed, 70 wounded

Source: "Global Terrorism Database," National Consortium for the Study of Terrorism and Responses to Terrorism, University of Maryland, accessed October 30, 2023, https://www.start.umd.edu/gtd.

Sadrist movement from armed resistance against IS to armed autonomy from the central government. Given the political power of the Sadrists within Baghdad's Shiʿa neighborhoods, it also demonstrates the potential for social movements to drive a change in survival repertoires among ordinary citizens. In other words, threat perception emerges through the interaction of individual decisions and group socialization.

A nationwide survey one year later found that while 81 percent of Shiʿa respondents believed that the Iraqi government would treat Sunnis and Shiʿa in the same manner, only half of Sunnis believed that to be true.[11] Concerns over the political future of the PMF also remained salient—45 percent of Sunnis said they should be integrated into the Iraqi Army while 35 percent argued they should be completely disbanded. With the demise of IS, many Iraqis expressed their political and economic grievances at the ballot box in the May 2018 parliamentary elections. While the Sadrists and Iran-backed Fatah Alliance won nearly one-third of the national vote, the next prime minister would be another Shiʿa technocrat, Adil Abdul-Mahdi.

Displacement, resettlement, and repatriation

How did IS terrorism affect forced displacement from and within Baghdad Governorate? Unlike northern and western communities—where the IS offensive drove residents from their homes at record rates—fleeing was the least common survival repertoire among Baghdad residents.

There are two main reasons Iraqis remained in their home neighborhoods during the conflict. First, forced displacement had already peaked during the height of the civil war in 2006. Between 2003 and 2006, Baghdad's neighborhoods were balkanized into sectarian enclaves with the Shiʿa majority controlling most subdistricts east of the Tigris, as well as Kadhamiya District on the west bank.[12] By 2007, Adhamiya was the last remaining Sunni-majority subdistrict east of the Tigris River. West of the Tigris, in historically diverse districts like Mansour, Baghdad's Sunni residents resettled in smaller subdistricts, including Amiriya, Ghazaliya, Khadra, Kindi, and Yarmuk. By the end of the U.S. troop surge in 2008, only Adhamiya and Mansour contained Sunni majorities. During this period, Assyrian Christians and Kurds all but disappeared from the capital with the exception of a handful of affluent neighborhoods in Karrada District. Between 2003 and 2009, Baghdad's Christian population decreased by 85 percent. By the time IS threatened the Baghdad Belt in late June 2014, only 50,000–75,000 Assyrian Christians remained (down from 500,000 during Saddam's reign).[13] Three years later, less than 3 percent of Baghdad residents belonged to ethnoreligious minorities.

The second reason for low internal displacement during the IS insurgency was the central government's ability to maintain territorial control of the capital. While sporadic suicide attacks targeted Shiʿa-majority neighborhoods throughout the city, the ISF stalled IS's June 2014 offensive at Samarra. Due to their relative insulation from political violence, it was more common for Baghdad residents to cooperate with coalition forces or to pursue autonomy. Outside of Baghdad's urban neighborhoods, nearly 500,000 internally displaced persons (IDPs) from surrounding governorates resettled in twenty temporary camps circling the Baghdad Belt.[14] Over the course of the conflict, Baghdad Governorate was one of the top five locations for those displaced by the conflict, alongside the Kurdistan Region, Anbar, and Kirkuk (see figure 4.2). According to the International Organization for Migration, nearly half of IDPs fled Anbar Governorate, with an additional quarter from Babil, and 20 percent from Ninewa.[15] The majority of IDPs were Sunnis, with a smaller number hailing from minority groups.

Figure 4.2 shows variation in Baghdad's district-level population between 2013 and 2018. Several findings are noteworthy. First, the majority of refugee inflows arrived in Sunni-majority communities on the periphery of the Baghdad Belt. Second, within urban Baghdad, most IDPs resettled in Sunni-majority subdistricts of Karkh and Rusafa, instead of Shiʿa-majority subdistricts in Adhamiya, Kadhamiya, or Sadr City. Third, IDP inflows leveled off by 2015 across Baghdad's subdistricts. After 2015, IDP inflows only increased in Karkh, perhaps indicating additional IDP arrivals from Anbar Governorate during the liberation of Ramadi (February 2016) and Fallujah (June 2016).

As figure 4.3 illustrates, a plurality of Baghdad Governorate's IDPs resettled within temporary camps in Abu Ghraib, Mahmoudiya, and Tarmiya. Among those who reached urban Baghdad, the majority resettled in six IDP camps in Sunni-majority neighborhoods west of the Tigris River. The single IDP camp in eastern Baghdad was located in the Zayuna neighborhood. IDPs seeking sanctuary in the capital required sponsorship by a local resident. Government criteria for sponsorship was arduous, including proof of residential property ownership within Baghdad. IDPs lacking family or social connections had to pay to secure a sponsor. As one Sunni IDP from Ramadi explained, "I paid IQD [Iraqi dinars] 150,000 ($120 USD) to my sponsor after tough negotiations.... It is a very hard situation as we are in

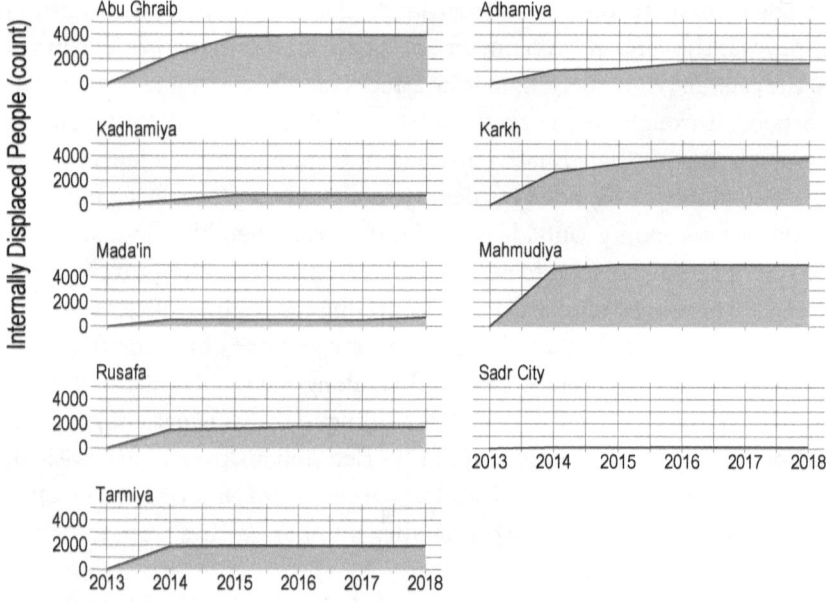

FIGURE 4.2 IDP arrivals by district over time across Baghdad Governorate (2013–2018).

Source: Displacement Tracking Matrix, International Organization for Migration, https://dtm.iom.int/iraq.

economic crisis. We could not afford paying such money. Due to these restrictions, those who have no money could not leave Ramadi, and remained there until the [Iraqi] Army came."[16]

Most IDPs who resettled in Baghdad struggled to sustain access to basic needs, including food, rudimentary medical care, and subsistence jobs. While security and personal safety were less of a concern than in IDP camps in western Iraq, restrictions on movement outside the camps further challenged people's ability to meet their basic needs. According to one Sunni IDP from Anbar, "We spent all our savings as my husband has been unemployed since our displacement. Due to the restrictions at checkpoints, my husband cannot search for a job outside the camp. He cannot move without his IDP identity card."[17] Bureaucratic hurdles—especially in the form of sectarian discrimination—prevented IDPs from obtaining official identity cards, citizenship certificates, passports, or food ration cards. According to one report, nearly three-quarters of Sunnis displaced from Anbar who

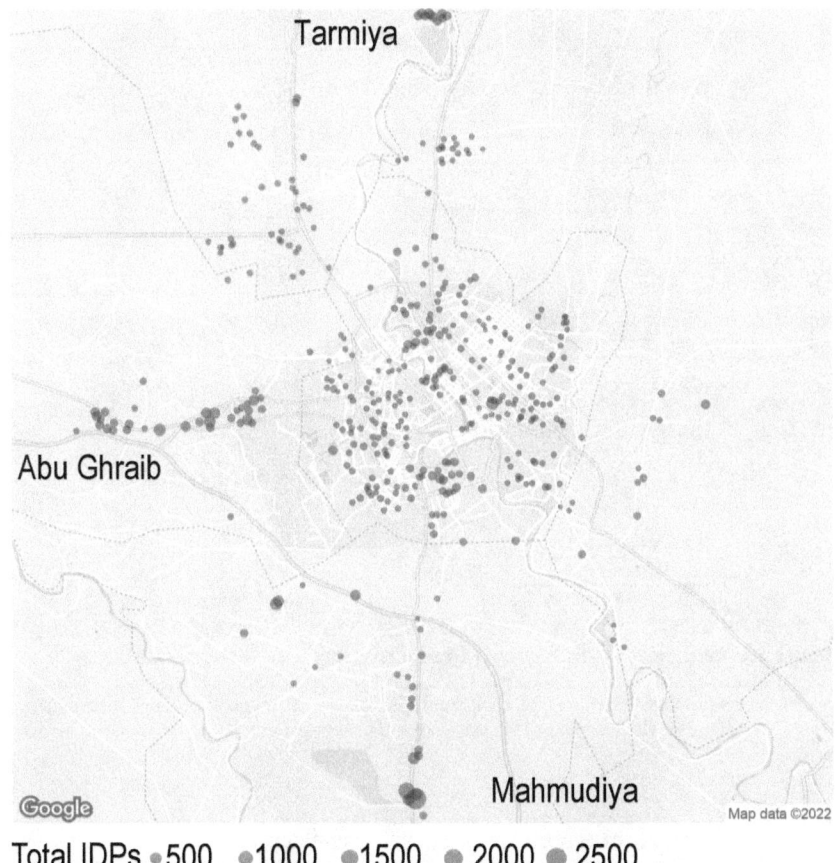

FIGURE 4.3 Network of IDP flows across Baghdad Governorate (2014–2018).

Source: Displacement Tracking Matrix, International Organization for Migration, https://dtm.iom.int/iraq; map underlayment from Google Maps.

resettled in Baghdad faced either administrative hurdles or active discrimination in obtaining humanitarian assistance.[18] Many IDPs attributed such obstacles to stigma related to their being perceived by capital residents as IS collaborators.

Figure 4.4 displays the rate of returnees to each district in Baghdad Governorate. Given the Sunni-majority composition of many rural communities surrounding the capital, only Abu Ghraib, Mahmoudiya, and Tarmiya saw significant return rates after IS's defeat in 2017. Each community also

82   BAGHDAD

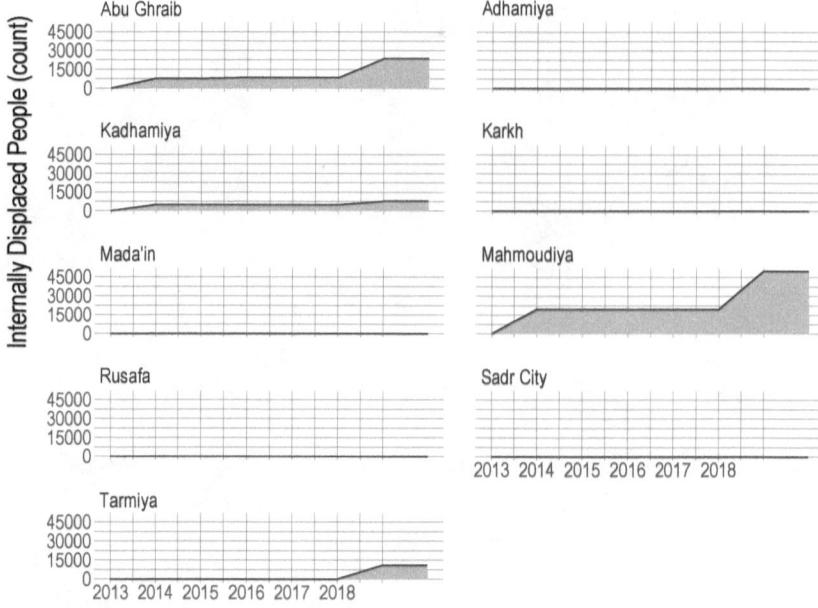

FIGURE 4.4 Returnees by district over time across Baghdad Governorate (2014–2018).

Source: Displacement Tracking Matrix, International Organization for Migration, https://dtm.iom.int/iraq.

stood at a critical transit point for entering the capital, making them strategic locations for insurgents and coalition members alike. As such, pressure on the delivery of humanitarian assistance, as well as public service provision, was most pronounced in rural communities along the periphery of the Baghdad Belt.

Studying those who stayed: A survey of Baghdad residents

How did Iraqis who remained in Baghdad during the war navigate the threat of IS terrorism? An original survey of Baghdad residents provides generalizable information about the beliefs, attitudes, and behaviors of those who stayed. The survey took place in November 2017, near the end of the coalition's counteroffensive but before IS's defeat. As such, it provides novel insights into respondents' motivations for survival during a period of conflict transition.

The survey questionnaire probed respondents' social, political, and economic attitudes, including their views about the current state of the conflict and the coalition's performance against IS. Given these topics' sensitive nature, the questionnaire included closed and open-ended questions, as well as a series of survey experiments. The survey experiments provided an indirect measure of respondents' attitudes toward different coalition members, as well as combatants' tactics during the anti-IS campaign. To test the validity of causal relationships, the questionnaire incorporated identical treatment categories and outcome questions in observational and experimental formats. At the end of the interview, enumerators collected respondents' demographic information.

The Independent Institute for Administration and Civil Society Studies—an Iraqi market research firm headquartered in Baghdad—enumerated the survey.[19] The survey team consisted of a project manager, three field supervisors, and ten enumerators. The author finalized the survey questionnaire in conjunction with the project manager and conducted enumerator training in Beirut, Lebanon. Prior to fielding the survey, the author and survey team revised a series of safety precautions to protect enumerators and respondents. Precautions included removing a series of sensitive topics from the questionnaire, checking local security conditions the day prior to interviewing, and sending enumerators to their home neighborhoods to defuse suspicion. During the two-week enumeration, local police or military personnel detained members of two fieldwork teams. In each case, local authorities released these individuals unharmed the same day they were detained.

The survey was representative of Baghdad's wartime population. It included a simple random sample of six hundred respondents from twenty-seven Sunni, Shiʿa, and mixed neighborhoods (also called subdistricts).[20] By November 2017, only two of Baghdad's ten districts—Adhamiya and Mansour—had Sunni-majority populations. Accordingly, the sample skews heavily Shiʿa, including neighborhoods exposed to higher levels of insurgent violence, as well as broader socioeconomic disparities.[21] Figure 4.5 displays the location of the twenty-seven primary sampling units. The gray scale indicates the total number of civilian fatalities in a given neighborhood between June 2014 and November 2017.

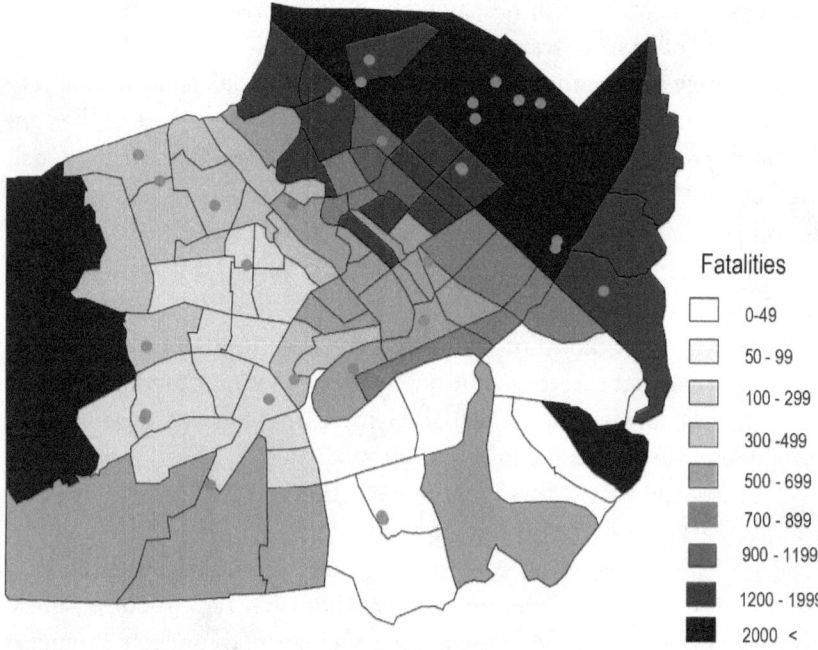

FIGURE 4.5 Survey interviews occurred across twenty-seven Baghdad neighborhoods. Gray circles indicate the locations of primary sampling units. Shading indicates the number of civilian fatalities in a given subdistrict (neighborhood) between June 2014 and November 2017.

Source: data on civilian fatalities from Iraq Body Count, https://www.iraqbodycount.org.

Among the six hundred respondents who completed the survey, 52 percent were male with an age distribution between eighteen and eighty-seven, with the mean respondent age being approximately forty years old (see figure 4.6). The majority of respondents identified as "just a Muslim," while 36 percent of respondents self-identified as Shiʿa and 5 percent self-identified as Sunni. With respect to education, 42 percent had at least a high school education. Thirty-one percent of respondents were employed, and among those not working, 25 percent were housewives. Roughly half of all respondents (55 percent) reported that their household income allowed them to pay for all expenses, with 38 percent responding that their current income level does not cover current expenses. When asked to compare their living conditions to that of their fellow Iraqis, 61 percent of

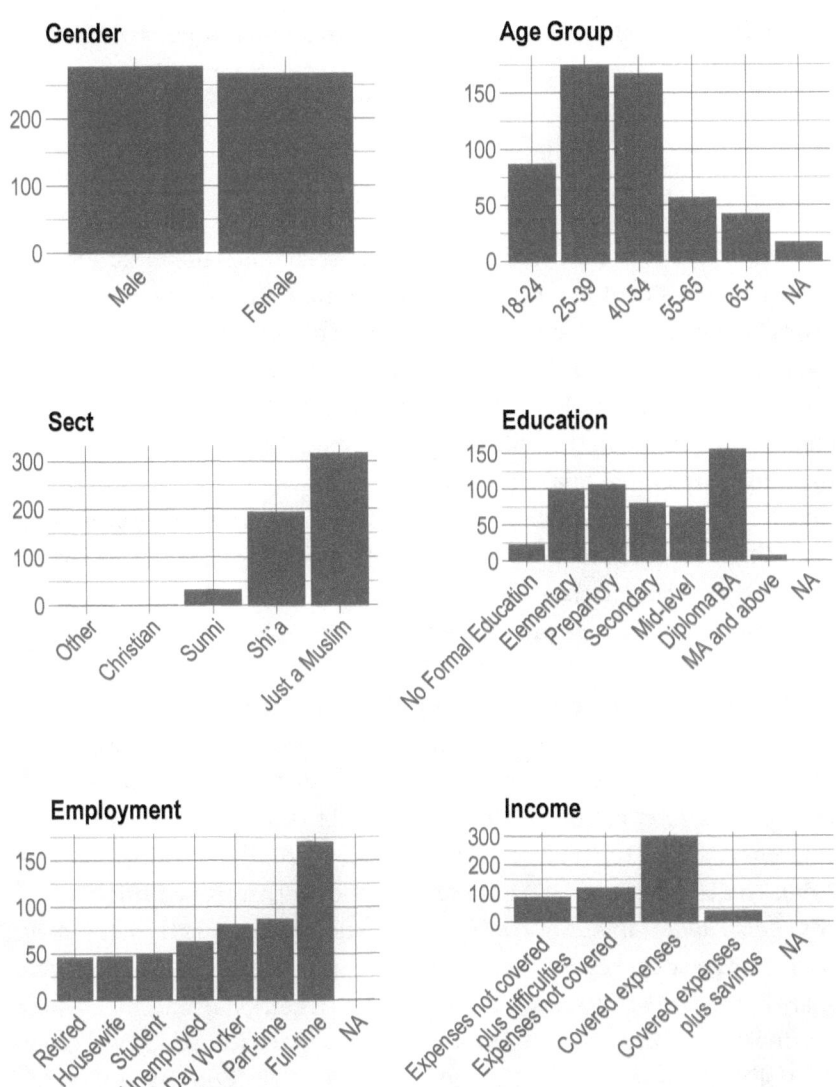

FIGURE 4.6 Respondent demographic characteristics.

Source: Author.

respondents recorded that their condition was similar, whereas 16 percent perceived themselves to be worse off. These demographics are consistent with prior academic surveys of Baghdad.[22]

CONTENTION

Contentious repertoires were among the most common means of survival for Baghdad residents over the course of the conflict. Despite confronting sporadic bouts of suicide terrorism, most Iraqis within the capital never were subject to IS control. As such, they resisted the Islamic State by supporting the anti-IS coalition. Baghdad residents did so by informing to the coalition, enlisting in the military, police, and militias, and participating in national and provincial elections. Despite drawing on a power base outside of the capital, the mobilization of PMF volunteers from within Baghdad's Shiʿa neighborhoods provides a parallel example of resistance through violent collective action.

Political participation provides evidence for Baghdad residents' perceptions of government performance. Figure 4.7 displays the vote share of the four largest Shiʿa parties—Daʿwa, the ISCI, National Accord, and the Sadrists—in federal and provincial elections between 2005 and 2021. Before the rise of IS, Maliki's State of Law Coalition enjoyed hegemonic success among Shiʿa voters in Baghdad. The ISCI and the Sadrists played the role of junior coalition partners, especially during Maliki's second term (2010–2014). The IS advance of 2014, however, not only threatened Iraqis' security, it also undermined Shiʿa voters' confidence in the central government. Over the course of the anti-IS campaign, the State of Law Coalition lost vote share to the ISCI and Sadrists. While Sadr was traditionally accustomed to playing the role of spoiler, after the defeat of IS his coalition enjoyed growing political success in the May 2018 provincial elections as well as the October 2021 parliamentary elections. Despite Prime Minister Abadi's success in leading the campaign against IS, his Victory Alliance coalition (Iʾtilaf al-Nasr) lost vote share to Sadr's Alliance Toward Reforms coalition (Saairun).

Consistent with electoral participation, survey evidence confirms public support for the anti-IS coalition, especially in the early years of the campaign. While no nationally representative surveys were enumerated between 2014 and 2016, the author's November 2017 survey provides novel evidence of Baghdad residents' support for specific coalition members.

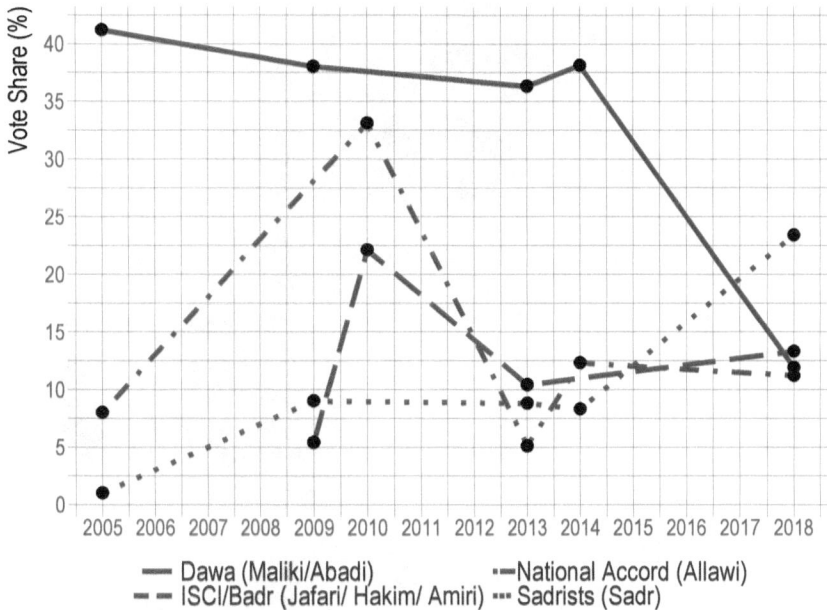

FIGURE 4.7 Iraq national election results (2005–2018). Parliamentary election turnout: 79 percent (December 2005), 62.4 percent (March 2010), 62 percent (April 2014), 44.5 percent (May 2018). Note: 2009 and 2013 represent provincial election years.

Source: "Council of Representatives of Iraq," IPU Parline, Inter-Parliamentary Union, accessed November 3, 2023, https://data.ipu.org/node/80/elections?chamber_id=13422.

Figure 4.8 displays the results from a question asking about security provision. Respondents' confidence in the performance of specific coalition members reveals a latent tension between support for combatants based on a common social identity, and support rooted in combatants' battlefield performance. In other words, is social identity or past performance a stronger heuristic for perceiving which combatants are most trustworthy?

Three out of four respondents had a great deal of confidence in the security provision of integrated fighting units such as the Iraqi Counter Terrorism Service and Federal Police. Similarly, the PMF received a level of support equal to that enjoyed by the state security forces. Public support for these units makes sense given the Shiʿa-majority share of survey respondents. However, public confidence in the Sunni tribes is mixed, despite their past success combatting al-Qaʿida in Iraq during the 2007 Anbar Awakening. Baghdadis' attitudes toward the Peshmerga

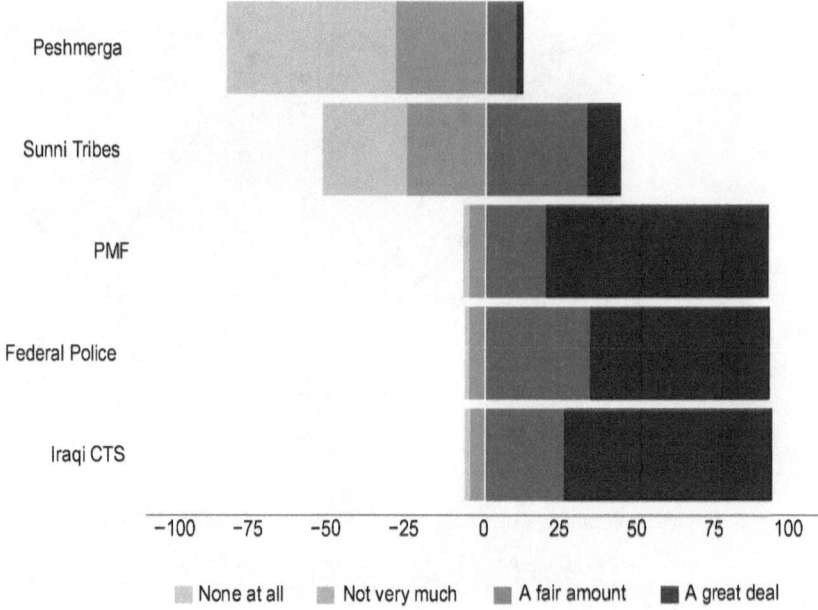

FIGURE 4.8 "How much confidence do you have in [group name] to improve the security situation in Iraq?"

Source: Baghdad survey enumerated by the author, November 2017.

are overwhelmingly negative, with two-thirds of respondents registering little or no confidence in the Kurds' ability to improve security in Iraq. Given the majority Arab representation in the sample, negative attitudes toward the Kurds remain consistent with previous survey research.

Even as the IS threat to Baghdad receded, respondents still evaluated combatants' battlefield performance through the lens of social identity. Crucially, the lack of support for the Sunni tribes among Sunni respondents is telling. It reveals the importance of geography in generating public support above and beyond diffuse ethnic or sectarian bonds. Given their presence outside of urban neighborhoods in Baghdad, most Baghdad Sunnis were hesitant to support tribal militias despite sharing a common sectarian identity. This result challenges the conventional wisdom that ingroup bias is one of the primary predictors of civilian support.[23]

Respondents' attitudes toward foreign intervention reveal a similar tension regarding the internal trade-offs individuals make between

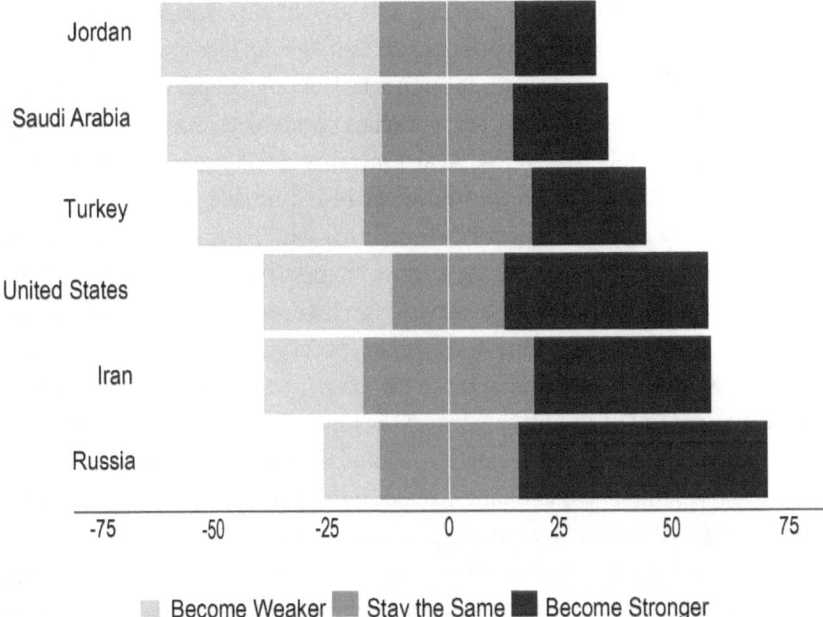

FIGURE 4.9 "Do you prefer that future security cooperation between Iraq and [country] [become stronger/become weaker/stay the same]?"

Source: Baghdad survey enumerated by the author, November 2017.

in-group bias and nationalist sentiment. In other words, when confronting an insurgent threat, do local residents prioritize identity or security provision? Figure 4.9 reveals that a majority of respondents would prefer for Iraqi security cooperation with Russia (55 percent), the United States (44 percent), and Iran (39 percent) to become stronger, even as cooperation with the United States was met with stronger negative ratings (28 percent preferred weaker cooperation). In fact, elsewhere in the survey, nearly half of all respondents (48 percent) said that the United States was responsible for the rise of IS. The relative parity of public support between the United States and Russia likely reflects respondents' instrumental support for intervention from great powers instead of regional states. Russia's performance in support of the Assad regime in Syria might have also influenced Baghdad residents' support for Moscow in November 2017.

Respondents were generally indifferent to the prospect of security cooperation with Turkey, whereas their views toward Saudi Arabia and Jordan were strongly negative, even among self-identifying Sunnis. These findings suggest an asymmetry with respect to in-group bias as a survival heuristic. While the majority of Shiʿa supported strong cooperation with Iran, Sunnis lacked corresponding co-sectarian bonds with Sunni patrons like Jordan, Saudi Arabia, the United Arab Emirates, or Qatar.[24] Results suggests that Iraq's Sunni and Shiʿa communities relied in different ways on sectarian identity as a heuristic for determining which combatants to trust.[25] By the end of the anti-IS campaign, most Baghdad residents supported the coalition but were also eager to see foreign interveners leave the country. While many previously supported foreign intervention to halt the IS offensive on Baghdad, they become more nationalistic as the insurgent threat subsided. Instead of supporting intervention from a shared in-group, they began to view foreign interveners as violating Iraqi sovereignty.

An endorsement experiment embedded within the survey provided a means of differentiating whether public support was purely a function of co-sectarian bias, or whether respondents updated their preferences based on changing security conditions in their neighborhoods. This design allowed enumerators to measure support based on pairs of foreign interveners and specific intervention tactics.[26]

Figure 4.10 visualizes how respondents' support for coalition members changed as a function of their ethnic and sectarian identity. In the control group, support for intervention by the United Nations has a mean of 0.62 (s.d. = 0.19). In comparison, the mean level of support for respondents in the treatment groups is 0.54 (s.d. = 0.19), resulting in a negative endorsement effect of -0.085 ($p < 0.001$). In substantive terms, support for foreign intervention dropped by an average of 8.5 percent when foreign interveners deployed identical tactics as United Nations forces.[27]

If co-sectarian bias was the most powerful heuristic predicting combatant support, one would expect to find a positive endorsement effect for Iran (especially among Shiʿa) and a negative endorsement effect vis-à-vis Turkey, Saudi Arabia, and Jordan. However, the observed findings support the prediction of opposition to out-group intervention, but remain ambiguous with respect to co-sectarian support. The absence of stronger public support for Iran is a function of the dissipating insurgent threat. By November 2017, given the choice between intervention by the UN or a regional country, the average Baghdad resident preferred the UN.

To directly test which heuristic is more influential in shaping survival, figure 4.11 displays the differential effects of neighborhood violence on

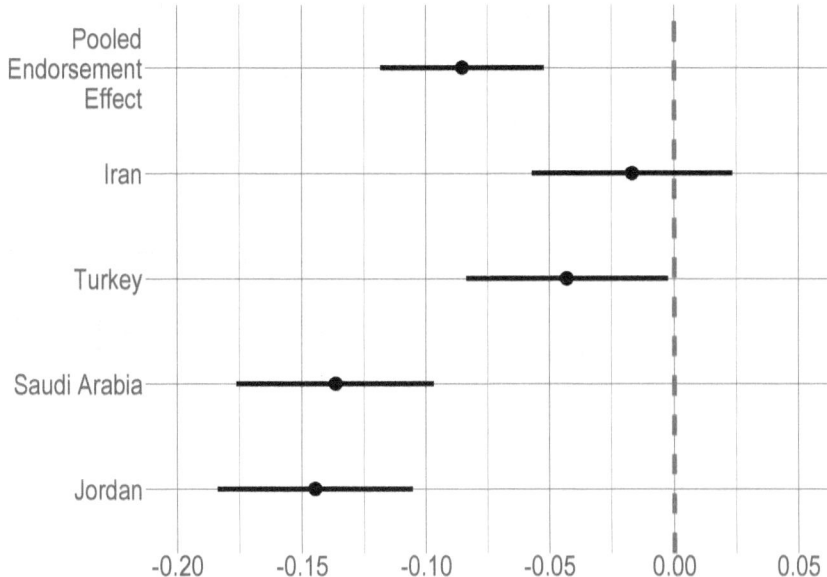

FIGURE 4.10 Respondents were opposed or indifferent to foreign intervention by neighboring states.

Source: Baghdad survey enumerated by the author, November 2017.

public support for foreign intervention. Do local security conditions change how residents respond to the presence of foreign troops? Within the survey sample, two of the five districts sampled experienced more severe terrorist violence relative to the mean. The most insecure Baghdad neighborhoods were located within the Shiʿa-majority districts of Sadr City and Kadhamiya.[28] If security conditions were the most influential heuristic, one would expect to find higher levels of support for foreign intervention among residents in the most violent neighborhoods (especially in Kadhamiya and Sadr City). However, the endorsement effects remained consistent across neighborhood-level violence.[29] Interestingly, Shiʿa respondents' opposition to Saudi and Jordanian intervention remained even in the most insecure neighborhoods. These findings are consistent with responses elsewhere in the questionnaire, where most respondents held Sunni states in the region responsible for IS's rise.[30]

Existing research on wartime survival suggests that civilians also make decisions based on how combatants behave in the community.[31] Combatant behavior informs survival by shaping the perceived risk attendant to

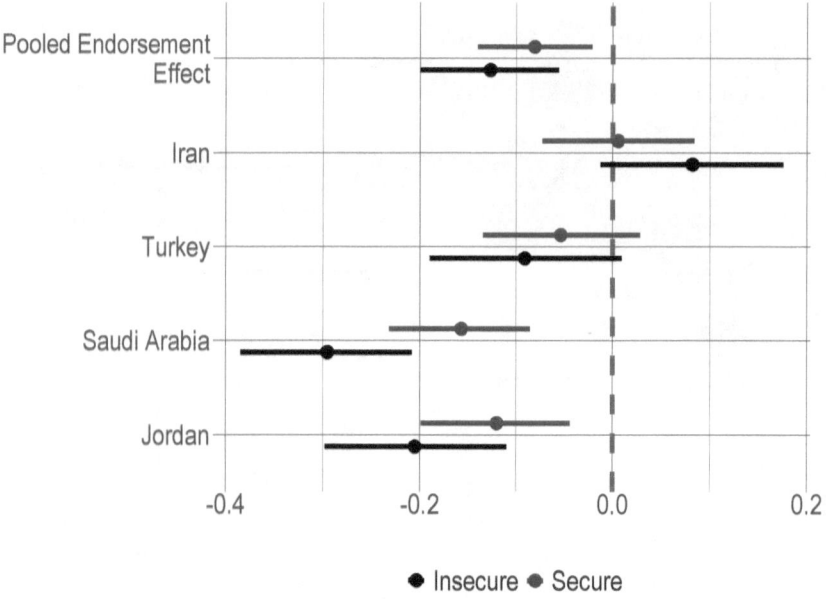

FIGURE 4.11 Support for foreign intervention changes based on local violence conditions.

Source: Baghdad survey enumerated by the author, November 2017.

accommodating insurgent or regime rule. If locals perceive that coalition members are more likely to engage in indiscriminate violence or other invasive forms of control, then the prospects of insurgent control become more attractive. Individuals will be especially sensitive to invasive tactics employed by out-group combatants.[32] In short, the heuristics of coercive behavior and combatant identity interact to inform the relative risk of supporting coalition versus insurgent forces.

Figure 4.12 visualizes support for intervention tactics based on the identity of the most and least popular foreign members of the anti-IS coalition.[33] If past research applies to the Iraq case, local residents should prefer more invasive tactics from in-group interveners, but oppose those same tactics from representatives of the out-group. While respondents were generally supportive of intervention by Iran, they were indifferent to specific intervention tactics. Similar trends hold for Saudi Arabia, with the exception of strong and significant opposition to the deployment of Saudi

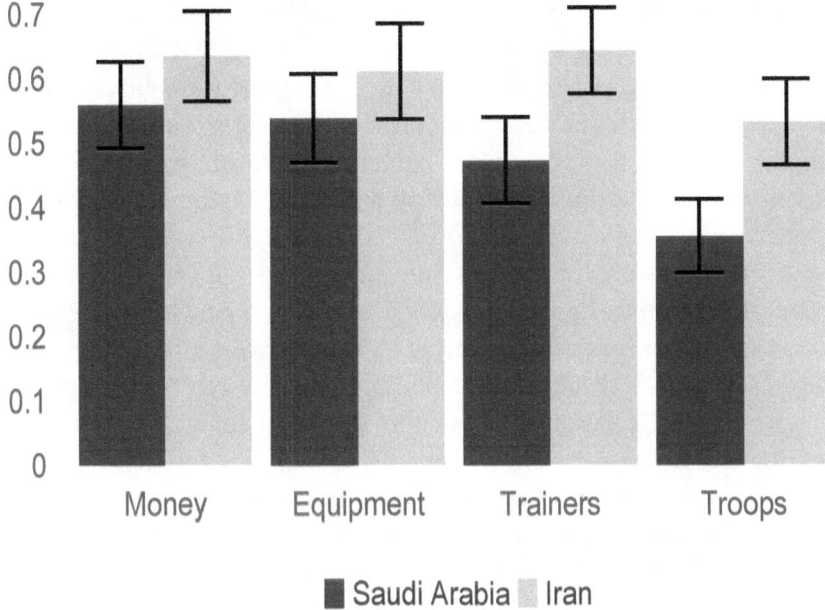

FIGURE 4.12 Support for intervention tactics changes based on intervener identity.

Source: Baghdad survey enumerated by the author, November 2017.

combat troops. Given the choice between intervention by Iran or Saudi Arabia, however, most respondents preferred Iran.

Consistent with this study's theoretical framework, respondents' aversion to invasive tactics is strongest for out-group interveners, especially when respondents live in communities effectively governed by in-group forces. The absence of an existential IS threat during the time of the survey thus explains respondents' sensitivity to invasive forms of foreign intervention. However, in cases where insurgent violence escalates over time, one would expect local residents to support invasive tactics regardless of combatant identity. The public will support whatever force is able to dampen insurgent violence without victimizing civilians. During the 2007 troop surge in Baghdad, for example, local residents supported the United States' invasive counterinsurgency tactics given escalating violence in the capital since March 2003.

The survey also included a conjoint experiment to understand how Baghdad residents made trade-offs with respect to their support for foreign interventions, intervention tactics, and local combatants.[34] A conjoint design provides evidence for whether survival heuristics interact with one another. For example, how do local security conditions shape support for specific coalition members and the intervention tactics they employ? The primary goal for the conjoint experiment was to compare Sunni and Shi'a respondents' differing preferences with respect to security provision. The marginal mean—or the average level of support for each attribute—provides a baseline measure of support (relative to chance) for each foreign intervener, local coalition unit, and intervention tactic. Attributes with marginal means above 0.5 indicate higher favorability, while those below 0.5 indicate lower favorability.[35]

Figure 4.13 displays the distribution of marginal means across each attribute of the conjoint experiment. Consistent with findings from the endorsement experiment, respondents registered above average support for Iranian and Russian intervention and strong opposition to Saudi

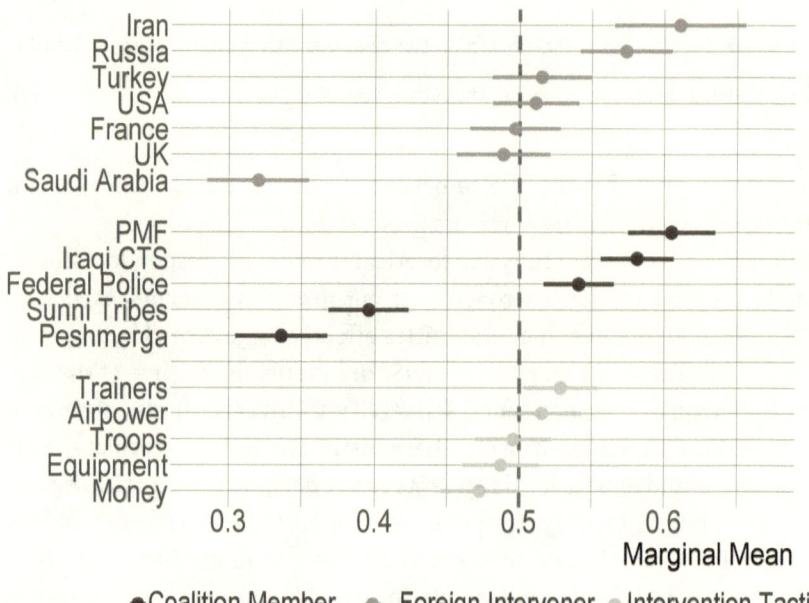

FIGURE 4.13 Support for the anti-IS coalition varies based on social identity and intervention tactics.

Source: Baghdad survey enumerated by the author, November 2017.

intervention. Interestingly, coalitions that included the United States, United Kingdom, France, and Turkey were not favored relative to chance. With respect to support for local clients, respondents strongly supported coalitions that included integrated fighting units like the Iraqi Counter Terrorism Service (CTS) and Federal Police, as well as the PMF. Respondents overwhelmingly opposed foreign support provided to the Sunni tribes and Peshmerga. Absent information about combatant identity, respondents were relatively indifferent to specific intervention tactics. More invasive tactics, including airpower, military trainers, and combat troops, received similar support to less invasive measures (e.g., foreign aid or military equipment).

If support for foreign intervention varied based on which coalition members received security assistance, then respondents should prefer more invasive tactics when foreign interveners assist a favored local coalition member. Strong public support should be evident for the Iraqi CTS and PMF, whereas there should be strong opposition to invasive tactics that assist the Peshmerga and Sunni tribes. Figure 4.14 visualizes the effect of intervention tactics on support for local coalition members. As predicted, popular support changes when coalition members are paired with specific intervention tactics. In the case of the Iraqi CTS, respondents preferred foreign airpower and military trainers, but continued to oppose the deployment of foreign troops. Conversely, respondents opposed a variety of intervention tactics when foreign interveners assisted the Peshmerga.

Consistent with the heuristics of combatant identity and coercive behavior, Iraqis living in neighborhoods secured by the central government opposed foreign troop deployments regardless of an intervener's ethnic or sectarian identity. Indeed, respondents' opposition to foreign intervention remained despite the countervailing influence of in-group favoritism. Shiʿa residents opposed the deployment of Iranian troops despite sharing a common sectarian identity. The indifference to foreign support for the Kurds suggests that local residents will provide limited support to interventions assisting an out-group if they perceive that foreign interveners can successfully monitor the behavior of local clients.

How does neighborhood insecurity affect public support? Are local residents exposed to insurgent violence more likely to support invasive intervention tactics? In November 2017, nearly half of the respondents lived

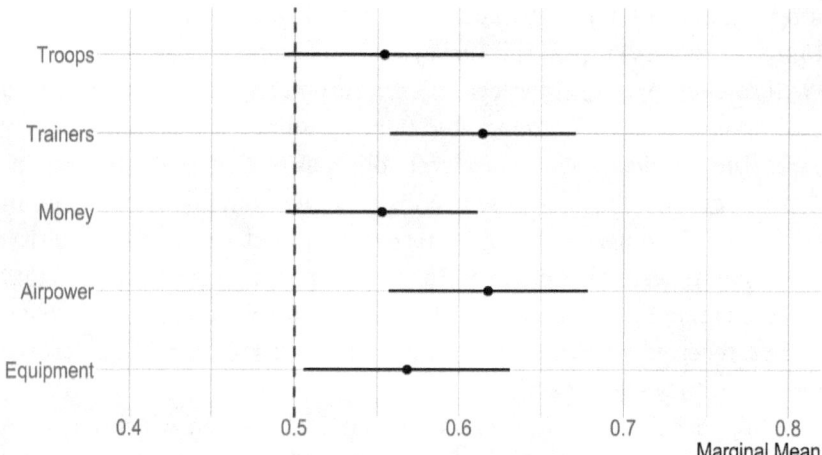

(a) Tactics employed by the Iraqi Counter-Terrorism Service

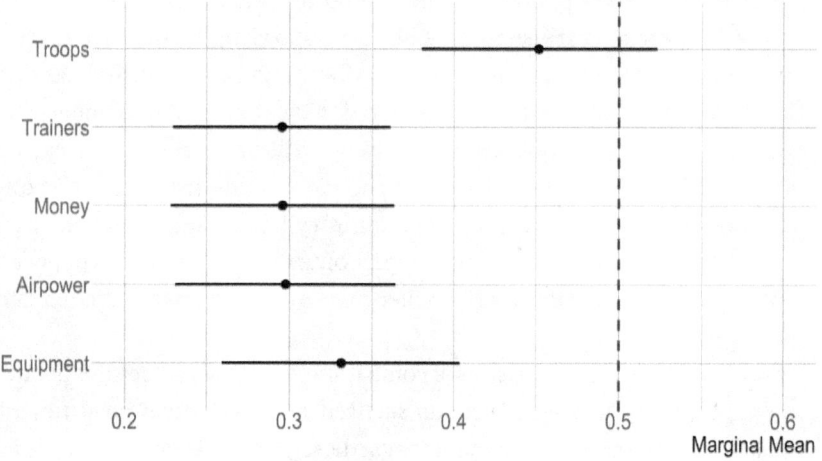

(b) Tactics employed by the Kurdish Peshmerga

FIGURE 4.14 Respondents preferred that foreign intervention assist the Iraqi Army instead of the Kurdish Peshmerga.

Source: Baghdad survey enumerated by the author, November 2017.

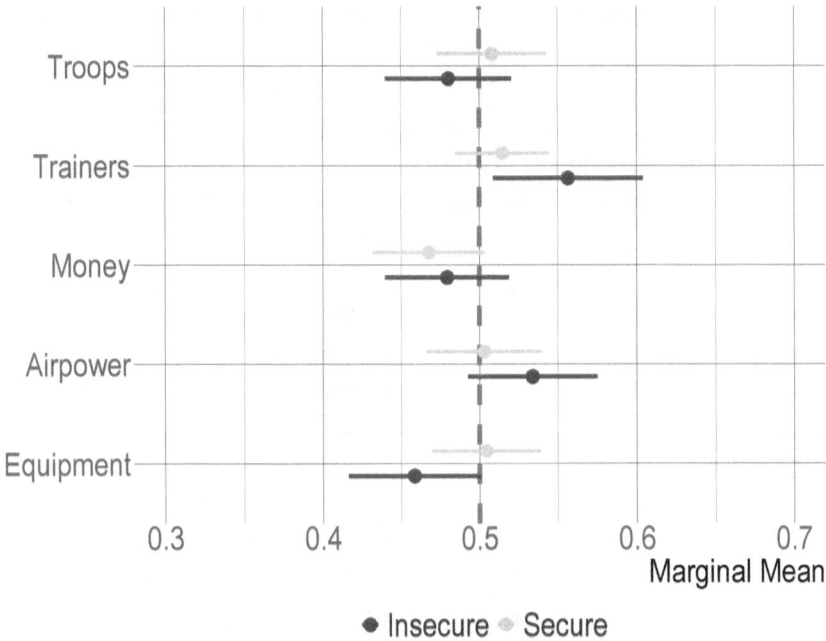

FIGURE 4.15 Respondents in insecure neighborhoods preferred the support of foreign military trainers.

Source: Baghdad survey enumerated by the author, November 2017.

in districts with a level of past fatalities above the mean for Baghdad (approximately thirty-six civilian fatalities in the previous nine months).

If perceptions of local violence affect survival decisions, then those residents living in the most violent neighborhoods should also support the most invasive foreign intervention tactics. For Baghdad's most vulnerable residents, the identity of the specific intervener should come second to whether an intervener has the motivation and ability to improve local security. Surprisingly, local insecurity had little effect on public attitudes toward intervention tactics. Secure and insecure respondents alike opposed the deployment of foreign combat troops. Among Iraqis in insecure districts, the average respondent preferred foreign military trainers to any other intervention tactic. Support for intervention through military training reflects a desire for improved local security without an increased risk of indiscriminate violence.

What does the Baghdad survey reveal about public support for the anti-IS coalition? First, local support for foreign intervention is a function of residents' relative vulnerability to insurgent violence. Baghdad residents perceived threats by drawing on heuristics about who controls their community and how foreign intervention is expected to alter the status quo. In regime-controlled neighborhoods throughout the capital, local residents supported intervention that bolstered the capacity of the in-group but opposed tactics that undermined their sovereignty.

Second, public aversion to indiscriminate violence tempers support for foreign intervention. Despite the strength of in-group bonds, there are tangible limits to the military tactics that local citizens were willing to tolerate. Even a reputation for resolve in assisting beleaguered regimes (e.g., Russian intervention in Syria) is insufficient to dampen nationalist sentiment.

Third, Sunni and Shiʿa respondents differed in how they weighed the role of social identity as a threat detection heuristic. While Iraqi Shiʿa value transnational sectarian attachments, Sunnis' social identity is parochial, rooted in attachments to local elites, tribes, and prominent families.[36] The logic outlined above also explains why Sadr was able to remobilize his followers into a formidable pro-government militia within the anti-IS coalition.

NEUTRALITY

Few Iraqis in Baghdad survived IS terrorism through repertoires of neutrality or autonomy. Unlike the Sunnis, Kurds, and Assyrian Christians—where autonomy emerged in the absence of coalition protection—Shiʿa residents pursued autonomy after the IS threat subsided. With the decline in insurgent violence came updated expectations about regime governance, especially as its related to public service provision, education, and employment. Increased security combined with electoral success incentivized many Shiʿa to update their expectations of co-sectarian elites within the Abadi regime.

During the height of the 2014 IS offensive, however, some Shiʿa neighborhoods mobilized PMF units that operated without Iranian support. The most prominent example is Muqtada al-Sadr's Peace Companies (Sarayya al-Salam), reconstituted from the Mahdi Army that mobilized to oppose the 2003 U.S.-led intervention. Sadr used his patronage networks to recruit economically disadvantage young men from Baghdad's poorer neighborhoods. During the anti-IS campaign, the Sadrists successfully mobilized more than twenty thousand Baghdad Shi'a to actively serve in different Peace Companies.[37] A lawyer in eastern Baghdad described the recruitment process to Renad Mansour in the following manner: "The poor are unable to get loans to gain a fixed resource. Most of the youth in our areas resort to being hired by the PMF and Sarayya al-Salam. Sometimes you think that this poverty is a methodology used by the factions to gain fighters. If job opportunities become available, they will go to the relatives and friends of the partisans."[38]

As the anti-IS campaign progressed, the Sadrists transitioned from cooperation to neutrality, seeking to guard their financial and operational autonomy from the Abadi regime as well as Iran's Islamic Revolutionary Guard Corps. When the defeat of IS became increasingly likely, Sadr called for the disbandment of the PMF, referring to them as "the Imprudent Militias" (*al-militiat al-waqiha*).[39] In practice, however, many Peace Companies took direction from Asa'ib Ahl al-Haq, the Badr Organization, and Kata'ib Hezbollah. Weak horizontal ties between units and a lack of integration into core state institutions would put the Sadrists at a financial and political disadvantage vis-à-vis the Iranian-backed PMF.

Public discontent with Iranian influence in the anti-IS coalition extended well beyond the PMF. In early November 2019, over two hundred thousand Baghdad residents came out to the streets in a wave of populist protest. Their grievances centered not only on the perceived incompetence of the prime minister, but also on Iran's meddling in Iraqi politics. One of the more prominent protest slogans was "Free, free Iraq . . . Iran get out, get out." As one Baghdad protestor put it, "All the ministries, all the civilian facilities in Iraq are run by Iran . . . still our passports are not good in almost any country. We want to get rid of this government, we want our country back, we want an independent president."[40] On rare occasions, public protests escalated into armed resistance against police or military forces.

In sum, Baghdad's Shi'a residents transitioned to repertoires of neutrality and even armed autonomy as the anti-IS campaign progressed. While Sadr's militias mobilized to protect their neighborhoods from insurgent violence, the Sadrists were also careful to preserve their autonomy from the Abadi regime as well as Tehran. As defeat of IS approached, autonomous repertoires became more pronounced, including escalating protests against Iran's involvement in Iraqi politics. The PMF and Peace Companies would also increasingly cooperate with political elites in the central government, allowing them to operate as the armed wings of political parties in the ruling coalition.

COOPERATION

Within Baghdad, cooperation with IS was even more rare than neutrality. Instead, as IS weakened, Iraqis updated their expectations of government performance beyond the security sector. While armed resistance against the central government was exceedingly rare, public protests became increasingly common. Tellingly, anti-regime protests peaked both before and after the zenith of IS control. The combination of decreasing security threats and increasing electoral success exacerbated internal divisions within Prime Minister Abadi's ruling coalition. The average Baghdadi's patience grew thin as high inflation, unemployment, rampant corruption, and poor public utilities (especially electricity provision) persisted. Iraqis within the capital registered their discontent with the Abadi regime through public acts of civil disobedience.

The first significant protest wave occurred when the Arab uprisings reached Baghdad in 2011. Much like the public protests that broke out in neighboring countries, Iraqis took to the streets of the capital in weekly protests between mid-February and late December 2011 (see figure 4.16). Like their counterparts in other Arab uprisings, Iraqis were fed up with their government's failure to address economic stagnation, unemployment, corruption, and lack of reliable public service provision.[41] Public concerns over the continued U.S. military presence also unified protesters across ethnic and sectarian divides. Seeing an opportunity to gain political leverage over Maliki, Muqtada al-Sadr organized a massive protest of nearly one hundred thousand followers on May 26, 2011, fueled by grievances related to the U.S. occupation.[42] Given his domestic popularity and reputation as a populist firebrand, Sadr leveraged his role as a political spoiler to bolster his image as an Iraqi nationalist free from manipulation from Baghdad or Tehran. Sadr's supporters, in turn, transitioned to neutrality and autonomy as

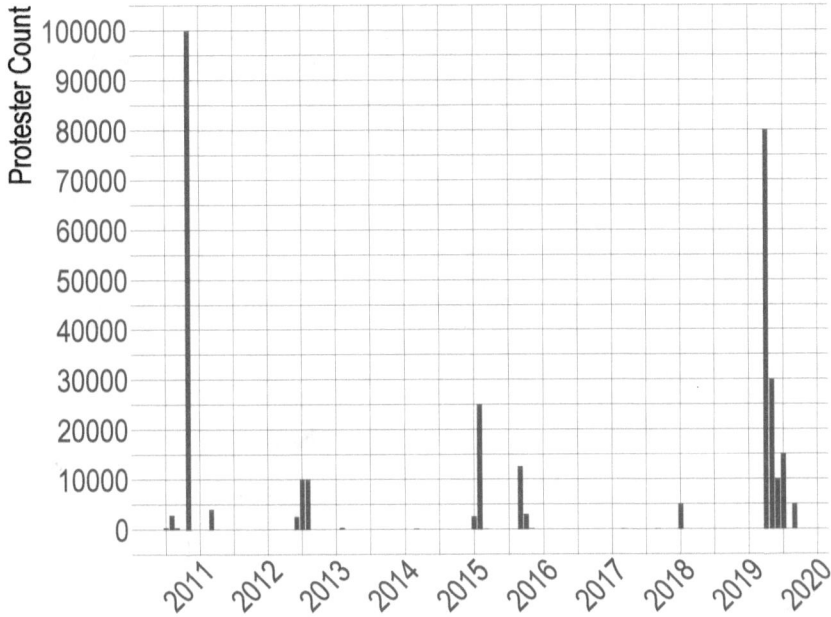

FIGURE 4.16 Major public protests in Baghdad (2011–2019).

Source: David Clark and Patrick Regan, "Mass Mobilization Protest Data," version 4.0 (1990–2019), Mass Mobilization Project, accessed November 3, 2023, https://massmobilization.github.io.

ongoing conflict revealed political infighting among the Sadrists, the Daʿwa movement, and the ISCI.

Over the following two years, Maliki's inability to improve governance outside of the security sector was a major motivation for public protests against the central government. The Sadrists, in particular, were able to voice opposition to the Maliki regime thanks to their electoral gains in the Council of Representatives during the March 2010 parliamentary elections. Electoral victories allowed the Sadrists to play the role of spoiler, even as they were a junior coalition partner. Public opinion data show that Baghdad residents expressed a desire for political change during periods of relative peace in the capital. These data also provide clues as to the underlying beliefs and attitudes that motivated a shift from supporting the government to neutrality and autonomy.

Figure 4.17 visualizes survey data from the Arab Barometer and the author's survey concerning changes in political attitudes over time. The

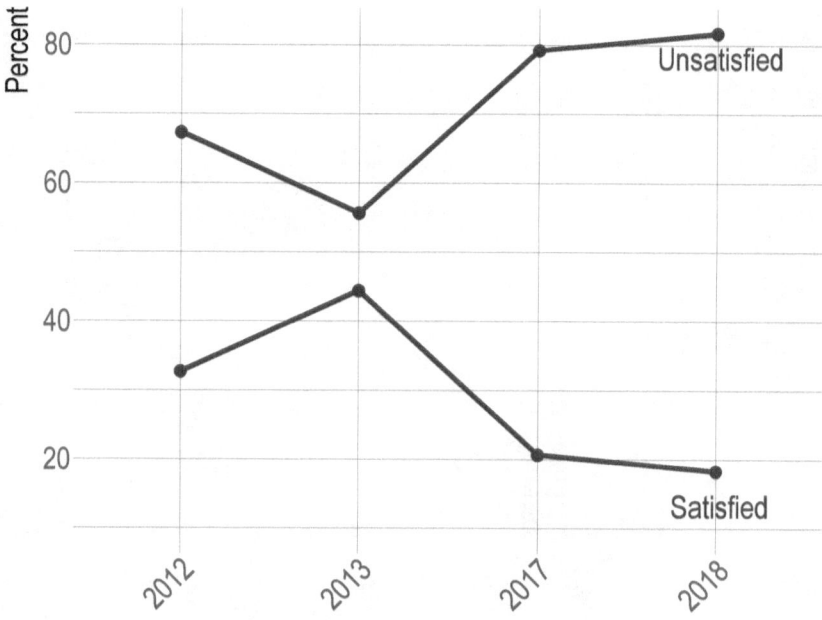

FIGURE 4.17 "To what extent are you satisfied with the government's performance?"

Source: Baghdad survey enumerated by the author, November 2017.

data relates to a subset of respondents from Baghdad and is taken from much larger, national survey waves. They demonstrate Baghdad residents' increasing dissatisfaction with the central government's performance across a number of areas over time. Respondent satisfaction was highest in 2013, and then dropped precipitously as the IS threat materialized in early 2014.

Despite sectarian differences, Iraqis across the country were largely unified when it came to identifying the primary challenges facing the country. As figure 4.18 highlights, public concerns over corruption took center stage, whereas one in ten respondents were most concerned about domestic security. Interestingly, respondents were increasingly concerned about the role of "foreign interference" over time, with a peak of 12 percent by the end of the anti-IS campaign in early 2018. In 2017 and 2018, 16 percent of Baghdad residents identified the United States as the country posing the

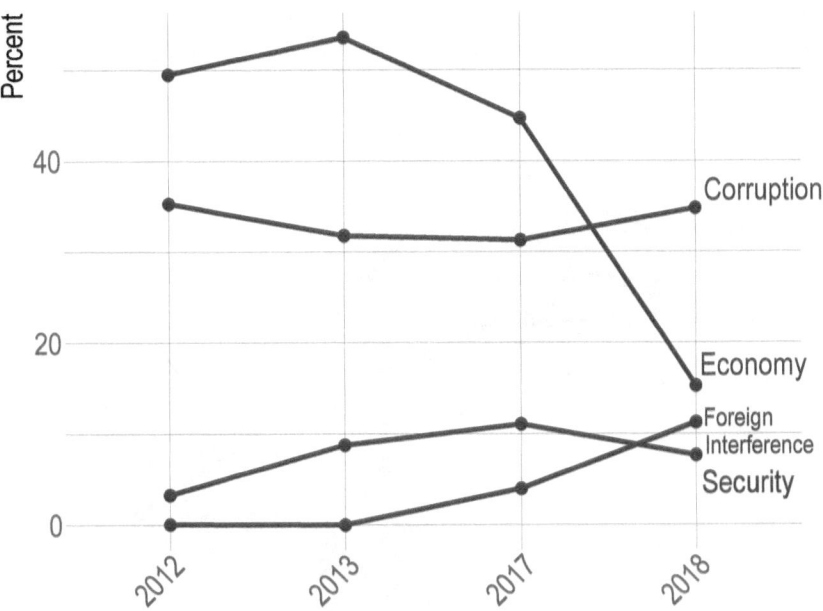

FIGURE 4.18 "What are the most important challenges Iraq is facing today?"

Source: Baghdad survey enumerated by the author, November 2017.

greatest threat to the stability of Iraq. Iran and Israel came in second and third, with 15.1 percent and 10.3 percent, respectively.

With respect to U.S.-Iraqi relations, a plurality of Baghdad residents supported establishing stronger security cooperation over time, despite the fact that many Iraqis blamed the United States for the security vacuum that enabled IS's rise (see figure 4.19). At the same time, 36 percent of respondents in 2018 supported weakening Iraq's security cooperation with the United States. Most respondents agreed that the status quo was untenable, and over time the percentage of respondents who answered "stay the same" decreased into the single digits.

What do these data reveal about Baghdad residents' shift toward noncooperation as the IS threat declined? First, despite strong Shiʿa majorities in the national and provincial governments, most of Baghdad's Shiʿa neighborhoods were unsatisfied with the government's performance beyond security provision. When economic concerns like unemployment,

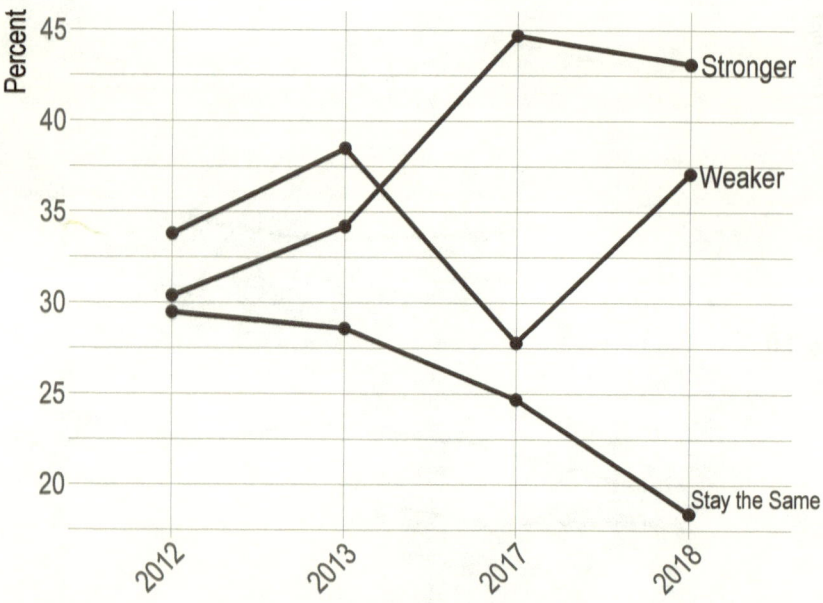

FIGURE 4.19 "Do you prefer future security relations between and Iraq and the U.S. to [become stronger/become weaker/stay the same]?"

Source: Baghdad survey enumerated by the author, November 2017.

corruption, and inflation took precedent over security, Iraqis were less willing to unconditionally support co-sectarian elites. Second, while Iraqis were generally unsatisfied with the country's relationship with the United States, many nonetheless wanted stronger bilateral security ties. They believed that the United States was responsible for eliminating the threat it created when it left Iraq a decade earlier. Moreover, in the absence of the IS threat, Iraqis became more sensitive to coercive behavior employed by foreign coalition members. Public opposition to Iraq's status of forces agreement with the United States grew as Baghdad became a less violent city beginning in 2010. Iraqis' growing nationalist sentiment translated into a greater desire for political autonomy from external states, on the one hand, and the excesses of the central government, on the other.

Finally, the Abadi regime's success at restoring security created higher expectations of government performance, especially among Shiʻa voters in Baghdad. As the IS threat subsided, Shiʻa increasingly voiced their frustration over the state of the economy as well as the government's increasing centralization. Abadi's inability to reform the economy, curb corruption and inflation, and deliver reliable public services led to the dissolution of his Shiʿa base. To make matters worse, Shiʿa factions outside of the party—including members of the ISCI and Sadrists—withdrew support from Abadi as public opinion began to turn.

Baghdad residents responded to the rise and fall of the Islamic State by drawing on a more limited range of repertoires than Iraqis living under insurgent control. During the anti-IS campaign, few residents fled the capital, but those who remained were affected by the influx of Sunni IDPs from neighboring governorates. Throughout the campaign, the most prominent survival repertoires included various forms of cooperation with the anti-IS coalition. Once the IS threat diminished, many Shiʿa transitioned to autonomy by publicly protesting against the Abadi regime for failing to curb corruption, unemployment, and poor service provision. As the central government aimed to reintegrate militias into the Interior Ministry, Sadr's supporters shifted from resisting IS to seeking autonomy from Baghdad and its foreign patrons.

A representative survey of Baghdad residents near the end of the anti-IS campaign reveals how Iraqis updated their beliefs and attitudes about survival as the IS threat dissipated. As the IS defeat neared, Baghdad residents sought greater autonomy, especially from foreign states and their perceived interference in Iraqi politics. Punctuated episodes of civil disobedience and public protest also emerged, as Iraqis updated their expectations about the central government's effectiveness and broader legitimacy.

How did Iraqis living under Islamic State control survive the conflict? The next chapter examines the experiences of Iraqis living under IS rule in Fallujah, Ramadi, and Tikrit. These Sunni-majority cities provide a complement to the Baghdad case study, as Sunnis in western Iraq had a history of resisting foreign occupiers through selective cooperation with insurgents. As such, the range of survival repertoires employed by Iraqis in these cities differed from those in Baghdad.

5

Fallujah, Ramadi, and Tikrit

Navigating Violence in the Sunni Triangle

Personally, I do not mind anyone coming in, dominating, and forcing security, but they have to be fair, am I correct? If I am cooperating with you, then I expect that you provide security and make life easy.
—CIVIL ADMINISTRATOR IN FALLUJAH (RESPONDENT B01)

They [Tikritis] joined Daʻesh because of starvation.... The world reached the stage of despair and its children reached the stage of death from starvation, so they had to go with Daʻesh.
—DAY LABORER IN TIKRIT (RESPONDENT B04)

There is a proverb that says, "Whoever changes their home becomes less valuable" (*min talaʻa min darih, qul miqdaruh*). This is the society that I can live in, whether I go to the north, the middle, or the south. I can adjust in a month. We are similar in morals, character, food, speech, generosity, responsibilities. Whatever I don't know I will learn. But if I leave my country, I will be a stranger no matter how much money I have.
—TRIBAL SHEIKH IN TIKRIT (RESPONDENT B20)

When Da'esh came as defenders of Sunnis, we knew that they were criminals, that they were not Sunni defenders. When they presented themselves, people said, 'Well, it may be possible to save us from the government, from the army which is not a professional national army, but one that killed and arrested Sunnis,'" explained Dr. Rafi al-Issawi.[1] Issawi's words aptly summarized the predicament confronting many Sunnis during the rise of the Islamic State. As an influential Sunni politician from the Albu Issa tribe, Issawi served as deputy prime minister as well as finance minister during Prime Minister Nouri al-Maliki's second term. Despite a string of assassination attempts by sectarian militias, he continued in the cabinet, encouraging Sunnis to remain engaged in national politics. Two years into Maliki's second term, however, the prime minister used a Ba'thist-era counterterrorism law to approve a raid on Issawi's home based on accusations of support for al-Qa'ida. While Issawi remained free, ten of his bodyguards were arrested. Three months later, in March 2013, Issawi resigned his post in protest and returned home to Fallujah. Issawi's return fueled the ongoing protests against the central government, which began in earnest after the emergence of the Arab uprisings in February 2011.

This chapter examines how Sunnis in western Iraq survived occupation of their communities by IS. It focuses on the "Sunni Triangle," the cluster of Sunni-majority communities hemmed in by the cities of Ramadi, Fallujah, and Tikrit (see figure 5.1). The Sunni Triangle is important for this study, because it was the location where al-Qa'ida transformed into the Islamic State during the summer of 2011. The region served as a proving ground not only for IS's military strategy, but also for how it would govern citizens living within the so-called caliphate.

Most importantly, the Sunni Triangle merits further investigation because it represents a case where cooperation with IS was a viable survival repertoire. Given the sectarian composition of these communities—in concert with Maliki's systematic political persecution after the 2011 U.S. departure—IS governance served as a viable alternative to that of the central government. Despite escalating insurgent violence throughout 2013, many residents perceived IS as less of a threat than the government in Baghdad. As Issawi would later explain, "People got very upset, very angry about the government's behavior and the Iraqi army's behavior.... The people started to look at the army as an enemy rather than as a national army."[2]

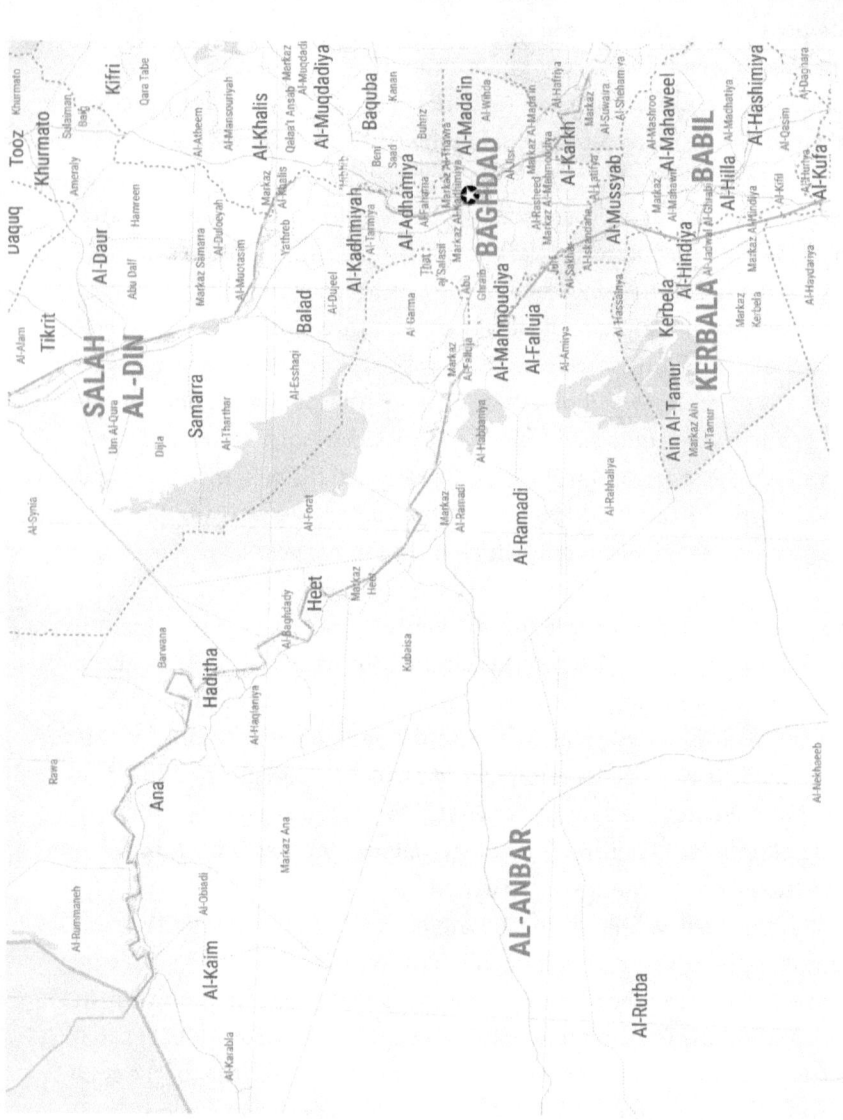

FIGURE 5.1 Map of the "Sunni Triangle."

Source: "Iraq: National Reference Map (as of 28 Sep 2021)," Office for the Coordination of Humanitarian Affairs, United Nations, September 28, 2021, https://reliefweb.int/map/iraq/iraq-national-reference-map-28-sep-2021.

The pages that follow draw on interviews from the field to explore how Iraqis in the Sunni Triangle survived the IS occupation. It shows that many residents' ability to initially accommodate IS control made neutrality and cooperation viable means of survival. For many, the best way to survive was to lay low or passively acquiesce as IS consolidated control. As one day laborer from Tikrit explained, "Daʿesh opened the closed streets and spoke in the name of humanity and said, 'We have nothing to do with the police and the army,' so the people remained silent" (respondent B04). Also unique to the region was the prevalence of fence-sitting and side-switching among the most powerful tribes. As IS brutality escalated, however, various forms of contention emerged, including armed resistance. The chapter concludes with a discussion of resettlement and reintegration for those Iraqis who fled their homes during the war.

A transformed insurgency in western Iraq (2011–2016)

The Islamic State evolved out of al-Qaʿida in Iraq six months prior to the withdrawal of the remaining U.S. forces in December 2011. During this period, two critical factors led IS to secure a foothold among Iraqis in the Sunni Triangle. First, Maliki's exclusion of Sunni elites and persecution of everyday citizens generated a collective sense of alienation (*mazlumiyya*), motivating Sunnis to search for viable alternatives to regime governance. In an encore to the Arab uprisings one year earlier, Sunnis and Kurds took to the streets to protest Maliki's policies.[3] Throughout 2013, tens of thousands of protestors in Ramadi, Fallujah, and Samarra chanted slogans such as "Nouri al-Maliki is a liar" (*jadhab Nouri al-Maliki*) and "No to corruption" (*kala lil fasad*).[4]

Table 5.1 provides a list of major protests throughout western Iraq since the U.S.-led intervention in March 2003. West of Baghdad, anti-regime protests increased after the 2010 parliamentary elections, escalating in frequency and intensity until February 2013. While the Maliki regime initially ignored public protests, it later took steps to violently repress large public demonstrations throughout Anbar, Diyala, and Salah al-Din. By the end of 2013, over two hundred Iraqis had been killed in the protests, significantly increasing animosity between Sunni communities in the west and the Iraqi Security Forces. As one Tikriti remarked, "They used to make arrests for the slightest reason, and they took people off the streets and put them in

TABLE 5.1 Anti-regime protests in western Iraq (2005–2018)

Date	Location(s)	Protestor count	Government response
9/4/2005	Ramadi	1,500	Ignore
8/29/2005	Tikrit	1,000	Ignore
12/25/2005	Baqubah, Fallujah	100	Beatings
6/24/2006	Tikrit	1,000	Ignore
1/2/2007	Tikrit	50	Ignore
2/9/2008	Diyala	300	Arrests
9/19/2008	Ad-Dawr	400	Ignore
3/1/2009	Diyala	100	Ignore
12/23/2011	Samara and Baqubah	1,000s	Arrests
12/21/2012	Fallujah and Baghdad	1,000s	Ignore
1/4/2013	Anbar, Tikrit, Mosul, and Baghdad	10,000s	Ignore
1/18/2013	Samarra and Abar	1,000s	Ignore
1/26/2013	Fallujah, Mosul, Ninewa, Salah al-Din, Diyala, and Kirkuk	1,000s	Shootings
2/1/2013	Fallujah and Ramadi	10,000s	Ignore
2/8/2013	Fallujah	100s	Ignore
2/15/2013	Fallujah, Ramadi, Samara, Mosul, Kirkuk, and Baghdad	10,000s	Ignore

Source: David Clark and Patrick Regan, "Mass Mobilization Protest Data," Version 4.0 (1990–2019), Mass Mobilization Project, accessed November 3, 2023, https://massmobilization.github.io.

prisons, without a court order. That is why there is hatred between the security forces and the citizenry" (respondent B04).

When Sunnis went to the streets, Maliki responded by using the Iraqi Army and Federal Police to victimize Sunni protesters. In April 2013, the regime crackdown in Hawija resulted in 200 dead and an additional 15 wounded.[5] In response to the violence, the speaker of the Iraqi parliament, Osama al-Najafi, called for Maliki's resignation. That same month, a government raid on a protest camp resulted in 44 civilian fatalities, though the regime admitted to only 3 civilian and 23 "terrorist" deaths.[6] "There was no direct relationship at all between the demonstrations and tribes from outside and Al Qaeda on the outside. People got very upset, very angry about the government's behavior and the Iraqi army's behavior. . . .

The people started to look at the army as an enemy rather than as a national army," observed Rafi al-Issawi.⁷ According to Toby Dodge, Maliki's campaign of sectarian exclusion "triggered a mobilization of a Sunni section of Iraqi society who, since the elections of 2010, had been feeling increasingly and deliberately excluded from Iraqi politics, and cut off from the benefits of oil wealth, and discriminated and targeted by Iraqi security forces."⁸

Maliki also alienated Sunnis in western Iraq by dismantling the Sons of Iraq instead of integrating the tribal militias into the Interior Ministry. IS used the government's vendetta against the tribes to co-opt or persuade tribal leaders. Those who refused to join the insurgents' ranks were identified and systematically assassinated.⁹ The combination of regime persecution and IS's leadership-decapitation strategy led to the near extinction of the Sahwa militias by 2013.

IS exploited Sunni grievances to win local "hearts and minds" to their cause. Their most successful political strategy during this period was tacitly participating in the broader protest movement. Given that many rank-and-file insurgents were Iraqi nationals, IS's support for the protests looked like grassroots opposition to the Maliki regime instead of foreign fighters fomenting unrest. Crucial to this effort was IS's support for local Islamists.

As Hoshyar Zebari, a Kurdish politician and former deputy prime minister, explained, "Many of those [protest] organizers were the Islamist scholars, the mullahs, the religious leader of the mosque of Najaf, of Anbar, of Mosul and so on. They were at the forefront, actually. The politicians were behind them. So that was not a positive image. It enhanced the sectarian feeling, and fed the minds of the Shiʻa and the others that really this is not clean. It has infiltrators and other people trying to benefit [from the protests]."¹⁰

IS also leveraged superior organization and combat tactics in order to secure an ideational and material advantage over state security forces. Beginning in the summer of 2012, IS launched its "Breaking the Walls" campaign, consisting of over two dozen suicide bombings and eight prison breaks, freeing hundreds of former al-Qaʻida insurgents imprisoned in Kirkuk, Tikrit, Taji, and Abu Ghraib.¹¹ On July 22, 2013, IS attacked Abu Ghraib prison, freeing between five hundred and a thousand inmates, including senior AQI leaders. At the same time, IS launched the "Soldiers' Harvest" campaign in an effort to recruit disaffected Baʻthists, military members, and tribal fighters to their ranks. The primary goal was to

112 FALLUJAH, RAMADI, AND TIKRIT

reignite sectarian strife in an effort to persuade Sunni communities that IS was a more reliable and effective source of governance than Baghdad.

By the beginning of 2014, a powerful Islamist insurgency had reemerged in western Iraq. During this period, the Sunni Triangle witnessed violence unseen since the peak of the civil war in 2006 (see figure 5.2).[12] In January, IS insurgents took advantaged of armed clashes between the Iraqi Army and Sunni tribes to launch an offensive on Ramadi. Ramadi would come fully under insurgent occupation by May, and by the end of the year, IS would also control Fallujah, the largest city in Anbar Governorate. By summer 2014, IS insurgents controlled nearly three-quarters of Anbar, including the cities of Fallujah, Al Qaʾim, Ar Rutba, and half of the provincial capital of Ramadi. From Ramadi, IS accessed the Baghdad Belt by infiltrating the capital's western district of Abu Ghraib. That October, IS insurgents hunted down and assassinated Sunni militiamen, culminating in the mass execution of between fifty and seventy-five Albu Nimr tribesman in Hit.[13]

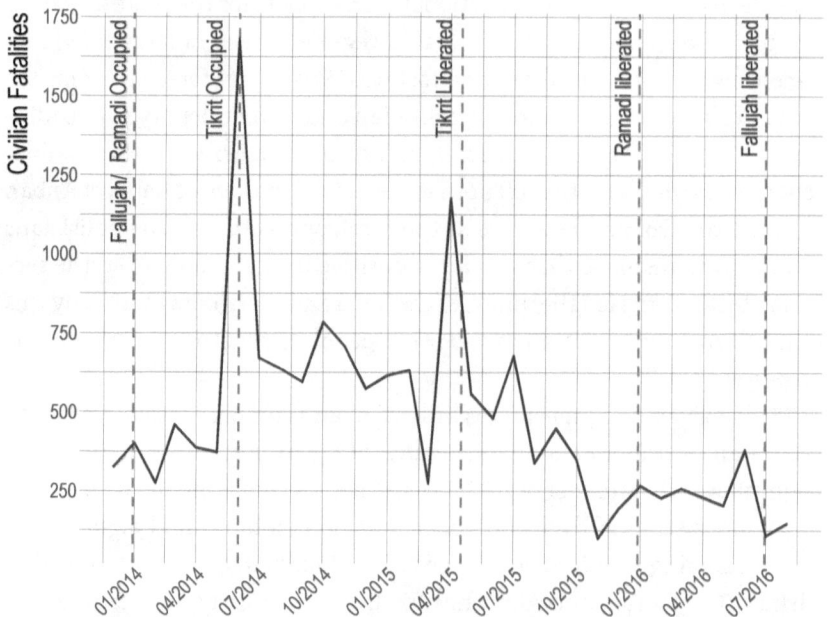

FIGURE 5.2 Civilian fatalities in western Iraq (2014–2016).

Source: Iraq Body Count, https://www.iraqbodycount.org.

As IS extended its western offensive throughout 2014, the security situation within the Sunni Triangle became increasingly fluid and complex. Much like other areas of Iraq, each "side" of the local conflict actually consisted of coalitions of opposing forces. While IS represented the largest and most capable opposition force, there also existed a series of intertribal disputes among Sunni tribes and smaller Islamist groups, such as the Naqshbandi Order (JRTN) and 1920 Revolution Brigades.[14]

Within the anti-IS coalition, there also existed intra-coalition violence among Shiʿa and Sunnis. Of particular importance are the armed clashes that occurred between the Popular Mobilization Forces and the Sunni tribal resistance organized under the Tribal Mobilization Force. While many elements of the latter organization would formally integrate into the PMF as the anti-IS campaign progressed, earlier periods of the conflict had seen violent exchanges between armed groups aligned against IS. By and large, international coalition members played a supporting role in the counter-IS campaign, including through the provision of air support, intelligence, and military equipment and ammunition to the Iraqi Army, the Counter Terrorism Service, and the Federal Police. For example, the U.S. military limited its role in Anbar to providing security assistance to Iraqi coalition members from its regional headquarters at Al Asad Airbase.[15]

By mid-2015, the anti-IS coalition had turned the tide against the Islamic State in western Iraq. In late December, coalition forces liberated Ramadi. Throughout Anbar, several tribal militias affiliated with the Sahwa began collaborating with the PMF. In some instances, the Sunni tribes formally integrated their militias into new PMF brigades.[16] Fierce fighting over the following six months resulted in a steady stream of victories by the anti-IS coalition, culminating in the liberation of Fallujah in June 2016. By the end of the summer, over 75 percent of Anbar and Salah al-Din had been cleared of IS insurgents. The anti-IS coalition would launch a northern offensive in Ninewa Governorate beginning in October 2016.

Displacement, resettlement, and repatriation

Forced displacement within the Sunni Triangle skyrocketed with IS's June 2014 offensive. At the height of the group's territorial control in autumn 2014, approximately 3.2 million Iraqis were internally displaced across three thousand communities in Anbar and Salah al-Din.[17] The IS offensive produced simultaneous outflows from urban centers like Fallujah, Ramadi, and Tikrit with inflows from the rural peripheries most vulnerable to insurgent violence. Six months prior to the June 2014 offensive, approximately 250,000 people had fled communities in and around Fallujah as IS insurgents launched an offensive to "defend Sunnis from the central government."[18] In the subsequent six months, an additional 500,000 Anbaris fled their homes, including nearly half of Ramadi's prewar population of 375,000.[19]

Figure 5.3 provides a network visualization of IDP flows originating from Anbar and Salah al-Din during the IS insurgency. Nodes correspond to

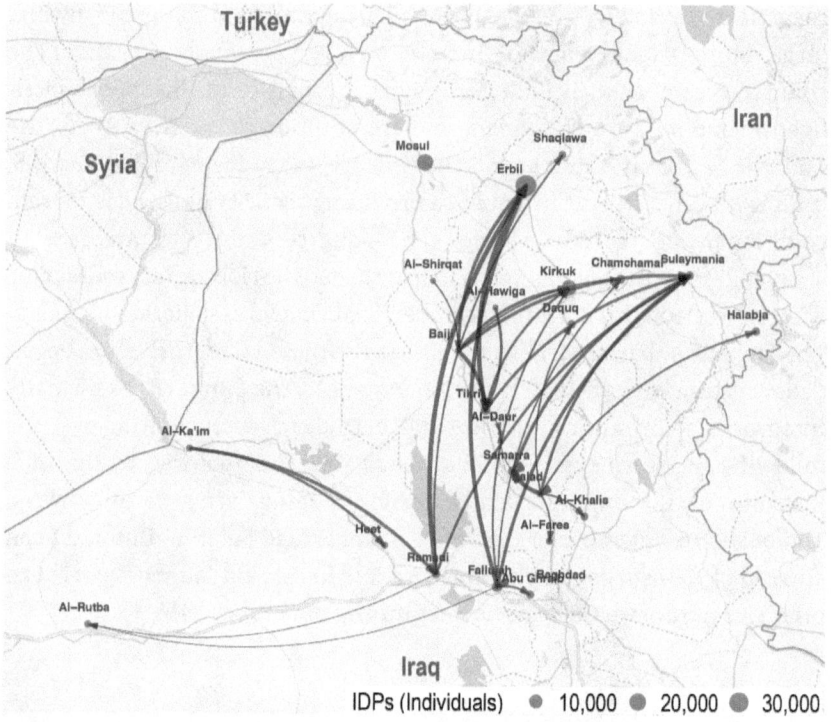

FIGURE 5.3 Network of IDP flows across Anbar and Salah al-Din Governorates (2014–2020).

Source: Displacement Tracking Matrix, International Organization for Migration, https://dtm.iom.int/iraq.

departure or arrival locations, and the size of each node reflects the aggregate inflow of IDPs throughout the conflict. Edges are represented by gray arrows connecting each node in the network. The width of each edge reflects the relative volume of IDP flows between locations. Edges are directed, indicating which communities sent IDPs and which ones received them.

During the IS offensive, nearly ten times as many Iraqis fled as resettled within the Sunni Triangle. Within Anbar and Salah al-Din, most IDPs originated from rural communities and fled to urban centers in search of security, jobs, and functioning public infrastructure. As displayed in figure 5.4, most IDPs resettled in Fallujah, Samarra, and Tikrit. Within these three arrival districts, the vast majority of IDPs originated from the same governorate. One of the primary drivers of internal resettlement was cost. For Tikritis, for example, it was easier and more affordable to

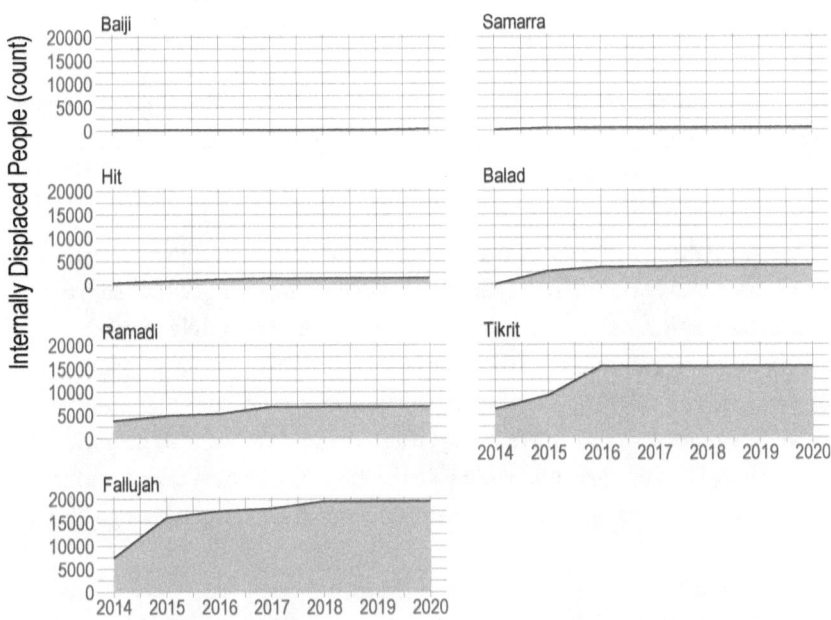

FIGURE 5.4 IDP arrivals by district over time across Anbar and Salah al-Din Governorates (2014–2018).

Source: Displacement Tracking Matrix, International Organization for Migration, https://dtm.iom.int/iraq; map underlayment from Google Maps.

make the two-hour journey to Kirkuk instead of resettling in Baghdad or Erbil. Even so, successful resettlement depended on one's ability to make a living in a new community. As one Tikrit resident recounted, "I cannot go to Kirkuk. The rents for the houses there are high; some houses, their rents reach 1 million dinars [approximately US$685]. If I decide to leave, I must have a salary in order to secure it, and I do not have this" (respondent B04). While most had a strong motivation to flee, for many families, the cost of safe resettlement inhibited their ability to leave.

At the same time, residents of the Sunni Triangle were fleeing their homes to safer communities in the Kurdistan Region. In Fallujah, approximately 98,000 Sunnis fled the district, with half resettling in Erbil and Sulaymania and 16 percent resettling within Anbar Governorate.[20] Similar trends are observed in Ramadi, where 100,000 individuals fled the city to find safe haven in Erbil, Sulaymania, and Shaqala.[21] Tikrit saw fewer residents displaced by insurgent violence, with 33,000 Iraqis relocating to the neighboring city of Kirkuk or the Kurdistan Region. Notably, over 95 percent of IDP households remained displaced for longer than three years.[22] Iraqis suffering from protracted displacement were forced to move locations multiple times throughout the conflict due to changing patterns of violence, as well as competition over access to humanitarian relief.

As one Sunni IDP who resettled in Baghdad noted,

> We were displaced from our areas three and half years ago and settled in the Al Takiya camp in Baghdad. We were then forcibly expelled from the campsite even though we cannot return to our areas. We are now living in the open 2 km away from our homes, and we want the government agencies to find a solution for us. Our number is nearly 3,000 families, and no one cares for us. We do not want any aid. We want to go back to our homes, which are near where we live now. The biggest crime against us is that we can see our homes with our own eyes, but we cannot go back to them.[23]

Three factors set displacement trends in western Iraq apart from other regions. First, unlike displacement trends in Baghdad and Ninewa, IDPs from the Sunni Triangle commonly resettled within their governorate of origin. While nearly one in three IDPs fled to the Kurdistan Region, a majority resettled within Anbar and Salah al-Din. One in four IDPs from Anbar remained in the governorates, whereas more than 90 percent of those displaced in Diyala fled to Erbil, Kirkuk, and Sulaymania.[24] Internal resettlement rates were even higher in Salah al-Din, with 40 percent of IDPs resettling within neighboring communities. Less than 5 percent relocated to Sunni-majority areas in west Baghdad.

Second, insurgent and government checkpoints and transit routes shaped refugee flows.[25] For many displaced Sunnis, the relative risk of fleeing was similar if IS insurgents or pro-government militias controlled the checkpoints. As local residents were fleeing the IS offensive in 2014, for example, the Al Razaza checkpoint in Amiriya—a town outside of Fallujah connecting Karbala and Anbar—became a central transit point where Kataʾib Hezbollah militiamen victimized and extorted IDPs. On October 26, 2014, for example, 192 residents of Jurf Al Sakhr (a small tribal community in Babil Governorate about fifty kilometers south of Baghdad) disappeared at the Al Razaza checkpoint. The checkpoint would later become known by local residents as a "crossing of death" (ʿubur al-mawt).[26] According to the MENA Rights Group and Al Wissam Humanitarian Assembly, "Far from being an isolated incident, the total number of individuals disappeared from the checkpoint is much higher, with some estimates stating that as many as 1,200 civilians went missing from the checkpoint in one year."[27]

Destruction of public infrastructure also shaped migration routes. As one IDP who resettled in Ramadi conveyed, "It was difficult to leave Al Hasa [a rural village in Anah District], our living conditions worsened a lot, and all the sites that were bombed by the [Iraqi Air Force] were not for Daʿesh but civilians" (respondent B02). Similarly, an IDP who resettled in Fallujah noted, "We left in daylight, but by chance there was bombing and civilian cars were burnt, so people left their cars and started running away . . . but since it is a crossing, you are able to cross it by foot" (respondent B01).

The availability and cost of smuggling routes further restricted displacement. In addition to paying a fee to drivers for safe passage, many IDPs successfully fled by bribing insurgents or coalition forces at security checkpoints. "At that time, the sums for leaving the city amounted to $500 and more. And the Daʿesh gangs themselves were taking money from people and allowing them to leave. . . . They arrange for them an exit permit from the hospital or for medical and health purposes and help the citizens escape from Fallujah," one respondent explained (respondent B11). Entering Baghdad was even more complicated. IDPs not only needed to navigate the network of checkpoints encircling the capital, they also had to secure the support of a sponsor within the city.[28] As one Fallujah resident conveyed, "The [relocation] process was similar to what happens when you try to enter Baghdad, so you have to pay money to the army in order for them to let you in" (respondent B05).

As soon as IDPs became mobile, their vulnerability to exploitation drastically increased. More often than not, the journey between one's former home and arrival location was the most dangerous part of resettlement. One Tikriti described the predicament well: "All the roads between the areas were blocked. Many people left and were trapped between the checkpoints and the safe areas. Sometimes the [coalition] air strikes hit them. Therefore, many families were harmed by bombing while leaving" (respondent B04). Another respondent from outside of Fallujah described a similar situation afflicting those fleeing to Baghdad: "The bridge [across the Euphrates] was closed, children were sleeping on the bridge, people were sick, and no one crossed into Baghdad without paying money. Those who did not have the money to cross had to wait for a sponsor and remained at the mercy of the Lord of the Worlds [*Rabb al-ʿAlamin*]. The situation was very dire" (respondent B05). Given public suspicion surrounding local collaboration with IS within the Sunni Triangle, opportunities to secure sponsorship were especially difficult for single Sunni women.

Those considering flight confronted a dilemma. While it took time to save enough money to safely flee, those departing at later stages faced a greater risk of being perceived by their new neighbors as IS collaborators. As one civil administrator who fled from a village near Al Obaidy (Al Qaʾim District) remarked, "Some of [the Iraqi Army] welcomed you, and some doubted you because of your delay in leaving. . . . We can say that they were blaming us. They did not accuse us directly, but they asked what took us so long to leave" (respondent B01). Another respondent fleeing from Al Hasa (Anah District) to Ramadi observed, "When we escaped, we couldn't shave off our beards. We tried to shave and cut the hair a little bit when we reached the house in [redacted], but we couldn't do it properly so it was uneven. Imagine that we couldn't shave off our beard for two years, how do you expect us to look?" (respondent B02). Instead of signaling a lack of hygiene, the length of a man's beard served as a visible sign of his adherence to a strict interpretation of shariʿa.

The arrival of IDPs also upended the social cohesion of the communities in which they resettled. In many cases, newly arrived IDPs were the objects of ostracism and suspicion, including the suspicion that they had collaborated with IS. Such accusations were particularly severe for Sunni women, especially those of reproductive age, who were often perceived as having the opportunity to exchange marriage or sex for physical protection.

By August 2016, coalition forces had expelled IS insurgents from most large communities within the Sunni Triangle. Over the following year, approximately 534,000 individuals returned to their home communities (see figure 5.5). By October 2021, 2.2 million IDPs and refugees had returned to their home communities in Anbar and Salah al-Din. In the cities of Fallujah, Al Qaʾim, and Ramadi, 90 percent of displaced households had returned to their homes after the liberation of their communities.[29] Ramadi

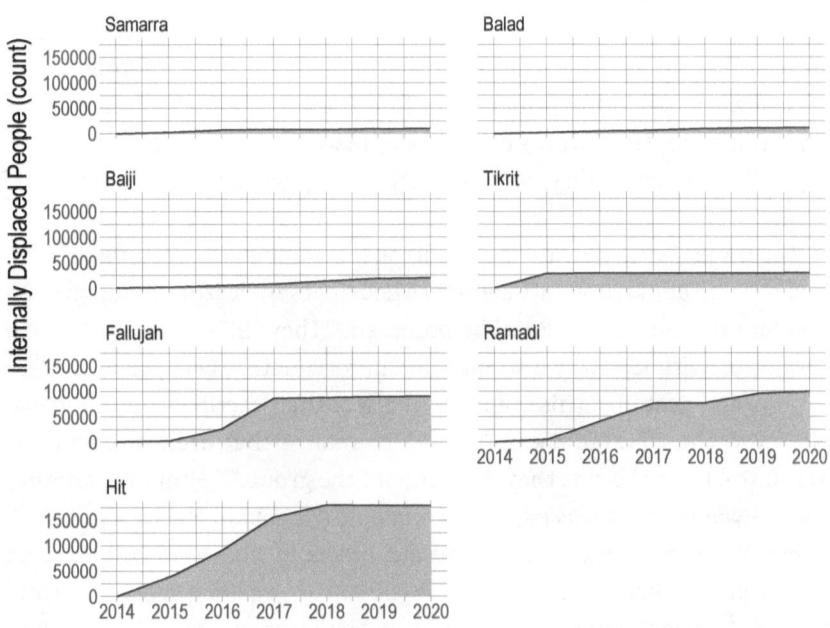

FIGURE 5.5 Returnees by district across Anbar and Salah al-Din Governorates (2014–2020).

Source: Displacement Tracking Matrix, International Organization for Migration, https://dtm.iom.int/iraq.

saw approximately 100,000 households return to the community after the liberation of the city in February 2015. In the districts of Hawija and Al Shirqat, north of Tikrit, over 55,000 households returned to their home communities.

Despite increasing returnee flows, barriers to resettlement and reintegration plagued many Sunni communities. In addition to a lack of access to basic needs—including reliable access to food, shelter, medical care, education, and public utilities—barriers to social cohesion were also present. As one IDP from a village in Anah District recounted, "We only see [local officials] during election periods. There also are not any health services there, not even medical clinics or ambulances. How do you expect people to go back to their homes? They won't" (respondent B02).

A key social barrier to reintegration was perceived collaboration with IS. As a 2020 report from the International Organization for Migration noted, "returned IDPs with perceived affiliation have been secondarily displaced after having been rejected by their communities of origin."[30] In most instances, perceived IS affiliation derived from a family's clan identity, the period in which they fled their home, or simple rumors and innuendo. For Sunni Arab women, mere accusations of IS support, regardless of credibility, were enough to trigger ostracism from their neighbors.[31]

For Iraqis living outside of IS control, the combination of gender, sect, and a "late" departure date served as heuristics indicating IS support. As one Sunni woman from Al Abba observed, "They [IDPs with a perceived affiliation with IS] carry a stigma, and unfortunately, because of the traditions and customs, this stigma will affect their families and the tribe. However, the community is starting to realize that each individual is accountable for the sins they commit, not the group."[32] Similarly, another Anbari woman who was expelled from an IDP camp in Habbaniya noted, "They closed our camp and took us out suddenly. I have six children and do not know where to go. My clan in the Anbar province accuses me and my family of belonging to IS. I fear for my children and husband. We cannot go back to our area. We are afraid that we will be hidden or liquidated."[33] As of August 2022, one-quarter of the 1.2 million Iraqis still displaced from their homes originated from communities within the Sunni Triangle.[34]

Contention

For those who stayed in their homes—either by necessity or by choice—resisting IS rule entailed significant risk. Those most likely to forcibly contend with IS rule had a prior history of resisting al-Qaʿida during the U.S. intervention. Despite sharing a similar social identity, contention emerged among tribal elites whose power was diminished by the arrival of foreign jihadists. The same dynamic emerged in 2014, when IS challenged the networks of tribal authority and influence in western Iraq. Resistance also emerged among Sunnis who initially welcomed IS as an alternative to the government in Baghdad, only to be later exploited by insurgents. Given a shared sectarian identity between IS and Sunni-majority communities, the heuristics of personal experience and coercive behavior were more relevant than in-group bias for judging insurgents' motives and intentions.

Despite the attendant risks, residents of the Sunni Triangle pursued various repertoires of contention, opposition, and resistance. Acts of everyday resistance were most common among Sunnis who were endangered by IS control, but who lacked viable alternatives for coalition protection. For communities directly under IS control, one of the most common forms of everyday resistance was informing to coalition forces. Confidential informing was a common way of cooperating during the previous civil war, especially during the 2007 troop surge.[35] The provision of tips by local residents took the form of direct and indirect communication with the coalition. Direct communication included secret phone calls and SMS messages to an individual's contacts in the Iraqi Army or Federal Police.

The ability to inform to the coalition depended on two key conditions. First, an individual had to have access to a reliable cellular or Internet connection. However, confidential informing was difficult given IS's monitoring and surveillance of public locations with reliable Internet connections (e.g., an Internet café or meeting hall). Second, an individual had to have connections to members of the state security forces through their social network. Given the mass desertion of Iraqi Army and police during the IS offensive, it was difficult for many to identify a trustworthy member of the coalition who could receive their tips. In the face of this suspicion, heuristics based on past interactions and social identity proved especially useful. As one Tikriti explained, "There were certain places where you could go and communicate. In addition to the presence of some relatives in the security forces outside, there was a kind of communication between them and calls. So, the government had specific points for [Daʿesh] and determined their locations, and there were specific operations and attacks against [Daʿesh] points. And the youth inside the city began to show the government the positions" (respondent B04). In other communities, such as rural Anbar, direct communication with the coalition was not feasible due to lack of reliable cell coverage and Internet access (respondent B01). In these circumstances private acts of everyday resistance were more common.

Individuals could also use indirect channels to communicate with coalition forces. Several respondents recounted how local residents would discreetly place compact discs near insurgent locations in order to provide targeting assistance to the Iraqi Air Force. "Those who had acquaintances in the army or security forces who worked with them began throwing CDs near [Daʿesh] homes as a signal for the air force to bomb them," explained one Tikriti (respondent B04). Other forms of indirect communication included marking IS locations with graffiti. Using graffiti to tag buildings with anti-IS messaging was also a common form of everyday resistance (respondent B03). Still others resisted IS by striving to keep their minds clear of Islamist propaganda. As one Ramadi resident related, "I believe I resisted them intellectually. Like the discussion I had with that person, and, in my mind I know these actions are wrong and do not represent Islam at all" (respondent B06). In such cases, perceived violations of sacred values made it difficult for Iraqis to accommodate IS control.

Higher-risk repertoires of contention included operating as a "fifth column" among the insurgent ranks, including volunteering to fight yet failing to perform assigned tasks or duties. According to one tribal sheikh in Tikrit, "Some [community members] escaped by accepting to fight with [Daʿesh], since many areas were cornered in between the clashes there was no way to escape. Taking up arms with them and pretending to fight in the battles was a way for some people to escape from Daʿesh during those clashes, without killing anyone or taking up the side of anyone in those clashes" (respondent B20). Similar accounts of internal sabotage and feigned collaboration exist but are difficult to corroborate. However, opportunistic resistance typically emerged when IS control was declining and local residents had an outside option for receiving protection from coalition forces.

Residents with a higher risk tolerance actively resisted IS control by mobilizing community self-defense groups.[36] As one tribal militiaman from Ramadi observed, "We weren't counted as martyrs and we couldn't prevent Daʿesh from getting in. We did what we had to do" (respondent B10). A tribal militia volunteer expressed a similar motivation, "If [Daʿesh] found me and my family, they would kill us. So, I made sure my family was safe, and then I stayed and fought with the security forces, the army, the police, and the ones who [remained] . . . until we left. We left after we were helpless" (respondent B09).

Other times, a desire to protect one's property from destruction or theft motivated armed resistance. "When I ask someone, 'What made you stay?' they tell me that they . . . only stay for the sake of their fortunes and their businesses and money as the ones who live in the deserts [Bedouins] with their sheep" (respondent B10). Individuals with illiquid assets such as farmland, livestock, or heavy equipment had the motivation and opportunity to resist IS since fleeing would result in the forfeiture of their livelihoods.[37]

The riskiest forms of armed resistance involved covert assassinations of IS leaders and rank-and-file fighters. A history of past victimization served as a particularly powerful heuristic motivating violent resistance. "They bought weapons and developed the plan. In addition to another targeting operation, they carried out [assassinations] at night under the control of Daʿesh. . . . They attacked and killed them and documented them with a video, and then the video was sent to the security forces," explained one Tikriti man (respondent B04). However, armed resistance efforts were also subject to internal sabotage by residents informing to IS. "They [resistance forces] failed, they put themselves in danger, and there were people from the inside who cooperated with them," recounted one IDP from Fallujah (respondent B01).

As the anti-IS counteroffensive gained momentum in western Iraq in the summer of 2015, many tribal militias switched to active collaboration with coalition forces (see table 5.2). On select occasions, tribal militias were formally integrated into the coalition, including through the formation of Sunni tribal brigades within the PMF.[38] Examples of collaboration included intelligence sharing, joint tactical exercises, patrolling checkpoints, and providing perimeter security. "The cooperation with the security forces was great, and they took up their weapons and crossed to the side of the forces and escaped by themselves and joined the PMF and fought back until

TABLE 5.2 Sunni tribal resistance against the Islamic State (2011–2017)

Tribe (clan)	Location	Alignment	Elites
Albu Risha	Ramadi	Iraq Army, Federal Police	Ahmed al-Alwani; Abdul Sattar Abu Risha (d. 2007)
Albu Thiyab	Ramadi	Iraq Army, Federal Police	Hamid Farhan al-Heiss; Colonel Tariq Yusef Muhammad
Albu Aetha (Hardan)	Anbar	Iraq Army, Federal Police	Sheikh Wissam Hardan al-Aethawi; Sheikh Ibrahim Nayef Mshhan al-Hardan
Albu Faraj	Ramadi	Iraqi local police	Sheikh Abdullah Jallal Mukhlif al-Faraji; Dr. Thamer Ibrahim Tahir al-Assafi
Albu Fahad	East Ramadi	Iraqi local police	Rafi al-Fahadawi; Mohammed Mahmoud Latif al-Fahadawi
Albu Mahal	Al Qaʿim	Iraq Army, Federal Police	Sheikh Sabah al-Mahalawi
Albu Nimr	Hit	Iraq Army, Federal Police	Sheikh Ghazi al-Kaoud; Sheikh Naim al-Kaoud; Sheikh Jalal al-Kaoud
Sunni Endowment Diwan	Tikrit; Baiji; Sufiya (Ramadi)	PMF (86th Brigade)	Mufti Sheikh Dr. Mahdi al-Sumaidaʿie
Azza	Hamrin; Muqdadiya	Iraqi Army, PMF (Badr Brigade)	Major General Muzhir al-Azzawi
Al Jabbour	Mosul; Shirqat; Tikrit	PMF (51st Brigade)	Abu Abir al-Jabbouri; Sheikh Jasim Jabbara; Ashem Sabhan al-Jabbouri; Major Sattam al-Jabbouri; Yazan al-Jabbouri

Sources: Martha L. Cottam and Joe W. Huseby, *Confronting Al Qaeda: The Sunni Awakening and American Strategy in Al Anbar* (Lantham, MD: Rowman & Littlefield, 2016); Michael Knights and Alexander Mello, "Losing Mosul, Regenerating in Diyala: How the Islamic State Could Exploit Iraq's Sectarian Tinderbox," *CTC Sentinel* 9, no 10. (October 2016): 1–7; Carter Malkasian, *Illusions of Victory: The Anbar Awakening and the Rise of the Islamic State* (New York: Oxford University Press, 2017); Joel D. Rayburn and Frank K. Sobchak, *The U.S. Army in Iraq: Surge and Withdrawal (2007-2011)* (Washington, DC: Operation Iraqi Freedom Study Group, Office of the Chief of Staff, U.S. Army, January 2019); Aymenn Jawad Al-Tamimi, "Hashd Formations of Iraq: Interview with Harakat Ahrar al-Iraq," *Pundicity*, January 18, 2019, https://www.aymennjawad.org/2019/01/hashd-formations-of-iraq-interview-with-harakat; Haian Dukhan, "Tribal Mobilisation Forces in Iraq: Subtleties of Formation and Consequential Power Dynamics," *British Journal of Middle Eastern Studies*, online first, June 14, 2022, https://doi.org/10.1080/13530194.2022.2087599.

all areas were liberated," explained one interviewee from Tikrit (respondent B04).

Another member of a PMF-aligned tribal militia explained, "They [the PMF unit] were resisting Daʿesh with communications and intelligence. They were providing intelligence with information about Daʿesh [to the Iraqi Security Forces]" (Respondent B14). Similar examples of intelligence sharing and security coordination occurred during the liberation of Fallujah in May 2016. As one member of a tribal PMF unit in Fallujah explained, "We cooperate. . . . There is coordination with tribal sheikhs and the city's *mukhtars* [village leaders]. We have civilian sources and collaborators. The *mukhtars* give us their phone numbers, and every Thursday we have a meeting. Every member has his own informants who share with us what they know."[39]

Despite active coordination with the coalition, internal divisions between the tribal resistance and Shiʿa-majority PMF undermined public trust. As one tribal fighter from Tikrit observed, "[Tikritis] only have tension against the al-Hashd ash-Shaʿbi [i.e., the PMF]. . . . The al-Hashd ash-Shaʿbi was putting pressure on people, and they were accusing people of being affiliated with Daʿesh" (respondent B14). Another Ramadi resident went so far as to argue that "Iran-backed militias [in this case, the Badr Brigades] are no less dangerous than Daʿesh" (respondent B06). As was the case in Baghdad during the U.S. intervention, once insurgents no longer presented an existential threat, sectarian infighting and local grievances undermined social cohesion.

In conclusion, despite the myriad risks, many Sunnis who remained in western Iraq resisted IS control. During the 2014 IS offensive and subsequent occupation, many individuals pursued low-risk or secret forms of everyday resistance, including the provision of tips to coalition forces. Those with a higher risk tolerance and access to greater resources remobilized tribal militias. As the anti-IS coalition gained momentum throughout 2015, armed resistance against insurgents became increasingly common.

Neutrality

Hiding or laying low represented the most common survival repertoire for residents of the Sunni Triangle. Even for those who would eventually flee their homes, the initial dilemma was whether it was possible to survive by keeping one's head down. The key heuristic motivating survival decisions was whether accommodating IS governance was possible given how insurgents were consolidating control. The anticipated costs of neutrality only increased as communities throughout the region witnessed the precipitous retreat of the Iraqi Army.

As a tribal sheikh from Tikrit remarked, "It was indescribable, I was stunned seeing with my own eyes the army retreating" (respondent B20). Trust in local elites—including sheikhs, mukhtars, and imams—also declined as local power brokers ceded influence as IS consolidated control. "People no longer trust the clergy and tribal leaders after they put their trust in them and obeyed their calls and went out in demonstrations.... People now think that the clergy are the reason behind what happened," explained a resident of Fallujah (respondent B05).

Most residents under IS control tried to avoid direct engagement with the insurgents. As one tribal militiaman from Ramadi observed, "Some people didn't leave their homes; they said that if they were going to get killed, they want to get killed in their homes" (respondent B10). A resident who remained in Tikrit during the IS offensive conveyed a similar sentiment: "I tell you that even leaving the house has become impossible, because they will hold you accountable for your beard and clothing, and if you violate their orders, they will flog you. There were people who died under [Daʿesh's] torment and flogging" (respondent B04).[40]

With dwindling food, supplies, and shelter, many people opted to leave their homes and pursue neutrality through movement. Given their shared ethno-sectarian identity, some residents bargained or negotiated with insurgents by communicating that they were not interested in choosing sides in the conflict. As one Fallujah resident stated, "As someone said to Daʿesh that I have nothing to do with you, I do not have any policeman or army in my family, and I am not against you and not with the state. I am with those who provide me with security and safety, with those who control the situation, but by peaceful and legal means" (respondent B08).

As many quickly found out, however, IS seldom tolerated neutrality from residents of communities they controlled. Sharing a social identity as Sunni Arabs did not exempt local residents from coercion or punishment. Once IS established control, it would send members of the *hisbah* door to door to ensure that citizens were abiding by shariʿa and attending Friday prayer services.⁴¹ "After the security forces had retreated, [Daʿesh] held a meeting in the market and started stating rules. This is when people were shocked," recounted one Fallujah resident (respondent B01).

When hiding or commuting became untenable, some residents pursued autonomy by forming community self-defense groups. In several rural villages south of Fallujah, such as Falahat, Husi, and Shamiya, community defense fell on those men who remained. As one Sunni woman from Falahat recounted, "Residents decided to organize night patrols to protect the region because it is exposed from the desert's side and [Daʿesh] elements could infiltrate our areas."⁴² A local militiaman in Ramadi recounted a similar story: "My uncle, the sheikh of the tribe, volunteered to buy weapons with his own money from the government, and they [members of the local militia] would actually take day and night shifts to keep the area secure . . . and also to help the security forces" (respondent B10). However, given the absence of coalition forces, autonomous resistance was short-lived prior to late 2015. As one tribal fighter in Fallujah recounted, [There were clans who got out there and fought them [IS], but only for a short period, because the whole fight lasted three to five days only" (respondent B01). In sum, the transition from neutrality to autonomy occurred when insurgents increased their victimization of Sunni residents to the point where accommodation became untenable. As noted above, most attempts at armed autonomy originated from older male tribal elites, especially those who could mobilize young men to fight and defend the community.

While several of the most powerful tribal militias violently resisted IS, others sought autonomy from insurgents and Baghdad alike. The motivation for this type of fence-sitting strategy came from the memory of Maliki's campaign of exclusion and marginalization during the post–Arab uprisings protests. As Carter Malkasian explains, "The Albu Fahad, for example, was deeply divided between pro-resistance and pro-AQI factions. This all serves to make the point that the tribal system was inherently unstable."⁴³ Past experience with AQI served as a useful heuristic for determining whether complete autonomy or regime collaboration was more desirable.

During the first coalition counteroffensive on Ramadi in late 2014, for example, some local militiamen recounted being told by coalition forces to retreat from the area. "The [Federal Police] told us to leave; they told everyone—the police, the clans, sons of clans, members of the Sahwa, and everyone else supporting. They told us that we are not allowed to stay. That is when we had to withdraw," said one member of the tribal resistance (respondent B10). On select occasions, self-defense groups would accuse Iraqi forces of friendly fire. "When our leader went there and [told] them that what happened isn't acceptable and that these are our people, they responded that it was a technical error. . . . [But] we don't believe that, and we can't trust them anymore" (respondent B10). As the conflict escalated, even tribal militias with sufficient arms and personnel felt hard-pressed to choose sides between the coalition and IS. As a result, repertoires of autonomy became increasingly untenable.

As the counteroffensive against IS in western Iraq advanced, internal tribal disputes caused autonomous resistance to fragment, rendering neutrality unsustainable. In the process, the heuristics of social identity, past experience, and current governance took on greater salience. Fragmentation within the Albu Alwan tribe led to some clans fighting alongside the Iraqi Army against IS, while other clans under the leadership of Sheikh Raad sought autonomy.[44] Clan-based militias in the Albu Fahad tribe also suffered internal fragmentation as coalition forces liberated Ramadi.[45]

A similar dilemma plagued clans within the Albu Nimr tribe during the IS offensive on Hit in October 2014. In the absence of coalition support, the Albu Nimr deployed militias to confront IS, suffering heavy casualties in the process, including the mass execution of two hundred fighters under the command of Sheikh Naim al-Kaoud in late October 2014.[46] Commenting on the fragmentation of tribal resistance in Anbar, Carter Malkasian observed, "At this critical moment, the tribes went their separate ways. The confusion of the situation afflicted the tribes as it had the army. The tribes were still confronting the army when the Islamic State attacked. Under untoward pressure, they succumbed to the fractures that curse tribalism."[47]

What do examples of neutrality and autonomy reveal about how Sunnis in western Iraq survived IS control? As many locals recounted, hiding was often their first choice prior to leaving their homes. When a strategy of waiting out the conflict became untenable, some transitioned to everyday resistance. The absence of coalition forces motivated the adoption of armed autonomy, which later transitioned into armed resistance during the anti-IS offensive beginning in 2015.

Cooperation

Between 2014 and 2015, passive acquiescence was the most common form of cooperation among Sunnis living under IS control. As the conflict intensified, most individuals had to come to terms with IS control. Believing that fellow Sunnis would be exempted from collective punishment, many residents shifted from neutrality to cooperation. This shift was most pronounced among residents who were insulated from past victimization by AQI during the 2003 civil war.

As one interviewee in Fallujah recounted, "[Daʿesh] imposed order on society. The organization came and imposed its control over the region by force of arms, so the citizens had to accept their presence and coexist with them in order to preserve themselves" (respondent B08). Another Fallujah resident shared a similar sentiment: "They [residents] remained obedient to Daʿesh's rules. We don't want to be unfair toward those who stayed—they couldn't go anywhere, they didn't have any alternatives, doors were closed in their faces, so they had to accept reality. It's not that they were welcoming them" (respondent B16). That person later observed, "As long as you're staying and they're around, so there's no other authority than theirs. You have to accept reality; cope with them, greet them, talk to them—not willingly, but you have to pretend affection. Deep inside you don't like them, but you're powerless" (respondent B16). Another Ramadi resident succinctly summed up the predicament as follows: "God protected us and we needed to go with the wind (*adhhab maʿa al-rih*)" (respondent B10).

As the conflict endured, the increasing scarcity of food, cooking fuel, and basic medical supplies motivated many to adopt various forms of transactional cooperation. One Tikrit resident bluntly stated the dilemma: "They joined Daʿesh because of starvation.... The world reached the stage of despair and its children reached the stage of death from starvation, so they had to go with Daʿesh" (respondent B04).[48] "If a person has a family and kids who are starving, he's compelled to ask [for help] from them [Daʿesh], there's no other option. So, that was the reason for people to communicate with them," explained another person from Fallujah (respondent B16). Similarly, a Ramadi resident recounted that "these poor people were defeated because of their financial statuses; they were very weak, they couldn't do anything but stay. They used to say, 'This is our house and we will stay right here'" (respondent B13). While it would be inaccurate to describe transactional cooperation as collaboration, such repertoires reflect the most common forms of engagement between locals and insurgents.

In other instances, insurgents extracted cooperation through a combination of threats and inducements. Mara Revkin and Elisabeth Wood argue that the social contract in IS-governed territories involved cooperation in exchange for not only access to basic needs, but also a withholding of punishment.[49] "Governance became such a high priority for ISIL that many Sunnis noted how services improved after ISIL captured their territory, with clean streets, functioning and improved infrastructure, and security from the criminality that plagued many citizens," notes Karl Kaltenthaler, Daniel Silverman, and Munqith Dagher.[50] Coercive threats included forced marriage, seizure of assets (e.g., real estate, livestock, and farmland), the use of public corporal punishment, and forced recruitment.[51] "For example, one of the IS members comes to [a villager under the group's control] and forcibly tells him, 'I want you to marry me to one of your daughters.' Or one of the mujahideen tells him he wants his daughter. Some people, fearing this matter, were forced to join. In general, there are things that happened during the rule of IS. If I tell you all about them, 'the hair of the children will turn gray' (*yaj'alu wildaana shiban*) from what I will say," observed a local sheikh in Fallujah (respondent B17).[52] For Sunni women confronting the threat of forced marriage, often the best way to survive was through passive acquiescence rather than everyday resistance.

Stories of insurgents forcibly seizing assets or property were also common. On several occasions interviewees noted the vulnerability of local farmers and herders. As one tribal militiaman recounted of one of his neighbors, "He was forced to cooperate with Da'esh because he could not leave his house and his sheep.... Therefore, his behavior was in order to preserve himself and his sheep, because this is the source of his livelihood, his children and grandchildren, and he is an old man. But he definitively does not join them and has never been with Da'esh, but he was forced to cooperate with Da'esh" (respondent B08). Another interviewee in Fallujah described the consequences of disobedience: "If you do not follow the rules, you will be humiliated, beaten up, and tortured if they expelled you from the area. Then all the people [who] would have done the same left peacefully" (respondent B01).

On other occasions, the IS incentivized cooperation through offers of food, cooking fuel, or monthly stipends. "Some were forced to join ISIS in order to secure a livelihood for their families because Daʿesh was giving money to those who joined them while there were no jobs at that time. In addition, they joined to protect their families from the threat of Daʿesh," explained one man from Fallujah (respondent B05). Another person explained, "People used to go to [Daʿesh] to take food from them. . . . Daʿesh had the fuel, so people went to them for this purpose" (respondent B11). The opportunity for a livable wage also attracted voluntary recruits to civil and combat roles. As one interviewee noted, "Others who were not convinced by this method [theological persuasion] were tempted by money, where they used to offer $1,000, and since the youth were desperate and unemployed, they drifted easily" (respondent B05). Another recounted the example of a young boy from his neighborhood: "So a boy wanted to volunteer to get a generator and $50–$100 salary, and food supply" (respondent B01).

IS's charity offices (Diwan al-Zakat wa al-Sadaqat) were particularly effective at inducing local cooperation. "[Daʿesh] used to look up the poor families and give them some aid . . . every five days or so. They talked to the family members; they tried to convince the son or the father to join," explained a local taxi driver (respondent B15). Reflecting on the goal of IS charity during the war, another Fallujah resident observed, "This is part of Daʿesh's plan to make us as citizens in constant need of them. He will withhold food for you unless you have to go to him and say hello or sympathize with them" (respondent B17).

Given how IS structured their threats and incentives, opportunistic collaboration was common among local tribal and religious elites who had a vested interested in maintaining their status in the community. Especially during the early IS offensive, opportunistic bandwagoning and side-switching was common among the most powerful tribes in Anbar, including clans affiliated with the Albu Fahad, Albu Faraj, and Albu Jumayli. In fact, many tribal leaders used the IS insurgency as an opportunity to settle past scores against other tribes, or even government forces. As Carter Malkasian explains,

> A set of tribal leaders, including those from former Awakening tribes such as the Albu Faraj, issued a public announcement of hostility against any tribe or group fighting the Islamic State or standing with the government. Certain tribal leaders swore loyalty to [IS leader] Baghdadi. Often,

these were the tribes and tribal leaders that had lost out in the spoils of the awakening. Leading awakening tribes such as the Albu Risha, Albu Nimr, and Albu Alwan had dominated since 2007 and sometimes mistreated other tribes (and even groups within their own tribes). The mistreated tribal leaders now exploited the opportunity to reorder the hierarchy.[53]

Opportunistic collaboration was a popular repertoire for tribal elites because IS initially branded themselves as "tribal revolutionaries" seeking to protect Sunnis from government persecution. As one Fallujah resident explained, "When they first came, they didn't come as Daʿesh, everybody knew them as 'revolutionaries of the clans' (*thuwar al-ʿashaʾir*). That was in the beginning" (respondent B16). Public support for antigovernment forces only increased after Maliki's persecution of prominent Sunni politicians, including Ahmed al-Alwani, a parliamentarian from Anbar who had appeared at antigovernment protests the previous year.[54]

While motivations for active collaboration differed, a common belief was that cooperation would increase an individual's status, wealth, or personal security. Some young men joined out of a desire for power, prestige, or personal significance. Much like the decision to join a gang, young men with few outside options for employment, education, or marriage turned to insurgent groups not only for a steady paycheck, but also out of a desire for a sense of belonging and purpose.[55] "There are young people who joined them in rashness in order to show off and carry weapons. I remember here at the time I met a twelve-year-old boy who . . . joined them," explained one respondent from Tikrit (respondent B04). Another Fallujah resident remarked, "Daʿesh came with the Afghani outfits, the hairstyle, and the weapons in their hands, and they're ignorant people who don't know religion, and they thought that it was prestige and something to show off, and hence they rode the wave with them. They thought that Daʿesh is going to keep ruling and it is an Islamic state, and they build it up in their minds. It's going to prevail in Iraq and we all need to be under the flag of the Islamic State" (respondent B16). Status, prestige, and self-esteem were among the most common motivations among military-age males with fewer prospects for further education, employment, or marriage.[56]

A smaller subset of collaborators shared an ideological affinity with IS: "There are people who are convinced for the sake of religion, and there were young men committed to religion, prayer, and fasting. When Daʿesh came, these people were the right people, but the path of Daʿesh is a one-line path ... it is never possible to return from it," explained one Tikriti (respondent B04). Another Fallujah resident observed, "People actually believed that it was a revolution. ... They [Daʿesh] were really good with the media. Back then all the Arabic TV news channels used to call them revolutionaries at the beginning, but when they entered the city, everyone was shocked" (respondent B01). Compared to the personal motivations of greed or status, ideological support was more evenly distributed among Sunni men and women.

Local religious elites were also co-opted by IS's ideology. One Ramadi militiaman noted the effects of IS's campaign of persuasion within rural communities: "I went to the imam of the mosque [in Ar Rutbah] to take an order for prosthetics [for wounded community members] and the imam actually helped find us a person to help. He [later] accused us of being with the crusaders (al-salibiyun), and he told us that he had a military uniform and ... that if we stayed in Ar Rutbah, he would kill us and put it on our chests" (respondent B10).

To summarize, many who remained in their communities during the IS occupation of Anbar and Salah al-Din either passively acquiesced or transactionally cooperated. One civil servant in Fallujah expressed this dilemma with pragmatic fatalism: "Personally, I do not mind anyone coming in, dominating, and forcing security, but they have to be fair, am I correct? If I am cooperating with you, then I expect that you provide security and make life easy" (respondent B01). Many who accommodated IS rule perceived that a shared sectarian identity would spare them from selective punishment or victimization. Over time, the conditions for cooperation became increasingly burdensome, which proved to be too difficult for many Sunni communities to endure.

"[Our] social reality has changed. We feel that all our days are the same. Previously, we used to remember events in history, but now there is nothing of that sort," recounted a tribal sheikh from Fallujah (respondent B17). For many communities, the demise of IS control only served to complicate the task of rebuilding. While relations between local residents and the central government improved, many Sunnis continued to fear the PMF. One Tikriti declared, "[The PMF] are worse than Daʿesh's handling [of problems].... The two have become two sides of the same coin. The people who survived by a miracle, when al-Hashd [the Kataʿib al-Imam Ali Brigade] came, they fabricated accusations and cases for people, who were then arrested" (respondent B04). The lack of economic and educational opportunities proved an even greater obstacle than security provision. "My only hope is for a job.... Many problems will be solved if they tackle the problem of unemployment in society," the same interviewee continued (respondent B04). While economic redevelopment accelerated after IS's formal defeat in December 2017, barriers to social cohesion and post-conflict reconciliation persisted.

6
Ninewa Plains, Sinjar, and Tal Afar
Resilience in the Land of Two Rivers

[The arrival of Daʿesh] was a shock. How can an entire province fall in a night and a day? In two or three days? Where were the security forces? Their numbers were very large and crowded. It was thousands upon thousands! How did they all disappear in a day and night? It was really a shock.

—UNIVERSITY STUDENT, MOSUL

We fear the possible war between the Iraqi Army and the Peshmerga. We fear we might be caught in the middle.

—SHABAK MEDICAL PROFESSIONAL, HAMDANIYA

We didn't have any name, but we fought Daʿesh.

—YAZIDI MILITIA LEADER, MOUNT SINJAR

At the height of the Islamic State's power, the eighty-kilometer drive from Mosul to Erbil might have taken two hours or two days. After clearing insurgent checkpoints surrounding the perimeter of the city, those fleeing would encounter separate checkpoints patrolled by community self-defense groups, the Iraqi Army or Federal

Police, or the Popular Mobilization Forces. A series of Peshmerga-controlled checkpoints presented a final hurdle at the Upper Zab River partitioning Ninewa Governorate from the Kurdistan Region.

Whether armed groups patrolling the checkpoints were trustworthy had little to do with the insignias sewn to their (makeshift) uniforms. While a combatant's identity as an Arab, Kurd, or Christian might provide some clue as to how one would be treated at a checkpoint, a shared ethnic or sectarian identity was never a perfect guarantee of protection against exploitation or harassment. Personal experience could serve as a basic heuristic for survival, but it was also an imperfect guide by which to navigate shifting conflict dynamics. Those with *wasta*—a web of social connections, influence, and material resources—had better odds of sustaining access to basic needs while on the road.

Najah is an Assyrian Christian from Qaraqosh (also called Bakhdida or Hamdaniya), an Assyrian-majority village about thirty-five kilometers southeast of Mosul. Despite family roots tracing back to the Ottoman occupation of Iraq in the nineteenth century, Najah and his family decided to leave Qaraqosh when the IS offensive extended to the Ninewa Plains after the occupation of Mosul. The cultural center of Christianity in Iraq, dating back to the fourth century, was once again threatened by Islamist violence.

As Najah explained,

> On June 8[, 2014], in the evening, we left Bakhdida [Qaraqosh], where we left everything we had, and we went out with only our clothes. We took the road linking Mosul to Erbil and crossed the [Khazar] Bridge with difficulty as a result of tens of thousands . . . [waiting] to cross. . . . When we arrived, Erbil's border control was blocked. . . . We remained out in the open all night without food, water, or a [place to sleep]. . . . It was a very difficult day. We wished we would die and not see such a sight.[1]

Najah's story is representative of many of Iraq's ethnoreligious minorities, including the Assyrians, Bahais, Kaka'is, (Sabian) Mandaeans, Shabaks, Turkmen, and Yazidis. While most people fled their homes, those who remained had limited survival repertoires at their disposal. Some Assyrian and Yazidi militias aligned with the Kurdistan Democratic Party (KDP), while others merged with the Popular Mobilization Forces. Other self-defense groups—such as a splinter faction of the Sinjar Resistance Units

(Yekîneyên Berxwedana Şengalê, or YBS)—sought autonomy from coalition forces. Still others, including some Shabak and Turkmen, took advantage of the security vacuum to exploit their neighbors or settle private scores.

What best explains the wide variation in survival repertoires pursued by ethnoreligious minorities throughout Ninewa Governorate? This chapter examines how residents of three communities across Ninewa survived IS rule. Evidence of survival repertoires from Ninewa highlight several unique features of wartime survival. First, the Ninewa case blurs the distinction between migration and forced displacement. At each stage in the conflict, territorial contestation and combatant realignment created new uncertainty related to the pivotal decision of whether to stay or flee. The Ninewa case also illustrates how intercommunal competition between Iraqi and Syrian IDPs shapes public engagement with government forces. As one Sunni Arab refugee in Erbil recounted, "There are many conflicts between Syrian and Iraqi refugees in Erbil. They are based on differences in language, culture, and community [of origin]" (respondent A06).

Second, Ninewans' experience highlights the negative, unintended consequences of the choice to resist insurgents by supporting coalition forces. Coalition cooperation created new obstacles for post-conflict reconstruction and refugee resettlement, especially for Assyrian Christians on the Ninewa Plains. Rather than confronting "Arabization" (*al-ta'rib*) during the Anfal campaign of the mid-1980s, minorities faced a similar "Kurdification" campaign after IS's defeat. Conflict-related sexual abuse and exploitation was also a threat for minority girls and women within IDP camps in Ninewa and the KRI.[2]

Third, the plight of Ninewa's minorities demonstrates the ethical dilemmas inherent to the pursuit of autonomy during wartime. Examples of forced marriages between Mosul residents and IS fighters show how communities can avoid insurgent victimization by outsourcing the risk of harm to a select few. Opportunistic and limited cooperation with IS among Turkmen and Shabak also highlights how minorities can secure protection by sitting on the fence or switching sides when the local balance of power shifts.

The chapter examines wartime survival through a mixed-method approach.[3] Field interviews with Iraqi peace builders shed light on how communities in Ninewa, Sinjar, and Tal Afar navigated IS control. Quantitative data on migration trends from the International Organization for

Migration show how shifting IDP populations complicated the survival calculus of those who remained. Secondary sources provide supporting evidence for armed repertoires of cooperation and contention among Assyrian, Shabak, and Turkmen communities. The chapter concludes with a summary of key findings and implications for post-conflict refugee resettlement and reintegration.

The Islamic State occupation of northern Iraq (June 2014–December 2017)

Ninewa is Iraq's third-largest and second most-populated governorate. As the regional capital, Mosul was home to approximately 1.5 million residents prior to the rise of IS.[4] Nestled between the Turkish and Syrian borders, it includes nine administrative districts spread across three distinct regions (see figure 6.1).[5] The first region includes the districts of Tal Afar, Sinjar, and Al Ba'aj, which border Turkey and Syria, respectively. Tal Afar and Sinjar are the most mountainous districts and are home to Turkmen and Yazidi communities. Al Ba'aj is less populous and flatter; it is home to a plurality of Sunni Arabs. The second region encompasses the district of Mosul, Iraq's second-largest city and home to a Sunni Arab majority with smaller communities of Assyrians, Kurds, and Turkmen. The Ninewa Plains constitute a subset of three districts sandwiched between Mosul and the Kurdistan Region, including Hamdaniya, Shekhan, and Tal Kaif. Each district hosts the historic homeland of a variety of Assyrian communities, including Eastern-Rite Christians and secular political parties such as the Assyrian Democratic Movement.[6]

Ninewa is home to some of the most ethnolinguistically diverse communities in the Middle East. Throughout Ninewa a plurality of Sunni Arabs and Kurmanji Kurds live alongside a diverse array of "second-order" or "micro-minorities": Assyrians, Bahais, Kaka'is, (Sabian) Mandaeans, Shabaks, Turkmen, and Yazidis.[7] Second-order minorities are distinct from their Arab and Kurdish neighbors because of their ethnic identities or native languages (distinct from local dialects of Iraqi Arabic, such as Moslawi). Some second-order minorities practice Islam (Shabaks and Turkmen), while others observe Eastern denominations of Christianity (Assyrians), and still others practice synchronistic or indigenous faiths (Mandeaens,

FIGURE 6.1 Map of Ninewa Governorate and the Kurdistan Region.

Source: "Iraq: National Reference Map (as of 28 Sep 2021)," Office for the Coordination of Humanitarian Affairs, United Nations, September 28, 2021, https://reliefweb.int/map/iraq/iraq-national-reference-map-28-sep-2021.

Kaka'i, and Yazidis). As such, the ethnic, sectarian, and geographic fault lines of Ninewa have informed local politics and social relations since the Neo-Assyrian Empire of the ninth century BCE.

Ninewa's physical geography is also distinct. It is predominantly rural and agricultural, unlike the neighboring Arab-majority governorates of Anbar and Salah al-Din, or the Kurdistan Region (encompassing Dahuk, Erbil, and Sulaymania). Prior to the 2003 civil war, approximately half of all Ninewa residents lived outside of major cities.[8] After the collapse of the Ba'thist regime, ethno-sectarian conflict drove increasing urbanization. Young men from rural communities came in ever larger numbers to Mosul and Tal Afar in search of work, education, and medical care. Internal displacement only intensified with the arrival of IS insurgents in June 2014.

Given its demographic and geographic diversity, overlapping social cleavages also plague Ninewa's local politics. The first cleavage involves territorial disputes between the Iraqi government and the Kurdistan Regional Government (KRG) in contested subdistricts within Tal Afar, Tal Kaif, Shekhan, Akre, and Hamdaniya. Forced displacement and ethnic cleansing have featured prominently in these disputes dating back to the Ba'thist period, including the Kurdish uprisings of the 1960s, the Anfal campaign carried out under Saddam Hussein, and the 1991 Kurdish uprisings.[9]

The second cleavage involve regional politics. Given Iraq's porous borders with Syria and Turkey, many Kurdish and minority communities maintain robust social networks with their coethnics in neighboring states. Coordination among Kurdish groups is a particular concern for political elites in Damascus and Ankara, as both states view Kurdish separatism as an internal security threat. For Ankara, in particular, the prospect of a safe haven for the Kurdistan Workers' Party (Partiya Karkerên Kurdistanê, or PKK) in western Ninewa is unacceptable.[10] Concerns about ethnic separatism have resulted in sporadic, unilateral military interventions into Ninewa, including Turkish ground offensives in February 2008 and October 2016, and air strikes in April 2017. Damascus has been similarly concerned with cooperation between Syrian Kurdish separatists—such as the Democratic Union Party and its military wing, the People's Defense Forces—and the YBS.[11]

A final cleavage divides local politics, including through internal disputes between the KRG and Arab and minority communities throughout Ninewa. At the center of such disputes are concerns voiced by local communities that the KRG is using the Peshmerga to free communities threatened by Islamists only to stay after liberation to lay claim to territory, resources, and political institutions. Victims claim that the KRG is attempting to "Kurdify" minority communities much like Baʿthist efforts toward "Arabization" during the Anfal campaign. Minority concerns over alleged Kurdification have only increased since 2003, with the mass displacement of minorities and the increasing presence of Peshmerga control beyond the KRI.

The collapse of the Baʿthist regime in 2003 fundamentally changed the balance of power among ethnic and sectarian groups in northern Iraq. The marginalization of Sunnis associated with the Baʿth Party generated concern within many Sunni communities in Ninewa—including Arab and Turkmen Sunnis—some of whom resorted to violence as a form of resistance. Districts like Tal Afar became critical nodes for Sunni resistance and Ninewa became a regional base for the Sunni insurgency. The violence committed over the course of this insurgency impacted relations between Shiʿa and Sunnis and intercommunal relations with other minority groups.[12] Only after the 2007–2008 troop surge progressed into Ninewa did Sunni Islamists lose their political influence.[13]

While the IS occupation of Mosul received global media attention in June 2014, the group's advance into northern Iraq began the nine months prior. In September 2013, IS insurgents initiated a wave of suicide attacks in the Kurdish regional capital of Erbil, killing six Peshmerga soldiers and wounding dozens of civilians. In the following two months, over nine hundred Iraqis fell victim to IS violence (see figure 6.2).

In the winter of 2014—as Prime Minister Maliki fought for a third term in the April parliamentary elections—IS continued to expand throughout Ninewa. It was the offensive on the northern city of Mosul in June 2014, however, that marked its emergence as an existential threat. On June 4, 2014, approximately fifteen hundred IS insurgents attacked and subsequently occupied Mosul. One month later, on July 4, 2014, IS leader Abu Bakr al-Baghdadi declared himself caliph of an Islamist empire stretching from Aleppo, Syria, to Diyala, Iraq. By summer's end, the IS offensive extended south into Salah al-Din and Diyala Governorates, bringing the group to within an hour's drive of Baghdad.

The Islamic State launched an offensive on Kurdish and minority communities in Sinjar and Zumar on August 2, 2014. The forced displacement

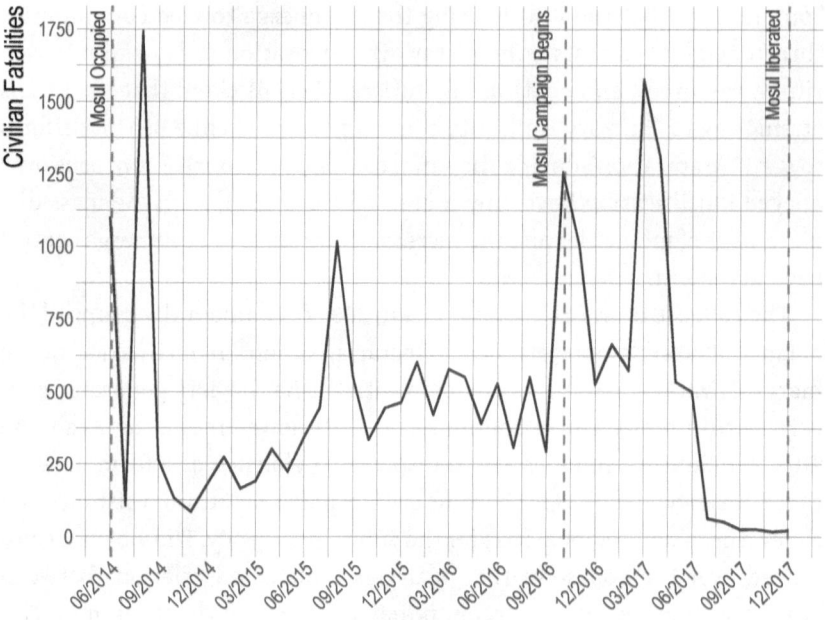

FIGURE 6.2 Civilian fatalities in Ninewa Governorate (2014–2018).

Source: Iraq Body Count, https://www.iraqbodycount.org.

and ethnic cleansing of Yazidi communities on Mount Sinjar, in particular, provided the clearest evidence of IS's intent to bring about the mass extermination of ethnoreligious minorities.[14] Later that month, IS insurgents seized the Mosul Dam, infrastructure responsible for supplying more than 1.5 million Iraqis with electricity.[15]

In response to the atrocities in Sinjar, the United States began a campaign of air strikes against IS-held armor and artillery in an effort to halt the offensive throughout Ninewa.[16] On the ground, the anti-IS coalition grew to incorporate the PMF, who were united in their efforts to defeat IS, but who also competed for popular support and political influence with the Iraqi government. Similar to the Sunni Triangle, there also existed dozens of community militias and local self-defense groups that loosely collaborated with coalition forces. Given the limited capabilities of these local groups, there was little cross-community coordination. Antagonism between the Peshmerga and Turkish security forces was also a unique feature of coalition politics in Ninewa Governorate. Despite being aligned against IS, Turkey and the KRG were reticent to fully coordinate with non-state armed groups, given Ankara's concerns regarding ethnic separatism.

The anti-IS coalition began to turn the tide on IS in Ninewa in October 2016. By the end of the year, coalition forces progressed into Ninewa Governorate, liberating minority communities on the southern periphery of Mosul, such as the Assyrian Christian community of Qaraqosh. The most significant anti-IS operation in Ninewa was the battle for Mosul, a nine-month effort to liberate the city from IS control. Starting in November 2016, the Iraqi Army advanced to the eastern suburbs of the city. By year's end, coalition forces had liberated approximately twenty neighborhoods (or roughly one-third of the city) in these eastern districts.

By the end of January 2017, coalition forces had consolidated control of eastern Mosul after a hundred days of pitched urban warfare assisted by Western airpower. In the process, Iraqi units—especially the Golden Division of the Iraqi Counter Terrorism Service (CTS)—suffered heavy casualties, including more than 40 percent of its personnel and combat equipment.[17] Between February and July, Iraqi CTS and Federal Police led ground operations supported by coalition artillery and airpower. Over the summer, IS insurgents held up in the Grand Mosque of al-Nouri, using residents as human shields against coalition artillery and air strikes.[18]

Iraqi troops captured the remains of the mosque on June 29 after an eight-month campaign in western Mosul. By July 21, 2017, coalition forces liberated the remaining western neighborhoods, including the Old City. By the end of combat operations, an estimated nine to eleven thousand civilians had died, a third of which were attributed to coalition air and artillery strikes.[19] By summer's end, coalition forces captured Tal Afar, Ninewa's remaining urban center under IS control.

Displacement, resettlement, and repatriation

Forced displacement has been an ever-present reality for Ninewa's ethnoreligious minorities. In the post-Baʿthist period, however, Ninewa hosted increasing numbers of displaced minorities from external communities in Baghdad, Anbar, Salah al-Din, and Diyala. Many Assyrians, for instance, departed their homes in Baghdad in order to resettle in Christian-majority communities on the Ninewa Plains.[20] An estimated 750,000 Iraqis were registered as IDPs in the period between the U.S. departure in December 2011 and IS's June 2014 offensive.[21]

The arrival of IS only exacerbated the forced displacement that plagued vulnerable Iraqis during the prior civil war. Throughout the country, an estimated 3.5 to 5 million Iraqis fled their homes over the course of the IS insurgency.[22] According to the United States Institute of Peace, "Between June 2014 and March 2015, over one million individuals [were] displaced from Ninewa Governorate, the majority of which were ethnoreligious minorities: 500,000 Yazidis, predominantly from Sinjar, 190,000 Turkmen Shiʿa from Tal Afar, 60,000 Shabak Shiʿa from Ninewa Plains, and 60,000 Christians from Ninewa Plains."[23] These figures include the ethnic cleansing of Yazidis from Mount Sinjar beginning on August 2, 2014. An estimated 200,000 individuals were displaced, amounting to approximately half of northern Iraq's Yazidi population. Insurgents killed an additional 4,200 Yazidis and abducted nearly 10,000 between August 3 and 8.[24] Sinjar also had the lowest rate of return of all of Iraq's districts, with approximately 16 to 18 percent of residents returning to their home communities.[25]

As figure 6.3 illustrates, the majority of IDPs resettled within the Kurdistan Region. By 2016, approximately 1.3 million Ninewa residents had relocated to Kurdish districts, concentrating in IDP camps in Erbil, Dahuk, Sumel, and Zakho.[26] As was the case during the 2003 civil war, a small subset of minority residents resettled in diasporic communities in Australia, North America, and western Europe.[27] Even for those fleeing to a bordering country, however, cost could be a significant barrier to exit. This included not only the fee an individual would pay for a driver or smuggler, but also the necessary cash on hand for bribing coalition forces stationed at security checkpoints and border crossings. As one Sunni from Mosul explained, "I had a friend who left. The night before we were together and he told me that he's going to leave for Turkey the next day. I asked him how. He said it costs US$6,000. I told him that I didn't have such an amount of money" (respondent B15).[28]

Figure 6.4 visualizes a network of IDP inflows and outflows from communities throughout Ninewa, Erbil, Dahuk, and Salah al-Din between 2014 and 2018. A spatial distribution of IDP flows reveals that refugee resettlement occurred in conflict-affected communities like Hamdaniya, as well as urban centers in Kurdistan (e.g., Dahuk, Erbil, Sumel, and Zakho), which were relatively insulated from insurgent violence. The network map also

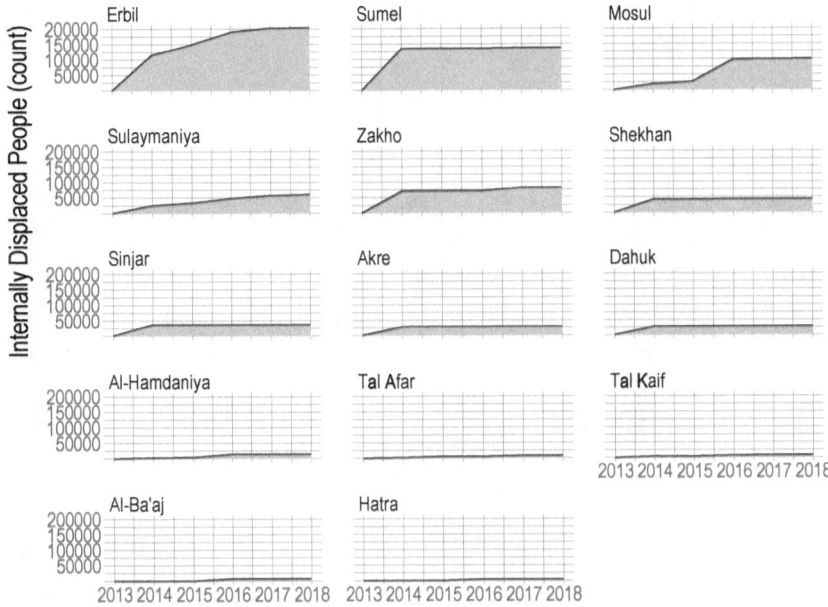

FIGURE 6.3 IDP arrivals by district over time across Ninewa Governorate and the Kurdistan Region (2013–2018).

Source: Displacement Tracking Matrix, International Organization for Migration, https://dtm.iom.int/iraq.

reveals that many Iraqis who were affected by the IS advance on Mosul were initially displaced to surrounding communities on the Ninewa Plains. Subsequent displacement is common for the most vulnerable members of conflict-affected communities, who must often flee several times before finding a safe location for resettlement.[29]

In the historically Christian town of Qaraqosh, for example, nearly 170,000 individuals from 28,000 households were displaced between June 2014 and October 2016, including over 95 percent of the population of 50,000 Assyrian Christians.[30] These figures represent over half the pre-IS population of the Ninewa Plains (estimated at approximately 226,500 residents in 2013).[31] Of those displaced, 20 percent resettled in IDP camps within the Kurdistan Region (especially in Dahuk and Erbil), whereas 80 percent resettled in private settings outside of camps. A total of one in three IDPs from the Ninewa Plains resettled in or near Erbil.[32] As Henriette Johansen

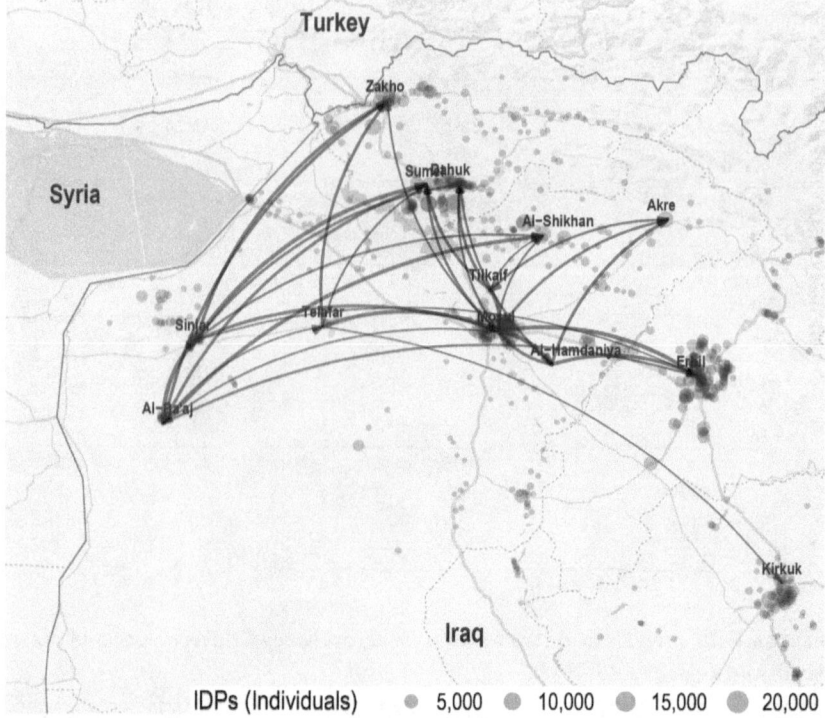

FIGURE 6.4 Network of IDP flows across Ninewa Governorate (2014–2018).

Source: Displacement Tracking Matrix, International Organization for Migration, https://dtm.iom.int/iraq.

and coauthors note, "In practical terms, displacement from the [Ninewa Plains] was absolute and remained so until the district was liberated by joint operations between the Kurdish forces and the Iraqi security forces (ISF) in late October 2016."[33] As of August 2021, approximately 170,000 individuals had returned to their homes, nearly 88 percent of the pre-IS population of the Ninewa Plains.[34]

Given the speed of the IS offensive, displaced families confronted many obstacles as they evacuated their communities, including traffic congestion, checkpoints, and a lack of reliable access to food, water, and shelter. Heuristics based on a combatant's ethnic or sectarian identity, as well as whether an individual had past encounters with armed groups, proved vital.

As one Moslawi university student conveyed,

> When [Daʿesh] took control over the city, they ruled it and no one was able to get out of the city of Mosul at that time except through smuggling, and the smuggling at that time was dangerous and risky to live based on luck. You have to be IS . . . [or] they will execute you. Therefore, I tried in every way, as I was a sixth-grade student at the time and wanted to complete my exams, so I went to IS to get a permit to go out and complete the exams, but they did not agree. (respondent B07)

A similar trend occurred within the Turkmen community in Ninewa. A week after the successful advance on Mosul, IS captured Tal Afar on June 16, 2014. Prior to IS's arrival, Tal Afar District had a population of approximately 300,000 residents (two-thirds of which resided in Tal Afar City). The district was 90 percent Turkmen, with roughly 75 percent identifying as Sunni and 25 percent Shiʿa. The non-Turkmen community included a mix of Sunni Arabs, Kurds, Yazidis, and Shabak. The majority of Shiʿa Turkmen in Tal Afar City fled to neighboring Sinjar by mid-June 2014, which fell to IS insurgents less than two months later. In the words of one Shiʿa Turkmen tribal leader, "When IS came, people immediately fled to Sinjar and that's where they stayed for a couple of months. In the unfinished buildings, houses, and other places. . . . The people there, especially the Eyzidis [an alternate spelling of "Yazidi"], they were very supportive and responded honourably to the influx of displaced people by welcoming and sheltering them."[35]

Over the course of the IS occupation of Ninewa—June 16, 2014, to September 2, 2017—over 420,000 residents were displaced, including the majority of Shiʿa Turkmen, Sunni Arabs, and Sunni Kurds. One in three homes were destroyed. As of summer 2022, the district still lacked functioning sewage networks, pumping stations, and wastewater treatment plants.[36] A second, smaller wave of displacement occurred during the liberation campaign in August 2017. During this period, an additional 20,000 residents fled Tal Afar City in anticipation of clashes between IS and coalition forces. As of September 2021, approximately 82 percent of IDPs have returned to Tal Afar District, encompassing nearly 358,000 displaced residents.[37]

While IS was defeated in December 2017, it took several years for IDPs to resettle in their home communities. Figure 6.5 displays the rate of return

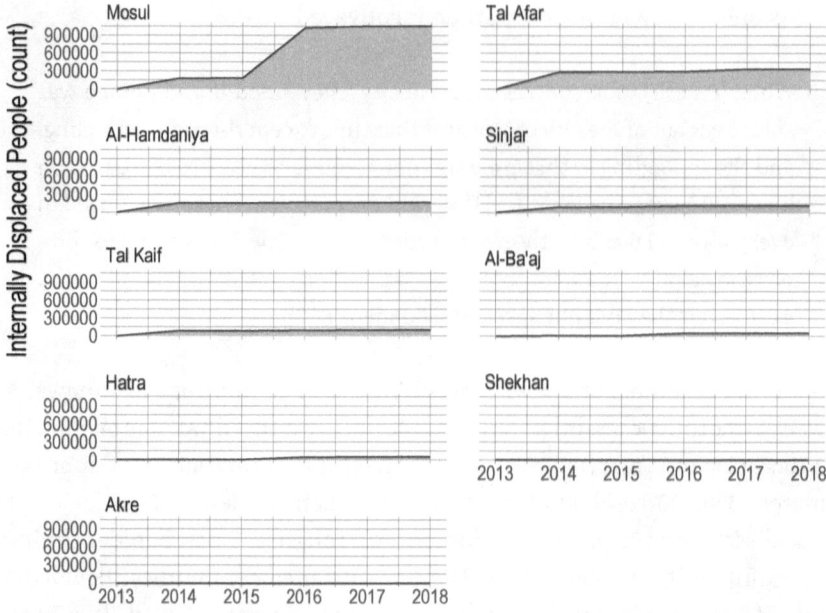

FIGURE 6.5 Returnees by district over time across Ninewa Governorate (2014–2018).

Source: Displacement Tracking Matrix, International Organization for Migration, https://dtm.iom.int/iraq.

for IDPs across Ninewa's nine districts. By summer 2019, nearly two-thirds of displaced Ninewa residents—approximately 1.6 million individuals—returned to their homes throughout the governorate. As figure 6.5 illustrates, the vast majority returned to the city of Mosul. In contrast, the Ninewa Plains, Sinjar, and Tal Afar welcomed relatively few returning families. Even four years after IS's defeat, approximately 250,000 Iraqis were still displaced throughout Ninewa Governorate.[38]

Contention

Contention served as a primary repertoire among local ethnoreligious minorities who survived IS's consolidation of control in northern Iraq. The presence of an existential threat, and the absence of viable alternatives for protection, dictated the choice of either flight or resistance. Suffering insurgent victimization during the 2003 civil war, and unable to accommodate IS's rules for non-Sunni subjects, those who remained after the Iraqi Army's retreat in June 2014 tended most often to adopt forms of everyday resistance.

However, this form of contention looked different for men and women in Ninewa. While men relied on a combination of civil and armed resistance repertoires, women relied primary on civil action. As one Moslawi explained, "I do not think that there was resistance inside Mosul. This is a difficult matter. At the time, as we say, one hand cannot clap [*yad wahidah ma tasqafish*]. That was hard. IS was a powerful organization because of the violence and crimes they committed against the people of Mosul; people had a very strong reaction toward them" (respondent B07). Mara Revkin also notes the limited availability of contentious repertoires in IS-occupied Syria: "Peaceful resistance was much less common given IS's harsh treatment of dissidents, but there were at least two such instances including one in which a group of women gathered outside of the IS court in al-Mayadin to demand the release of their imprisoned sons."[39]

As the campaign to liberate Ninewa began, covert informing to coalition forces became more common. As one interviewee in Mosul put it, "It was not resistance in the true sense of the word, but they told the army about the locations where IS fighters are located and the homes they live in" (respondent B12). "They were observing IS, knowing their movements, and setting up an ambush . . . then there was the opportunity to kill an IS element," explained another Moslawi (respondent B07). Yet another described using his smartphone to text the coordinates of insurgent locations to the Iraqi Air Force. "For instance, if they find a base, they define its location; they give its GPS to the air force and the aircrafts bomb them," he recounted (respondent B14). Other forms of everyday resistance included the use of graffiti to mark IS houses (respondent B03), as well as the secret distribution of CDs with audio and video content opposing IS rule. "CDs with recordings of the resistance of the *Sarayas* [Muqtada al-Sadr's Peace Companies] were going around at that time," explained another resident (respondent B18). In short, given the opportunity, many Iraqi men took risks to resist IS by assisting coalition forces. Accounts of covert informing are less common among Iraqi women in Ninewa, but evidence from the field is still incomplete.

As coalition forces liberated Mosul's rural periphery, armed resistance also began to emerge. The most coordinated and capable forms of armed resistance originated in communities with strong local parties whose elites enjoyed ties to power brokers in Baghdad or Erbil. Given the prewar cleavages present within most minority communities, two distinct logics dictated patterns of coalition support. First, minorities integrated their self-defense groups into coalition units with a shared ethnic or sectarian identity. In-group bias provided a reliable heuristic for determining which coalition units were perceived to be most trustworthy or reliable. For example, Shiʿa militias within the Shabak and Turkmen communities—including volunteer units aligned with Hunain al-Qaddo's Shabak Democratic Gathering (e.g., the Ninewa Plains Forces) and Yilmaz an-Najjar's Turkmen militias—aligned with the PMF, including units with close ties to the Badr Organization.[40] As the campaign progressed, Turkmen and Shabak militias were formally integrated into the PMF as distinct brigades. Similarly, Yazidi units who identified as Kurdish—including volunteers loyal to the Qasim and Haydar Shesho's Êzîdihan Protection Units—integrated into KDP-affiliated Peshmerga units. In-group attachments between local parties and political elites made collaboration with the anti-IS coalition more likely. As one tribal militiaman from outside of Mosul noted, "I work for al-Hashd [the PMF], so families may call us for food or to buy them groceries, not necessarily having a problem . . . even if it's humanitarian aid" (respondent B15).

Other minorities formed neighborhood self-defense groups with the hopes of later coordinating with coalition forces. Repertoires of armed resistance were most common among young men, especially those with patronage connections to prominent elites or influential local families. One Moslawi—a taxi driver who also moonlighted for a local PMF unit—recounted, "My father's cousin and my uncle created the Ahrar al-Mosul [the Mosul Freemen]. They killed thirty of Daʿesh, but then they were caught and killed; my father's cousin in Al Khafsa and my uncle in Bab Al Tob. [They resisted] with guns. At the time of Daʿesh, people could buy guns for forty or fifty thousand dinars [thirty-five U.S. dollars]. Don't think that it was a real state where there aren't any uncontrolled weapons; on the contrary, there was a lot of corruption" (respondent B15). Another man recounted a family member who volunteered for the same self-defense group: "My uncle, who was executed by them, used to sneak in and take them by surprise at night time and kill four or five of them and sneak back. Those were Al Ahrar [the Mosul Freemen], by the way; the media was unfair regarding them. Because at that time they didn't have mobile phones with them, they were afraid to take videos with their mobiles" (respondent B14).

Table 6.1 provides an overview of the alignment between minority self-defense groups and the anti-IS coalition.

Other minorities opportunistically resisted IS once coalition forces arrived in their communities. Aligned short-term interests—primarily the expulsion of IS insurgents from Ninewa—were crucial. Prominent examples within the Assyrian Christian community on the Ninewa Plains include collaboration between Riyan al-Kildani's Babylon Brigade and Badr Organization units of the PMF. The Ninewa Plains Protection Units—affiliated with General Behnam Aboosh and the Assyrian Democratic Movement—also aligned with the PMF. Smaller and less capable Assyrian militias coordinated with KDP-affiliated Peshmerga, and on rare occasion, formally integrated into KRG security institutions. In some cases, minorities joined Peshmerga, Zeravani (military police), or Asayish (military intelligence) units, while others acquiesced to Peshmerga control. Prominent examples include the Ninewa Plains Force headed by Romeo Hakari (of the Beth Nahrain Party), the Assyrian Patriotic Party commanded by Lieutenant Colonel Odisho, Dwekh Nawsha (The Sacrificers), and Ninewa Plains Guard Force—known as the Church Guards—under Sarkis Aghajan Mamendo (of the Chaldean Syriac Assyrian Popular Council) and operating out of Erbil.[41]

After the successful liberation of Ninewa in 2017, many minorities shifted toward neutral repertoires. Exploitation by coalition forces who remained in liberated communities, including PMF and Peshmerga units, incentivized a shift in survival repertoires.[42] On the Ninewa Plains, Assyrian Christians were particularly worried about the impending "Kurdification" of their communities by KDP-aligned Peshmerga.[43] For example, a Shabak detachment of the PMF—the 30th Brigade under the command of Waad Qado—was accused of extortion, illegal arrests, and kidnapping Assyrians in Bartalla.[44] Residents of Sinjar, including several of the peace builders I interviewed, also expressed concern about the effects of indiscriminate violence between competing units within the coalition. One Yazidi peace builder from Sinjar noted that hate speech and intimidation between PMF and PKK units was a major obstacle preventing the return

TABLE 6.1 Collaboration between Ninewa self-defense groups and the anti-IS coalition

Unit	Social identity	District	Alignment	Party & elites
Dwek Nawsha*	Assyrian Christian	Hamdaniya	KRG (KDP)	Lieutenant Colonel Yousef Odisho (Assyrian Patriotic Party)
Ninewa Plains Protection Units	Assyrian Christian	Hamdaniya	Iraqi Army; PMF	General Behnam Aboosh (Assyrian Democratic Movement)
Ninewa Plains Forces	Assyrian Christian	Hamdaniya	KRG (KDP)	Romeo Hakari (Beth Nahrain Democratic Party); Safaa Khamro (military commander)
Ninewa Plains Guard Forces	Assyrian Christian	Hamdaniya	KRG (KDP)	Sarkis Aghajan Mamendo (Chaldean Syriac Assyrian Popular Council)
Sinjar Resistance Units	Yazidi	Sinjar	PMF (80th Brigade)	Êzîdi Freedom and Democracy Party
Sinjar Resistance Units (Splinter faction)	Yazidi	Sinjar	PKK/HPG	Khiary Khedar (d. October 22, 2014)
Babylon Brigades	Assyrian Christian	Hamdaniya	PMF (50th Brigade)	Riyan al-Kildani
Lalish Battalion	Yazidi	Sinjar	PMF (36th Brigade)	Ali Khali
Turkmen Brigades	Turkman	Tal Afar	PMF (16th and 52nd Brigades)	Said Yilmaz an-Najjar
Ninewa Plains Forces	Shabak	Hamdaniya	PMF (30th Brigade)	Hunain and Waad Qaddo (Shabak Democratic Gathering)
Êzîdihan Protection Units	Yazidi	Sinjar	KRG (KDP)	Qasim and Haydar Shesho

*Dwek Nawsha (The Sacrificers) was formally disbanded prior to the liberation campaign of the Ninewa Plains in 2016.

and resettlement of community members (respondent A01). "The KDP Peshmerga are the ones who abandoned us to genocide and made this catastrophe possible. They promise us freedom, but their promises are empty. They have established Yazidi units not because they care about Yazidis, but for their own benefit and because they want to use us to control Sinjar for their own ends," explained another Sinjari.[45] Despite the defeat of IS, many communities confronted the dilemma of how to acclimate to coalition control.

Neutrality

Unlike Shiʿa or Kurdish communities, Ninewa's ethnoreligious minorities lacked the protection of powerful patrons in Baghdad or Erbil. Moreover, hiding, laying low, or strategic commuting were more difficult given the limited size and rural locations of most communities in the Ninewa Plains, Tal Afar, and Sinjar. Given the severity of the IS threat and the absence of coalition forces, most minorities pursued flight over neutrality. This was especially true for minority women, who faced the threat of sexual and gender-based violence from local insurgents. Those women who stayed were often referred to by IS as ʿawrah, a term denoting the parts of a woman's body that must remain covered according to orthodox Sunni practice. The implicit meaning, however, was that "those who are shameful should remain hidden."

Among those who stayed, repertoires of autonomy stemmed from necessity rather than choice. For those lacking the motivation or opportunity to exit, the combination of proximate threats and a lack of viable alternatives incentivized minorities to pursue autonomy. As a peace builder in Hamdaniya explained, the IS presence necessitated that "local teachers, social workers, and community organizers and others work as peace builders, even though they lacked formal training and experience" (respondent A03). Another Moslawi remarked, "It was Allah who saved us. . . . We were almost dead by the liberation. It was the will of the Almighty [al-Aziz] that we are still alive: missiles, killing, etc. IS killed and forcibly moved people out, slaughtered them" (respondent B15).

Given the severity of IS's ethnic cleansing, the mobilization of autonomous self-defense groups was also common. The Ninewa Plains and Sinjar, in particular, saw a proliferation of local self-defense groups. During the August 2014 IS offensive on Yazidi communities in Sinjar, Wana, and Zumar, for example, local communities mobilized self-defense groups loosely aligned with the PKK. The two most capable Yazidi self-defense groups included the Êzîdxan Protection Force (Hêza Parastina Êzîdxanê, or HPE)—mobilized by Qasim and Haydar Shesho—and the YBS. As one Yazidi militiaman in Sinjar explained, "We didn't have any name, but we fought Daʿesh."[46] During the counter-IS offensive in November 2017, the HPE was integrated into the Ministry of Peshmerga Affairs, and the majority of YBS fighters joined the "Lalish Battalion" (36th Brigade of the PMF). Only a splinter group of the YBS would remain entirely autonomous from either Baghdad or Erbil. In the latter case, autonomy was only viable through coordination with anti-IS rebel groups, such as PKK affiliates in Turkey and Syria.[47]

Beyond the battlefield, ethnoreligious minorities pursued autonomy through support from the diaspora. Transnational advocacy networks—composed of political activists, foreign lobbyists, media figures, nongovernmental organizations, and political allies in foreign governments in Australia, North America, and western Europe, among other places—provided financial and political support for many minority communities.[48] These networks mobilized support through public awareness campaigns, government petitions, media coverage, donations, and direct financial assistance to self-defense groups.[49] While most communities did not achieve complete autonomy from Baghdad or Erbil, diaspora support did provide limited bargaining power to resist IS and negotiate with the coalition. Transnational advocacy networks also provide international support for Iraqi men *and* women to collaborate on an equal footing in activism and awareness campaigns. Perhaps the most prominent example is the 2018 Nobel Peace Prize winner, Nadia Murad, a Yazidi activist from Kocho.[50]

Assyrians and Yazidis were particularly effective at leveraging their diasporic networks to draw attention to IS atrocities. For example, in late June 2017 the author was a participant observer at a conference in Brussels organized by representatives of the European Parliament. Titled "A Future for Christians in Iraq," the conference aimed to draw awareness to the plight of Iraqi Christians on the Ninewa Plains. The organizers called for the victimization of Assyrian Christians to be recognized as an act of genocide, as well as proposing political autonomy for the Ninewa Plains. However, while seven Iraqi political parties attended the conference, the two most influential political actors in Ninewa, the Assyrian Democratic Movement and the Chaldean Catholic Church, boycotted it.[51]

Worse yet, on the final day of the conference, KRG representatives stormed out of the room and refused to sign the position paper. What emerged was a political consensus among seven of the weakest minority parties around a position paper with little binding authority in Brussels, Baghdad, or Erbil. As such, the 2017 Brussels statement on "A Future for Christians in Iraq" demonstrates how diaspora activists can create undue risk for local partners by advocating for positions—such as political autonomy—that have little chance of succeeding on the ground.

In short, Ninewa's ethnoreligious minorities pursued autonomy out of necessity rather than by choice. Past experience and current circumstances informed how residents perceived the relative threats posed by IS and coalition forces. Some communities mobilized self-defense groups to guard against insurgent violence, while others actively collaborated with the coalition. Some communities, including Assyrian Christians on the Ninewa Plains, maintained autonomy through assistance from the diaspora. In the end, many communities simply substituted support from Baghdad or Erbil for foreign patronage.

Cooperation

Ethnoreligious minorities lacked motivation and opportunity to collaborate with IS given insurgents' strategy of displacing or subjugating non-Sunnis under their control.[52] By definition, IS's rigid criteria excluded Assyrians, Kurds, and Yazidis, as well as Shiʿa members of Shabak and Turkmen communities. Accordingly, only Sunni Arabs, Shabak, and Turkmen had the ability to accommodate IS rule without facing extermination.

Cooperation with IS emerged in communities where prewar social cleavages accelerated internal fragmentation within minority constituencies. Competition over access to basic needs further degraded social trust, community resilience, and social cohesion. The lack of a superseding social identity strong enough to mend second-order cleavages further exacerbated security concerns. As a result, subgroups with a shared ethnic identity—such as Turkmen or Shabak—pursued divergent survival repertoires. Heuristics based on shared identity and past experience were less informative than internal calculations about whether one could accommodate IS rule. Insurgents' reputation and coercive behavior served as more informative survival heuristics.

Given overlapping social cleavages, it is difficult to differentiate opportunistic cooperation from forced compliance based on behavior alone.[53] Who was collaborating to promote their own interests or to seek revenge, and who was forced, against their will, to victimize or exploit their neighbors? "Distinctions should be made between those who were forced to join IS, those who merely assisted IS and committed material crimes such as looting, and those who embraced IS's extremist ideology and committed violent crimes or mobilised others to do so," argue Dave van Zoonen and Khogir Wirya.[54] Similarly, a civil servant from Tal Afar observed, "The issue is about differentiating between who is IS and who is not. The Sunnis themselves know who are the collaborators but there are people who might have become part of IS under duress. Those people should be freed and given amnesty."[55] Sunni Arab and Turkmen women also reported confronting community suspicion that they were actively collaborating with IS. "Any way you can think they [single women] can be exploited, they are," explained one woman from Tal Afar.[56]

Interviewees had a range of perspectives on why their Sunni neighbors either passively acquiesced or actively supported IS. The most common explanation was transactional cooperation—an exchange of loyalty for food, jobs, money, or protection. "They were hopeful that Daʿesh will save them, provide security and jobs, and respect the citizens.... They wanted a savior and thought that Daʿesh will save them. They thought that Daʿesh will make the country settled and end bribes and bring a good government. They were fooled by them," explained one Mosul resident (respondent B18). Another Moslawi explained, "People were convinced that IS came to support the oppressed and restore people's rights. They will also stand with the people and support them. That is why people stood with them. After people discovered the intentions of IS, their violence and means of killing, and they knew the truth, some people retreated" (respondent B07). By appealing to a shared social identity and history of past grievances, Sunni residents could appeal to insurgents for protection even when they privately disagreed with IS's ideology, goals, or tactics.

Other residents benefited from IS's provision of social services. "[Daʿesh] had a *diwan* called 'Office of Charity' [Diwan al-Zakat wa al-Sadaqat], they used to look out for the poor families and give them some aid, and whenever they do so, every five days or so, they talk to the family members; they try to convince the son or the father, [and] hence they join.... They didn't assist them out of charity, but for attracting more to be recruited. Sometimes I used to think that they were willingly joining, and some other times I feel they were tempted to do so" (respondent B15). A resident from a neighboring area concurred: "If you're a poor woman with a starving family, and you have young, thoughtless sons, and I come to assist you once, twice, without saying anything, and then I come and give 50,000 dinars or 100,000 dinars to each of your sons—can you imagine how big this amount of money is for them?" (respondent B15). A tribal sheikh from outside of Mosul offered a similar rationale for IS recruitment: "Many people joined them for 100,000 dinars, 150,000 dinars [approximately US$105], and a sack of flour. They joined them just to support their families" (respondent B18).[57] In many instances, families who benefited from insurgent assistance would reciprocate by sending a brother, husband, or son to enlist in IS in a civil or combat role.

Other residents noted the temptation for young men to join or support IS based on a desire for a sense of community and/or personal purpose. Appealing to shared religious commitments provided another wellspring of support. One Moslawi woman explained the motivation to collaborate in the following way:

> People were not forced to be fighters with Daʿesh; instead, Daʿesh forced young men to always gather in mosques for prayers. They had a way to persuade people.... They convinced and used people in the name of religion, and since people of the community were conservatives, many of them were convinced that way.... [IS] would gather people and preach religion to them and give them instructions on how not to do wrong, to not go to hell. They called it "spreading awareness," and they used religion, the Prophet's sayings [hadith], and things like that. (respondent B03)

As another Moslawi observed, "Young men used to go willingly. And that was how they approached people; first as assistance and then to meet for 5,000 IQD, to be given to them at the mosque, to listen and get educated about the religion and the right path" (respondent B15). Yet another described the misperception that prompted some people to celebrate the arrival of IS insurgents: "They welcomed them, thinking that they were an organization of an Islamic state, and that they came to support the oppressed. When they discovered them, they were shocked!" (respondent B07). In short, residents described various motives for active cooperation, each addressing different basic needs, ranging from physical and social needs to existential ones. Given preexisting disparities in friendship and marriage networks between men and women, men benefited more from the social and relationship networks that came with IS membership than their female collaborators did.

Armed collaboration between minority groups and IS was exceedingly rare. However, existing accounts suggest two cases of voluntary collaboration in Ninewa Governorate. In both instances, collaboration emerged through political opportunism rather than any explicit commitment to Islamist ideology on the part of the minority partner. The first account consists of Sunni Shabak militias exploiting Assyrian Christian neighborhoods in Hamdaniya. Prior to IS's arrival, intercommunal tension drove a wedge between Shabaks and Assyrians. Many Assyrians in the Ninewa Plains worried that the influx of Shabak in the post-Saddam period would undermine the cultural and social identity of historically Christian neighborhoods in towns like Bartalla, Qarambles, and Qaraqosh.[58]

Social cleavages within Shabak communities over ethnic identity and political alignment also contributed to internal fragmentation. Shabak nationalists—such as Hunain al-Qaddo and the Shabak Democratic Gathering—contend that Shabaks are ethnically distinct from Arabs or Kurds. They tended to align with the central government, including supporting Nouri al-Maliki's State of Law Coalition, and advocated for the political autonomy of the Ninewa Plains. Other Shabaks align with the KDP. The pro-KDP contingent of Shabak saw alignment with the Barzani regime as the best path for improving local governance. Outside of local elites, however, many Shabaks felt caught in the middle of a political tug-of-war between Baghdad and Erbil. As two Shabak women explained, "We notice that our representatives in Baghdad and the KRG don't have the rights to express our needs and ideas. They have to express the ideology that their parties have. . . . They don't represent us; they represent their parties."[59]

Eyewitness accounts of the IS offensive through the Ninewa Plains suggest that Sunni Shabak militias used the chaos to settle scores, redress grievances, and extract private rents from their Assyrian neighbors. As Salma Mousa notes, "Stronger than their Christian counterparts, it is alleged that Shabak militia looted and damaged Qaraqosh" with the goal of deterring the return of Christian residents.[60] In the words of one resident of Qaraqosh, "They [the Shabak] lived with us for the past 100 years. And yet they went with IS and sold us cheaply; stealing our houses, animals and other properties."[61] In the author's interviews with peace builders from Qaraqosh, accusations of exploitation by Shabak residents were common, including complaints about property theft, looting, and squatting in neighbors' homes (respondent A07).

The second account of opportunistic collaboration occurred in Tal Afar. Much like Shabaks in Al Hamdaniya, Tal Afar's Turkmen community suffered from intercommunal strife dating back to the 2003 U.S.-led intervention. Sunni Turkmen (roughly 70–75 percent of the total community) mistrusted their Shiʿa neighbors due to their supposed political and financial ties to Iran. Likewise, Shiʿa Turkmen mistrusted their Sunni neighbors based on suspicions of Turkish influence. Shiʿa Turkmen also accused their Sunni neighbors of active collaboration with IS. According to one Shiʿa Turkmen civil servant, "The majority [of Sunnis] was supportive of the terrorist groups ideologically and in practice. In addition, around 90 percent of the Sunnis joined IS. . . . Only 10 percent of them left Tal Afar when IS invaded the city."[62] Similarly, in the post-IS period, Sunni Turkmen who returned to Tal Afar were equally worried about the prolonged presence of the PMF, including fears of economic exploitation, revenge killings, and other forms of violent reprisal.[63]

Despite foreign direct investment during the interwar period (2011–2013), IS's arrival in Tal Afar on June 16, 2014, further escalated internal tensions within Turkmen communities. During the IS offensive on Tal Afar, approximately half a million Turkmen residents—nearly 90 percent of the existing community—fled the district.[64] During the occupation, Tal Afar became a central node in IS's network of control within Ninewa. Specifically, the city of Tal Afar served as a temporary transit point for the exploitation and trafficking of Yazidi women and girls.[65] While systematic data is lacking, current evidence suggests that splinter groups within the fifty thousand Sunni Turkmen residents who remained collaborated with IS insurgents.[66] As Henriette Johansen and coauthors explain, "Although much is still unclear, it is widely believed that a number of Sunni Turkmen from Tal Afar joined IS and stand accused of having committed war crimes in their name."[67]

Shabak and Turkmen collaboration also highlights the limitations of relying on heuristics alone to explain wartime survival. In each case, internal social cleavages undermined the cohesion created by a superseding social identity. Past experience was of limited utility as well, since the internal divisions that divided minority communities only became salient after the de-escalation of the 2003 civil war. Consequently, assessments of insurgents' coercive behavior centered on whether cooperation would enhance one's chances of survival.

Significant barriers to return, resettlement, and reintegration remain for minority communities in the aftermath of IS's defeat. Nonetheless, local residents emphasized the necessity of reinvestments in peace building alongside economic development. An activist in Qaraqosh noted, "The return home was very hard, but the insistence on returning was the main motive for making us work in the most difficult circumstances. We had to clean the streets of unexploded shells, booby traps, and the remains of those who were killed by Daʿesh" (respondent A10). Ninewa residents also expressed hope that their communities could be transformed in the aftermath of nearly two decades of war. As one peace builder from Bashiqa said, "Peace building is a daily need, just like water or food" (respondent A02). Another, from Qaraqosh, observed, "People in the community want to make things better, but they don't know how" (respondent A07).

This chapter's findings suggest two key lessons for post-conflict reconstruction in northern Iraq. First, successful resettlement and reintegration relies on local actors and institutions committed to an extended process of transitional justice and political reconciliation.[68] Interviewees frequently stated that the primary barriers to resettlement included deficits of social trust, solidarity, and social cohesion. While long-standing efforts to reintegrate ex-combatant men do exist (e.g., disarmament, demobilization, and reintegration initiatives), equally important are programs directed at repairing the ostracism, stigmatization, and suspicion directed toward women who remained under IS occupation. Accordingly, return and resettlement is only sustainable with investment in a "triple nexus" of humanitarian assistance, economic development, and local peace building.[69] Each leg of the triad represents a necessary yet insufficient means of restoring peace in the aftermath of war.

What lessons do Iraqis' experience with Islamic State control hold for the issue of wartime survival more broadly? The next chapter concludes by summarizing the argument, highlighting key findings, and discussing future prospects for the growing research program on civilian survival during wartime.

7

"We Have on This Land That Which Makes Life Worth Living"

Be of the disciples of Aaron, loving peace and pursuing peace, loving your fellow creatures and bringing them close to the Torah.
—HILLEL THE ELDER, *PIRKEI AVOT* 1:12
("CHAPTERS OF THE FATHERS")

Blessed are the peacemakers, for they will be called sons of God.
—JESUS OF NAZARETH, GOSPEL OF MATTHEW 5:9

For indeed, with hardship [there will be] ease (*fa inna maʿal ʿusri yusran*).
—QURʾAN 94:5, *SURAH ASH-SHARH* ("THE RELIEF")

Mosul's Grand Mosque of al-Nuri, with its iconic leaning minaret known as "the Hunchback" (*al-Hadbaʾ*), bears witness to Iraqis' suffering under the Islamic State. Constructed by Seljuk Turks in the late twelfth century CE, it served as a focal point for Muslim devotion within various multiethnic empires spanning across the Middle East. For the next eight hundred years it withstood subsequent occupations by Safavids, Ottomans, British, and Americans. As the medieval geographer Ibn Jubayr (1145–1217) observed, "The city is a large and ancient one, fortified and imposing, and prepared against the strokes of adversity."¹

By the time IS arrived in June 2014, Moslawis were well acquainted with foreign occupation. On July 4, 2014—the first Friday of Ramadan—the Grand Mosque's pulpit (*minbar*) was the scene of a thirteen-minute sermon by IS's self-appointed caliph. "I was appointed as a leader for you, although I am not the best of you, nor am I better than you. . . . Obey me as long as I obey Allah in your regards," Abu Bakr al-Baghdadi proclaimed.² As a final act of defiance, insurgents attempted to destroy *al-Hadbaʾ* as IS was losing control of Mosul in summer 2017. "Blowing up the al-Hadbaʾ minaret and the al-Nuri Mosque amounts to an official acknowledgment of defeat [by Daʿesh]," reflected Prime Minister Haider al-Abadi.³ While reconstruction began in autumn 2018, it was not until 2022 that wealthy Gulf benefactors funded a UNESCO-led initiative to rebuild the mosque.

This book has explored how Iraqis from different parts of the country survived the rise and fall of the Islamic State. Motivated by a concern for the lived experience of ordinary Iraqis, it described the range of survival repertoires deployed by local residents to navigate violent situations in their communities. Why did survival repertoires vary across different communities at various points in the conflict? Iraqis confronting similar threats within the same communities responded by deploying different repertoires. Some fled their homes while others remained. Among those who stayed, most hid, others resisted, some remained neutral, and a select few collaborated. None were left unaffected by IS's brutal regime.

This chapter revisits key claims and highlights how the book's findings complement and challenge existing research on civilian survival. It then explores the challenges facing Iraqis who seek to return and reintegrate into their home communities before widening the aperture by exploring key implications for civilian survival beyond Iraq. The chapter finishes with a brief discussion of avenues for expanding the growing research program on civilian survival in wartime.

Revisiting key claims: How heuristics shape survival repertoires

This book analyzed how ordinary people survive wartime violence. In particular, it examined how individuals adopt survival repertoires—social practices, tools, organized routines, symbols, and rhetorical strategies—to navigate violent situations in their communities. Distinct from rational strategies, repertoires are creative, flexible, and often contradictory. They are based on intuitions informed by personal experience, as opposed to a set of rational rules dictating one's decisions. Most importantly, survival repertoires provide a means of coping with the inherent stress, uncertainty, and volatility of war.

Existing accounts of wartime survival either essentialize social identity or ignore it altogether by reducing survival to the result of political opportunism or cost-benefit calculations. Historical grievances, perceptions of relative deprivation, social norms, and cost-benefit calculations undoubtedly influence how people make life-and-death decisions. Nevertheless, this book sought to investigate the scope of conditions that shape the adoption of specific repertoires. In so doing, it eschewed a monocausal explanation of wartime survival.

Heuristics—or decision-making shortcuts—shape the adoption of repertoires by considering insurgents' social identities, reputations, and behavior in the community. In the face of impending violence, individuals subconsciously reflect on their past experiences with armed groups, especially if previous encounters resulted in exploitation or victimization. Experiences that left a vivid impression—either for good or for ill—are more readily available in people's memories, and thus more likely to influence how individuals appraise their current circumstances.

For those confronting wartime violence, the central question is whether one can acclimate to or accommodate insurgent rule without sacrificing access to basic needs or violating sacred values. The answer varies based on relative vulnerability, largely a function of age, gender, socioeconomic status, and worldview. Flight is the preferred means of survival for those unwilling or unable to accommodate insurgent governance. For men facing forced conscription or women risking sexual assault or rape, the danger of life on the road is preferable to bargaining with local insurgents. Facing higher barriers to flight, the most vulnerable are prone to passive acquiescence and everyday resistance. Those with a higher threshold for risk—especially military-age males—are more likely to pursue armed collaboration and resistance. The rarest forms of collaboration involve the "true believers," or those dedicated to the cause despite mortal risk and social ostracism.

Individuals update and refine their heuristics based on how insurgents govern. Most people will leave their communities when they are unable or unwilling to accommodate insurgent control, yet lack access to alternative sources of basic needs. An imminent and credible threat of violence against oneself or a family member is the strongest motivation to flee. Those who remain confront existential decisions about how they will navigate insurgent control. The initial decision to acclimate to insurgent control by laying low, hiding, or adjusting one's movement soon gives way to cooperation or contention. Those with a viable alternative for protection will pursue repertoires of contention, such as "everyday resistance," active opposition, and armed resistance. Those who are unable or unwilling to accommodate insurgent rule—but lack viable alternatives for protection— are more likely to passively acquiesce to insurgents' rules and demands. Others seek to avoid future exploitation by engaging in transactional cooperation. More often than not, a more vulnerable third party will pay higher costs, as was the case with the sexual exploitation of Yazidi girls and women throughout Ninewa Governorate. Tragically, the threats to life and limb are rarely evenly distributed.

Chapter 3 surveyed the rise and fall of IS in Iraq over three acts. Act 1 begins with the United States' de-escalation starting in 2009. It focused, in particular, on the political and security effects of the departure of U.S. forces in December 2011. Rather than conclusively defeating insurgents, the United States' transition to a population-centric counterinsurgency (or "COIN") strategy temporarily suppressed a more fundamental conflict between insurgent groups, sectarian militias, and paramilitary organizations. Act 2 examined the "interwar" period between the 2011 Arab uprisings and beginning of IS's military offensive in June 2014. It focused on the nascent rise of the Islamic State, and Nouri al-Maliki's transformation into a sectarian autocrat. It also offered a comprehensive picture of how IS governed its newly captured territories through a regimen of coercion, co-option, and persuasion. Act 3 analyzed the anti-IS offensive, including the formation, operations, and internal politics of the anti-IS coalition. It also explored how ordinary Iraqis navigated the threat of violence as coalition forces and insurgents fought for control of their communities.

Chapter 4 examined how Iraqis in Baghdad navigated the threat of IS terrorism. Unlike communities elsewhere in the country, Baghdad residents never directly confronted IS control. As a result, they primarily relied on contention and neutrality to navigate wartime violence. Support for the central government was highest during the peak of the IS threat, and gradually dissipated as the anti-IS campaign progressed. In the process, many Baghdad residents adopted neutrality or autonomy as a way to express their discontent with the Abadi regime's inability (or unwillingness) to curb corruption, unemployment, and poor service provision. While few Iraqis directly collaborated with IS, pubic opposition to the central government—especially public protests—became increasingly common. Despite the military defeat of IS in December 2017, waves of Iraqis would return to the streets in October 2019 for a reprisal of the Arab uprising known as the Tishreen movement.[4]

Chapter 5 explored how Sunnis in Fallujah, Ramadi, and Tikrit navigated IS control. Unlike in Baghdad, persecution and political exclusion by the central government initially made the prospects of IS governance more appealing in these areas. Despite escalating insurgent violence throughout 2014, many residents perceived IS as less of a threat than the central government. Passive acquiescence, transactional cooperation, and even active collaboration provided repertoires for surviving insurgent control and government contestation. However, as IS consolidated control, the price of cooperation became more than most local residents could bear. Passive acquiescence and neutrality gave way to flight and contention. Those who remained and who were most threatened by IS rule pursued armed resistance, mobilizing local self-defense groups and community militias. As coalition forces dismantled insurgent control, the allure of autonomy increased due to the risk of exploitation by coalition forces.

Chapter 6 presented a case study of minority survival in Ninewa, Sinjar, and Tal Afar. Unlike in western Iraq, ethnoreligious minorities in these areas could not cooperate with IS due to their status as non-Arabs and non-Sunnis. While some Sunni Shabak and Turkmen communities opportunistically collaborated with IS, most Ninewa residents fled or pursued forms of everyday resistance. Later in the occupation, armed resistance arose as local self-defense groups coordinated with coalition forces. Some Assyrians and Yazidi militias aligned with the Kurdistan Democratic Party, while others opted to join the Popular Mobilization Forces. Still other groups—such as a splinter faction of the Sinjar Resistance Units—sought autonomy from the anti-IS coalition. As the campaign progressed, however, many minorities felt caught in the middle of a political struggle between

Baghdad and Erbil. Once the coalition dislodged IS control in Ninewa, however, the desire for political autonomy from Arabs and Kurds returned.

Expanding the research program on civilian survival in wartime

The theory and evidence offered in this book challenge existing work on wartime survival by showing that three key assumptions are actually empirical questions. First, past research assumes that information about territorial control and military capabilities are legible to ordinary people. In reality, the boundaries between territorial control and the scope of armed groups' coercive power are elusive. Past encounters with insurgents are not always indicative of territorial control as many armed groups are able to influence local populations without controlling territory. In Afghanistan, for example, the Taliban's mobile shariʿa courts allowed insurgents to monitor and enforce Islamic law without deploying fighters to every community it wanted to influence.[5] Similarly, this book has demonstrated how IS was able to control local residents through a combination of coercion, co-option, and persuasion. Controlling territory allowed for more effective governance, but this was not a necessary condition for enforcing the group's draconian system of laws, norms, and practices.

Second, previous studies have assumed that local residents assign blame for wartime violence based on proximity to violence and past interactions with armed groups. This assumption rests on the belief that individuals assign blame by seeking accurate information instead of relying on implicit bias or motivated reasoning. However, findings from Iraq show that many people have difficulty determining who is responsible for fomenting violence in their communities. Not only are insurgents' social identities obscure (e.g., Iraqi nationals versus foreign fighters), but fighters can moonlight for different groups, wage private vendettas, and pursue revenge. As a result, the correspondence between insurgents' social identities and their organizational affinities is often ambiguous, complicating how local residents detect and respond to threats.

Finally, this book's findings address whether the expected benefits of military intervention overcome foreign aversion rooted in nationalism. While the Shiʿa majority initially welcomed Iranian assistance to the PMF, as the IS threat dissipated, many Iraqis began to resent Tehran's meddling in Iraqi politics. During the 2019 Tishreen protests, for example, protestors in Karbala set fire to the Iranian consulate while shouting "Karbala is free, Iran out, out!"[6] Sunnis in western Iraq had a reputation for resisting the 2003 U.S.-led intervention, as well as the presence of the Iraqi Army and Federal Police. However, they later collaborated with foreign interveners and government forces once their relationships with local insurgents soured. In each case, in-group bias and security-seeking behavior tempered patterns of cooperation, contention, and neutrality.

Economic, political, and social challenges in postwar Iraq

Despite the military defeat of IS in mid-December 2017, several challenges remain for postwar Iraq. The top three material challenges relate to security provision, economic development, and post-conflict reconstruction. Specifically, the security landscape across Iraq remains fragmented and fragile. Despite its loss of territory, IS and allied insurgent groups are abandoning conventional violence and returning to insurgent tactics such as nighttime raids and suicide attacks. The Hamrin Mountains—separating the regional capital of Kirkuk from communities along the Tigris River—continue to provide a safe haven for the IS remnant.[7]

Parallel to the latent threat of insurgent violence, Iraq is also witnessing the fragmentation of the anti-IS coalition.[8] For example, Iran and Turkey continue to conduct illicit military operations inside Iraq, often targeting their ethnic, sectarian, or political opponents. Iranian-backed PMF units attacked U.S. military facilities at Camp Tajj in March 2020.[9] Similarly, in July 2022, an artillery strike attributed to Turkey and targeting Kurdish separatists killed eight Iraqis vacationing at a resort near Dahuk.[10]

The PMF's growing political power and operational autonomy is also a concern. As a Kurdish resident of Kirkuk explained, "In every country, there is a law and a system that holds the security authorities accountable when they do not perform their duties properly. But who is holding the security forces accountable here?"[11] Since March 2018, the PMF has been integrated in the Ministry of Interior, securing an annual budget of approximately $1.5 billion. Since that time, PMF leaders have captured the principal leadership positions within the Interior Ministry and have formed a political coalition (the Fatah Alliance), which has since won seats in the Council of Representatives.[12]

Despite the PMF's electoral success, the central government faces public pressure to disarm, demobilize, or reintegrate militias into the Ministry of Interior. In July 2019, Prime Minister Adil Abdul-Mahdi signed a new decree calling for the PMF to become "an inseparable part of the armed forces. All rules applied to the armed forces will be applied to them."[13] Abdul-Mahdi's decree symbolizes the pressure and competition the PMF face as they seek to survive as an independent armed force, while the failure to implement the decree shows the political power that the PMF have achieved. As a result, they continue to operate as an autonomous security force within Iraq.[14] Many Iraqis view the PMF as a way to bypass government red tape and solve problems. "A tribal leader—who was previously critical of the PMF for blackmailing his neighbors in Kirkuk—acknowledged that if he encountered any trouble, his first resort was to go to the local PMF detachment. He found them quicker to respond and more effective because they were from the local area, unlike the Federal Police, who included officers from all over the country."[15] Iraqis also spoke of PMF assistance in securing loans and building permits. Like all political institutions, "PMF networks employ communications strategies, including a host of television channels, newspapers, and social media groups," and these allow the PMF to advertise their activities and strengthen ties with local citizens.[16]

Economic instability presents a second key challenge in postwar Iraq.[17] At the national level, corruption, inflation, and unemployment continue to plague the economy, despite increasing foreign direct investment and rising oil prices. One in four Iraqis live at or below the poverty line, with the World Bank estimating that over two million citizens have returned to poverty since onset of the global COVID-19 pandemic in 2020.[18] Average life expectancy has dropped to 70 years in 2021, compared to 79 in neighboring Lebanon.[19] The unemployment rate has risen since IS's defeat, including a 15 percent national average. Youth unemployment is grimmer still: over one in four Iraqis between the ages of 16 and 25 with at least a high-school degree are unemployed.[20]

Inflation has averaged between 6 and 8 percent, weakening the dinar against regional currencies such as its Jordanian counterpart.[21] The

Consumer Price Index—a measure of the change in the prices paid by consumers for a weighted average of goods and services—increased by 34 percent, from 86 in 2009 to 116 in 2021.[22] Inflation has also affected the cost and supply of food staples such as wheat, rice, and cooking oil. For example, between 2020 and 2022 the price of a bag of wheat (fifteen kilograms) doubled to thirty-five U.S. dollars, while the price of a liter of cooking oil tripled to one dollar.[23]

Federal and local corruption also continue to destabilize the Iraqi economy. Transparency International's "Corruption Perceptions Index" scores Iraq at a 21 (or 157 out of 180 countries ranked), compared to 18 in 2011.[24] "Politically sanctioned corruption is facilitated in part through the 'special grades' (*al-darajat al-khasa*) scheme, in which ruling parties compete to appoint senior civil servants to oversee, among other things, the tendering of contracts. Operating under the protection of the political parties, these bureaucrats ensure that resources flow from ministries and state institutions to their patrons. They also serve as chokepoints, blocking contracts if they do not benefit the parties concerned," explain Toby Dodge and Renad Mansour.[25] An Iraqi journalist reporting in Basra explained a similar problem: "The government prioritizes giving resources to populations who they think will support them in elections."[26]

In the Arab Barometer's spring 2021 nationwide survey of Iraq, 88 percent of respondents recorded that "corruption pervades national and state agencies" to a medium or large extent, a statistic similar to that of neighboring fragile democracies such as Lebanon and Tunisia.[27] As one Kurdish focus group participant in Kirkuk concluded, "We are a people who sell principle for money (*nahnu shaʿb nabie al-mabdaʾ min ajl al-mal*)."[28] By October 2019, grievances regarding politically sanctioned corruption became so severe as to motivate a months-long series of public protests, demonstrations, sit-ins, and acts of civil disobedience.[29] The Tishreen protests resulted in the resignation of Prime Minister Abdul-Mahdi in November 2019 and the appointment of Mustafa Al-Kadhimi in May 2020.

At the local level, many communities in the seven governorates affected by IS violence continue to suffer from poor public service provision.[30] One pressing issue is the lack of funds and political resolve to rebuild damaged public infrastructure, including roads, utilities, schools, hospitals, and residential areas. The World Bank has estimated that Iraq's education and health sectors have suffered more than US$5 billion in damage since the

2003 civil war.[31] By the time the COVID-19 pandemic arrived in Iraq in spring 2020, two-thirds of those surveyed stated that the central government was doing a poor job responding to the crisis.[32]

Lagging public service provision is especially severe in Ninewa Governorate, where the IS occupation was most brutal and local communities lack access to foreign direct investment from wealthy Gulf states.[33] Even when international agencies and nongovernmental organizations are present and investing at the local level, a lack of coordination between nonprofit and community leaders produces inefficiency, time delays, and public frustration. According to a needs-based assessment of Hamdaniya, Sinjar, and Tal Afar conducted by the United States Institute of Peace, the primary barriers to reconstruction and resettlement include the destruction of the housing stock, a lack of livelihood opportunities and services, and deficient investment into reconciliation and trauma treatment.[34] As one Kurdish resident of Kirkuk reflected, "We only want services, security and safety. We want roads, bridges, a successful health sector and health services, but it is difficult to obtain them. We want universities and schools to improve and job opportunities to be available regardless of who governs."[35]

Even in major cities like Baghdad, insufficient electricity, water, sewage, and trash services plague residents' daily lives. Rolling brownouts and electricity shortages remain severe in urban areas such as Baghdad, Fallujah, Mosul, and Ramadi, especially during the summer months, when air conditioning usage peaks. In 2019, the International Energy Association reported a twelve-gigawatt gap between peak demand and electricity production.[36]

Equally important as a lack of public governance, formerly occupied communities also suffer from deficits in social trust and community cohesion. Those who remained in their homes during the IS occupation are often perceived by returnees and outsiders as likely collaborators. According to USIP, discrimination and harassment are especially severe for single female–headed households (SFHH)—especially among Sunni Arabs—some of whom entered into arranged marriages and bore children with IS fighters. Mere rumor or innuendo is often sufficient to block SFHHs from movement, job opportunities, or social commitments in their communities. As USIP explains, "Rumoring women of such affiliation is easy and has been used as an intimidation tool by tribal leaders in the Anbar region to push SFHHs and other women back to their AoO [area of origin]."[37] Gender affects not only the threats confronting wartime survivors, but also how survival repertoires change as violence de-escalates in the post-conflict period.

Returnees also confront fear, suspicion, and ostracism among their neighbors who remained. Social tensions arise as returnees seek to resecure ownership of their homes, agricultural land, and businesses that were appropriated under IS control. A November 2020 USIP survey of Ninewa found that 71 percent of respondents agreed that "no family with members with perceived ISIS affiliation should be allowed to return."[38] Returnees also face fears over demographic change and future political marginalization, driving further uncertainty and competition over access to basic needs. In the Ninewa Plains, for example, Assyrian Christians perceive the increasing rate of Shabak returnees as competition for accessing resources in the community.[39] A similar set of fears affects returnees to Sinjar, where historically Yazidi-majority communities are contested among Kurdish and PMF-aligned militias.

Insufficient investment in transitional justice and post-conflict reconciliation also stymies the restoration of social cohesion. As the mayor of one Ninewa community noted, "The problem is that the Iraqi government has no unified decision towards the issue of reconciliation and displacement. There is much interference in Iraq and belonging and loyalty are divided. Iraq lacks a common identity and sense of belonging. In Iraq everyone, every community works for their own interests."[40] Another Yazidi community leader from Sinjar concurred: "Without justice, there is no reconciliation with Sunni tribes."[41] Although most Iraqi citizens endorse a blend of governmental and tribal justice for IS fighters and collaborators, there is substantial disagreement regarding the legacy of human rights violations perpetrated by the coalition. IDPs, in particular, reported that human rights violations by state security forces undermine their ability to either safely remain in their camps or return home. Even for IDPs in relatively safe camps under Kurdish control, reports of harassment, unjust detention, and torture by Peshmerga and Asayish units are prevalent.[42] The approximately 1.3 million victims of sexual and gender-based violence continue to face disproportionate challenges in achieving justice.[43]

Human rights violations by the PMF also pose a political challenge to provincial and local authorities. As Fanar Haddad notes, "When it comes to the question of human rights violations and the *Hashd* [i.e., PMF], there is little room for debate: the *Hashd* have undoubtedly and repeatedly committed gross human rights violations."[44] During the spring 2016 counteroffensive in western Iraq, for example, PMF units were accused of looting and destroying civilian buildings in Tikrit, as well as practicing mass detention, forced displacement, and ethnic cleansing of Sunni men from Fallujah and Saqlawiya.[45] PMF units in Tal Afar have been accused of stoking sectarian tensions between Sunni and Shiʿa Turkmen after the liberation of the district from IS in October 2017.[46] According to the Iraqi Commission for Human Rights, during the 2019–2020 Tishreen protests, PMF units were responsible for the deaths of over five hundred Iraqis, with an additional twenty-three thousand injuries reported as a result of the state's repression against protestors.[47] Despite extensive documentation of human rights abuses, political leaders lack the resolve or ability to hold PMF units accountable for atrocities committed on the battlefield.

Implications for civilian protection

What implications do findings from Iraq have for broader policies related to civilian protection in other conflict zones? With respect to international humanitarian law, legal scholars, policy makers, and practitioners should refine how they define "civilians" and "noncombatants." International humanitarian law currently defines "civilians" as those who are not members of a state or non-state armed group, or who do not actively participate in hostilities.[48] The joint criteria of group membership and behavior are central to this definition. In practice, however, civilian status is often assigned based on ascriptive characteristics—such as age or gender—with the default assumption being that such actors are peaceful, innocent, and unarmed.[49] Similarly, male civilians are often viewed as "imperfect victims," given prevailing norms surrounding the feminization of victimhood and the legitimacy of targeting military-age males.[50]

As Iraq's experience with the IS illustrates, membership and behavior criteria are often fluid. Individuals transition between armed and unarmed status, as well as group membership, based on conflict dynamics in their communities. The choice to take up arms or actively participate in hostilities can emerge in response to insurgent coercion, as well as co-option, and persuasion. Is the teenager in Ramadi who buys arms in order to defend his relatives no longer a civilian?[51] What about IDPs who arm themselves for protection as they travel to a safer community? The fluid boundary between combatants and noncombatants is hardly unique to Iraq or even the wider Middle East. The Russian occupation of Ukraine, the border war between Ethiopia and Eritrea, and post-conflict politics in Colombia all present cases where individuals adopt multiple roles in order to survive war.[52]

A core implication of this research is that legal and customary definitions of "civilian" should be restricted to behavioral criteria instead of ascriptive traits or group membership. Civilians abandon their status as noncombatants during the period in which they participate in hostilities, as opposed to when they affiliate with a specific group or decide to procure arms or other protective measures. As a UN guidance note on civilian protection argues, "Civilians who directly participate in hostilities are excluded from protection for such time as they do so. This may include civilians in self-defense groups. However, once they cease to engage in violence they should be protected."[53] Prosecution for past actions belongs in the domains of conflict mediation and transitional justice.

A second core requirement of effective civilian protection is the monitoring, collection, and distribution of real-time data from conflict-affected communities. State and non-state actors each have a unique role to play in collecting and distributing data related to human rights violations by armed actors, as well as incidents of civilian victimization. Since the 2011 Arab uprisings, information and communications technology also allowed outside observers to record, analyze, and disseminate the experiences of civilians in real time. Advances in social media and mobile Internet technology have also equipped individuals in conflict zones to act as citizen journalists, informing both locals and outsiders about the security and humanitarian conditions within their communities.

In Iraq's confrontation with IS, Omar Mohammad's journalism for the *Mosul Eye* provided policy makers and everyday observers a personal account of the group's control through the lens of local residents in Mosul. Aymenn Jawad Al-Tamimi's original research on IS control in Iraq and Syria, as well as the human rights violations committed by armed groups, has provided scholars, policy makers, and advocates with local data to inform civilian protection. Tamimi has been particularly effective at distributing his research findings through social media channels and a subscription-based newsletter.[54] At the international level, nongovernmental organizations in the United States and Europe connected to minority communities in Ninewa—including the Assyrian Policy Institute, In Defense of Christians, Sallux, and Yazda—have supplied real-time updates on the persecution of minority communities as well as humanitarian relief for those displaced by the conflict.

A key implication is that NGOs and individual activists can engage in "networked advocacy" by highlighting the contributions of local journalists, aid workers, and peace builders in conflict-affected communities.[55] Such efforts would not only increase public awareness, but would also provide credible and hard-to-acquire data on humanitarian needs and human rights violations in vulnerable communities. In fact, the collection and distribution of information on local conflict dynamics is often more effective than direct policy advocacy. As a participant observer to the European Union's advocacy for Iraqi Christians, the author found that the diaspora activists' policy demands—while well-meaning (and financially strategic)—actually put local partners at risk by advancing demands unlikely to be accepted by political stakeholders in Baghdad and Erbil.

Public-private partnerships are also effective mechanisms for collecting and distributing real-time data on threats to noncombatants. The USIP's Conflict and Stabilization Monitoring Framework, for example, provides a compelling model of how public funding can support data collection and analysis within partner communities.[56] Through regular waves of surveys, focus group discussion, key informant interviews, and event history data, the framework provides time-series data on the beliefs, attitudes, and behaviors of Iraqis affected by IS violence across Ninewa Governorate. These data were particularly useful in informing policy related to transitional justice and reconciliation advanced by USIP and its partner organizations, such as the Erbil-based Middle East Research Institute.

A third policy domain of civilian protection is the safe evacuation of individuals seeking to exit conflict-affected communities. With the increasing urbanization of many conflicts, the risk of indiscriminate violence for city-dwelling residents has risen, thus emphasizing the need for safe and effective humanitarian evacuation procedures. In Iraq, humanitarian evacuations played a marginal role given fluid conflict dynamics and the rapid mobilization of the anti-IS coalition. The August 2014 air strikes and humanitarian air drop to Yazidis trapped atop Mount Sinjar provides a notable exception. Between August 7 and 10, coalition aircraft targeted insurgent positions while cargo planes dropped over 35,000 gallons of fresh water and 114,000 prepackaged meals.[57] Coalition air strikes created a humanitarian corridor that allowed more than 30,000 Yazidis to evacuate with the assistance of U.S. special operations forces and local Peshmerga units.[58]

Humanitarian evacuations have played a more prominent role in Syria, where the United States and various European states negotiated with Russia and the Assad government to create humanitarian corridors adjacent to large urban centers such as Aleppo, Hama, and Homs.[59] Humanitarian corridors evolved out of the Bosnian civil war and resemble no-fly zones or safe zones, but are distinct as they involve a temporary cessation of hostilities and demilitarization of specific territory aimed at providing humanitarian assistance and safe evacuation of noncombatants. During the 2016 regime counteroffensive on Aleppo, as well as a subsequent operation in April 2017, humanitarian corridors were established prior to escalation in order to allow local residents to escape the crossfire.[60] Humanitarian corridors have been less effective in the 2022 Russian invasion of Ukraine, where the Russian military has intentionally relied on indiscriminate violence to weaken Ukrainians' resolve.[61] The creation of humanitarian corridors is an imperfect policy: while they can accelerate demographic change and inadvertently enable ethnic cleansing, they can also equip belligerents to coordinate policies that avoid further civilian victimization.

Finally, this study points to the negative, unintended consequences of airpower as a tool of civilian protection. While a "light footprint" strategy of advising, assisting, and equipping local clients proved politically tenable for the anti-IS coalition, a reliance on offshore airpower also produced civilian casualties.[62] In Iraq, the U.S.-led air campaign against IS resulted in over 14,000 air strikes between August 2014 and January 2018.[63] While U.S. officials state that 1,417 Iraqi noncombatants died during coalition air strikes, outside observers estimate the real figure to be between 8,000 and 13,000.[64] In the liberation of Mosul, for example, 103 civilian deaths can be directly attributed to coalition air strikes, while an additional 2,500–3,000 Iraqis died through artillery shelling.[65]

To compensate for unintended casualties, coalition members should follow through on a commitment to provide condolence (*ex gratia*) payments to victims. In the United States, Congress authorized condolence payments for "property damage, personal injury, or death" as a part of the 2015 National Defense Authorization Act.[66] To date, however, only $4.9 million has been distributed to verified victims, including only six payments to Iraqi victims as of 2021.[67] Condolence payments distributed by the United States Agency for International Development account for higher annual contributions, but these lag behind commitments stipulated in subsequent legislation.

Avenues for future research

This book contributes to a growing, multidisciplinary research program on wartime survival. While it is not the first account of survival under the Islamic State, it sets the stage for new theoretical and empirical analysis.

Evidence from Iraq shows that ordinary people adopt a number of different repertoires, often simultaneously, as conflicts evolve. Under IS control, Iraqis could be victims of violence in one instance and perpetrators of violence in the next. Those who took up arms also adopted different roles, as members of state security forces could also moonlight for militias, self-defense groups, or even criminal organizations in order to earn extra income, influence, or status. The International Committee of the Red Cross identifies this trend as the "civilianization of armed conflicts," while Médecins Sans Frontières (Doctors Without Borders) has developed a "practical guide to humanitarian law" outlining civilian protection in complex conflicts.[68]

Scholars and practitioners should also refine the theoretical and empirical differences between coerced and voluntary collaboration. In Iraq, there were few cases of unencumbered, voluntary support for IS. Those under the group's control—especially in Sunni communities in western Iraq—supported insurgents as a result of coercion, co-option, and persuasion. While acknowledging the role of complex motivations in shaping support for armed groups, scholars still lack a conceptual and moral vocabulary for describing different forms of "collaboration." Moving forward, it would be useful for us to draw on existing research in the just war tradition—such as Michael Walzer's discussion of "the problem of dirty hands"—to describe the mixed motivations of collaboration and resistance during wartime.[69]

While this book explores the conditions under which specific survival repertoires emerge, for the sake of parsimony it spends less time looking at how repertoires interact and evolve over time. Evidence from fieldwork reveals how ordinary people simultaneously deploy different repertoires depending on who they are engaging on a particular day. While some repertoires emerged from careful deliberation, others were spontaneous. Passive cooperation (such as adhering to IS's morality code) would be paired with acts of everyday resistance, such as secretly informing to coalition members. Future research should refine this study's typology by describing which repertoires most often appear in combination, including why contradictory repertoires (e.g., passive acquiescence *and* everyday resistance) simultaneously emerge when confronting insurgent control.

Finally, the book describes how Iraqis adapted and modified their survival repertoires in the face of evolving conflict dynamics. Beyond the balance of territorial control, local residents modify repertoires based on how insurgents govern. In other words, repertoires changed based on insurgents' specific combination of coercion, co-option, and persuasion. Similar to Roger Petersen's study of Lithuanian resistance to Nazi Germany and the Soviet Union, this book finds that neutrality, nonalignment, and autonomy are transitory tactics.[70] Very few Iraqis could credibly sustain neutrality—let alone autonomy—as IS consolidated control. More often than not, neutrality evolved into passive acquiescence or everyday resistance as the conflict continued.

Future research should outline pathways and processes by which repertoire change occurs. Specifically, how do repertoires evolve as conflicts de-escalate and ordinary people prepare themselves for life after war? Does neutrality, nonalignment, and autonomy become more common, or do individuals rally around armed groups that will increase their power or status in the post-conflict period? Such questions are especially pressing in the MENA region, where pro-government militias often develop political parties in order to compete in peacetime elections. While such parties need public support in order to challenge the incumbent regime, local citizens also face decisions about how they will relate to such parties (and their armed wings) in the absence of insurgent threats.

Above all else, studies of wartime survival must maintain an emphasis on the lived experience of ordinary people. Scholars must resist the temptation to abstract away the rich details of people's lives in favor of theoretical parsimony or methodological sophistication. By foregrounding the everyday experiences of local people, scholars can not only advance research on wartime survival, but also safeguard the dignity of their research subjects. As Anne Frank noted in her journal on June 6, 1944, "Where there's hope, there's life. It fills us with fresh courage and makes us strong again."[71]

Appendix A
Survey Methodology

This appendix provides technical details related to the design, enumeration, and analysis of the author's November 2017 Baghdad survey. Replications files and data are available at http://www.austinknuppe.com/book.

Questionnaire design

Measuring sensitive beliefs and attitudes in conflict zones presents methodological, logistical, and ethical challenges.[1] The risk of social desirability bias, refusals and item nonresponse, and preference falsification are especially acute for questions about trust in local security providers. Combining identification strategies not only mitigates threats to causal inferences, but also protects the safety of enumerators and respondents. To that end, the Baghdad questionnaire employs a multifaceted identification strategy consisting of direct and indirect techniques, as well as observational and experimental questions (see figure A.1).

To capture baseline attitudes toward different members of the anti-IS coalition, the questionnaire included open- and closed-ended observational questions about transnational cooperation and local security provision. Survey experiments indirectly measure respondent preferences by asking them to make structured trade-offs among competing foreign

	Observational	Experimental
Direct	Close-ended and self-report questions	Conjoint analysis, vignette experiments, and priming techniques
Indirect	Self-administered questionnaires	Endorsement, list, and randomization experiments

FIGURE A.1 How can researchers measure sensitive beliefs and attitudes using surveys in conflict zones?

Source: Author.

interveners, local coalition members, and intervention tactics. The questionnaire includes identical treatment categories and outcome questions across observational and experimental settings to decompose the effects of potentially confounding treatments.[2]

The questionnaire also included an endorsement experiment to probe whether local support for foreign intervention reduces to in-group favoritism. Endorsement experiments allow an analyst to indirectly measure respondent support for sensitive actors or policies.[3] An endorsement design is ideal in this setting because it allows for the indirect estimation of respondent support for pairs of foreign patrons and intervention tactics. Table A.1 displays the control and treatment vignettes for the endorsement experiment.

The setup of the endorsement experiment goes as follows. Prior to enumeration, respondents were randomly assigned with equal probability to either the control or treatment group. Within the control group, respondents rated their support for security assistance policies provided by the United Nations. The United Nations was chosen as the control condition because it represents a politically neutral organization that is well-known for its capacity to deliver security and development assistance in fragile

TABLE A.1 Question wording for the endorsement experiment (English)

Control	Treatment
As you may know, in recent months many countries have offered security assistance to Iraq. I am going to describe various proposals, and I want you to tell me how much you support each one: • United Nations providing financial aid • United Nations providing military equipment • United Nations providing military adviser • United Nations providing foreign troops	As you may know, in recent months many countries have offered security assistance to Iraq. I am going to describe various proposals, and I want you to tell me how much you support each one: • [Iran/Saudi Arabia/Turkey/Jordan] providing financial aid • [Iran/Saudi Arabia/Turkey/Jordan] providing military equipment • [Iran/Saudi Arabia/Turkey/Jordan] providing military adviser • [Iran/Saudi Arabia/Turkey/Jordan] providing foreign troops

states. Respondents in the treatment group were told that one of four regional patrons—Iran, Saudi Arabia, Turkey, or Jordan—was supplying the security assistance in question. The patron associated with each assistance form was randomly assigned within each questionnaire in the treatment group.[4] These four patrons were chosen as endorsers based on their visible participation in anti-IS operations in Iraq.

Each respondent answered four endorsement questions during the course of the interview (drawn from a pool of twenty-four patron-assistance combinations). Differences in support between the control and treatment groups can be attributed to the identity of the foreign patron because respondents in both groups are exposed to the same four forms of assistance. As a result, the relevant inference is between intervention tactics deployed by the United Nations and one of four regional interveners.

Following Graeme Blair and coauthors, the author measured respondent support by capturing an individual endorsement effect for each regional patron.[5] The endorsement effect for a given patron is estimated though the difference in mean support for respondents in the control group (P_j) and mean support for responses within one of four endorsement conditions (T_j). Endorsement effects are estimated via ordinary least squares regression, including one outcome for the pooled endorsement effect as well as separate models associated with each endorser. To capture how respondent-level traits shape support for foreign patronage, I also estimated additional specifications of the following regression:

$$P_i = \beta T_i + \eta x_i + \gamma T_i x_i + \alpha_p + T_i \alpha_p + \epsilon_i$$

where x_i represents the respondent-level traits (i.e., age, gender, ethnicity, religion, education, and employment), η, captures how these traits affect support in the control condition, and $T_i \alpha_p$ accounts for the possibility of district-specific treatment effects. In turn, γ, provides estimates of heterogeneous treatment effects conditional on confounders. In other words, γ captures how individual-level traits shape observed differences in endorsement effects.

The second embedded survey experiment was based on a conjoint design. Conjoint experiments measure how respondents make trade-offs across and within each attribute class.[6] Enumerators presented respondents with a pair of coalition profiles—consisting of a randomly assigned patron, client, and tactic—and were then asked which coalition they most

TABLE A.2 Conjoint experiment attributes

Attribute	Levels
Foreign intervener	• United States • Russia • United Kingdom • France • Iran • Saudi Arabia • Turkey
Coalition member	• Iraqi Counter Terrorism Service • Iraqi Federal Police • Popular Mobilization Forces • Kurdish Peshmerga • Sunni tribes
Intervention tactic	• Financial assistance • Military equipment sales • Foreign airpower • Military trainers • Foreign troops

TABLE A.3 Censored conjoint profiles

Foreign intervener	Coalition member	Intervention tactic
Iran	Peshmerga	Money
Iran	Peshmerga	Military equipment
Iran	Peshmerga	Trainers
Iran	Peshmerga	Troops
Iran	Sunni Tribes	Money
Iran	Sunni Tribes	Military equipment
Iran	Sunni Tribes	Trainers
Iran	Sunni Tribes	Troops
Saudi Arabia	Popular Mobilization Forces	Money
Saudi Arabia	Popular Mobilization Forces	Military equipment
Saudi Arabia	Popular Mobilization Forces	Trainers
Saudi Arabia	Popular Mobilization Forces	Troops
Turkey	Peshmerga	Money
Turkey	Peshmerga	Military equipment
Turkey	Peshmerga	Trainers
Turkey	Peshmerga	Troops

support to lead combat operations against the Islamic State (see table A.3). Each profile represented an actual patron-client relationship operating in Iraq, with the exception of twenty profiles censored due to their implausibility based on preexisting ethno-sectarian cleavages (e.g., Saudi patronage for Shiʿa militias or Turkish support for the Peshmerga).[7]

After their initial selection, respondents were asked to rate their support for each coalition profile on an ordinal scale (rescaled 0–1 for analysis). Respondents completed five choice tasks, ranking a total of ten unique coalition profiles per interview. The unit of analysis is the coalition profile and each coalition attribute represents an independent variable. Each respondent completed five choice tasks with two profiles per round, yielding a total of ten observations per respondent. Attributes were randomized within and across coalition profiles and standard errors are clustered at the level of the respondent to account for multiple comparisons.

To make comparisons among subgroups, I also examine the distribution of marginal means, which provide a measure of attribute favorability relative to chance.[8] For a given attribute level, the marginal mean represents the mean outcome across all appearances of that attribute level, averaging across all the other attributes. In other words, it conveys the absolute level of attribute favorability among respondents for all levels of a given attribute. Attribute levels with marginal means above 0.5 indicate higher favorability, while those lower than 0.5 indicate lower favorability. As a descriptive measure, marginal means are ideal for studying preference heterogeneity within attributes because they are not reliant on a reference category.

Table A.4 lists the respondent-level covariates used as control variables in the modeling of the conjoint and endorsement experiments.

Sampling procedure and enumeration process

In order to accurately reflect the ethnic sorting that occurred in Baghdad during the 2003 civil war, the survey team sampled Sunni, Shiʿa, and mixed neighborhoods. A 2010–2011 household census served as the sampling frame for a five-stage proportional probability sample. In stage one, the team distributed potential interviews equally among Baghdad's ten districts (*qadaʾ*), repeating the process across the city's eighty-nine subdistricts (*nahiyah*). Within each subdistrict, neighborhood blocks were selected using a probability-proportional-to-size procedure. The primary sampling unit consisted of clusters of ten to thirty interviews distributed equally among several streets within a given block (*zukak*) (see table A.5). Streets were selected via simple random sample, taking into account updated spot maps. The spot maps were then used to randomly select households. Within each household, adult respondents were randomly selected based on the last birthday method. Responses were recorded using Samsung Galaxy tablets.

Enumerators were assigned to their home neighborhoods to defuse the effects of social desirability bias and fieldwork teams included female enumerators to comply with local gender norms. Demographic information for each enumerator and field supervisor was recorded prior to enumeration to account for enumerator-driven effects.[9] Tables A.6 and A.7 provide a description of enumerator characteristics, as well as enumeration trends by enumerator.

Additional quality-control measures included GPS coordinates for the start and end of each interview, survey duration (as well question time and

TABLE A.4 Description of control variables in survey experiments

Variable	Description	Measurement
Gender	Male/female	Indicator variable; Male = 1
Age	Birth year	integer
Education	"What is the highest level of education that you have completed?"	Seven-point Likert; rescaled 0–1
Income	"I will read you some statements related to your household income. Which of these statements comes closest to describing your household income?"	Four-point Likert; rescaled 0–1
Sect	Respondent's religious sect	Indicator variable; Shiʿa = 1
District	Administrative district where interview took place	Nine-point factor
Anti-American	"Who or what do you think is responsible for creating Daʿesh?"	Open response, recoded as indicator; 1 for U.S.
Nationalism	(1) "If I ask you about your identity, how do you prefer to identify yourself?" (2) "To what extent do you agree with the following statement: 'My religious identity is more important than my national identity'?" (3) "If you have been asked to identify yourself, with which of the following do you most closely identify yourself?"	Additive index; rescaled 0–1
Right direction	"Generally speaking, do you think that things in Iraq are going in the right direction, or do you think things are going in the wrong direction?"	Indicator variable, coded 1 for "right direction"
Political Influence	"In your opinion, how likely is it that Iraqis can influence government decisions?"	Four-point factor, 4 for "very likely;" recoded 0–1
Election Opinion	"Regardless of whether you voted or not, how would you characterize the last parliamentary elections?"	Four-point Likert scale; recoded 0–1

TABLE A.5 Overview of multistage sampling design

District	Subdistrict Total	Subdistrict Sample	Census block Total	Census block Sample	Individuals Total	Individuals Sample	Fatalities
Rusafa	13	6	34	7	183,065	104	47
Adhamiya	11	4	27	4	315,337	72	8
Sadr City	13	7	68	7	1,456,700	103	95
Kadimiya	17	4	58	4	716,815	67	13
Kharkh	18	10	22	10	155,827	190	15
9 Nissan	8	–	76	–	967,955	–	1,915
Karada	5	–	42	–	310,300	–	727
Zafraniya	7	–	N/A	–	N/A	–	251
Mansour	13	–	55	–	535,925	–	676
Rashid	15	–	N/A	–	N/A	–	1,877

Note: Civilian fatalities data collected from Iraq Body Count, accessed November 3, 2023, https://www.iraqbodycount.org.

TABLE A.6 Enumerator characteristics

Enumerator ID	Gender	Age	Sect	Religious clothing	Education	Home neighborhood
15	Female	30	Sunni	Yes	College or above	Jamʿa
35	Female	28	Sunni	Yes	College or above	Adhamiya
55	Female	24	Shiʿa	Yes	College or above	Bunook
108	Male	29	Sunni	No	College or above	Jihad
111	Female	24	Sunni	Yes	College or above	Abu Gharaib
113	Female	26	Sunni	Yes	College or above	Hurria
114	Male	27	Shiʿa	No	College or above	Iʾlam
116	Male	21	Shiʿa	No	College or above	Bayaʿa
128	Male	54	Sunni	No	Professional school	Ateefia
162	Male	21	Sunni	No	High school	Karrada
329	Female	26	Shiʿa	Yes	College or above	Bayaʿa
351	Female	27	Shiʿa	Yes	College or above	New Baghdad
365	Female	33	Shiʿa	Yes	Professional school	Shaʿab
368	Male	25	Shiʿa	No	Professional school	Kahira

the time between completed interviews), and audio data from a randomly selected subset of interviews. In addition to the quality-control checks implemented by the survey firm, I used the "percentmatch" algorithm outlined in Noble Kuriakose and Michael Robbins's research to check for abnormal questionnaire falsification (see figure A.2).[10]

TABLE A.7 Enumerator effects

EID	Interview count	Completion rate	Question mean	Question SD	Avg. nonresponse
15	44	74.57	0.40	0.23	7.35
35	42	57.53	0.34	0.26	5.47
55	33	50.76	0.38	0.28	4.79
108	41	59.42	0.44	0.25	4.81
111	53	64.63	0.38	0.21	5.48
113	49	73.13	0.36	0.22	5.73
114	54	77.14	0.41	0.27	5.18
116	37	80.43	0.37	0.28	4.60
128	40	76.92	0.44	0.25	7.50
329	36	78.26	0.40	0.26	5.22
351	27	69.23	0.44	0.27	4.49
365	37	64.91	0.48	0.21	9.33
368	51	71.83	0.32	0.20	5.41

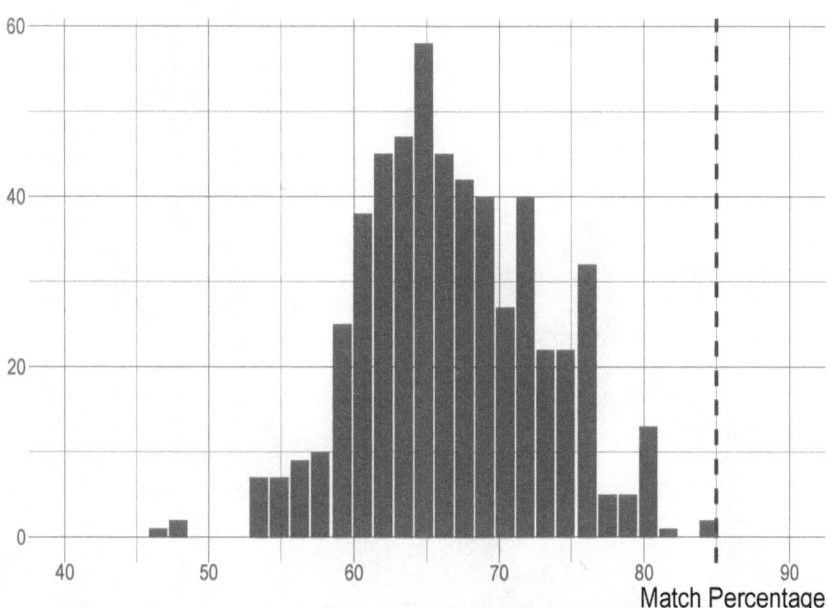

FIGURE A.2 Distribution of questionnaire response similarity.

Source: Baghdad survey enumerated by the author, November 2017.

TABLE A.8 Description of incomplete interviews

Randomization failure*	68	26.8%
Refusal/not reachable	127	50%
Quality control concern	59	23.2%
Total	254	100%

* Conditional on successful randomization, the survey response rate increases to 74.6%.

The Baghdad survey's margin of error was ± 4.4 percent ($n = 545$) calculated to incorporate the clustering effects of multistage sample design, as well as provide statistical reliability at the 95 percent confidence level. The overall completion rate was 68.3 percent, consisting of 545 complete interviews out of a total of 799 attempts. Tables A.8 provides a description of survey nonresponse by category and frequency.

Endorsement experiment

The following subsections include additional analyses, sensitivity analysis, and robustness checks for the endorsement experiment.

ENDORSEMENT EFFECTS BY FOREIGN INTERVENER

TABLE A.9 Support for security assistance by foreign intervener

	Panel A: Unconditional Means			
	Iran	Saudi Arabia	Turkey	Jordan
β: Group cue	−0.017	−0.136***	−0.043***	0.145***
	(0.021)	(0.020)	(0.021)	(0.020)
Constant	0.621***	0.621***	0.621***	0.621***
	(0.014)	(0.014)	(0.014)	(0.014)
Adjusted R^2	0.085	0.085	0.085	0.085
N	536	536	536	536
	Panel B: Conditional Means			
	Iran	Saudi Arabia	Turkey	Jordan
β: group cue	−0.015	−0.220***	−0.082**	−0.161***
	(0.032)	(0.031)	(0.033)	(0.031)
Constant	0.595***	0.623***	0.556***	0.561***
	(0.075)	(0.078)	(0.083)	(0.074)
Adjusted R^2	0.139	0.310	0.104	0.215
N	199	199	199	199
District fixed effects	Y	Y	Y	Y
Demographic Controls	Y	Y	Y	Y
Attitudinal controls	Y	Y	Y	Y

***$p < 0.001$, **$p < 0.01$, *$p < 0.05$ (two-tailed). Heteroskedastic-consistent standard errors in parentheses.

ENDORSEMENT EFFECTS BY RESPONDENT SECT

TABLE A.10 Respondent sect and support for foreign intervention

	Iran	Saudi Arabia	Turkey	Jordan
β: group cue	−0.186*	−0.140	−0.027	−0.139
	(0.083)	(0.078)	(0.089)	(0.084)
η: Shiʿa	0.001	−0.024	0.009	−0.006
	(0.070)	(0.066)	(0.075)	(0.071)
γ: group cue × Shiʿa	0.227**	−0.092	−0.062	−0.026
	(0.087)	(0.082)	(0.093)	(0.088)
Shiʿa treatment effect ($\beta + \gamma$)	0.040	−0.231**	−0.089*	−0.164*
	(0.033)	(0.030)	(0.035)	(0.033)
Sunni treatment effect (β)	−0.186*	−0.140	−0.027	−0.139
	(0.083)	(0.078)	(0.089)	(0.084)
Constant	0.715***	0.571***	0.528***	0.546***
	(0.090)	(0.085)	(0.096)	(0.092)
District fixed effects	Y	Y	Y	Y
Demographic controls	Y	Y	Y	Y
Attitudinal controls	Y	Y	Y	Y
Adj. R^2	0.171	0.315	0.107	0.216
N	199	199	199	199

***$p < 0.001$, **$p < 0.01$, *$p < 0.05$ (two-tailed). Heteroskedastic-consistent standard errors in parentheses.

ENDORSEMENT EFFECTS BY DISTRICT-LEVEL INSECURITY

TABLE A.11 District-level insecurity and support for foreign intervention

	Iran	Saudi Arabia	Turkey	Jordan
β: group cue	0.024	−0.216***	−0.093**	−0.162***
	(0.033)	(0.031)	(0.034)	(0.033)
η_1: low insecurity	0.070	0.073*	0.064	0.075*
	(0.038)	(0.036)	(0.040)	(0.038)
η_1: high insecurity	−0.016	−0.003	−0.007	−0.008
	(0.033)	(0.030)	(0.034)	(0.033)
γ_1: group cue × low insecurity	−0.070	−0.037	0.054	0.006
	(0.055)	(0.051)	(0.057)	(0.054)
γ_2: group cue × high insecurity	0.018	0.014	−0.053	−0.002
	(0.049)	(0.046)	(0.052)	(0.049)
Low-insecurity treatment effect $(\beta + \gamma_1)$	−0.046	−0.253	−0.038	−0.156
	(0.058)	(0.052)	(0.061)	(0.056)
Middle-insecurity treatment effect (β)	0.024	−0.216***	−0.093***	−0.162***
	(0.033)	(0.031)	(0.034)	(0.033)
High-insecurity treatment effect $(\beta + \gamma_2)$	0.042	−0.201	−0.145	−0.164
	(0.064)	(0.085)	(0.067)	(0.091)
Constant	0.588***	0.616***	0.572***	0.561***
	(0.079)	(0.073)	(0.082)	(0.079)
District fixed effects	Y	Y	Y	Y
Demographic controls	Y	Y	Y	Y
Attitudinal controls	Y	Y	Y	Y
Adj. R^2	0.143	0.309	0.108	0.211
N	199	199	199	199

***$p < 0.001$, **$p < 0.01$, *$p < 0.05$ (two-tailed). Heteroskedastic-consistent standard errors in parentheses.

COVARIATE BALANCE

TABLE A.12 Covariate balance in endorsement experiment

	Control	Treatment
PSU count	31.0	29.0
Percent male	49.3	52.8
Mean age	40.7	40.7
Mean education	3.9	4.3
Mean income	2.5	2.6
Percent Shiʿa	36.6	32.8

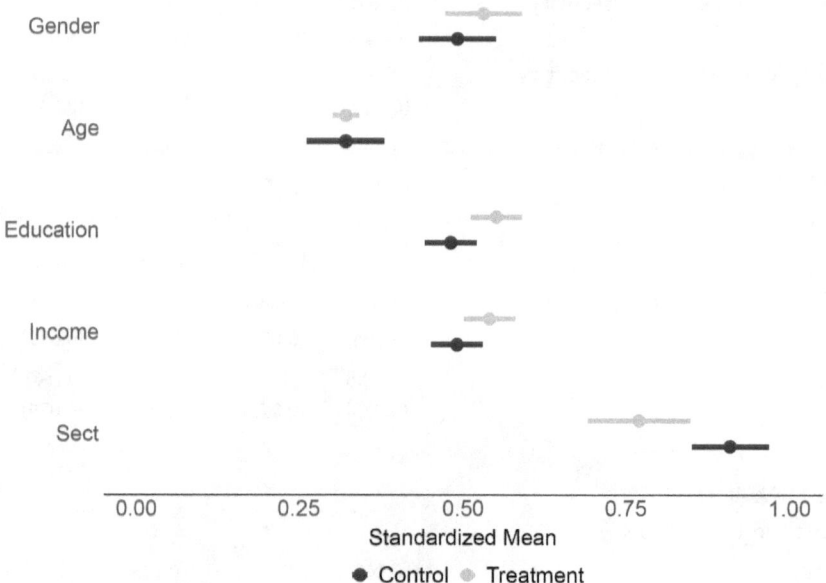

FIGURE A.3 Covariate balance for endorsement experiment.

Source: Baghdad survey enumerated by the author, November 2017.

SENSITIVITY ANALYSIS

As demonstrated by table A.13, the endorsement effects are robust to specific intervention tactics. In other words, when we remove questions related to specific tactics (e.g., money, equipment, trainers, and troops), the endorsement effect remains negative and statistically significant. These negative endorsement effects are also substantively significant relative to the control group (UN as endorser). Figure A.4 provides a graphical representation of the endorsement effects.

TABLE A.13 Sensitivity analysis for endorsement experiment

	Full data	No money	No equipment	No trainers	No troops
(Intercept)	-0.62***	0.45***	0.44***	0.45***	0.52***
	(0.01)	(0.01)	(0.01)	(0.01)	(0.01)
Treatment	-0.09***	-0.06***	-0.05***	-0.05***	-0.09***
	(0.02)	(0.01)	(0.01)	(0.01)	(0.01)
AIC	-231.28	-518.55	-528.75	-543.00	-389.26
BIC	-218.43	-505.69	-515.90	-530.15	-376.41
Log likelihood	118.64	262.27	267.38	274.50	197.63
Deviance	20.16	11.79	11.57	11.27	15.01
N	536	536	536	536	536

***$p < 0.001$, **$p < 0.01$, *$p < 0.05$ (two-tailed). Heteroskedastic-consistent standard errors are in parentheses.

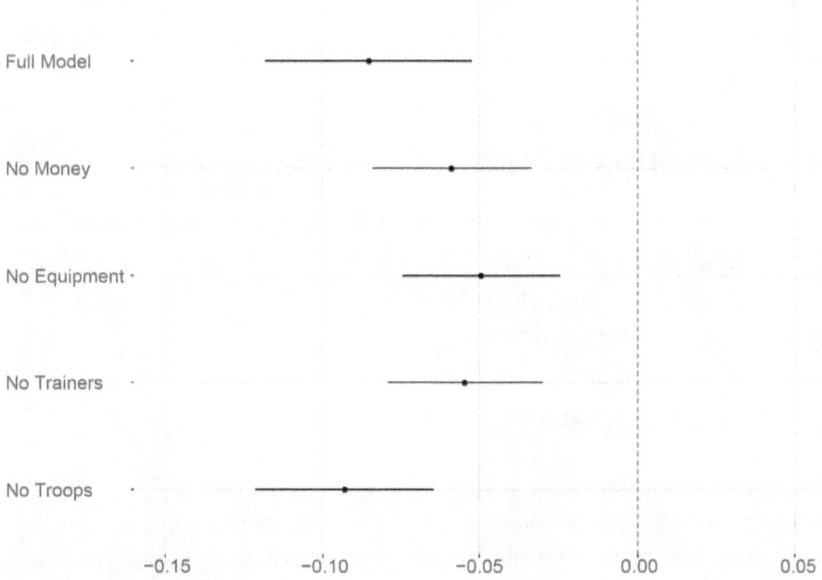

FIGURE A.4 Sensitivity analysis for endorsement experiment.

Source: Baghdad survey enumerated by the author, November 2017.

Conjoint experiment

The following subsections include additional analyses, sensitivity analysis, and robustness checks for the conjoint experiment.

SENSITIVITY ANALYSIS

The following rule of thumb determines the minimum sample sizes for aggregate-level, full-profile, choice-based conjoint modeling:

$$\frac{n \times t \times a}{c} \geq 500$$

Where n is the number of respondents, t is the number of tasks, a is number of alternatives per task (not including the "none" alternative), and c is the number of analysis cells.[11] When considering main effects, c is equal to the largest number of levels for any one attribute. In this study,

$$\frac{540 \times 5 \times 2}{7} = 711.42$$

Table A.14 demonstrates how sensitive the results of the conjoint analysis are to changes in sample size (holding the choice task and profile pairs constant).

RANDOMIZATION CHECKS

Randomization checks were carried out for the three conjoint attributes along three covariates: gender, age, and education. The results from tables A.15, A.16, and A.17 demonstrate that there is covariate balance across each attribute in the conjoint analysis.

CARRYOVER ASSUMPTION TEST

A key assumption of conjoint experiments is that respondents' choices do not display time dependencies, allowing analysts to pool responses across multiple choice tasks. Figure A.5 presents the average marginal component effect (AMCE) within each choice task, with each abbreviation depicting a different attribute level (e.g., for patron, "RU" = Russia, "GB" = United

TABLE A.14 How sensitive is conjoint analysis to sample size?

	N = 150	N = 300	N = 540
United States	—	—	—
Russia	0.48*	0.53***	0.27**
	(0.19)	(0.14)	(0.10)
United Kingdom	0.27	0.04	−0.10
	(0.20)	(0.01)	(0.10)
France	−0.08	0.01	−0.08
	(0.20)	(0.14)	(0.10)
Iran	0.35	0.24	0.02
	(0.23)	(0.16)	(0.12)
Saudi Arabia	−0.89***	−0.88***	−0.78***
	(0.23)	(0.16)	(0.11)
Turkey	−0.14	−0.15	−0.17
	(0.21)	(0.15)	(0.11)
Iraqi CTS	—	—	—
Federal Police	−0.13	−0.28*	−0.21*
	(0.16)	(0.11)	(0.08)
Peshmerga	−1.07***	−1.05***	−1.11***
	(0.20)	(0.14)	(0.10)
PMF	0.26	0.21	−0.04
	(0.17)	(0.12)	(0.09)
Sunni Tribes	−0.33	−0.76***	−0.93***
	(0.22)	(0.14)	(0.10)
Money	—	—	—
Equipment	−0.07	−0.09	0.05
	(0.17)	(0.12)	(0.09)
Trainers	0.46*	0.17	0.23*
	(0.18)	(0.12)	(0.09)
Troops	0.03	0.05	0.09
	(0.03)	(0.12)	(0.09)
AIC	947.03	1,872.28	3,417.26
Log Likelihood	−459.51	−922.14	−1,694.63
N	1,500	3,000	3,000

***$p < 0.001$, **$p < 0.01$, *$p < 0.05$ (two-tailed). Heteroskedastic-consistent standard errors are in parentheses.

TABLE A.15 Foreign intervener randomization

	Russia	United Kingdom	France	Iran	Turkey	Saudi Arabia
Intercept	[-0.073, 0.601]	[-0.569, 0.050]	[-0.527, 0.270]	[-0.920, -0.129]	[-0.794, -0.053]	[-0.338, 0.349]
Male	[-0.242, 0.130]	[-0.208, 0.152]	[-0.279, 0.153]	[-0.395, 0.054]	[-0.257, 0.165]	[-0.273, 0.116]
Age	[-0.006, 0.005]	[-0.005, 0.008]	[-0.008, 0.006]	[-0.008, 0.007]	[-0.007, 0.008]	[-0.007, 0.007]
Education	[-0.105, 0.012]	[-0.009, 0.098]	[-0.041, 0.093]	[-0.056, 0.085]	[-0.030, 0.097]	[-0.111, 0.013]

TABLE A.16 Coalition member randomization

	Federal Police	PMF	Peshmerga	Sunni tribes
Intercept	[-0.252, 0.314]	[-0.780, -0.144]	[-0.905, -0.253]	[-0.830, 0.080]
Male	[-0.188, 0.121]	[-0.249, 0.123]	[-0.173, 0.183]	[-0.377, 0.145]
Age	[-0.006, 0.004]	[-0.006, 0.005]	[-0.007, 0.005]	[-0.009, 0.007]
Education	[-0.028, 0.061]	[-0.008, 0.097]	[0.042, 0.153]	[0.011, 0.162]

TABLE A.17 Intervention tactic randomization

	Equipment	Airpower	Trainers	Troops
Intercept	[-0.298, 0.296]	[-0.343, 0.253]	[-0.099, 0.413]	[-0.099, 0.413]
Male	[-0.294, 0.044]	[-0.417, -0.087]	[-0.003, 0.007]	[-0.358, -0.041]
Age	[-0.006, 0.005]	[-0.003, 0.008]	[-0.358, -0.041]	[-0.003, 0.007]
Education	[-0.038, 0.061]	[-0.033, 0.064]	[-0.069, 0.018]	[-0.069, 0.018]

Kingdom, "FR" = France, "IR" = Iran, "SA" = Saudi Arabia, and "TR" = Turkey). The dashed horizontal line indicates the AMCE average across all ten profiles (five choice tasks of two profiles each).

Figure A.5 demonstrates that the results are relatively stable over time: for the security assistance attribute (the bottom-most figure), for example, the AMCEs are tightly clustered within and across each round. As discussed in chapter 4, respondents slightly prefer foreign military trainers to other forms of security assistance. The clustering across choice tasks indicates that respondents are evaluating the various

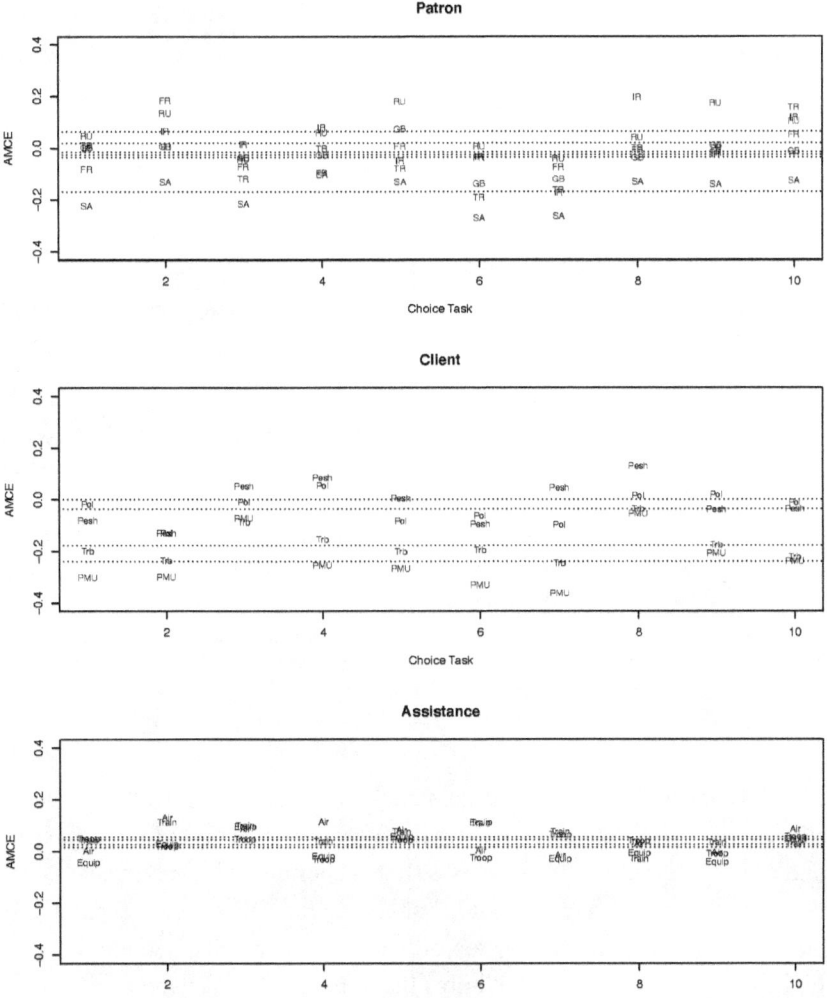

FIGURE A.5 Treatment effects of each attribute level remain stable across five choice tasks.

Source: Baghdad survey enumerated by the author, November 2017.

TABLE A.18 Randomization in average marginal component effects by choice task

Attribute	Levels	Coef.	Min.	Max.
Foreign intervener	(1) United States	—	—	—
	(2) Russia	0.064	−0.043	0.180
	(3) Great Britain	−0.026	−0.139	0.074
	(4) France	−0.016	−0.096	0.184
	(5) Iran	0.019	−0.174	0.196
	(6) Saudi Arabia	−0.169	−0.272	−0.103
	(7) Turkey	−0.035	−0.192	0.156
Coalition member	(1) CTS	—	—	—
	(2) Federal Police	−0.035	−0.130	0.054
	(3) Peshmerga	−0.238	−0.361	−0.054
	(4) PMF	0.001	−0.129	0.130
	(5) Sunni Tribes	−0.177	−0.246	−0.036
Intervention tactic	(1) money	—	—	—
	(2) equipment	0.016	−0.045	0.109
	(3) airpower	0.045	−0.013	0.132
	(4) trainers	0.056	−0.029	0.112
	(5) troops	0.027	−0.033	0.062

Reference Categories: United States/Iraqi CTS/financial aid

attribute levels consistently across each of the five rounds. In comparison, there is more variation within and across choice tasks for the patron and client attributes. This suggests that respondents have stronger preferences for these attributes, and that their preferences for a given attribute (e.g., a Russian intervener or Iraqi Army coalition member) are highly contingent on the attributes listed in the comparison profile.

Appendix B
Interview Methodology

The fieldwork for this book occurred between 2017 and 2021. During this period, the author conducted or facilitated thirty key informant interviews among Iraqis who lived in Anbar, Baghdad, Erbil, Ninewa, and Salah al-Din Governorates during the Islamic State insurgency. The A-series interviews occurred in December 2019 during fieldwork to the Kurdistan Region. The B-series interviewed occurred in October 2021 in Anbar and Salah al-Din Governorates.

The relevant interview pool included Iraqi peace builders and civil society activists from across Ninewa Governorate. Within Ninewa Governorate, the author interviewed Iraqi peace builders representing minority communities in Hamdaniya (Ninewa Plains), Sinjar, and Tal Afar. The author was introduced to interviewees through a collaboration with Tearfund, a London-based NGO that conducts peace building, economic development, and humanitarian assistance work in fragile and conflict-affected states. Tearfund provided a conference room in their regional office in Erbil to conduct interviews, including a local interpreter for Kurdish speakers. Interviews lasted between sixty and ninety minutes and were conducted in a mix of Modern Standard Arabic, Iraqi Arabic, or Kurdish, depending on the interviewee's native language and prior education. While having a gender balance enabled the interviewing of female peace builders, it likely influenced how interviewees discussed sexual and gender-based violence.

Informed consent was obtained through a written instructional form in each interviewee's native language. To respect interviewees' confidentiality, audio recordings of interviews were omitted, as well as written notes related to sensitive details of their peace-building programs (e.g., opposition to the program by a community's political or religious elites). Follow-up clarifications were obtained via encrypted SMS messages on WhatsApp between the author and each interviewee. Due to their ongoing relationships with Tearfund—as well as their role as community leaders—most interviewees had higher levels of education, income, and social status when compared to their neighbors and family members. As such, these interviews represent the perspective of community elites as opposed to the more vulnerable residents of their respective communities. Members of the armed forces, as well as pro-government militias, were intentionally excluded from the interview pool.

In October 2021, an additional twenty key informant interviews were conducted among Iraqis in Anbar and Salah al-Din Governorates (B-series interviews). The interview pooled differed from the Ninewa fieldwork, in that it included members of local influential families and tribes, as well as volunteers enlisted in pro-government militias and community self-defense groups. Due to the COVID-19 pandemic, the author did not conduct these key informant interviews in person. Rather, enumerators were hired to conduct face-to-face interviews in locations across Fallujah, Mosul, Ramadi, and Tikrit.

The author conducted online enumerator training in Arabic via Zoom video calls with assistance from a local project manager. Similar to the Ninewa fieldwork, interviews lasted between sixty and ninety minutes and covered the same list of questions related to security, politics, and economic development before, during, and after the IS occupation. In contrast to the Ninewa interviews, the research team purposely recruited members of non-state security forces aligned with the anti-IS coalition. By drawing on members who voluntarily mobilized to fight IS, these key informants provide insights into the beliefs and motivations of individuals who pursued armed resistance to defend their home communities.

Table B.1 provides the descriptive statistics for all thirty key informant interviews.

TABLE B.1 Descriptive statistics for key informant interviews

ID	Gender	Age	Identity	Location	Job/role
A01	Male	40–50	Sunni Arab	Qaraqosh	Parent-teacher association (PTA) in local school district
A02	Male	40–50	Yazidi	Bashiqa	PTA in local school district
A03	Male	40–50	Sunni Kurd	Erbil	University student group for interreligious dialogue
A04	Female	30–40	Sunni Arab	Bashiqa	Women's community group
A05	Female	20–30	Assyrian Christian	Qaraqosh	PTA in local school district; school guidance councilor
A06	Female	20–30	Assyrian Christian	Qaraqosh	Women's association; community garden initiative
A07	Female	20–30	Sunni Kurd	Erbil	University student group
A08	Female	20–30	Sunni Kurd	Erbil	Peace builder for international NGO
A09	Male	20–30	Sunni Kurd	Erbil	Journalist for *Rudaw*
A10	Male	30–40	Assyrian Christian	Qaraqosh	Local business owner and city council member
B01	Male	30–40	Sunni Arab	Obaidy	Local government agency
B02	Male	30–40	Sunni Arab	Hasa	High school teacher
B03	Female	40–50	Sunni Arab	Mosul	N/A
B04	Male	30–40	Sunni Arab	Tikrit	Intermittent day laborer
B05	Male	30–40	Sunni Arab	Fallujah	Intermittent/freelance work
B06	Male	30–40	Sunni Arab	Ramadi	Intermittent day laborer
B07	Male	20–30	Sunni Arab	Mosul	University student
B08	Male	N/A	Sunni Arab	Fallujah	Tribal militia volunteer (Sahwa)
B09	Male	40–50	Sunni Arab	Ramadi	Tribal militia volunteer (Sahwa)
B10	Male	40–50	Sunni Arab	Ramadi	Tribal militia volunteer (Sahwa)
B11	Male	30–40	Sunni Arab	Fallujah	Tribal militia volunteer (Sahwa)
B12	Male	20–30	Sunni Arab	Mosul	Tribal militia volunteer (PMF)
B13	Male	30–40	Sunni Arab	Ramadi	Tribal militia volunteer (PMF)
B14	Male	30–40	Sunni Arab	Tikrit	Tribal militia volunteer (PMF)
B15	Male	30–40	Sunni Arab	Mosul	Tribal militia volunteer (PMF)
B16	Male	40–50	Sunni Arab	Fallujah	Tribal militia volunteer (PMF)
B17	Male	50–60	Sunni Arab	Fallujah	Tribal sheikh
B18	Male	50–60	Sunni Arab	Mosul	Tribal sheikh
B19	Male	30–40	Sunni Arab	Ramadi	Tribal sheikh
B20	Male	50–60	Sunni Arab	Tikrit	Tribal sheikh

Note: A-series interviews conducted in December 2019; B-series interviews conducted in October 2021.

Notes

1. How Do Ordinary People Survive War?

1. Kareem Fahim and Suadad Al-Salhy, "Exhausted and Bereft, Iraqi Soldiers Quit Fight," *New York Times*, June 10, 2014, https://www.nytimes.com/2014/06/11/world/middleeast/exhausted-and-bereft-iraqi-soldiers-quit-fight.html.
2. See "Iraq," Displacement Tracking Matrix, International Organization for Migration, accessed October 11, 2023, https://dtm.iom.int/iraq.
3. IS referred to Yazidis as "devil worshippers" (ʿabdat al-Shaytan) and polytheists (*mushrikun*) due to the influence of Zoroastrianism—including fallen angels and other deities—into their religious observance. Such distinctions would place them outside of the realm of protection afforded to monotheists (i.e., Jews and Christians).
4. Stathis N. Kalyvas and Matthew Adam Kocher, "Ethnic Cleavages and Irregular War: Iraq and Vietnam," *Politics & Society* 35, no. 2 (2007): 183–223; James Habyarimana et al., *Coethnicity: Diversity and the Dilemmas of Collective Action* (New York: Russell Sage Foundation, 2009); Luke N. Condra et al., "The Effect of Civilian Casualties in Afghanistan and Iraq," Working Paper 16152, National Bureau of Economic Research, 2010; Jason Lyall, Kosuke Imai, and Graeme Blair, "Explaining Support for Combatants in Wartime: A Survey Experiment in Afghanistan," *American Political Science Review* 107, no. 4 (2013): 679–705; Jason Lyall, Yuki Shiraito, and Kosuke Imai, "Coethnic Bias and Wartime Informing," *Journal of Politics* 77, no. 3 (2015): 833–848; Daniel Silverman, "What Shapes Civilian Beliefs About Violent Events? Experimental Evidence from Pakistan," *Journal of Conflict Resolution* 63, no. 6 (2019): 1460–1487.

1. HOW DO ORDINARY PEOPLE SURVIVE WAR?

5. Kalyvas observes that micro-level cleavages rarely correspond to macro-level narratives because civil wars occur in a "context that places a premium on the joint action of local and supralocal actors, insiders and outsiders, individuals and organizations, civilians and armies: action (including violence) results from their alliance in pursuit of their diverse goals—whose main empirical manifestation is ambiguity." Stathis N. Kalyvas, "The Ontology of 'Political Violence': Action and Identity in Civil Wars," *Perspectives on Politics* 1, no. 3 (2003): 487.
6. Stathis N. Kalyvas, *The Logic of Violence in Civil War* (New York: Cambridge University Press, 2006); Eli Berman, Joseph H. Felter, and Jacob N. Shapiro, *Small Wars, Big Data: The Information Revolution in Modern Conflict* (Princeton, NJ: Princeton University Press, 2018); Justin Schon, *Surviving the War in Syria* (New York: Cambridge University Press, 2020); Munqith Dagher et al., *ISIS in Iraq: The Social and Psychological Foundations of Terror* (New York: Oxford University Press, 2023).
7. Roger Mac Ginty, *Everyday Peace: How So-Called Ordinary People Can Disrupt Violent Conflict* (New York: Oxford University Press, 2021), 30.
8. Karl Kaltenthaler, Daniel Silverman, and Munqith Dagher note limited Kurdish support for IS (between 5 and 8 percent) primarily in rural communities outside of Erbil or Sulaymaniyah. The authors note that a "substantial minority of Kurds living in the KRG region have turned to Salafist Islam because of the influence of radical mullahs and Salafi student networks as well as their unfavorable view of the status quo in Iraqi Kurdistan. Many see a blighted future if they are not part of the ruling elite's power structure, and have turned to Salafism and even jihadism as an alternative to the status quo. Thus, voicing positive views of ISIL does not mean a Kurdish respondent is necessarily desirous of joining the group or even wants it controlling his or her territory. Positive views of ISIL can be a way to show extreme displeasure with the status quo for the 'have-nots' in KRG." Karl Kaltenthaler, Daniel Silverman, and Munqith Dagher, "Identity, Ideology, and Information: The Sources of Iraqi Public Support for the Islamic State," *Studies in Conflict & Terrorism* 41, no. 10 (2018): 808–809.
9. Ana Arjona, "Civilian Cooperation and Non-cooperation with Non-state Armed Groups: The Centrality of Obedience and Resistance," *Small Wars & Insurgencies* 28, nos. 4–5 (2017): 755–778.
10. Elisabeth Jean Wood, "The Social Processes of Civil War: The Wartime Transformation of Social Networks," *Annual Review of Political Science* 11 (2008): 548.
11. Oliver Kaplan, *Resisting War: How Communities Protect Themselves* (New York: Cambridge University Press, 2017), 3.
12. Roger D. Petersen, *Resistance and Rebellion: Lessons of Eastern Europe* (New York: Cambridge University Press, 2001); Evgeny Finkel, *Ordinary Jews: Choice and Survival During the Holocaust* (Princeton, NJ: Princeton University Press, 2017); Kaplan, *Resisting War*; Schon, *Surviving the War in Syria*; Ashley Jackson, *Negotiating Survival: Civilian-Insurgent Relations in Afghanistan* (London: Hurst, 2021); Aidan Milliff, "Facts Shape Feelings: Information, Emotions, and the Political Consequences of Violence," *Political Behavior* 45, no. 3 (2022): 1169–1190; Anastasia Shesterinina, *Mobilizing in*

Uncertainty: Collective Identities and War in Abkhazia (Ithaca, NY: Cornell University Press, 2021).
13. Marika Landau-Wells, "Dealing with Danger: Threat Perception and Policy Preferences" (PhD diss., Massachusetts Institute of Technology, 2018), 3.
14. Shesterinina, *Mobilizing in Uncertainty*.
15. Finkel, *Ordinary Jews*, 52.
16. Aidan Milliff, "Making Sense, Making Choices: How Civilians Choose Survival Strategies during Violence," *American Political Science Review*, October 24, 2023, https://aidanmilliff.com/media/Milliff_JMP.pdf.
17. Kalyvas, *The Logic of Violence in Civil War*, 103.
18. Stathis N. Kalyvas, "Ethnic Defection in Civil War," *Comparative Political Studies* 41, no. 8 (2008): 1043–1068.
19. David A. Lake, *The Statebuilder's Dilemma: On the Limits of Foreign Intervention* (Ithaca, NY: Cornell University Press, 2016); Berman, Felter, and Shapiro, *Small Wars, Big Data*; Eli Berman and David A. Lake, *Proxy Wars: Suppressing Violence Through Local Agents* (Ithaca, NY: Cornell University Press, 2019).
20. Betcy Jose and Peace A. Medie, "Understanding Why and How Civilians Resort to Self-Protection in Armed Conflict," *International Studies Review* 17, no. 4 (2015): 515–535; Betcy Jose and Peace A. Medie, "Civilian Self-Protection and Civilian Targeting in Armed Conflicts: Who Protects Civilians?," in *Oxford Research Encyclopedia of Politics* (December 22, 2016), https://doi.org/10.1093/acrefore/9780190228637.013.216.
21. Shane Joshua Barter, *Civilian Strategy in Civil War: Insights from Indonesia, Thailand, and the Philippines* (New York: Palgrave Macmillan, 2014); Albert O. Hirschman, *Exit, Voice, and Loyalty: Responses to Decline in Firms, Organizations, and States* (Cambridge, MA: Harvard University Press, 1970).
22. Milton Lodge and Charles S. Taber, *The Rationalizing Voter* (New York: Cambridge University Press, 2013); Dan M. Kahan, "Misconceptions, Misinformation, and the Logic of Identity-Protective Cognition" (Cultural Cognition Project Working Paper Series No. 164, Yale Law School, May 24, 2017), https://papers.ssrn.com/sol3/papers.cfm?abstract_id=2973067.
23. Habyarimana et al., *Coethnicity*; Condra et al., *The Effect of Civilian Casualties in Afghanistan and Iraq*; Lyall, Shiraito, and Imai, "Coethnic Bias and Wartime Informing."
24. Francisco Gutiérrez-Sanín and Elisabeth Jean Wood, "What Should We Mean by 'Pattern of Political Violence?' Repertoire, Targeting, Frequency, and Technique," *Perspectives on Politics* 15, no. 1 (2017): 20–41; Laia Balcells and Jessica A. Stanton, "Violence Against Civilians During Armed Conflict: Moving Beyond the Macro- and Micro-Level Divide," *Annual Review of Political Science* 24 (2020): 45–69; Livia Isabella Schubiger, "State Violence and Wartime Civilian Agency: Evidence from Peru," *Journal of Politics* 83 (4 2021): 1383–1398.
25. Kalyvas, *The Logic of Violence in Civil War*.
26. John Bellows and Edward Miguel, "War and Local Collective Action in Sierra Leone," *Journal of Public Economics* 93, nos. 11–12 (2009): 1144–1157; Christopher Blattman,

"From Violence to Voting: War and Political Participation in Uganda," *American Political Science Review* 103, no. 2 (2009): 231–247; Maarten J. Voors et al., "Violent Conflict and Behavior: A Field Experiment in Burundi," *American Economic Review* 102, no. 2 (2012): 941–964; Michael Callen et al., "Violence and Risk Preference: Experimental Evidence from Afghanistan," *American Economic Review* 104, no. 1 (2014): 123–148.

27. Barter, *Civilian Strategy in Civil War*; Kaplan, *Resisting War*; Abbey Steele, *Democracy and Displacement in Colombia's Civil War* (Ithaca, NY: Cornell University Press, 2017); Jana Krause, *Resilient Communities: Non-violence and Civilian Agency in Communal War* (New York: Cambridge University Press, 2018); Schon, *Surviving the War in Syria*; Shesterinina, *Mobilizing in Uncertainty*.

28. Lisa Blaydes, *State of Repression: Iraq Under Saddam Hussein* (Princeton, NJ: Princeton University Press, 2018); Samuel Helfont, *Compulsion in Religion: Saddam Hussein, Islam, and the Roots of Insurgencies in Iraq* (New York: Oxford University Press, 2018); Caroleen Marji Sayej, *Patriotic Ayatollahs: Nationalism in Post-Saddam Iraq* (Ithaca, NY: Cornell University Press, 2018); David S. Patel, *Order Out of Chaos: Islam, Information, and the Rise and Fall of Social Orders in Iraq* (Ithaca, NY: Cornell University Press, 2022); Isak Svensson et al., *Confronting the Caliphate: Civil Resistance in Jihadist Proto-States* (New York: Oxford University Press, 2022); Dagher et al., *ISIS in Iraq*.

29. Barter, *Civilian Strategy in Civil War*; Kaplan, *Resisting War*; Steele, *Democracy and Displacement in Colombia's Civil War*; Krause, *Resilient Communities*; Schon, *Surviving the War in Syria*; Sarah E. Parkinson, *Beyond the Lines: Social Networks and Palestinian Militant Organizations in Wartime Lebanon* (Ithaca, NY: Cornell University Press, 2023).

30. Appendix A provides technical details about the design and enumeration of the Baghdad survey. Appendix B outlines the interview methodology.

31. I am indebted to my colleagues from Tearfund, Search for Common Ground, and the United States Institute of Peace for providing assistance in the field, but also an education on responsible research practices in conflict-affected settings. Teri Murphy—a colleague at Ohio State University—was a particularly helpful guide in thinking through conflict-sensitivity considerations. Manuel Almeida of ARK Group DMCC has also been helpful on thinking through research design from a conflict-sensitivity perspective. See Manuel Almeida, "Conducting Primary Research in Yemen: Challenges and Lessons," ARK Group International, June 15, 2020, https://www.ark.international/ark-blog/conducting-primary-research-in-yemen-challenges-and-lessons.

32. Dyan Mazurana, Karen Jacobsen, and Lacey Andrews Gale, eds., *Research Methods in Conflict Settings: A View from Below* (London: Cambridge University Press, 2013).

33. Mary B. Anderson, *Do No Harm: How Aid Can Support Peace—or War* (London: Lynne Rienner, 1999); United State Institute of Peace, *Conflict Sensitivity in Peacebuilding* (Washington, DC: Gandhi-King Global Academy, 2021). For some recent examples in political science, see Diana Kapiszewski, Lauren M. MacLean, and Benjamin L. Read, *Field Research in Political Science: Practices and Principles* (New York: Cambridge University Press, 2015); Kate Cronin-Furman and Milli Lake, "Ethics Abroad:

Fieldwork in Fragile and Violent Contexts," *PS: Political Science & Politics* 51, no. 3 (2018): 607–614; Anastasia Shesterinina, "Ethics, Empathy, and Fear in r-Research on Violent Conflict," *Journal of Peace Research* 56, no. 2 (2019): 190–202; Kevin Koehler et al., *Safer Field Research in the Social Sciences: A Guide to Human and Digital Security in Hostile Environments* (London: Sage, 2020), 1–176; Peter Krause and Ora Szekely, *Stories from the Field: A Guide to Navigating Fieldwork in Political Science* (New York: Columbia University Press, 2020); Mara Redlich Revkin, "Competitive Governance and Displacement Decisions Under Rebel Rule: Evidence from the Islamic State in Iraq," *Journal of Conflict Resolution* 65, no. 1 (2020): 46–80; Séverine Autesserre, *The Frontlines of Peace: An Insider's Guide to Changing the World* (Oxford: Oxford University Press, 2021); Jesse Driscoll, *Doing Global Fieldwork: A Social Scientist's Guide to Mixed-methods Research Far from Home* (New York: Columbia University Press, 2021); Roger Mac Ginty, Roddy Brett, and Birte Vogel, *The Companion to Peace and Conflict Fieldwork* (London: Springer, 2021); Sarah E. Parkinson, "(Dis)courtesy Bias: 'Methodological Cognates,' Data Validity, and Ethics in Violence-Adjacent Research," *Comparative Political Studies* 55, no. 3 (March 2022): 420–450.
34. IIACSS is also referred to as Al Mustakella for Research.
35. Interviewees are referred to by either pseudonyms or interview numbers (e.g., respondent A01) in order to protect their privacy. Table B.1 in appendix B provides descriptive statistics for each interviewee.
36. Members of the Iraqi Army, Iraqi Federal Police, and pro-government militias were intentionally excluded from the interviewee pool.

2. Survival Repertoires in Wartime

1. Ben Birnbaum, "Allawi Cites 'Dictatorship,' Iranian Control in Iraq," *Washington Times*, March 22, 2012, https://www.washingtontimes.com/news/2012/mar/22/allawi-cites-dictatorship-iranian-control-iraq.
2. Ralph Sundberg, Kristine Eck, and Joakim Kreutz, "Introducing the UCDP Non-state Conflict Dataset," *Journal of Peace Research* 49, no. 2 (2012): 351–362.
3. "Refugee Data Finder," United Nations High Commissioner for Refugees, accessed November 5, 2023, https://www.unhcr.org/refugee-statistics.
4. John Mueller, "The Banality of 'Ethnic War,'" *International Security* 25, no. 1 (2000): 42–70; Kalyvas, *The Logic of Violence in Civil War*; Jason Lyall, Kosuke Imai, and Graeme Blair, "Explaining Support for Combatants in Wartime"; Berman, Felter, and Shapiro, *Small Wars, Big Data*.
5. Kaplan, *Resisting War*; Schon, *Surviving the War in Syria*; Jeffrey K. Hass, *Wartime Suffering and Survival: The Human Condition Under Siege in the Blockade of Leningrad, 1941-1944* (New York: Oxford University Press, 2021); Jackson, *Negotiating Survival*; Shesterinina, *Mobilizing in Uncertainty*.
6. Scholars have conceptualized contemporary civil wars as "new new" civil wars, "multi-party" civil wars, "complex conflicts," "asymmetric conflicts," "hybrid" or

"grey zone" conflicts, and "surrogate warfare." For example, see Mary Kaldor, *New and Old Wars: Organised Violence in Global Era* (Stanford, CA: Stanford University Press, 2006); Fotini Christia, *Alliance Formation in Civil Wars* (New York: Cambridge University Press, 2012); Adam Day, Vanda Felbab-Brown, and Fanar Haddad, *Mastering the Gray Zone: Understanding a Changing Era of Conflict* (Carlisle, PA: Strategic Studies Institute, U.S. Army War College, December 2014); Nynke Salverda, "Complex Conflicts: Causes and Consequences of Multiparty Civil Wars" (PhD diss., Queensland University of Technology, 2017); Barbara F. Walter, "The New New Civil Wars," *Annual Review of Political Science* 20 (2017): 469–486; Berman, Felter, and Shapiro, *Small Wars, Big Data*; Andreas Krieg and Jean-Marc Rickli, *Surrogate Warfare: the Transformation of War in the Twenty-First Century* (Washington, DC: Georgetown University Press, 2019); Laia Balcells and Jessica A. Stanton, "Violence Against Civilians During Armed Conflict: Moving Beyond the Macro- and Micro-Level Divide," *Annual Review of Political Science* 24 (2020): 45–69; Adam Day, Vanda Felbab-Brown, and Fanar Haddad, *Hybrid Conflict, Hybrid Peace: How Militias and Paramilitary Groups Shape Post-conflict Transitions* (New York: United Nations University, April 2020); J. Andrés Gannon et al., "The Shadow of Deterrence: Why Capable Actors Engage in Contests Short of War," *Journal of Conflict Resolution*, online first, April 20, 2023, https://doi.org/10.1177/00220027231166345.

7. Jeffrey T. Checkel, *Transnational Dynamics of Civil War* (New York: Cambridge University Press, 2013).
8. Marc Lynch, *The New Arab Wars: Uprisings and Anarchy in the Middle East* (New York: PublicAffairs, 2016), 4.
9. Ariel Ahram, *Proxy Warriors: the Rise and Fall of State-Sponsored Militias* (Palo Alto, CA: Stanford University Press, 2011); Andrew Mumford, *Proxy Warfare* (Cambridge: Polity Press, 2013); Tyrone L. Groh, *Proxy War: The Least Bad Option* (Palo Alto, CA: Stanford University Press, 2019).
10. Marc Lynch, "The End of the Middle East: How an Old Map Distorts a New Reality," *Foreign Affairs* 101, no. 2 (April 2022): 58–67.
11. Adam Baczko, Gilles Dorronsoro, and Arthur Quesnay, *Civil War in Syria: Mobilization and Competing Social Orders* (New York: Cambridge University Press, 2018), 90.
12. Stathis N. Kalyvas and Laia Balcells, "International System and Technologies of Rebellion: How the End of the Cold War Shaped Internal Conflict," *American Political Science Review* 104, no. 3 (August 2010): 415–429.
13. Prakash Adhikari, "Conflict-Induced Displacement, Understanding the Causes of Flight," *American Journal of Political Science* 57, no. 1 (2013): 82–89; Schon, *Surviving the War in Syria*; Akisato Suzuki, Djordje Stefanovic, and Neophytos Loizides, "Displacement and the Expectation of Political Violence: Evidence from Bosnia," *Conflict Management and Peace Science* 38, no. 5 (2020): 1–19.
14. Walter, "The New New Civil Wars."
15. R. Charli Carpenter, "Recognizing Gender-Based Violence Against Civilian Men and Boys in Conflict Situations," *Security Dialogue* 37, no. 1 (2106): 83–103; Magdalena Suerbaum, *Masculinities and Displacement in the Middle East: Syrian Refugees in Egypt*

(London: Bloomsbury, 2020); Anne-Kathrin Kreft and Mattias Agerberg, "Imperfect Victims? Civilian Men, Vulnerability, and Policy Preferences," *American Political Science Review*, online first, April 19, 2023, https://doi.org/10.1017/S0003055423000345.

16. Torunn Wimpelmann, *The Pitfalls of Protection: Gender, Violence, and Power in Afghanistan* (Berkeley: University of California Press, 2017).
17. Rebecca Horn et al., "Women's Perceptions of Effects of War on Intimate Partner Violence and Gender Roles in Two Post-conflict West African Countries: Consequences and Unexpected Opportunities," *Conflict and Health* 8, no. 1 (2014): 1–13; Beth L. Rubenstein et al., "Predictors of Interpersonal Violence in the Household in Humanitarian Settings: A Systematic Review," *Trauma, Violence, & Abuse* 21, no. 1 (2020): 31–44; Linda Jolof et al., "Experiences of Armed Conflicts and Forced Migration Among Women from Countries in the Middle East, Balkans, and Africa: A Systematic Review of Qualitative Studies," *Conflict and Health* 16, no. 46 (2022): 1–16.
18. Jose and Medie, "Understanding Why and How Civilians Resort to Self-Protection in Armed Conflict"; Jose and Medie, "Civilian Self-Protection and Civilian Targeting in Armed Conflicts"; Marie E. Berry, "Radicalising Resilience: Mothering, Solidarity, and Interdependence Among Women Survivors of War," *Journal of International Relations and Development* 25, no. 4 (2022): 946–966.
19. Jakana L. Thomas, "Sisters Are Doing It for Themselves: How Female Combatants Help Generate Gender-Inclusive Peace Agreements in Civil Wars," *American Political Science Review*, online first, June 26, 2023, https://doi.org/10.1017/S0003055423000461.
20. Ana Arjona, "Civilian Cooperation and Non-cooperation with Non-state Armed Groups"; Jackson, *Negotiating Survival*.
21. Article 3 of the 1958 Geneva Convention defines noncombatants as "persons taking no active part in the hostilities." See Jean Pictet, *The Geneva Conventions of 12 August 1949: Geneva Convention Relative to the Protection of Civilian Persons in Time of War*, vol. 4 (Geneva: International Committee of the Red Cross, 1958).
22. Conflict to Peace Lab, *Report: Exploring Obstacles to Social Cohesion in the Aftermath of Violent Conflict* (Columbus: Mershon Center for International Security Studies, Ohio State University, November 2019), https://mershoncenter.osu.edu/sites/default/files/2020-02/C2P%20Report_Interactive.pdf.
23. Landau-Wells, "Dealing with Danger"; Milliff, "Facts Shape Feelings"; Alex Mintz, Nicholas A. Valentino, and Carly Wayne, *Beyond Rationality: Behavioral Political Science in the 21st Century* (New York: Cambridge University Press, 2021).
24. Gerd Gigerenzer and Wolfgang Gaissmaier, "Heuristic Decision Making," *Annual Review of Psychology* 62 (2011): 454.
25. Petersen, *Resistance and Rebellion*, 101.
26. Richard H. Thaler, *Misbehaving: The Making of Behavioral Economics* (New York: W. W. Norton, 2015).
27. Ellen Peters et al., "Numeracy and Decision Making," *Psychological Science* 17, no. 5 (2006): 407–413.

28. Gerd Gigerenzer and Reinhard Selten, *Bounded Rationality: The Adaptive Toolbox* (Cambridge, MA: MIT Press, 2002); Daniel Kahneman, *Thinking, Fast and Slow* (New York: Farrar, Strauss and Giroux, 2011).
29. Walter B. Cannon, "The James-Lange Theory of Emotions: A Critical Examination and an Alternative Theory," *American Journal of Psychology* 39, nos. 1–4 (1927): 106–124; Jeffrey Alan Gray, *The Psychology of Fear and Stress* (New York: Cambridge University Press, 1987); Danielle J. Maack, Erin Buchanan, and John Young, "Development and Psychometric Investigation of an Inventory to Assess Fight, Flight, and Freeze Tendencies: The Fight, Flight, Freeze Questionnaire," *Cognitive Behaviour Therapy* 44, no. 2 (2015): 117–127.
30. George Loewenstein and Jennifer S. Lerner, "The Role of Affect in Decision Making," in *Oxford Handbook of Affective Sciences*, ed. K. R. Scherer, R. J. Davidson, and H. H. Goldsmith (New York: Oxford University Press, 2003), 619–642; Dacher Keltner and Jennifer S. Lerner, "Emotion," in *Handbook of Social Psychology*, vol. 1, ed. Susan T Fiske, Daniel T. Gilbert, and Gardner Lindzey (New York: Wiley Online Library, 2010), 317–352, https://psycnet.apa.org/record/2010-03505-009.
31. Paul Slovic et al., "Risk as Analysis and Risk as Feelings: Some Thoughts About Affect, Reason, Risk, and Rationality," *Risk Analysis: An International Journal* 24, no. 2 (2004): 311–322.
32. Jennifer S. Lerner et al., "Emotion and Decision Making," *Annual Review of Psychology* 66 (2015): 799–823.
33. Landau-Wells, "Dealing with Danger."
34. Gerd Gigerenzer and Peter M. Todd, "Fast and Frugal Heuristics: The Adaptive Toolbox," in *Simple Heuristics That Make Us Smart*, ed. Gerd Gigerenzer and Peter M. Todd (New York: Oxford University Press, 1999), 3–34.
35. Gerd Gigerenzer, "Dread Risk, September 11, and Fatal Traffic Accidents," *Psychological Science* 15, no. 4 (2004): 286–287.
36. Wendy Pearlman, "Emotions and the Microfoundations of the Arab Uprisings," *Perspectives on Politics* 11, no. 2 (2013): 387–409.
37. Finkel, *Ordinary Jews*, 52.
38. Milliff, "Making Sense, Making Choices."
39. Shesterinina, *Mobilizing in Uncertainty*.
40. Marie E. Berry, *War, Women, and Power: From Violence to Mobilization in Rwanda and Bosnia-Herzegovina* (New York: Cambridge University Press, 2018).
41. Kanchan Chandra, "What Is Ethnic Identity and Does It Matter?," *Annual Review Political Science* 9 (2006): 397–424; James Habyarimana et al., *Coethnicity: Diversity and the Dilemmas of Collective Action* (New York: Russell Sage Foundation, 2009); Michael Kalin and Nicholas Sambanis, "How to Think About Social Identity," *Annual Review of Political Science* 21 (2018): 239–257.
42. Lyall, Shiraito, and Imai, "Coethnic Bias and Wartime Informing."
43. Omar Shahabudin McDoom, "The Psychology of Threat in Intergroup Conflict: Emotions, Rationality, and Opportunity in the Rwandan Genocide," *International Security* 37, no. 2 (2012): 119–155.

44. Christopher Blattman, *Why We Fight: The Roots of War and the Paths to Peace* (New York: Viking, 2022), 153.
45. Elinor Ostrom, "A Behavioral Approach to the Rational Choice Theory of Collective Action: Presidential Address, American Political Science Association, 1997," *American Political Science Review* 92, no. 1 (1998): 1–22.
46. Rachel M. Stein, *Vengeful Citizens, Violent States: A Theory of War and Revenge* (New York: Cambridge University Press, 2019).
47. Individuals devoted to sacred values or causes are more likely than their secular compatriots to make costly sacrifices, including radical acts of altruism such as fighting and dying to protect one's community. Scott Atran, *In Gods We Trust: The Evolutionary Landscape of Religion* (New York: Oxford University Press, 2002); Philip E. Tetlock, "Thinking the Unthinkable: Sacred Values and Taboo Cognitions," *Trends in Cognitive Sciences* 7, no. 7 (2003): 320–324.
48. Laia Balcells, *Rivalry and Revenge: The Politics of Violence During Civil War* (New York: Cambridge University Press, 2017).
49. Lisa Wedeen, *Ambiguities of Domination: Politics, Rhetoric, and Symbols in Contemporary Syria* (Chicago: University of Chicago Press, 1999); Christia, *Alliance Formation in Civil Wars*; Wendy Pearlman, "Narratives of Fear in Syria," *Perspectives on Politics* 14, no. 1 (2016): 21–37; Lisa Wedeen, *Authoritarian Apprehensions: Ideology, Judgment, and Mourning in Syria* (Chicago: University of Chicago Press, 2019).
50. A community's collective memory can be shaped and spread by local elites and formal institutions (official memory) or perpetuated informally by community members and informal institutions (unofficial memory). Geneviève Zubrzycki and Anna Woźny, "The Comparative Politics of Collective Memory," *Annual Review of Sociology* 46 (2020): 175–194.
51. Carlos Bozzoli, Tilman Brueck, and Tony Muhumuza, "Does War Influence Individual Expectations?," *Economics Letters* 113, no. 3 (2011): 288–291.
52. Kurt Weyland, "The Arab Spring: Why the Surprising Similarities with the Revolutionary Wave of 1848?," *Perspectives on Politics* 10, no. 4 (2012): 917–934.
53. Jason Lyall, Yang-Yang Zhou, and Kosuke Imai, "Can Economic Assistance Shape Combatant Support in Wartime? Experimental Evidence from Afghanistan," *American Political Science Review* 114, no. 1 (2020): 126–143.
54. Abraham H. Maslow, *Motivation and Personality* (New York: Harper and Row, 1954); Arie W. Kruglanski, Jocelyn J. Bélanger, and Rohan Gunaratna, *The Three Pillars of Radicalization: Needs, Narratives, and Networks* (New York: Oxford University Press, 2019); Munqith Dagher et al., *ISIS in Iraq*.
55. Pearlman, "Emotions and the Microfoundations of the Arab Uprisings"; Lerner et al., "Emotion and Decision Making."
56. Insurgents can effectively govern without maintaining physical control of territory. Remote monitoring and enforcement work through selective deploying incentives and punishments. In Afghanistan, the Taliban introduced mobile shariʿa courts as a means of providing governance without maintaining a constant presence in the community, thereby exposing themselves to ISAF counterinsurgency

operations. The mobile courts not only facilitated Taliban control in communities beyond their immediate sphere of influence, but also delegitimated public courts by adjudicating disputes more transparently and effectively than the government. Antonio Giustozzi, "The Taliban's 'Military Courts,'" *Small Wars & Insurgencies* 25, no. 2 (2014): 284–296; Florian Weigand, "Afghanistan's Taliban—Legitimate Jihadists or Coercive Extremists?," *Journal of Intervention and Statebuilding* 11, no. 3 (2017): 359–381; Donald Grasse, Renard Sexton, and Austin Wright, "The Logic and Impacts of Rebel Public Services Provision: Evidence from Taliban Courts in Afghanistan" (Unpublished manuscript, 2022).

57. Robert A. Pape, *Dying to Win: The Strategic Logic of Suicide Terrorism* (New York: Random House, 2005); Luke N. Condra et al., "The Effect of Civilian Casualties in Afghanistan and Iraq" (Working Paper 16152, National Bureau of Economic Research, 2010), https://www.nber.org/papers/w16152; Jason Lyall, "Are Coethnics More Effective Counterinsurgents? Evidence from the Second Chechen War," *American Political Science Review* 104, no. 1 (2010): 1–20.

58. David M. Edelstein, *Occupational Hazards: Success and Failure in Military Occupation* (Ithaca, NY: Cornell University Press, 2011); Alexander B. Downes and Jonathan Monten, "Forced to Be Free?: Why Foreign-Imposed Regime Change Rarely Leads to Democratization," *International Security* 37, no. 4 (2013): 90–131; Alexander B. Downes and Lindsey A. O'Rourke, "You Can't Always Get What You Want: Why Foreign-Imposed Regime Change Seldom Improves Interstate Relations," *International Security* 41, no. 2 (2016): 43–89; Matthew Adam Kocher, Adria K. Lawrence, and Nuno P. Monteiro, "Nationalism, Collaboration, and Resistance: France Under Nazi Occupation," *International Security* 43, no. 2 (2018): 117–150; Karl C. Kaltenthaler, Daniel M. Silverman, and Munqith M. Dagher, "Nationalism, Threat, and Support for External Intervention: Evidence from Iraq," *Security Studies* 29, no. 3 (2020): 1–25.

59. Lyall, Imai, and Blair, "Explaining Support for Combatants in Wartime."

60. Luke N. Condra and Jacob N. Shapiro, "Who Takes the Blame? The Strategic Effects of Collateral Damage," *American Journal of Political Science* 56, no. 1 (2012): 167–187.

61. Sidney G. Tarrow and Charles Tilly, "Contentious Politics and Social Movements," in *The Oxford Handbook of Comparative Politics*, ed. Carlos Boix and Susan Stokes (New York: Oxford University Press, 2007), 435–460; Lorenzo Bosi and Stefan Malthaner, "Political Violence," in *The Oxford Handbook of Social Movements*, ed. Donatella Della Porta and Mario Diani (New York: Oxford University Press, 2015), 439–451; Charles Tilly and Sidney G. Tarrow, *Contentious Politics*, 2nd ed. (New York: Oxford University Press, 2015); Mac Ginty, *Everyday Peace*.

62. Charles Tilly, "To Explain Political Processes," *American Journal of Sociology* 100, no. 6 (1995): 1594–1610; Andrew Abbott, *Time Matters: On Theory and Method* (Chicago: University of Chicago Press, 2001); Charles Tilly, "Social Boundary Mechanisms," *Philosophy of the Social Sciences* 34, no. 2 (2004): 211–236; Rawi Abdelal et al., *Measuring Identity: A Guide for Social Scientists* (New York: Cambridge University Press, 2009).

63. Bosi and Malthaner, "Political Violence," 440.

64. Special thanks to Tiina Hyyppä for challenging the author on this point.

65. In the MENA region, the most common forms of autonomy involve ethnic separatism and secession, two repertoires that fall outside of the range of autonomous strategies analyzed in the existing literature. See, for example, Avant et al., *Civil Action and the Dynamics of Violence*.
66. Jose and Medie, "Understanding Why and How Civilians Resort to Self-Protection in Armed Conflict"; Jose and Medie, "Civilian Self-Protection and Civilian Targeting in Armed Conflicts."
67. Rose McDermott, *Risk-Taking in International Politics: Prospect Theory in American Foreign Policy* (Ann Arbor: University of Michigan Press, 2001); Kahneman, *Thinking, Fast and Slow*.
68. Lucy Foulkes and Sarah-Jayne Blakemore, "Studying Individual Differences in Human Adolescent Brain Development," *Nature Neuroscience* 21, no. 3 (2018): 315–323; Lisa J. Knoll et al., "Age-Related Differences in Social Influence on Risk Perception Depend on the Direction of Influence," *Journal of Adolescence* 60 (2017): 53–63.
69. Dustin Pardini et al., "Risk and Protective Factors for Gun Violence in Male Juvenile Offenders," *Journal of Clinical Child & Adolescent Psychology* 50, no. 3 (2021): 337–352; Ilana Seff et al., "Predicting Adolescent Boys' and Young Men's Perpetration of Youth Violence in Colombia," *International Journal of Injury Control and Safety Promotion* 29, no. 1 (2022): 123–131.
70. Sheryl Silver Ochayon, "Armed Resistance in the Ghettos: The Dilemma of Revolt," Yad Vesham: The World Holocaust Remembrance Center, accessed October 17, 2023, https://www.yadvashem.org/articles/general/armed-resistance-dilemma-of-revolt.html; Emily Fishbein and Nu Nu Lusan, "Young, Rebellious and the Myanmar Military's 'Worst Enemy,'" *Al Jazeera*, October 5, 2022, https://www.aljazeera.com/news/2022/10/5/young-rebellious-and-the-myanmar-militarys-worst-enemy.
71. Hass, *Wartime Suffering and Survival*, 9. Emphasis in the original.
72. James C. Scott, *Weapons of the Weak: Everyday Forms of Peasant Resistance* (New Haven, CT: Yale University Press, 1985); James C. Scott, *Domination and the Arts of Resistance: Hidden Transcripts* (New Haven, CT: Yale University Press, 1990); James C. Scott, *The Art of Not Being Governed* (New Haven, CT: Yale University Press, 2010).
73. Cassy Dorff observes that nonviolent resistance is often more effective in prolonged civil conflicts, as it is better able to mobilize broader segments of society and gain international support. See Dorff, "Violent and Nonviolent Resistance in Contexts of Prolonged Crisis."
74. Anna Johansson and Stellan Vinthagen, *Conceptualizing "Everyday Resistance": A Transdisciplinary Approach* (London: Routledge, 2019), 19.
75. Omar Mohammad, "Cycling Against the Islamic State," *Mosul Eye*, December 7, 2016, https://mosuleye.wordpress.com/2016/12/07/cycling-against-the-islamic-state.
76. "The Sex State" (*ad-dawlah al-jinsiyya*) is a double entendre primarily used as an insult for IS fighters who engaged in the anti-Islamic practices of human trafficking, forced marriage, and rape. Ahmed Al-Rawi, "Anti-ISIS Humor: Cultural

Resistance of Radical Ideology," *Politics, Religion & Ideology* 17, no. 1 (2016): 52–68; Balsam Mustafa, "The Bigh Daddy Show: The Potentiality and Shortcomings of Countering Islamic State Through Animated Satire," *Digest of Middle East Studies* 31, no. 2 (2022): 113–130.

77. Erika Chenoweth, *Civil Resistance: What Everyone Needs to Know* (New York: Oxford University Press, 2021).
78. Sebastian Van Baalen, "Civilian Protest in Civil War: Insights from Côte d'Ivoire," *American Political Science Review*, online first, June 14, 2023, https://doi.org/10.1017/S0003055423000564.
79. Svensson et al., *Confronting the Caliphate*, 108.
80. Svensson et al., 121–122.
81. Mai Hassan and Ahmed Kodouda, "Sudan's Uprising: The Fall of a Dictator," *Journal of Democracy* 30, no. 4 (2019): 89–103.
82. Andrew Marantz, "How to Stop a Power Grab," *New Yorker*, November 16, 2020, https://www.newyorker.com/magazine/2020/11/23/how-to-stop-a-power-grab.
83. Ghaith Abdul-Ahad, "After the Liberation of Mosul, an Orgy of Killing," *The Guardian*, November 21, 2017, https://www.theguardian.com/world/2017/nov/21/after-the-liberation-of-mosulan-orgy-of-killing.
84. Edelstein, *Occupational Hazards*; Michael Hechter, *Alien Rule* (New York: Cambridge University Press, 2013); Alexander B. Downes, *Catastrophic Success: Why Foreign-Imposed Regime Change Goes Wrong* (Ithaca, NY: Cornell University Press, 2021).
85. Callen et al. "Violence and Risk Preference"; Bellows and Miguel, "War and Local Collective Action in Sierra Leone"; Christopher Blattman, "From Violence to Voting: War and Political Participation in Uganda," *American Political Science Review* 103, no. 2 (2009): 231–247; Voors et al., "Violent Conflict and Behavior."
86. Austin J. Knuppe, "Blowback or Overblown? Why Civilians Under Threat Support Invasive Foreign Intervention," *Journal of Peace Research* 59, no. 4 (2022): 478–494.
87. Jonah Schulhofer-Wohl, *Quagmire in Civil War* (New York: Cambridge University Press, 2020); Nils Hägerdal, *Friend or Foe: Militia Intelligence and Ethnic Violence in the Lebanese Civil War* (New York: Columbia University Press, 2021); Munira Khayyat, *A Landscape of War: Ecologies of Resistance and Survival in South Lebanon* (Berkeley: University of California Press, 2022); Sarah E. Parkinson, *Beyond the Lines: Social Networks and Palestinian Militant Organizations in Wartime Lebanon* (Ithaca, NY: Cornell University Press, 2023).
88. "West Bank Anger Boils as Jenin Becomes Hotbed of Resistance," *Al Jazeera*, January 9, 2021, https://www.aljazeera.com/news/2021/9/1/west-bank-anger-boils-as-jenin-becomes-hotbed-of-resistance.
89. Stephen Biddle, Jeffrey A. Friedman, and Jacob N. Shapiro, "Testing the Surge: Why Did Violence Decline in Iraq in 2007?," *International Security* 37, no. 1 (2012): 7–40; Carter Malkasian, *Illusions of Victory: The Anbar Awakening and the Rise of the Islamic State* (New York: Oxford University Press, 2017).

90. Erin Baines and Emily Paddon, "'This Is How We Survived': Civilian Agency and Humanitarian Protection," *Security Dialogue* 43, no. 3 (2012): 236.
91. Kaplan, *Resisting War*, 43.
92. Kateryna Kibarova, "We Did Not Ask for 'Liberation': A Resident of Bucha Tells Her Story," *Persuasion*, May 4, 2022, https://www.persuasion.community/p/bucha-testimony.
93. Ana Arjona, "Subnational Units, the Locus of Choice, and Theory Building: The Case of Civilian Agency in Civil War," in *Subnational Research in Comparative Politics*, ed. Agustina Giraudy, Eduardo Moncada, and Richard Snyder (New York: Cambridge University Press, 2019), 224.
94. Kaplan, *Resisting War*, 45–46.
95. Ana Arjona, *Rebelocracy: Social Order in the Colombian Civil War* (New York: Cambridge University Press, 2016).
96. Jana Krause, *Resilient Communities: Non-violence and Civilian Agency in Communal War* (New York: Cambridge University Press, 2018).
97. Jackson, *Negotiating Survival*.
98. Christopher Zürcher, "Nonviolent Communal Strategies in Insurgencies: Case Study on Afghanistan," in *Civil Action and the Dynamics of Violence*, ed. Deborah Avant et al. (New York: Oxford University Press, 2019), 211–212.
99. Tiina Hyyppä, "Council in War: Civilocracy, Order and Local Organisation in Daraya During the Syrian War," *Small Wars & Insurgencies* 34, no. 1 (2023): 52–80; Sebastian Van Baalen, "Local Elites, Civil Resistance, and the Responsiveness of Rebel Governance in Côte d'Ivoire," *Journal of Peace Research* 58, no. 5 (2021): 930–944.
100. Elisabeth Jean Wood, *Insurgent Collective Action and Civil War in El Salvador* (New York: Cambridge University Press, 2003), 136–137.
101. Ahram, *Proxy Warriors*; Krieg and Rickli, *Surrogate Warfare*.
102. Helen Lackner, *Yemen: Poverty and Conflict* (London: Routledge, 2022); Stacey Philbrick Yadav, *Yemen in the Shadow of Transition: Pursuing Justice Amid War* (New York: Oxford University Press, 2022).
103. Benny Morris, *1948: A History of the First Arab-Israeli War* (New Haven, CT: Yale University Press, 2008).
104. Ahmed Fouad, "Egypt's Copts Have No Plans to Arm Youth Groups," *Al Monitor*, July 3, 2017, https://www.al-monitor.com/originals/2017/07/egypt-scouts-christians-military-training-militias-security.html.
105. Martin Roux, "Securing Coptic Churches: The Necessary Role of the Scouts," *Mada*, August 8, 2018, https://www.madamasr.com/en/2018/04/08/feature/society/securing-coptic-churches-the-necessary-role-of-the-scouts/#:~:text=The%20role%20of%20the%20scouts,those%20who%20volunteer%20at%20St.
106. Yaniv Voller, "Rethinking Armed Groups and Order: Syria and the Rise of Militiatocracies," *International Affairs* 98, no. 3 (2022): 853–871.
107. Krause, *Resilient Communities*, 78.
108. Ami C. Carpenter, "Havens in a Firestorm: Perspectives from Baghdad on Resilience to Sectarian Violence," *Civil Wars* 14, no. 2 (2012): 196.

109. Jackson, *Negotiating Survival*, 6.
110. Schubiger, "State Violence and Wartime Civilian Agency," 5.
111. Finkel, *Ordinary Jews*; Hass, *Wartime Survival and Suffering*.
112. Kalyvas, *The Logic of Violence in Civil War*, 119.
113. Kalyvas, 103.
114. Kalyvas, "Ethnic Defection in Civil War"; Lyall, "Are Coethnics More Effective Counterinsurgents?"; Jennifer M. Larson, "Networks and Interethnic Cooperation," *Journal of Politics* 79, no. 2 (2017): 546–559.
115. Kalyvas, *The Logic of Violence in Civil War*, 40.
116. Mara Redlich Revkin, "Competitive Governance and Displacement Decisions Under Rebel Rule: Evidence from the Islamic State in Iraq," *Journal of Conflict Resolution* 65, no. 1 (2020): 46–80; Revkin and Wood, "The Islamic State's Pattern of Sexual Violence."
117. Victoria Cetorelli and Sareta Ashraph, *A Demographic Documentation of ISIS's Attack on the Yazidi Village of Kocho* (London: London School of Economics, Middle East Centre, June 2019), https://www.un.org/sexualviolenceinconflict/wp-content/uploads/2019/08/report/a-demographic-documentation-of-isiss-attack-on-the-yazidi-village-of-kocho/Cetorelli_Demographic_documentation_ISIS_attack.pdf.
118. Arjona, "Subnational Units, the Locus of Choice, and Theory Building."
119. Hägerdal, *Friend or Foe*, 57–60.
120. Kocher, Lawrence, and Monteiro, "Nationalism, Collaboration, and Resistance," 126.
121. Bruce Hoffman, *Anonymous Soldiers: The Struggle for Israel, 1917-1947* (New York: Vintage, 2016).
122. Helen Lackner, *Yemen in Crisis: Road to War* (London: Verso Books, 2019), 177–181.
123. Sigrid Weber, "Controlling a Moving World: Territorial Control, Displacement and the Spread of Civilian Targeting in Iraq" (unpublished manuscript, 2023); Wood, "The Social Processes of Civil War"; Christia, *Alliance Formation in Civil Wars*; Abbey Steele, *Democracy and Displacement in Colombia's Civil War* (Ithaca, NY: Cornell University Press, 2017).
124. Devorah Manekin, "Violence Against Civilians in the Second Intifada: The Moderating Effect of Armed Group Structure on Opportunistic Violence," *Comparative Political Studies* 46, no. 10 (2013): 1273–1300.
125. Atran, *In Gods We Trust*; Kruglanski, Bélanger, and Gunaratna, *The Three Pillars of Radicalization*; Dagher et al., *ISIS in Iraq*.
126. Clara Pretus et al., "Neural and Behavioral Correlates of Sacred Values and Vulnerability to Violent Extremism," *Frontiers in Psychology* 9 (2018), https://doi.org/10.3389/fpsyg.2018.02462; Ángel Gómez et al., "Why People Enter and Embrace Violent Groups," *Frontiers in Psychology* 11 (2021) https://doi.org/10.3389/fpsyg.2020.614657; Jonathan Pickney, Michael Niconchuk, and Sarah Ryan, *Motives, Benefits, and Sacred Values: Examining the Psychology of Nonviolent Action and Violent Extremism*, Peaceworks Report No. 170 (Washington, DC: United States Institute of Peace, November 2021).

127. Anne Speckhard and Molly D. Ellenberg, "ISIS in Their Own Words: Recruitment History, Motivations for Joining, Travel, Experiences in ISIS, and Disillusionment Over Time-Analysis of 220 In-Depth Interviews of ISIS Returnees, Defectors and Prisoners," *Journal of Strategic Security* 13, no. 1 (2020): 82–127.
128. Kalyvas, "The Ontology of 'Political Violence,'" 481.

3. The Rise and Fall of the Islamic State, 2011–2017

Epigraphs: Fallujah Memorandum (author unknown), quoted in Haroro J. Ingram, Craig Whiteside, and Charlie Winter, *The ISIS Reader: Milestone Texts of the Islamic State Movement* (New York: Oxford University Press, 2020), 122. Lieutenant Colonel Muntadher, quoted in Ghaith Abdul-Ahad, *A Stranger in Your Own City: Travels in the Middle East's Long War* (New York: Knopf, 2023), 315.

1. Kalyvas, "The Ontology of 'Political Violence,'" 476.
2. Iraqi minorities in Kirkuk expressed a similar sentiment after the defeat of IS in their community. As one focus group participant explained, "I was born in 2003, I don't know what happened during Saddam Hussein's rule, but from what I hear from my parents and grandparents, the time period during which Saddam Hussein ruled was better than now. We [as Sabeans] want to move outside the governorate and live in Erbil." Matthew Cancian, Richard Nielsen, and Austin Knuppe, "Deliberation and Ethnic Cooperation in Kirkuk."
3. Kanan Makiya, *Republic of Fear: The Politics of Modern Iraq* (Berkeley: University of California Press, 1998); Fanar Haddad, *Sectarianism in Iraq: Antagonistic Visions of Unity* (New York: Oxford University Press, 2011); Amatzia Baram, *Saddam Husayn and Islam, 1968-2003: Baʿthi Iraq from Secularism to Faith* (Washington, DC: Woodrow Wilson Center Press, 2014); Lisa Blaydes, *State of Repression: Iraq Under Saddam Hussein* (Princeton, NJ: Princeton University Press, 2018); Samuel Helfont, *Compulsion in Religion: Saddam Hussein, Islam, and the Roots of Insurgencies in Iraq* (New York: Oxford University Press, 2018).
4. For recent research on the surge, see Peter D. Feaver, "The Right to Be Right: Civil-Military Relations and the Iraq Surge Decision," *International Security* 35, no. 4 (2011): 87–125; Stephen Biddle, Jeffrey A. Friedman, and Jacob N. Shapiro, "Testing the Surge: Why Did Violence Decline in Iraq in 2007?," *International Security* 37, no. 1 (2012): 7–40; Peter R. Mansoor, *Surge: My Journey with General David Petraeus and the Remaking of the Iraq War* (New Haven, CT: Yale University Press, 2013); Malkasian, *Illusions of Victory*; Joel D. Rayburn and Frank K. Sobchak, *The U.S. Army in Iraq: Surge and Withdrawal (2007-2011)* (Washington, DC: Operation Iraqi Freedom Study Group, Office of the Chief of Staff, U.S. Army, January 2019); Timothy Andrews Sayle et al., *The Last Card: Inside George W. Bush's Decision to Surge in Iraq* (Ithaca, NY: Cornell University Press, 2019).
5. Andrew W. Bausch, "Coup-Proofing and Military Inefficiencies: An Experiment," *International Interactions* 44, no. 1 (2018): 1–32.

6. Malkasian, *Illusions of Victory*, 167.
7. The Supreme Council for the Islamic Revolution in Iraq changed its name to the Islamic Supreme Council of Iraq in May 2007 to reflect its perceived success in the revolution to overthrow the Baʿthist regime. Caroleen Marji Sayej, *Patriotic Ayatollahs: Nationalism in Post-Saddam Iraq* (Ithaca, NY: Cornell University Press, 2018), 74–75.
8. Sayej, *Patriotic Ayatollahs*, 75.
9. Fearing increasing Iranian hegemony over Iraqi politics, the Obama administration also publicly supported a second Maliki term. Emma Sky, *The Unraveling: High Hopes and Missed Opportunities in Iraq* (New York: PublicAffairs, 2015), 330.
10. "Arab Barometer Wave III (2012–2014)," Arab Barometer, accessed October 19, 2023, http://www.arabbarometer.org/content/arab-barometer-iii-0.
11. Toby Dodge, *Iraq—From War to a New Authoritarianism* (London: Routledge, 2013).
12. By 2013, dissenters within the Daʿwa movement worked with Sistani to prevent Maliki for securing a third term in the 2014 parliamentary elections.
13. Ibrahim Al-Marashi, "Iraq and the Arab Spring: From Protests to the Rise of ISIS," in *The Arab Spring: The Hope and Reality of the Uprisings*, ed. Mark L. Haas and David W. Lesch, 2nd ed. (London: Routledge, 2016), 147–164.
14. Marc Lynch, *The Arab Uprising: The Unfinished Revolutions of the New Middle East* (New York: PublicAffairs, 2013), 115.
15. R. Chuck Mason, *U.S.-Iraq Withdrawal/Status of Forces Agreement: Issues for Congressional Oversight*, CRS Report No. R40011 (Washington, DC: Congressional Research Service, January 2011).
16. Neta C. Crawford, "Blood and Treasure: United States Budgetary Costs and Human Costs of 20 Years of War in Iraq and Syria: 2003–2023," Costs of War Project, Watson Institute of International Affairs, Brown University, March 15, 2023, https://watson.brown.edu/costsofwar/papers/2023/IraqSyria20.
17. Nir Rosen, "No Going Back: Little Relief in Sight for Millions of Displaced Iraqis," *Boston Review* 32, no. 5 (2007): 19–26.
18. Elizabeth Ferris, "Remembering Iraq's Displaced," Brookings Institution, March 18, 2013, https://www.brookings.edu/articles/remembering-iraqs-displaced.
19. By February 2014, al-Qaʿida would officially cut ties with IS over disagreements about the legitimacy of targeting Shiʿa and Sufis.
20. Al-Marashi, "Iraq and the Arab Spring."
21. "Iraq: Investigate Deadly Raid on Protest," Human Rights Watch, April 24, 2013, https://www.hrw.org/news/2013/04/24/iraq-investigate-deadly-raid-protest.
22. October 2014 would see the mass execution of between fifty and seventy-five Albu Nimr tribal fighters in Hit, further degrading the capabilities and resolve of Sunni tribal militias. Daveed Gartenstein Ross and Sterling Jensen, "The Role of Iraqi Tribes After the Islamic State's Ascendance," *Military Review*, July 2015, https://www.fdd.org/analysis/2015/07/27/the-role-of-iraqi-tribes-after-the-islamic-states-ascendance.

23. On July 22, 2013, IS attacked Abu Ghraib prison freeing between five hundred and a thousand inmates, including senior AQI commanders.
24. Daniel Milton, "The Islamic State: An Adaptive Organization Facing Increasing Challenges," in *The Group That Calls Itself a State: Understanding the Evolution and Challenges of the Islamic State*, ed. Bryan Price et al. (West Point, NY: Combating Terrorism Center, United States Military Academy, 2014), 39.
25. Weiss and Hassan, *ISIS*, 209.
26. The retreat of Iraqi forces represented over one-third of Iraqi Army and Federal Police brigades. Keren Fraiman, Austin Long, and Caitlin Talmadge, "Why the Iraqi Army Collapse (and What Can Be Done About It)," *Washington Post*, June 14, 2014, https://www.washingtonpost.com/news/monkey-cage/wp/2014/06/13/why-the-iraqi-army-collapsed-and-what-can-be-done-about-it.
27. The massacre of approximately fifteen hundred unarmed Iraqi Air Force cadets at Camp Speicher near Tikrit on June 12 further degraded the ISF's morale and capacity. Taif Alkhudary, "Five Years On, Still No Justice for Iraq's Camp Speicher Victims," *Al Jazeera*, December 6, 2019, https://www.aljazeera.com/opinions/2019/6/12/five-years-on-still-no-justice-for-iraqs-camp-speicher-victims.
28. Omar Mohammad, Haroro J. Imgram, and Andrew Mines, "Episode 4, Part 2: Never Again, Silence," September 21, 2021, in *Mosul and the Islamic State*, podcast, MP3 audio, 39:00, https://extremism.gwu.edu/mosul-and-the-islamic-state.
29. Haroro J. Ingram, *The Long Jihad: The Islamic State's Method of Insurgency: Control, Meaning, & the Occupation of Mosul in Context* (Washington, DC: Program on Extremism, George Washington University, September 2021), https://doi.org/10.4079/poe.05.2021.03.
30. Seth G. Jones et al., *Rolling Back the Islamic State* (Santa Monica, CA: RAND Corporation, April 2017), https://www.rand.org/pubs/research_reports/RR1912.html.
31. "Iraq," Displacement Tracking Matrix, International Organization for Migration, accessed October 11, 2023, https://dtm.iom.int/iraq.
32. Peter Krause, "A State, an Insurgency, and a Revolution: Understanding and Defeating the Three Faces of ISIS," in *The Future of ISIS: Regional and International Implications*, ed. Feisal al-Istrabadi and Sumit Ganguly (Washington, DC: Brookings Institution Press, 2018), 235.
33. Ingram, *The Islamic State's Method of Insurgency*, 54.
34. Aaron Y. Zelin, "The Islamic State's Territorial Methodology," *Research Notes* 29, Washington Institute for Near East Policy (January 15, 2016), https://www.washingtoninstitute.org/policy-analysis/islamic-states-territorial-methodology; Mara R. Revkin, "When Terrorists Govern: Protecting Civilians in Conflicts with State-Building Armed Groups," *Harvard National Security Journal* 9 (2018): 100; Ingram et al., *The ISIS Reader*; Craig Whiteside and Anas Elallame, "Accidental Ethnographers: The Islamic State's Tribal Engagement Experiment," *Small Wars & Insurgencies* 31, no. 2 (2020): 219–240; Matthew Bamber-Zryd, "Cyclical Jihadist Governance: The Islamic State Governance Cycle in Iraq and Syria," *Small Wars & Insurgencies* 33, no. 8 (2022): 1314–1344; Svensson et al., *Confronting the Caliphate*.

35. Respondent B20, December 2021.
36. Matthew Levitt, "Terrorist Financing and the Islamic State," Washington Institute for Near East Policy, November 13, 2014, https://www.washingtoninstitute.org/policy-analysis/terrorist-financing-and-islamic-state; Ingram, *The Islamic State's Method of Insurgency*; Svensson et al., *Confronting the Caliphate*.
37. Michaela Martin and Hussein Solomon, "Islamic State: Understanding the Nature of the Beast and Its Funding," *Contemporary Review of the Middle East* 4, no. 1 (2017): 18–49.
38. Levitt, *Terrorist Financing and the Islamic State*.
39. *Terrorism and Global Oil Markets: Hearing Before the Committee on Energy and Natural Resources*, 114th Cong., 1st sess. (2015) (testimony of Jamie Webster, senior director of global oil markets, IHS); Lukáš Tichý, "The IS and Attacks on the Oil and Gas Sector in Iraq," *Central European Journal of International & Security Studies* 12, no. 3 (2018): 106–127.
40. Mara Redlich Revkin and Ariel I. Ahram, "Perspectives on the Rebel Social Contract: Exit, Voice, and Loyalty in the Islamic State in Iraq and Syria," *World Development* 132 (August 2020): 104981, https://doi.org/10.1016/j.worlddev.2020.104981.
41. Patrick B. Johnston et al., *Foundations of the Islamic State Management, Money, and Terror in Iraq, 2005-2010* (Santa Monica, CA: RAND Corporation, May 2016), https://www.rand.org/pubs/research_reports/RR1192.html.
42. Weiss and Hassan, *ISIS*, 209.
43. Will McCants and Aaron Zelin, "Experts Weight in (Part 3): Is ISIS Good at Governing?," Brookings Institution, February 9, 2016, https://www.brookings.edu/blog/markaz/2016/02/09/experts-weigh-in-part-3-is-isis-good-at-governing.
44. Ingram, *The Islamic State's Method of Insurgency*, 21.
45. Mara Revkin and Will McCants, "Experts Weigh in (Part 1): Is ISIS Good at Governing?," Brookings Institution, November 20, 2016, https://www.brookings.edu/blog/markaz/2015/11/20/experts-weigh-in-is-isis-good-at-governing.
46. Ingram, *The Islamic State's Method of Insurgency*.
47. Revkin, "Competitive Governance and Displacement Decisions Under Rebel Rule."
48. James Verini, *They Will Have to Die Now: Mosul and the Fall of the Caliphate* (New York: Simon and Schuster, 2019).
49. Nadia Murad and Jenna Krajeski, *The Last Girl: My Story of Captivity, and My Fight Against the Islamic State* (New York: Tim Duggan Books, 2017); Revkin and Wood, "The Islamic State's Pattern of Sexual Violence."
50. Scott Gates and Sukanya Podder, "Social Media, Recruitment, Allegiance and the Islamic State," *Perspectives on Terrorism* 9, no. 4 (2015): 107–116.
51. Revkin and Ahram, "Perspectives on the Rebel Social Contract," 5.
52. Hassan Hassan and Will McCants, "Experts Weigh in (Part 7): Is ISIS Good at Governing?," Brookings Institution, April 18, 2016, https://www.brookings.edu/blog/markaz/2016/04/18/experts-weigh-in-part-7-is-isis-good-at-governing.
53. Ingram, *The Islamic State's Method of Insurgency*.
54. Revkin and Wood, "The Islamic State's Pattern of Sexual Violence."

55. Ingram, *The Islamic State's Method of Insurgency*.
56. IS media agencies include al-Furqan (video content across the Web and social media), *al-Hayat* (print and online magazines such as *Dabiq*), Ajnad (producing and distributing *nashids*), Bayan Broadcasting (responsible for radio and audio broadcasts), Wakalat Aʿmaq al-Ikhbariyah (daily news updates for foreign audiences), al-Himmah (public relations), and al-Naba (responsible for newsletters).
57. Haroro J. Ingram, "Three Traits of the Islamic State's Information Warfare," *RUSI Journal* 159, no. 6 (2014): 4–11; Craig Whiteside, "Lying to Win: The Islamic State Media Department's Role in Deception Efforts," *RUSI Journal* 165, no. 1 (2020): 130–141.
58. Iraq's Federal Police operate as the paramilitary wing of the Ministry of Interior, as opposed to a national law enforcement agency.
59. Michael Knights and Alexander Mello, "Losing Mosul, Regenerating in Diyala: How the Islamic State Could Exploit Iraq's Sectarian Tinderbox," *CTC Sentinel* 9, no. 10 (October 2016): 1–8.
60. C.J. Chivers, "Answering a Cleric's Call, Iraqi Shiites Take Up Arms," *New York Times*, June 9, 2014, https://www.nytimes.com/2014/06/22/world/middleeast/iraq-militia.html.
61. Renad Mansour, "Your Country Needs You: Iraq's Faltering Military Recruitment Campaign" *Diwan: Middle East Insights from Carnegie* (blog), Malcom H. Kerr Carnegie Middle East Center, July 22, 2015, https://carnegie-mec.org/diwan/60810.
62. "Iraq's Sadr Warns Will 'Shake the Ground' Against Militants," *Al Arabiya*, June 26, 2014, https://english.alarabiya.net/News/middle-east/2014/06/26/Iraq-s-Sadr-warns-will-shake-the-ground-against-militants-.
63. Michael R. Gordon, *Degrade and Destroy: The Inside Story of the War Against the Islamic State, from Barack Obama to Donald Trump* (New York: Macmillan, 2022), 15.
64. United Nations High Commissioner for Refugees, *"They Came to Destroy": ISIS Crimes Against the Yazidis* (New York: United Nations, June 2016), https://digitallibrary.un.org/record/843515?ln=en; Valeria Cetorelli et al., "Mortality and Kidnapping Estimates for the Yazidi Population in the Area of Mount Sinjar, Iraq, in August 2014: A Retrospective Household Survey," *PLoS Medicine* 14, no. 5 (2017): 1–15.
65. Saman Dawod, "Neglected Yazidi Mass Graves Finally Exhumed in Iraq," *Al-Monitor*, October 30, 2020, https://www.al-monitor.com/originals/2020/10/iraq-sinjar-yazidis-mass-graves.html.
66. As early as 2016, AQI sought to make Ramadi its putative capital. Gordon, *Degrade and Destroy*, 130.
67. Hassan Hassan, "More Than ISIS, Iraq's Sunni Insurgency," *Sada* (blog), Carnegie Endowment for International Peace, June 17, 2014, https://carnegieendowment.org/sada/55930.
68. "Ruinous Aftermath: Militias Abuses Following Iraq's Recapture of Tikrit," Human Rights Watch, September 20, 2015, https://www.hrw.org/report/2015/09/20/ruinous-aftermath/militias-abuses-following-iraqs-recapture-tikrit.
69. Gordon, *Degrade and Destroy*, 199.

70. Inna Rudolf, "The Sunnis of Iraq's 'Shia' Paramilitary Powerhouse," Century Foundation, February 14, 2020, https://tcf.org/content/report/sunnis-iraqs-shia-paramilitary-powerhouse.
71. Caroline Gluck, "Thousands of Civilians Flee Raging Battle for Falluja," United Nations High Commissioner for Refugees, May 31, 2016, https://www.unhcr.org/news/stories/thousands-civilians-flee-raging-battle-falluja.
72. "Fallujah: Anti-ISIL Drive Displaces 30,000 More Iraqis," *Al Jazeera*, June 19, 2016, https://www.aljazeera.com/news/2016/6/19/fallujah-anti-isil-drive-displaces-30000-more-iraqis.
73. Annie Slemrod, "The Failure in Fallujah: And How Lessons Must Be Learnt for Mosul," *New Humanitarian*, June 28, 2016, https://www.thenewhumanitarian.org/2016/06/28/failure-fallujah.
74. Qaraqosh is the Eastern Aramaic name for the village, while it is known in Arabic as Al Hamdaniya, and Bakhdida in Syriac.
75. Gordon, *Degrade and Destroy*, 490.
76. Tamer El-Ghobashy, "Iraq's Elite Special Forces Struggle to Regroup After Bloody Fight for Mosul," *Washington Post*, July 21 2017, https://www.washingtonpost.com/news/worldviews/wp/2017/07/21/iraqs-elite-special-forces-struggle-to-regroup-after-bloody-fight-for-mosul.
77. Abdul-Ahad, *A Stranger in Your Own City*, 307.
78. Abdul-Ahad, 326.
79. Verini, *They Will Have to Die Now*; Anthony King, *Urban Warfare in the Twenty-First Century* (Cambridge: Polity, 2021).
80. Samuel Oakford, "Counting the Dead in Mosul," *The Atlantic*, April 2018, https://www.theatlantic.com/international/archive/2018/04/counting-the-dead-in-mosul/556466.
81. Gordon, *Degrade and Destroy*, 540.
82. Gordon, 542.
83. Stephen Kalin, "Basic Infrastructure Repair in Mosul Will Cost Over $1 Billion: U.N.," Reuters, July 5, 2017, https://www.reuters.com/article/us-mideast-crisis-iraq-aid/basic-infrastructure-repair-in-mosul-will-cost-over-1-billion-u-n-idUSKBN19Q28F.
84. "UN: Mosul Repairs Will Cost $1bn," *Middle East Monitor*, July 7, 2017, https://www.middleeastmonitor.com/20170707-un-mosul-repairs-will-cost-1bn.
85. Abdul-Ahad, *A Stranger in Your Own City*, 304.
86. Margaret Coker and Falih Hassan, "Iraq Prime Minister Declares Victory Over ISIS," *New York Times*, December 9, 2017, https://www.nytimes.com/2017/12/09/world/middleeast/iraq-isis-haider-al-abadi.html.
87. Haider al-Abadi, *Impossible Victory: How Iraq Defeated the Islamic State* (London: Biteback, 2022), 251.
88. "Iraq," Displacement Tracking Matrix, International Organization for Migration, accessed October 11, 2023, https://dtm.iom.int/iraq. Coalition airstrikes are estimated to have killed between 1,500 and 2,000 civilians between 2014 and 2017.

Azmat Khan and Anand Gopal, "The Uncounted," *New York Times*, November 16, 2017, https://www.nytimes.com/interactive/2017/11/16/magazine/uncounted-civilian-casualties-iraq-airstrikes.html; Missy Ryan, Mustafa Salim, and Harry Stevens, "Behind the Tally, Names and Lives," *Washington Post*, November 18, 2020, https://www.washingtonpost.com/graphics/2020/world/coalition-airstrikes-isis-civilian-death-toll.

89. Jacob Eriksson and Ahmed Khaleel, *Iraq After ISIS: The Challenges of Post-war Recovery* (Cham, CH: Palgrave Pivot, 2018).
90. Andrew Mumford, *The West's War Against Islamic State: Operation Inherent Resolve in Syria and Iraq* (London: Bloomsbury, 2021), 66.
91. Derek Henry Flood, "From Caliphate to Caves: The Islamic State's Asymmetric War in Northern Iraq," *CTC Sentinel* 11, no. 8 (2018): 30–34.
92. "Islamic State Group Claims Responsibility for Deadly Attack on Iraqi Police," *France 24*, December 18, 2022, https://www.france24.com/en/middle-east/20221218-islamic-state-group-claim-responsibility-for-deadly-attack-on-iraq-police.
93. "Country Reports on Terrorism 2019: Iraq," Bureau of Counterterrorism, U.S. Department of State, accessed October 19, 2023, https://www.state.gov/reports/country-reports-on-terrorism-2019/iraq/#:~:text=2019%20Terrorist%20Incidents%3A%20According%20to,2019%20as%20of%20December%201.

4. Baghdad

Epigraph: Sadiq al-Saigh, "This Is Baghdad," in *Baghdad: The City in Verse*, ed. Reuven Snir (Cambridge, MA: Harvard University Press, 2013), 257.

1. Ghazwan Hassan, "Iraq Insurgents Take Saddam's Home Town in Lightning Advance," Reuters, June 11, 2014, https://www.reuters.com/article/us-iraq-security/iraq-insurgents-take-saddams-home-town-in-lightning-advance-idUKKBN0EM11U20140611.
2. "ISIS Urges Militants to March to Baghdad," *Al Arabiya News*, December 6, 2014, https://english.alarabiya.net/News/2014/06/12/ISIS-militants-plan-to-march-on-Baghdad.
3. Portions of the survey analysis are drawn from Austin J. Knuppe, "Blowback or Overblown? Why Civilians Under Threat Support Invasive Foreign Intervention," *Journal of Peace Research* 59, no. 4 (2022): 478–494.
4. Harith Hasan al-Qarawee, *Iraq's Sectarian Crisis: A Legacy of Exclusion* (Washington, DC: Carnegie Endowment for International Peace, April 2014), https://carnegieendowment.org/files/iraq_sectarian_crisis.pdf.
5. As Matthijs Bogaards notes, "the constitution only talks about proportionality in the armed forces and, for the moment, distribution of revenue from natural resources, it does not mention political proportionality. This leaves segmental autonomy, or self-rule, as the main consociational feature of the 2005 Iraq

constitution." Matthijs Bogaards, "Iraq's Constitution of 2005: The Case Against Consociationalism 'Light,'" *Ethnopolitics* 20, no. 2 (2021): 186–202.

6. James T. Quinlivan, "Coup-Proofing: Its Practice and Consequences in the Middle East," *International Security* 24, no. 2 (1999): 131–165; Toby Dodge, "Can Iraq Be Saved?," *Survival* 56, no. 5 (2014): 7–20.

7. Dodge, "Can Iraq Be Saved?"; Joel Rayburn, *Iraq After America: Strongmen, Sectarians, Resistance* (Palo Alto, CA: Hoover Institution Press, 2014); Quint Hoekstra, "How Mosul Fell: The Role of Coup-Proofing in the 2014 Partial Collapse of the Iraqi Security Forces," *International Politics* 57, no. 4 (2020): 684–703.

8. See statistics collected by the Iraq Body Count project, available at https://www.iraqbodycount.org.

9. Munquith Dagher and Karl Kaltenthaler, "A Striking Positive Shift in Sunni Opinion in Iraq Is Underway. Here's What It Means," *Washington Post*, September 14, 2017, https://www.washingtonpost.com/news/monkey-cage/wp/2017/09/14/iraqi-sunnis-are-impressed-by-the-defeat-of-isis-heres-what-that-could-mean.

10. Falih Hassan, Omar Al-Jawoshy, and Tim Arango, "Protesters Storm Baghdad's Green Zone to Denounce Corruption," *New York Times*, April 30, 2016, https://www.nytimes.com/2016/05/01/world/middleeast/iraq-protesters-storm-parliament-demanding-end-to-corruption.html.

11. Dagher and Kaltenthaler, "A Striking Positive Shift in Sunni Opinion in Iraq Is Underway."

12. Stephen Biddle, Jeffrey A. Friedman, and Jacob N. Shapiro, "Testing the Surge: Why Did Violence Decline in Iraq in 2007?," *International Security* 37, no. 1 (2012): 7–40; Nils B. Weidmann and Idean Salehyan, "Violence and Ethnic Segregation: A Computational Model Applied to Baghdad," *International Studies Quarterly* 57, no. 1 (2013): 52–64; Stephen Biddle, *Nonstate Warfare: The Military Methods of Guerillas, Warlords, and Militias* (Princeton, NJ: Princeton University Press, 2021).

13. Department of State, Office of International Religious Freedom, *2019 Report on International Religious Freedom: Iraq* (Washington, DC: United States Department of State, June 2019), https://www.state.gov/reports/2019-report-on-international-religious-freedom/iraq. "Situation of Christians in Baghdad," United Nations High Commissioner for Refugees, January 15, 2018, https://www.refworld.org/docid/5a66f80e4.html.

14. By the end of 2020, however, all but two IDP camps, Latifya 1 and 2, were closed. United Nations Office for the Coordination of Humanitarian Affairs, *January 2021 Humanitarian Bulletin* (Baghdad: United Nations Office for the Coordination of Humanitarian Affairs, January 2021). Riyadh Lafta et al., "Needs of Internally Displaced Women and Children in Baghdad, Karbala, and Kirkuk, Iraq," *PLoS Currents* 8 (2016), https://doi.org/10.1371/currents.dis.fefc1fc62c02ecaedec2c25910442828.

15. "Iraq," Displacement Tracking Matrix, International Organization for Migration, accessed October 11, 2023, https://dtm.iom.int/iraq.

16. Ahmed Hassin and Mays Al-Juboori, *Humanitarian Challenges in Iraq's Displacement Crisis* (London: Ceasefire Centre for Civilian Rights, December 2016), 8,

https://minorityrights.org/wp-content/uploads/2016/12/MRG-report-A4
   _english-DECEMBER-2016_WEB-2.pdf.
17. Hassin and Al-Juboori, *Humanitarian Challenges in Iraq's Displacement Crisis*, 8.
18. Hassin and Al-Juboori.
19. More information on the Independent Institute for Administration and Civil Society Studies is available at the institute's website, https://iiacss.org.
20. At the time of enumeration, Baghdad had ten districts and eighty-nine subdistricts encompassing an urban population of approximately six and a half million residents.
21. For a summary of survey nonresponse trends, see table A.8 of appendix A.
22. "Arab Barometer Wave III (2012–2014)," Arab Barometer, accessed October 19, 2023, https://www.arabbarometer.org/surveys/arab-barometer-wave-iii; Matthew J. Nanes, *Policing for Peace: Institutions, Expectations, and Security in Divided Societies* (New York: Cambridge University Press, 2021); Dagher et al., *ISIS in Iraq*.
23. Condra and Shapiro, "Who Takes the Blame?"; Lyall, Imai, and Blair, "Explaining Support for Combatants in Wartime"; Lyall, Shiraito, and Imai, "Coethnic Bias and Wartime Informing."
24. See Christopher Barrie's research for a similar finding relating to the asymmetric nature of in-group favoritism among Mosul residents. Christopher Barrie, "Sect, Nation, and Identity After the Fall of Mosul: Evidence from a Natural Experiment," *American Journal of Sociology* 127, no. 3 (2021): 695–738.
25. Fanar Haddad, "Sectarian Relations in Arab Iraq: Contextualising the Civil War of 2006–2007," *British Journal of Middle Eastern Studies* 40, no. 2 (2013): 115–138.
26. Technical information about the endorsement experiment is available in appendix A.
27. Results remain consistent when adjusting for respondent-level covariates such as gender, age, education, and sect (see panel B of table A.9 in appendix A).
28. The author constructed a measure of district-level insecurity by aggregating the number of civilian fatalities between June 2014 and November 2017 by district as recorded by Iraqi Body Count. An indicator for "high" and "low" insecurity districts was created by splitting along the median number of civilian fatalities. Among the five districts sampled, two were high-insecurity districts (Kadhimiya and Sadr City) and three were low-insecurity districts (Adhamiya, Karakh, and Rusafa).
29. Respondent preferences remained consistent when the author used a self-report measure of perceived physical insecurity (e.g., "high," "medium," and "low") instead of data on civilian fatalities.
30. Nearly half of all respondents said the United States was responsible for the rise of the Islamic State, whereas 20 percent of respondents identified Saudi Arabia or the Gulf states as responsible, and only 2.8 percent identified Iran as the primary culprit.
31. Bellows and Miguel, "War and Local Collective Action in Sierra Leone"; Blattman, "From Violence to Voting;" Voors et al., "Violent Conflict and Behavior"; Callen et al., "Violence and Risk Preference."

32. Pape, *Dying to Win*; Luke N. Condra et al., "The Effect of Civilian Casualties in Afghanistan and Iraq"; Lyall, "Are Coethnics More Effective Counterinsurgents?"
33. Table A.9 in appendix A provides a comparison of tactics across treatment groups.
34. Technical information about the conjoint experiment is available in appendix A.
35. As a descriptive measure, marginal means are ideal for studying preference heterogeneity within attributes because they are not reliant on a reference category. Thomas Leeper, *Cregg: Simple Conjoint Tidying, Analysis, and Visualization*, R package version 0.3.0 (2018), https://cran.r-project.org/web/packages/cregg/cregg.pdf; Thomas J. Leeper, Sara B. Hobolt, and James Tilley, "Measuring Subgroup Preferences in Conjoint Experiments," *Political Analysis* 28, no. 2 (2020): 207–221.
36. Haddad, "Sectarian Relations in Arab Iraq"; Nader Hashemi and Danny Postel, *Sectarianization: Mapping the New Politics of the Middle East* (New York: Oxford University Press, 2017).
37. Renad Mansour, *Networks of Power: The Popular Mobilization Forces and the State in Iraq* (London: Chatham House, February 2021), 28.
38. Mansour, *Networks of Power*, 15.
39. Renad Mansour and Faleh A. Jabar, "The Popular Mobilization Forces and Iraq's Future," Carnegie Middle East Center, April 28, 2017, https://carnegie-mec.org/2017/04/28/popular-mobilization-forces-and-iraq-s-future-pub-68810.
40. Alissa J. Rubin, "Iraqis Rise Against a Reviled Occupier: Iran," *New York Times*, November 4, 2019, https://www.nytimes.com/2019/11/04/world/middleeast/iraq-protests-iran.html.
41. Ibrahim Al-Marashi, "Iraq and the Arab Spring: From Protests to the Rise of ISIS," in *The Arab Spring: The Hope and Reality of the Uprisings*, ed. Mark L. Haas and David W. Lesch, 2nd ed. (London: Routledge, 2016), 147–164.
42. "Sadr Supporters Rally Over US Troops in Iraq," *Al Jazeera*, May 26, 2011, https://www.aljazeera.com/news/2011/5/26/sadr-supporters-rally-over-us-troops-in-iraq.

5. Fallujah, Ramadi, and Tikrit

1. Malkasian, *Illusions of Victory*, 179.
2. Malkasian, 178–179.
3. Ibrahim Al-Marashi, "Iraq and the Arab Spring: From Protests to the Rise of ISIS," in *The Arab Spring: The Hope and Reality of the Uprisings*, ed. Mark L. Haas and David W. Lesch, 2nd ed. (London: Routledge, 2016), 147–164.
4. Ahmed K. Al-Rawi, "The Arab Spring & Online Protests in Iraq," *International Journal of Communication* 8 (2014): 916–942.
5. "Iraq: Investigate Deadly Raid on Protest," Human Rights Watch, April 24, 2013, https://www.hrw.org/news/2013/04/24/iraq-investigate-deadly-raid-protest.

6. Tim Arango, "Dozens Killed in Battles Across Iraq as Sunnis Escalate Protests Against Government," *New York Times*, April 23, 2013, https://www.nytimes.com/2013/04/24/world/middleeast/clashes-at-sunni-protest-site-in-iraq.html.
7. Priyanka Boghani, "In Their Own Words: Sunnis on Their Treatment in Maliki's Iraq," *PBS Frontline*, October 28, 2014, https://www.pbs.org/wgbh/frontline/article/in-their-own-words-sunnis-on-their-treatment-in-malikis-iraq.
8. Louise Redvers, "Old Fault Lines, New Flash Points in Iraq's Anbar," *New Humanitarian*, July 2, 2014, https://www.thenewhumanitarian.org/analysis/2014/02/07/old-fault-lines-new-flashpoints-iraq-s-anbar.
9. Malkasian, *Illusions of Victory*, 176–177.
10. Boghani, "In Their Own Words."
11. Weiss and Hassan, *ISIS: Inside the Army of Terror*, 95–97.
12. In June 2014 alone, for example, IS insurgents killed over 1,7000 Sunni civilians throughout the region. "Iraq: UN Envoy Urges Political Leaders to Help End Bloodshed Following Latest Bombings," UN News, May 17, 2013, https://news.un.org/en/story/2013/05/439922.
13. Daveed Gartenstein-Ross and Sterling Jensen, "The Role of Iraqi Tribes After the Islamic State's Ascendance," *Military Review*, July–August 2015, https://www.armyupress.army.mil/Portals/7/military-review/Archives/English/MilitaryReview_20150831_art018.pdf.
14. Aymenn Jawad Al-Tamimi, "Sunni Opposition to the Islamic State," *Middle East Review of International Affairs* 18, no. 3 (2014): 1–13; Nadeem Elias Khan and Craig Whiteside, "State Accompli: The Political Consolidation of the Islamic State Prior to the Caliphate," *Studies in Conflict & Terrorism*, online first, December 16, 2021, https://doi.org/10.1080/1057610X.2021.2013755.
15. Gordon, *Degrade and Destroy*, 354.
16. For example, the Sunni grand mufti of Iraq, Sheikh Abdul-Mahdi al-Sumaidaie, mobilized his own unit of the PMF, the 86th Brigade, known as the Quwwat Ahrar al-ʿIraq. Inna Rudolf, "The Sunnis of Iraq's 'Shia' Paramilitary Powerhouse," Century Foundation, February 13, 2020, https://tcf.org/content/report/sunnis-iraqs-shia-paramilitary-powerhouse.
17. "Iraq," Displacement Tracking Matrix, International Organization for Migration, accessed October 11, 2023, https://dtm.iom.int/iraq.
18. "Situation Report: Anbar Humanitarian Crisis," Situation Report No. 6, United Nations High Commissioner for Refugees, February 4, 2014, https://reliefweb.int/report/iraq/anbar-humanitarian-crisis-situation-report-6.
19. United Nations International Organization for Migration, *Managing Return in Anbar: Community Responses to the Return of IDPs with Perceived Affiliation* (Baghdad: IOM Iraq, March 2020), https://reliefweb.int/report/iraq/managing-return-anbar-community-responses-return-idps-perceived-affiliation.
20. United Nations International Organization for Migration, *Managing Return in Anbar*.
21. United Nations International Organization for Migration.

22. "Iraq," Displacement Tracking Matrix, International Organization for Migration, accessed October 11, 2023, https://dtm.iom.int/iraq.
23. Euro-Mediterranean Human Rights Monitor, *Exiled at Home: Internal Displacement Resulted from the Armed Conflict in Iraq and Its Humanitarian Consequences* (Geneva: Euro-Mediterranean Human Rights Monitor, June 2021), https://reliefweb.int/report/iraq/exiled-home-internal-displacement-resulted-armed-conflict-iraq-and-its-humanitarian.
24. "Iraq," Displacement Tracking Matrix, International Organization for Migration, accessed October 11, 2023, https://dtm.iom.int/iraq.
25. These findings are consistent with prior research, including Nils Hägerdal, "Ethnic Cleansing and the Politics of Restraint: Violence and Coexistence in the Lebanese Civil War," *Journal of Conflict Resolution* 63, no. 1 (2019): 59–84; Abbey Steele, "Civilian Resettlement Patterns in Civil War," *Journal of Peace Research* 56, no. 1 (2019): 28–41; Adam G. Lichtenheld, "Explaining Population Displacement Strategies in Civil Wars: A Cross-National Analysis," *International Organization* 74, no. 2 (2020): 253–294; Justin Schon, *Surviving the War in Syria* (New York: Cambridge University Press, 2020); Adam G. Lichtenheld and Justin Schon, "The Consequences of Internal Displacement on Civil War Violence: Evidence from Syria," *Political Geography* 86 (2021): 102346.
26. Shelly Kittleson, "Iraqi Army, Non-local PMUs at Cross-Purposes in Western Anbar," *Al-Monitor*, October 21, 2018, https://www.al-monitor.com/originals/2018/10/iraq-anbar-syria-shiite-militias-tufuf.html.
27. "192 Internally Displaced Persons Disappeared from Infamous Al Razaza Checkpoint in Iraq in a Single Day," MENA Rights Group, May 10, 2019, https://menarights.org/en/articles/192-internally-displaced-persons-disappeared-infamous-al-razaza-checkpoint-iraq-single-day.
28. Similar residency permits were required for IDPs seeking resettlement in the Kurdistan Region. Michael Knights and Alexander Mello, *Losing Mosul, Regenerating in Diyala: How the Islamic State Could Exploit Iraq's Sectarian Tinderbox*, CTC Sentinel 9, no. 10 (2016): 3.
29. "Iraq," Displacement Tracking Matrix, International Organization for Migration, accessed October 11, 2023, https://dtm.iom.int/iraq.
30. United Nations International Organization for Migration, *Managing Return in Anbar*, 4.
31. "Iraq: Sunni Women Tell of ISIS Detention, Torture," Human Rights Watch, February 20, 2017, https://www.hrw.org/news/2017/02/20/iraq-sunni-women-tell-isis-detention-torture.
32. United Nations International Organization for Migration, *Managing Return in Anbar*, 11.
33. Euro-Mediterranean Human Rights Monitor, *Exiled at Home*.
34. "Iraq," Displacement Tracking Matrix, International Organization for Migration, accessed October 11, 2023, https://dtm.iom.int/iraq.

35. Andrew C. Shaver and Jacob N. Shapiro, "The Effect of Civilian Casualties on Wartime Informing: Evidence from the Iraq War," *Journal of Conflict Resolution* 65, nos. 7–8 (March 2021): 1–41.
36. Tribal militias fighting Daʿesh in Ramadi, including clans loyal to Muhammad Khamis Abu Risha, leader of the Ramadi Awakening Council (Majlis Sahwat al-Ramadi). Abu Risha was later assassinated in an IS suicide attack in Ramadi on June 4, 2014.
37. Sigrid Weber and Alexandra Hartman, "Property Rights and Post-conflict Recovery: Theory and Evidence from IDP Return Movements in Iraq" (unpublished manuscript, 2023).
38. According to Inna Rudolf, by autumn 2016, nearly 50,000 Sunni tribal fighters were integrated into the PMF, forming distinct tribal brigades. By the end of the anti-IS campaign, approximately 8 of 92 PMF brigades were tribal militias originating from subdistricts within Anbar, Salah al-Din, and Ninewa Governorates. Rudolf, "The Sunnis of Iraq's 'Shia' Paramilitary Powerhouse"; Mansour, *Networks of Power*. See also, Erica Gaston, "Sunni Tribal Forces," Global Public Policy Institute, August 30, 2017, https://www.gppi.net/2017/08/30/sunni-tribal-forces.
39. Rudolf, "The Sunnis of Iraq's 'Shia' Paramilitary Powerhouse."
40. Another Tikriti stated, "I did not do anything. I stayed in my house and did not go outside" (respondent B14).
41. Andrew F. March and Mara Revkin, "Caliphate of Law: ISIS' Ground Rules," *Foreign Affairs* 15, no. 4 (2015), https://www.foreignaffairs.com/articles/syria/2015-04-15/caliphate-law.
42. United Nations International Organization for Migration, *Managing Return in Anbar*, 11.
43. Malkasian, *Illusions of Victory*, 204.
44. Malkasian, 183.
45. Malkasian, 204.
46. "Islamic State 'Kills 322' from Single Sunni Tribe," *BBC News*, November 2, 2014, https://www.bbc.com/news/world-middle-east-29871068#.
47. Malkasian, *Illusions of Victory*, 181.
48. The interviewee continued, "No water, no electricity, no services! This was the feeling of the people who supported Daʿesh, and the army was pressing them, and they rejoiced in Daʿesh because they are better off" (respondent B04).
49. Revkin and Wood, "The Islamic State's Pattern of Sexual Violence," 15.
50. Kaltenthaler, Silverman, and Dagher, "Identity, Ideology, and Information," 807.
51. Revkin, "Competitive Governance and Displacement Decisions Under Rebel Rule"; Svensson et al., *Confronting the Caliphate*; Dagher et al., *ISIS in Iraq*.
52. Mara Revkin and Elisabeth Wood recount a similar bargaining dynamic in Syria: "According to a Syrian man from IS-controlled Manbij, 'Many parents felt that it was important for at least one of their daughters to marry an IS member as a kind of protection bargain.'" Revkin and Wood, "The Islamic State's Pattern of Sexual

Violence," 4. "The hair of the children will turn gray" is a reference to the Qu'ran, Surah 73:17, "The Enshrouded One."
53. Malkasian, *Illusions of Victory*, 182.
54. Malkasian, 180.
55. Kruglanski, Bélanger, and Gunaratna, *The Three Pillars of Radicalization*.
56. Svensson et al., *Confronting the Caliphate*; Dagher et al., *ISIS In Iraq*.

6. Ninewa Plains, Sinjar, and Tal Afar

Epigraphs: Shabak medical professional quoted in Dave van Zoonen and Khogir Wirya, *The Shabaks: Perceptions of Reconciliation and Conflict* (Erbil, IQ: Middle East Research Institute, July 2017), 13. Yazidi militia leader quoted in Hannah Lynch, "The Budding Kurdish-Iranian Alliance in Northern Iraq," *New Lines Magazine*, June 24, 2021, https://newlinesmag.com/reportage/the-budding-kurdish-iranian-alliance-in-northern-iraq.

1. Follow-up correspondence with respondent A10 (November 2021).
2. Henriette Johansen, Kamaran Palani, and Dlawer Ala'Aldeen, *Ninewa Plains and Western Ninewa: Barriers to Return and Community Resilience* (Washington, DC: United States Institute of Peace; Erbil, IQ: Middle East Research Institute, April 2020), 42–43.
3. Parts of this chapter are adapted from Austin Knuppe, "The Civilians' Dilemma: How Religious and Ethnic Minorities Survived the Islamic State Occupation of Northern Iraq," *Journal of the Middle East and Africa* 14, no. 1 (2023): 37–67.
4. Mosul was a regional capital of the Ottoman Empire before its collapse in the aftermath of the First World War. After the war, the British occupied Mosul due to their interest in potential oil reserves. The League of Nations was responsible for adjudicating border disputes between Iraq and the newly formed Republic of Turkey and Iraq, and it ruled that Iraq should retain sovereignty over Mosul. The signing of the "Frontier Treaty" in 1926, as well as Turkey's recognition of Iraqi independence in October 1932, ended territorial disputes over the so-called Mosul Question. Nevin Coşar and Sevtap Demirci, "The Mosul Question and the Turkish Republic: Before and After the Frontier Treaty, 1926," *Middle Eastern Studies* 42, no. 1 (2006): 123–132.
5. The district of Aqra is contested between the Government of Iraq and Kurdistan Region, though it has been under the political control of Erbil since 2010.
6. Ninewa's Christian denominations include the Chaldean Catholic Church (in fellowship with Rome), Assyrian Church of the East, the Ancient Church of the East, the Syriac Orthodox Church, and the Syriac Catholic Church. Alda Benjamen, *Assyrians in Modern Iraq: Negotiating Political and Cultural Space* (New York: Cambridge University Press, 2022).
7. Shane Joshua Barter, "Second-Order Ethnic Minorities in Asian Secessionist Conflicts: Problems and Prospects," *Asian Ethnicity* 16, no. 2 (2015): 123–135; Bethany

Lacina, *Rival Claims: Ethnic Violence and Territorial Autonomy Under Indian Federalism* (Ann Arbor: University of Michigan Press, 2017); Gregory J. Kruczek, "Christian (Second-Order) Minorities and the Struggle for the Homeland: The Assyrian Democratic Movement in Iraq and the Nineveh Plains Protection Units," *Journal of the Middle East and Africa* 12, no. 1 (2021): 1–29.
8. United Nations International Organization for Migration, *Rural Areas in Ninewa: Legacies of Conflict on Rural Economies and Communities in Sinjar and the Ninewa Plains* (Baghdad: IOM Iraq, November 2019), https://iraqdtm.iom.int/files/Durable Solutions/20224113849859_IOM_Iraq_Rural_Areas_in_Ninewa_Legacies_of _Conflict_Rural_Economies_Communities_Sinjar_Ninewa_Plains.pdf.
9. Sean Kane, *Iraq's Disputed Territories: A View of Political Horizon and Implications for U.S. Policy*, Peaceworks Report No. 69 (Washington, DC: United States Institute of Peace, March 2011).
10. Julie Ahn, Maeve Campbell, and Peter Knoetgen, *The Politics of Security in Ninewa: Preventing an ISIS Resurgence in Northern Iraq* (Cambridge, MA: Kennedy School of Government, Harvard University, May 2018).
11. The Kurdistan Free Life Party is the PKK affiliate located on the Iranian side of the Iraq-Iran border.
12. Matthew Barber, "They That Remain: Syrian and Iraqi Christian Communities Amid the Syria Conflict and the Rise of the Islamic State," in *Christianity and Freedom*, ed. Allen D. Hertzke and Timothy Samuel Shah (New York: Cambridge University Press, 2016), 453–488.
13. Johansen, Palani, and Ala'Aldeen, *Ninewa Plains and Western Ninewa*.
14. Current estimates include more than 4,440 Yazidi fatalities and as many as 10,8000 forced abductions. Valeria Cetorelli et al., "Mortality and Kidnapping Estimates for the Yazidi Population in the Area of Mount Sinjar, Iraq, in August 2014: A Retrospective Household Survey," *PLoS Medicine* 14, no. 5 (2017): 1–15. An estimated 200,000 residents were displaced, approximately half of the broader community's population. UNHCR, *"They Came to Destroy": ISIS Crimes Against the Yazidis*, A/HRC/32/CRP.2 (New York: United Nations, June 2016).
15. Alex Milner, "Mosul Dam: Why the Battle for Water Matters in Iraq," *BBC News*, August 18, 2014, https://www.bbc.com/news/world-middle-east-28772478.
16. Gordon, *Degrade and Destroy*, chap. 7.
17. El-Ghobashy, "Iraq's Elite Special Forces Struggle to Regroup."
18. King, *Urban Warfare in the Twenty-First Century*.
19. Oakford, "Counting the Dead in Mosul."
20. Johansen, Palani, and Ala'Aldeen, *Ninewa Plains and Western Ninewa*.
21. Lahib Higel, *Iraq's Displacement Crisis: Security and Protection* (London: Ceasefire Centre for Civilian Rights and Minority Rights Group International, March 2016).
22. Mansour and Celiku, *Breaking Out of Fragility*, 43.
23. Johansen, Palani, and Ala'Aldeen et al., *Ninewa Plains and Western Ninewa*.
24. Cetorelli et al., "Mortality and Kidnapping Estimates for the Yazidi Population in the Area of Mount Sinjar."

25. "Iraq," Displacement Tracking Matrix, International Organization for Migration, accessed October 11, 2023, https://dtm.iom.int/iraq.
26. Johansen, Palani, and Ala'Aldeen, *Ninewa Plains and Western Ninewa*.
27. Approximately 25–30 percent of the Iraqi diaspora in the United States (totaling around 400,000 people) belong to ethnoreligious minorities. These communities are concentrated in California, Illinois, and Michigan, with smaller communities in Arizona, Nebraska, and Tennessee. Eleni Diker et al., *Iraqi Minorities in Diaspora Mapping of Community Structures, Perceptions on Return, and Connections to the Homeland* (New York: United Nations International Organization for Migration, 2020); Dalia Abdelhady, *Routledge Handbook on Middle Eastern Diasporas* (London: Taylor & Francis, 2022).
28. Another interviewee also mentioned livelihoods as a major barrier to leaving the community: "And those who didn't leave couldn't because of their properties and jobs. They were concerned about how they could make a living if they left" (respondent B03).
29. Xavier Devictor, *Forcibly Displaced: Toward a Development Approach Supporting Refugees, the Internally Displaced, and Their Hosts* (Washington, DC: World Bank, 2017).
30. "Iraq," Displacement Tracking Matrix, International Organization for Migration, accessed October 11, 2023, https://dtm.iom.int/iraq.
31. Erica Gaston, *Iraq After ISIL: Qaraqosh, Hamdaniya District* (Berlin: Global Public Policy Institute, August 2017).
32. Assyrian communities from the Ninewa Plains largely relocated to Erbil because of the preexisting social capital of the Christian community (including local elites, such as the Chaldean archbishop, Bashar Warda).
33. Johansen, Palani, and Ala'Aldeen, *Ninewa Plains and Western Ninewa*, 24.
34. "Iraq," Displacement Tracking Matrix, International Organization for Migration, accessed October 11, 2023, https://dtm.iom.int/iraq.
35. Dave van Zoonen and Khogir Wirya, *Turkmen in Tal Afar: Perceptions of Reconciliation and Conflict* (Erbil, IQ: Middle East Research Institute, July 2017), 12.
36. Mansour and Bledi Celiku, *Breaking Out of Fragility*, 144.
37. "Iraq," Displacement Tracking Matrix, International Organization for Migration, accessed October 11, 2023, https://dtm.iom.int/iraq.
38. "Iraq," Displacement Tracking Matrix, International Organization for Migration, accessed October 11, 2023, https://dtm.iom.int/iraq.
39. Revkin, "What Explains Taxation by Resource-Rich Rebels?"
40. András Derzsi-Horváth, Erica Gaston, and Bahra Saleh, *Who's Who: Quick Facts About Local and Sub-state Forces* (Berlin: Global Public Policy Institute, August 2017).
41. Reine Hanna and Gregory J. Kruczek, *Contested Control: The Future of Security in Iraq's Nineveh Plain* (Chicago: Assyrian Policy Institute, June 2020).
42. William Reno, "Protectors and Predators: Why Is There a Difference Among West African Militias?," in *Fragile States and Insecure People?*, ed. Louise Anderson, Bjorn Moller, and Finn Stepputat (London: Palgrave Macmillan, 2007), 99–121.

43. Barber, "They That Remain"; Kent R. Hill, "On the Brink of Extinction Christians in Iraq and Syria," in *Under Caesar's Sword: How Christians Respond to Persecution*, ed. Daniel Philpott and Timothy Samuel Shah (New York: Cambridge University Press, 2018), 30–69.
44. United Nations High Commissioner for Refugees, *International Protection Considerations with Regard to People Fleeing the Republic of Iraq* (New York: United Nations, May 2019), https://www.refworld.org/pdfid/5cc9b20c4.pdf.
45. Bradley Brincka, "Yazidi PMU Fighters Face Uncertainty in the KRG," *1001 Iraqi Thoughts*, August 22, 2017, https://1001iraqithoughts.com/2017/08/22/yazidi-pmu-fighters-face-uncertainty-in-the-krg.
46. Lynch, "The Budding Kurdish-Iranian Alliance in Northern Iraq."
47. Dave van Zoonen and Khogir Wirya, *The Yazidis: Perceptions of Reconciliation and Conflict* (Erbil, IQ: Middle East Research Institute, July 2017).
48. Margaret E. Keck and Kathryn Sikkink, *Activists Beyond Borders: Advocacy Networks in International Politics* (Ithaca, NY: Cornell University Press, 1998).
49. For example, the Nineveh Plain Defense Fund, a U.S.-registered nonprofit supported by the Assyrian diaspora in suburban Chicago, allowed donors to make tax-deductible donations to support the Nineveh Plains Protection Units.
50. Nadia Murad and Jenna Krajeski, *The Last Girl: My Story of Captivity, and My Fight Against the Islamic State* (New York: Tim Duggan Books, 2017).
51. The seven parties that participated in the proceedings included the Beth Nahrain Democratic Party, the Beth Nahrain Patriotic Union Party, the Chaldean National Congress, the Chaldean Democracy Movement, the Chaldean-Syriac-Assyrian Popular Council, Chaldo-Ashour, and the Syriac Assembly Movement. Those groups that boycotted included the Assyrian Democratic Movement, the Sons of Mesopotamia, the Assyrian Patriotic Party, the Chaldean Catholic Church, and the Assyrian Church of the East.
52. Nicole Kikoler, *Our Generation Is Gone: The Islamic State's Targeting of Iraqi Minorities in Ninewa* (Washington, DC: United States Holocaust Museum, Simon-Skjodt Center for the Prevention of Genocide, 2015).
53. One Mosul resident referred to "the veil [or niqab], the beard, the long dress, and many other things that we had to implement at that time, and since we were besieged, and this is the ruling of the strong over the weak at that time, so we were forced to implement everything they asked for. That is why the people of Mosul submitted to IS" (respondent B07).
54. Dave van Zoonen and Khogir Wirya, *The Shabaks: Perceptions of Reconciliation and Conflict* (Erbil, IQ: Middle East Research Institute, July 2017), 9.
55. Zoonen and Wirya, *Turkmen in Tal Afar*.
56. Johansen, Palani, and Ala'Aldeen, *Ninewa Plains and Western Ninewa*, 19.
57. Respondent B12 mentioned a recruitment rate of 60,000 dinars (U.S.$42).
58. Zoonen and Wirya, *The Shabaks*, 10–11.
59. Zoonen and Wirya, 11.

60. Salma Mousa, "Building Social Cohesion Between Christians and Muslims Through Soccer in Post-ISIS Iraq," *Science* 369, no. 6505 (2020): 866–870.
61. Zoonen and Wirya, *The Shabaks*, 9.
62. Zoonen and Wirya, *Turkmen in Tal Afar*, 10.
63. "Turning a Blind Eye: The Arming of the Popular Mobilization Units," Amnesty International, January 5, 2017, https://www.amnesty.org/en/documents/mde14/5386/2017/en.
64. More than 20 percent, or 100,000 IDPs, belonged to Shiʿa Turkmen community. Johansen, Palani, and Ala'Aldeen, *Ninewa Plains and Western Ninewa*.
65. "Amid Iraq's Turmoil, Tal Afar Builds Peace," United States Institute of Peace, November 5, 2020, https://www.usip.org/publications/2020/11/amid-iraqs-turmoil-tal-afar-builds-peace.
66. An estimated 75,000 residents remained in Tal Afar city during the IS occupation. Johansen, Palani, and Ala'Aldeen, *Ninewa Plains and Western Ninewa*.
67. Zoonen and Wirya, *Turkmen in Tal Afar*, 5.
68. Khitam Alkhayanee, *Justice and Security Needs in Iraq after ISIL*, Special Report 389 (Washington, DC: United State Institute of Peace, August 2016).
69. Paul Howe, "The Triple Nexus: A Potential Approach to Supporting the Achievement of the Sustainable Development Goals?" *World Development* 124 (2019): 104629, https://doi.org/10.1016/j.worlddev.2019.104629.

7. "We Have on This Land That Which Makes Life Worth Living"

1. Chiara Pellegrino, "The Golden Age of a City Beyond Compare in the Narrative of an Arab Writer of the Twelfth Century," Fondazione Oasis, April 4, 2022, https://www.oasiscenter.eu/en/mosul-fortress-charmed-travelers.
2. Gordon, *Degrade and Destroy*, 149.
3. Martin Chulov and Kareem Shaheen, "Destroying Great Mosque of al-Nuri 'Is Isis Declaring Defeat,'" *The Guardian*, June 22, 2017, https://www.theguardian.com/world/2017/jun/21/mosuls-grand-al-nouri-mosque-blown-up-by-isis-fighters.
4. Marsin Alshamary, "The Iraq Invasion at Twenty: Iraq's Struggle for Democracy," *Journal of Democracy* 34, no. 2 (2023): 150–162.
5. Antonio Giustozzi, "The Taliban's 'Military Courts,'" *Small Wars & Insurgencies* 25, no. 2 (2014): 284–296; Florian Weigand, "Afghanistan's Taliban—Legitimate Jihadists or Coercive Extremists?," *Journal of Intervention and Statebuilding* 11, no. 3 (2017): 359–381; Grasse, Sexton, and Wright, "The Logic and Impacts of Rebel Public Services Provision."
6. "Three Killed as Iraq Protesters Attack Iran Consulate in Karbala," *Al Jazeera*, November 4, 2019, https://www.aljazeera.com/news/2019/11/4/three-killed-as-iraq-protesters-attack-iran-consulate-in-karbala#:~:text=At%20least%20three%20Iraqi%20protesters,the%20building%20late%20on%20Sunday.

7. Derek Henry Flood, "From Caliphate to Caves: The Islamic State's Asymmetric War in Northern Iraq," *CTC Sentinel* 11, no. 8 (September 2018): 30–34.
8. Mara R. Revkin, "How Does Subnational Variation in Repression Affect Attitudes Toward Police? Evidence from Iraq's 2019 Protests," *Violence: An International Journal* 3, no. 1 (2022): 85–99.
9. Dan Lamothe and Louisa Loveluck, "U.S. and Coalition Troops Killed in Rocket Attack in Iraq, Potentially Spiking Tensions with Iran," *Washington Post*, November 3, 2020, https://www.washingtonpost.com/national-security/2020/03/11/us-coalition-troops-killed-rocket-attack-iraq-potentially-spiking-tensions-with-iran.
10. Louisa Loveluck and Mustafa Salim, "Turkish Strike Kills at Least 8 Iraqi Tourists in Northern Resort," *Washington Post*, July 20, 2022, https://www.washingtonpost.com/world/2022/07/20/iraq-turkey-strike-tourists.
11. Cancian, Nielsen, and Knuppe, "Deliberation and Ethnic Cooperation in Kirkuk."
12. Although Iraq's 2015 Law on Political Parties banned parties from working with militias, this provision was widely ignored. Fatah finished second in the May 2018 elections (with 48 parliamentary seats) but suffered a setback in October 2021 when it finished fifth, accruing only 17 out of 329 parliamentary seats.
13. Mohammed Rwanduzy, "Iraqi PM Decrees Full Integration of PMF Into Iraqi Forces," *Rudaw*, January 7, 2019, https://www.rudaw.net/english/middleeast/iraq/01072019.
14. Michael Knights, "Iraq Is Quietly Falling Apart: Iran's Proxies Have Seized Power in Baghdad—and Are Gutting the State," *Foreign Affairs*, June 5, 2023, https://www.foreignaffairs.com/iran/iraq-quietly-falling-apart.
15. Toby Dodge and Renad Mansour, *Politically Sanctioned Corruption and Barriers to Reform in Iraq* (London: Middle East & North Africa Programme, Chatham House, June 2021), https://www.chathamhouse.org/sites/default/files/2021-06/2021-06-17-politically-sanctioned-corruption-iraq-dodge-mansour.pdf.
16. Dodge and Mansour, *Politically Sanctioned Corruption*, 26.
17. Haddad, "Turbulent Times for the 'New Iraq'"; Marsin Alshamary and Hamzeh Hadad, "The Collective Neglect of Southern Iraq: Missed Opportunities for Development and Good Governance," *International Peacekeeping*, online first, February 16, 2023, https://doi.org/10.1080/13533312.2023.2177640.
18. "Global Multidimensional Poverty Index," Oxford Poverty and Human Development Initiative, accessed October 30, 2023, https://ophi.org.uk/multidimensional-poverty-index.
19. "Life Expectancy at Birth, Total (Years)," World Bank Group, accessed January 13, 2022, https://data.worldbank.org/indicator/SP.DYN.LE00.IN.
20. "Unemployment, Youth Total (% of Total Labor Force, Ages 15–24)," World Bank Group, accessed January 13, 2022, https://data.worldbank.org/indicator/SL.UEM.1524.ZS.
21. "Inflation, Consumer Prices (Annual Percentage)," World Bank Group, accessed January 13, 2022, https://data.worldbank.org/indicator/FP.CPI.TOTL.ZG.

22. "Iraq Consumer Price Index (CPI)," Trading Economics, accessed October 30, 2023, https://tradingeconomics.com/iraq/consumer-price-index-cpi.
23. "Iraq—Food Prices," Humanitarian Data Exchange, accessed October 30, 2023, https://data.humdata.org/dataset/wfp-food-prices-for-iraq.
24. "Corruption Perception Index (2021): Middle East & North Africa," Transparency International, accessed January 14, 2022, https://www.transparency.org/en/cpi/2021.
25. Dodge and Mansour, *Politically Sanctioned Corruption*, 2.
26. "'If I Leave . . . I Cannot Breathe': Climate Change and Civilian Protection in Iraq," Center for Civilians in Conflict, July 6, 2022, https://civiliansinconflict.org/if-i-leave-i-cannot-breathe-climate-change-and-civilian-protection-in-iraq.
27. In this same survey, half of all respondents listed the economy and corruption as the country's most important challenges.
28. Matthew Cancian, "The Impact of Modern-System Training on Battlefield Participation by Kurdish Soldiers," *Journal of Conflict Resolution* 66, nos. 7–8 (2022): 1449–1480.
29. Irene Costantini, "The Iraqi Protest Movement: Social Mobilization Amidst Violence and Instability," *British Journal of Middle Eastern Studies* 48, no. 5 (2021): 832–849; Taif Alkhudary, "'We Want a Country': The Urban Politics of the October Revolution in Baghdad's Tahrir Square," *Third World Quarterly*, 2022, online first, December 2, 2022, https://doi.org/10.1080/01436597.2022.2141219; Vera Mironova and Sam Whitt, "Maintaining Nonviolent Self-Discipline in Hostile Protest Environments: Evidence from the 2019 Baghdad Protests," *Social Movement Studies*, online first, May 4, 2022, https://doi.org/10.1080/14742837.2022.2070466; Balsam Mustafa, "All About Iraq: Re-modifying Older Slogans and Chants in Tishreen (October) Protests," *Journal of Asian and African Studies* 58, no. 3 (2022): 401–420.
30. Communities in Anbar, Baghdad, Diyala, Erbil, Kirkuk, Ninewa, and Salah al-Din were affected by either IS occupation or insurgent violence.
31. Wael Mansour and Bledi Celiku, *Breaking Out of Fragility: A Country Economic Memorandum for Diversification and Growth in Iraq* (Washington, DC: World Bank Group, September 2020), https://openknowledge.worldbank.org/server/api/core/bitstreams/0d8484f9-90ee-5aa4-b821-92c3add840ef/content.
32. *Arab Barometer VI: Iraq Country Report* (Princeton, NJ: Arab Barometer, March 2021), https://www.arabbarometer.org/wp-content/uploads/Iraq-Arab-Barometer-Public-Opinion-2021-ENG.pdf.
33. Ramadi and Fallujah, in turn, have seen increasing rates of foreign direct investment and private equity from wealthy Gulf benefactors. "Iraq: Anbar's Post-ISIL Reconstruction Spawns Autonomy Debate," *Al Jazeera*, January 27, 2021, https://www.aljazeera.com/economy/2021/1/27/iraq-anbars-post-isil-reconstruction-spawns-autonomy-debate.
34. Johansen, Palani, and Ala'Aldeen, *Ninewa Plains and Western Ninewa*, 4–5.
35. Matthew Cancian, "The Impact of Modern-System Training on Battlefield Participation by Kurdish Soldiers," *Journal of Conflict Resolution* 66, nos. 7–8 (2022): 1449–1480.

36. "Iraq's Electricity Supply and Demand, 2018–2030," International Energy Association, accessed February 21, 2022, https://www.iea.org/data-and-statistics/charts/iraqs-electricity-supply-and-demand-2018-2030.
37. Johansen, Palani, and Ala'Aldeen, *Ninewa Plains and Western Ninewa*, 19.
38. "Conflict and Stabilization Monitoring Framework," United States Institute of Peace (USIP), accessed November 27, 2023, https://www.usip.org/programs/conflict-and-stabilization-monitoring-framework.
39. USIP, "Conflict and Stabilization Monitoring Framework."
40. Johansen, Palani, and Ala'Aldeen, *Ninewa Plains and Western Ninewa*, 57.
41. Johansen, Palani, and Ala'Aldeen.
42. "Iraq: Marked for life: Displaced Iraqis in Cycle of Abuse and Stigmatization," Amnesty International, November 24, 2020, https://www.amnesty.org/en/documents/mde14/3318/2020/en.
43. "First Gender-Based Violence Strategic Plan launched in Iraq," United Nations Iraq Press Office, February 2, 2022, https://iraq.un.org/en/170563-first-gender-based-violence-strategic-plan-launched-iraq.
44. Fanar Haddad, "Understanding Iraq's Hashd al-Sha'bi: State and Power in Post-2014 Iraq," Century Foundation, May 5, 2018, https://tcf.org/content/report/understanding-iraqs-hashd-al-shabi.
45. Michael Knights, "Back into the Shadows? The Future of Kata'ib Hezbollah and Iran's Other Proxies in Iraq," *CTC Sentinel* 13, no. 10 (October 2020): 1–22; Beston Husen Arif, "Pro-Government Militias in Iraq: A Threat to Human Rights and Stability," *Asian Affairs* 52, no. 2 (2021): 312–326.
46. Osama Gharizi and Joshua Lebowitz, "Four Years After ISIS, Iraq's Tal Afar Remains Riven by Communal Divisions," United States Institute of Peace, August 2, 2021, https://www.usip.org/publications/2021/08/four-years-after-isis-iraqs-tal-afar-remains-riven-communal-divisions.
47. Joanne Serrieh, "Over 500 People Killed Since Protests Erupted in Iraq: Human Rights Commission," *Al Arabiya News (English)*, March 2, 2020, https://english.alarabiya.net/News/middle-east/2020/02/03/Over-500-people-killed-since-protests-erupted-in-Iraq-Iraqi-Human-Rights-Commission.
48. "Humanitarian Evacuations in Violence and Armed Conflict," Internal Note for Internal Displacement Section, Division of International Protection, United Nations High Commissioner on Refugees, June 2016, https://www.unhcr.org/sites/default/files/legacy-pdf/4794a5512.pdf; "Civil Society Statement on the Protection of Civilians in Urban Conflict," International Rescue Committee, May 17, 2022, https://www.rescue.org/press-release/civil-society-statement-protection-civilians-urban-conflict-2022.
49. R. Charli Carpenter, "'Women, Children and Other Vulnerable Groups': Gender, Strategic Frames and the Protection of Civilians as a Transnational Issue," *International Studies Quarterly* 49, no. 2 (2005): 295–334; Shane Joshua Barter, "The Partisans: Civilian Support and Indirect Violence in Civil War" (working paper, 2022).

50. Kreft and Agerberg, "Imperfect Victims," 3.
51. See interview with respondent B10 in chapter 5.
52. A. Mark Clarfield et al., "An Appeal to World Leaders: Health Care for Ethiopians in Tigray," *The Lancet* 399, no. 10323 (January 2022): 433; Dominique Arel and Jesse Driscoll, *Ukraine's Unnamed War: Before the Russian Invasion of 2022* (New York: Cambridge University Press, 2023); Erica De Bruin et al., "The Partisans: Civilian Support and Indirect Violence in Civil War" (working paper, February 2023).
53. United Nations University, *The Protection of Civilians in United Nations Peacekeeping Handbook* (New York: United Nations Press, 2020), 10–11.
54. See Tamimi's blog at https://aymennjawad.org.
55. Margaret E Keck and Kathryn Sikkink, "Transnational Advocacy Networks in International and Regional Politics," *International Social Science Journal* 68, nos. 227–228 (2019): 65–76.
56. USIP, "Conflict and Stabilization Monitoring Framework."
57. Gordon, *Degrade and Destroy*, 197–212.
58. "Displacement from Sinjar: 3–14 August," REACH Initiative, August 18, 2014, https://reliefweb.int/report/iraq/displacement-sinjar-3-14-august.
59. Shannon Doocy and Emily Lyles, "Humanitarian Needs in Government-Controlled Areas of Syria," *PLoS Currents* 10 (February 2018), https://currents.plos.org/disasters/article/humanitarian-needs-in-government-controlled-areas-of-syria; Kevin Mazur, *Revolution in Syria: Identity, Networks, and Repression* (New York: Cambridge University Press, 2021); Alex J. Bellamy, *Syria Betrayed: Atrocities, War, and the Failure of International Diplomacy* (New York: Columbia University Press, 2022).
60. Benjamin Hubbard and Hwaida Saad, "More Than 7,000 People Evacuated From 4 Besieged Syrian Towns," *New York Times*, April 14, 2017, https://www.nytimes.com/2017/04/14/world/middleeast/syria-towns-sieges-population-transfers-assad.html.
61. David P. Southall et al., "The UN Must Provide Secure Medical and Humanitarian Assistance in Ukraine," *The Lancet* 399, no. 10332 (2022): 1301–1302.
62. Berman and Lake, *Proxy Wars: Suppressing Violence Through Local Agents*.
63. "US-led Coalition Airstrikes in Iraq and Syria," Airwars, accessed October 30, 2023, https://airwars.org/conflict/coalition-in-iraq-and-syria.
64. Azmat Khan, "The Civilian Casualty Files: Hidden Pentagon Records Reveal Patterns of Failure in Deadly Airstrikes," *New York Times*, December 18, 2021, https://www.nytimes.com/spotlight/the-civilian-casualty-files-pentagon-reports.
65. Azmat Khan and Anand Gopal, "The Uncounted," *New York Times*, November 17, 2017, https://www.nytimes.com/interactive/2017/11/16/magazine/uncounted-civilian-casualties-iraq-airstrikes.html.
66. In 2009, the Iraqi government adopted Law 20—"Compensating the Victims of Military Operations, Military Mistakes and Terrorist Actions"—to compensate for deaths, injuries, and damage affecting work, study, or property. The law was amended in 2015 to apply retroactively to the period 2003 through 2018 to account for the U.S.-led intervention and subsequent anti-IS campaign.

67. Matt Gluck, "An Examination of U.S. Military Payments to Civilians Harmed During Conflict in Afghanistan and Iraq," *Lawfare*, October 8, 2020, https://www.lawfareblog.com/examination-us-military-payments-civilians-harmed-during-conflict-afghanistan-and-iraq.
68. "A Practical Guide to International Humanitarian Law," Médecins Sans Frontières, accessed October 30, 23, https://guide-humanitarian-law.org/content/article/3/civilians; Andreas Wenger and Simon J. A. Mason, "The Civilianization of Armed Conflict: Trends and Implications," *International Review of the Red Cross* 90, no. 872 (2008): 835–852.
69. Michael Walzer, *Just and Unjust Wars: A Moral Argument with Historical Illustrations*, 5th ed. (New York: Basic Books, 2015).
70. Roger Petersen, *Resistance and Rebellion*.
71. Anne Frank, *The Diary of a Young Girl*, ed. Otto M. Frank and Mirjam Pressler, trans. Susan Massotty (New York: Bantam Books, 1997).

Appendix A. Survey Methodology

1. The Baghdad survey was covered under Ohio State University IRB Protocol #2016B0455. An anonymized version of the pre-analysis plan was preregistered with Experiments in Governance in Politics (Protocol No. 20171023AA).
2. Allan Dafoe, Baobao Zhang, and Devin Caughey, "Information Equivalence in Survey Experiments," *Political Analysis* 26, no. 4 (2018): 399–416.
3. Will Bullock, Kosuke Imai, and Jacob N. Shapiro, "Statistical Analysis of Endorsement Experiments: Measuring Support for Militant Groups in Pakistan," *Political Analysis* 19, no. 4 (2011): 363–384; Graeme Blair, Kosuke Imai, and Jason Lyall, "Comparing and Combining List and Endorsement Experiments: Evidence from Afghanistan," *American Journal of Political Science* 58, no. 4 (2014): 1043–1063; C. Christine Fair et al., "Relative Poverty, Perceived Violence, and Support for Militant Politics: Evidence from Pakistan," *Political Science Research and Methods* 6, no. 1 (2016): 1–25.
4. Randomization checks and covariate balance across control and treatment groups is available in the appendix.
5. Graeme Blair et al., "Poverty and Support for Militant Politics: Evidence from Pakistan," *American Journal of Political Science* 57, no. 1 (2013): 30–48.
6. Jens Hainmueller, Dominik Hangartner, and Teppei Yamamoto find that conjoint designs predict preferences that are largely consistent with respondents' observed behavior. Scott F. Abramson, Korhan Koçak, and Asya Magazinnik argue that obstacles remain in substantively interpreting conjoint experiments. Jens Hainmueller, Dominik Hangartner, and Teppei Yamamoto, "Validating Vignette and Conjoint Survey Experiments Against Real-World Behavior," *Proceedings of the National Academy of Sciences* 112, no. 8 (2015), 2395–2400; Scott F. Abramson, Korhan Koçak, and Asya Magazinnik, "What Do We Learn About Voter Preferences from Conjoint Experiments?," *American Journal of Political Science* 66, no. 4 (2022): 1008–1020.

7. Table A.3 presents a list of censored profiles.
8. Thomas Leeper, *Cregg: Simple Conjoint Tidying, Analysis, and Visualization*, R package version 0.3.0 (2018); Leeper, Hobolt, and Tilley, "Measuring Subgroup Preferences in Conjoint Experiments."
9. Claire L. Adida et al., "Who's Asking? Interviewer Coethnicity Effects in African Survey Data," *Comparative Political Studies* 49, no. 12 (2016): 1630–1660; Justine M. Davis and Martha Wilfahrt, "Enumerator Experiences in Violent Research Environments," *Comparative Political Studies*, online first, June 8, 2023, https://doi.org/10.1177/00104140231178735.
10. Noble Kuriakose and Michael Robbins, "Don't Get Duped: Fraud Through Duplication in Public Opinion Surveys," *Statistical Journal of the IAOS* 32, no. 3 (2016): 283–291.
11. Bryan K. Orme, *Getting Started with Conjoint Analysis: Strategies for Product Design and Pricing Research* (Madison, WI: Research Publishers, 2010), 64.

Bibliography

Abadi, Haider al-. *Impossible Victory: How Iraq Defeated the Islamic State*. London: Biteback Publishing, 2022.

Abbott, Andrew. *Time Matters: On Theory and Method*. Chicago: University of Chicago Press, 2001.

Abdelal, Rawi, Yoshiko M Herrera, Alastair Iain Johnston, and Rose McDermott. *Measuring Identity: A Guide for Social Scientists*. New York: Cambridge University Press, 2009.

Abdelhady, Dalia. *Routledge Handbook on Middle Eastern Diasporas*. London: Taylor and Francis, 2022.

Abdul-Ahad, Ghaith. "After the Liberation of Mosul, an Orgy of Killing." *The Guardian*, November 21, 2017. https://www.theguardian.com/world/2017/nov/21/after-the-liberation-of-mosul-an-orgy-of-killing.

———. *A Stranger in Your Own City: Travels in the Middle East's Long War*. New York: Knopf, 2023.

Abramson, Scott F., Korhan Koçak, and Asya Magazinnik. "What do We Learn About Voter Preferences from Conjoint Experiments?" *American Journal of Political Science* 66, no. 4 (2022): 1008–1020.

Adhikari, Prakash. "Conflict-Induced Displacement, Understanding the Causes of Flight." *American Journal of Political Science* 57, no. 1 (2013): 82–89.

Adida, Claire L., Karen E. Ferree, Daniel N. Posner, and Amanda Lea Robinson. "Who's Asking? Interviewer Coethnicity Effects in African Survey Data." *Comparative Political Studies* 49, no. 12 (2016): 1630–1660.

Ahn, Julie, Maeve Campbell, and Peter Knoetgen. *The Politics of Security in Ninewa: Preventing an ISIS Resurgence in Northern Iraq*. Cambridge, MA: Kennedy School of Government, Harvard University, May 2018.

Ahram, Ariel. *Proxy Warriors: The Rise and Fall of State-Sponsored Militias.* Palo Alto, CA: Stanford University Press, 2011.

Ali, Zahra. "From Recognition to Redistribution? Protest Movements in Iraq in the Age of 'New Civil Society.'" *Journal of Intervention and Statebuilding* 15, no. 4 (2021): 528–542.

———. *Women and Gender in Iraq: Between Nation-Building and Fragmentation.* New York: Cambridge University Press, 2018.

Alkhayanee, Khitam. *Justice and Security Needs in Iraq After ISIL.* Special Report 389. Washington, DC: United State Institute of Peace, August 2016.

Alkhudary, Taif. "Five Years On, Still No Justice for Iraq's Camp Speicher Victims." *Al Jazeera*, June 12, 2019. https://www.aljazeera.com/opinions/2019/6/12/five-years-on-still-no-justice-for-iraqs-camp-speicher-victims#:~:text=In%20no%20way%20do%20such,that%20unfolded%20in%20June%202014.

———. "'We Want a Country': The Urban Politics of the October Revolution in Baghdad's Tahrir Square." *Third World Quarterly*, online first, December 2, 2022. https://doi.org/10.1080/01436597.2022.2141219.

Almeida, Manuel. "Conducting Primary Research in Yemen: Challenges and Lessons." ARK Group DMCC, June 15, 2020. https://www.ark.international/ark-blog/conducting-primary-research-in-yemen-challenges-and-lessons.

Alshamary, Marsin. "The Iraq Invasion at Twenty: Iraq's Struggle for Democracy." *Journal of Democracy* 34, no. 2 (2023): 150–162.

Alshamary, Marsin, and Hamzeh Hadad. "The Collective Neglect of Southern Iraq: Missed Opportunities for Development and Good Governance." *International Peacekeeping*, online first, February 16, 2023. https://doi.org/10.1080/13533312.2023.2177640.

"Amid Iraq's Turmoil, Tal Afar Builds Peace." United States Institute of Peace, November 5, 2020. https://www.usip.org/publications/2020/11/amid-iraqs-turmoil-tal-afar-builds-peace.

Anderson, Mary B. *Do No Harm: How Aid Can Support Peace—or War.* London: Lynne Rienner Publishers, 1999.

Arab Barometer. *Arab Barometer VI: Iraq Country Report.* Princeton, NJ: Arab Barometer. https://www.arabbarometer.org/wp-content/uploads/Iraq-Arab-Barometer-Public-Opinion-2021-ENG.pdf.

"Arab Barometer Wave III (2012–2014)." Arab Barometer, accessed October 19, 2023. https://www.arabbarometer.org/surveys/arab-barometer-wave-iii.

Arango, Tim. "Dozens Killed in Battles Across Iraq as Sunnis Escalate Protests Against Government." *New York Times*, April 23, 2013. https://www.nytimes.com/2013/04/24/world/middleeast/clashes-at-sunni-protest-site-in-iraq.html.

Arel, Dominique, and Jesse Driscoll. *Ukraine's Unnamed War: Before the Russian Invasion of 2022.* New York: Cambridge University Press, 2023.

Arif, Beston Husen. "Pro-Government Militias in Iraq: A Threat to Human Rights and Stability." *Asian Affairs* 52, no. 2 (2021): 312–326.

Arjona, Ana. "Civilian Cooperation and Non-cooperation with Non-state Armed Groups: The Centrality of Obedience and Resistance." *Small Wars & Insurgencies* 28, nos. 4–5 (2017): 755–778.

———. *Rebelocracy: Social Order in the Colombian Civil War*. New York: Cambridge University Press, 2016.

———. "Subnational Units, the Locus of Choice, and Theory Building: The Case of Civilian Agency in Civil War." In *Inside Countries: Subnational Research in Comparative Politics*, edited by Agustina Giraudy, Eduardo Moncada, and Richard Snyder, 214–242. New York: Cambridge University Press, 2019:

Atran, Scott. *In Gods We Trust: The Evolutionary Landscape of Religion*. Oxford University Press, 2002.

Atran, Scott, Hammad Sheikh, and Ángel Gómez. "For Cause and Comrade: Devoted Actors and Willingness to Fight." *Cliodynamics* 5, no. 1 (2014): 41–57.

Autesserre, Séverine. *The Frontlines of Peace: An Insider's Guide to Changing the World*. New York: Oxford University Press, 2021.

Avant, Deborah, Marie Berry, Erica Chenoweth, Rachel Epstein, Cullen Hendrix, Oliver Kaplan, and Timothy Sisk, eds. *Civil Action and the Dynamics of Violence*. New York: Oxford University Press, 2019.

Baczko, Adam, Gilles Dorronsoro, and Arthur Quesnay. *Civil War in Syria: Mobilization and Competing Social Orders*. New York: Cambridge University Press, 2018.

Baines, Erin, and Emily Paddon. "'This Is How We Survived' Civilian Agency and Humanitarian Protection." *Security Dialogue* 43, no. 3 (2012): 231–247.

Balcells, Laia. *Rivalry and Revenge: The Politics of Violence During Civil War*. New York: Cambridge University Press, 2017.

Balcells, Laia, and Jessica A. Stanton. "Violence Against Civilians During Armed Conflict: Moving Beyond the Macro- and Micro-Level Divide." *Annual Review of Political Science* 24 (2020): 45–69.

Bamber-Zryd, Matthew. "Cyclical Jihadist Governance: The Islamic State Governance Cycle in Iraq and Syria." *Small Wars & Insurgencies* 33, no. 8 (2022): 1314–1344.

Baram, Amatzia. *Saddam Husayn and Islam, 1968-2003: Ba'thi Iraq from Secularism to Faith*. Washington, DC: Woodrow Wilson Center Press, 2014.

Barber, Matthew. "They That Remain: Syrian and Iraqi Christian Communities Amid the Syria Conflict and the Rise of the Islamic State." In *Christianity and Freedom*, edited by Allen D. Hertzke and Timothy Samuel Shah, 453–488. New York: Cambridge University Press, 2016.

Barrie, Christopher. "Sect, Nation, and Identity after the Fall of Mosul: Evidence from a Natural Experiment." *American Journal of Sociology* 127, no. 3 (November 2021): 695–738.

Bar-Tal, Daniel, ed. *Intergroup Conflicts and Their Resolution: A Social Psychological Perspective*. New York: Psychology Press, 2011.

Barter, Shane Joshua. *Civilian Strategy in Civil War: Insights from Indonesia, Thailand, and the Philippines*. New York: Palgrave Macmillan, 2014.

———. "The Partisans: Civilian Support and Indirect Violence in Civil War." Unpublished manuscript, 2022.

———. "Second-Order Ethnic Minorities in Asian Secessionist Conflicts: Problems and Prospects." *Asian Ethnicity* 16, no. 2 (2015): 123–135.

"Battle for Mosul: IS 'Blows Up' al-Nuri Mosque." *BBC News*, June 22, 2017. https://www.bbc.com/news/world-middle-east-40361857#.

Bausch, Andrew W. "Coup-Proofing and Military Inefficiencies: An Experiment." *International Interactions* 44, no. 1 (2018): 1–32.

Bellamy, Alex J. *Syria Betrayed: Atrocities, War, and the Failure of International Diplomacy*. New York: Columbia University Press, 2022.

Bellows, John, and Edward Miguel. "War and Local Collective Action in Sierra Leone." *Journal of Public Economics* 93, nos. 11–12 (2009): 1144–1157.

Benjamen, Alda. *Assyrians in Modern Iraq: Negotiating Political and Cultural Space*. New York: Cambridge University Press, 2022.

Berman, Eli, Joseph H. Felter, and Jacob N. Shapiro. *Small Wars, Big Data: The Information Revolution in Modern Conflict*. Princeton, NJ: Princeton University Press, 2018.

Berman, Eli, and David A. Lake. *Proxy Wars: Suppressing Violence Through Local Agents*. Ithaca, NY: Cornell University Press, 2019.

Berry, Marie E. "Radicalising Resilience: Mothering, Solidarity, and Interdependence Among Women Survivors of War." *Journal of International Relations and Development* 25, no. 4 (2022): 946–966.

———. *War, Women, and Power: From Violence to Mobilization in Rwanda and Bosnia Herzegovina*. New York: Cambridge University Press, 2018.

Biddle, Stephen. *Nonstate Warfare: The Military Methods of Guerillas, Warlords, and Militias*. Princeton, NJ: Princeton University Press, 2021.

Biddle, Stephen, Jeffrey A. Friedman, and Jacob N. Shapiro. "Testing the Surge: Why Did Violence Decline in Iraq in 2007?" *International Security* 37, no. 1 (2012): 7–40.

Birnbaum, Ben. "Allawi Cites 'Dictatorship,' Iranian Control in Iraq." *Washington Times*, March 22, 2012. https://www.washingtontimes.com/news/2012/mar/22/allawi-cites-dictatorship-iranian-control-iraq.

Blair, Graeme, C. Christine Fair, Neil Malhotra, and Jacob N. Shapiro. "Poverty and Support for Militant Politics: Evidence from Pakistan." *American Journal of Political Science* 57, no. 1 (2013): 30–48.

Blair, Graeme, Kosuke Imai, and Jason Lyall. "Comparing and Combining List and Endorsement Experiments: Evidence from Afghanistan." *American Journal of Political Science* 58, no. 4 (2014): 1043–1063.

Blattman, Christopher. "From Violence to Voting: War and Political Participation in Uganda." *American Political Science Review* 103, no. 2 (2009): 231–247.

———. *Why We Fight: The Roots of War and the Paths to Peace*. New York: Viking, 2022.

Blaydes, Lisa. *State of Repression: Iraq Under Saddam Hussein*. Princeton, NJ: Princeton University Press, 2018.

Bogaards, Matthijs. "Iraq's Constitution of 2005: The Case Against Consociationalism 'Light.'" *Ethnopolitics* 20, no. 2 (2021): 186–202.

Boghani, Priyanka. "In Their Own Words: Sunnis on Their Treatment in Maliki's Iraq." *PBS Frontline*, October 28, 2014. https://www.pbs.org/wgbh/frontline/article/in-their-own-words-sunnis-on-their-treatment-in-malikis-iraq.

Bosi, Lorenzo, and Stefan Malthaner. "Political Violence." In The *Oxford Handbook of Social Movements*, edited by Donatella Della Porta and Mario Diani, 439–451. New York: Oxford University Press, 2015.

Bozzoli, Carlos, Tilman Brueck, and Tony Muhumuza. "Does War Influence Individual Expectations?" *Economics Letters* 113, no. 3 (2011): 288–291.

Brincka, Bradley. "Yazidi PMU Fighters Face Uncertainty in the KRG." *1001 Iraqi Thoughts*, August 22, 2017. https://1001iraqithoughts.com/2017/08/22/yazidi-pmu-fighters-face-uncertainty-in-the-krg.

Bullock, Will, Kosuke Imai, and Jacob N. Shapiro. "Statistical Analysis of Endorsement Experiments: Measuring Support for Militant Groups in Pakistan." *Political Analysis* 19, no. 4 (2011): 363–384.

Callen, Michael, Mohammad Isaqzadeh, James D. Long, and Charles Sprenger. "Violence and Risk Preference: Experimental Evidence from Afghanistan." *American Economic Review* 104, no. 1 (2014): 123–48.

Cancian, Matthew. "The Impact of Modern-System Training on Battlefield Participation by Kurdish Soldiers." *Journal of Conflict Resolution* 66, nos. 7–8 (2022): 1449–1480.

Cancian, Matthew, Richard Nielsen, and Austin Knuppe. "Deliberation and Ethnic Cooperation in Kirkuk." Unpublished manuscript, 2023.

Cannon, Walter B. "The James-Lange Theory of Emotions: A Critical Examination and an Alternative Theory." *American Journal of Psychology* 39, nos. 1–4 (1927): 106–124.

Carpenter, Ami C. "Havens in a Firestorm: Perspectives from Baghdad on Resilience to Sectarian Violence." *Civil Wars* 14, no. 2 (2012): 182–204.

Carpenter, R. Charli. "Recognizing Gender-Based Violence Against Civilian Men and Boys in Conflict Situations." *Security Dialogue* 37, no. 1 (2006): 83–103.

———. "'Women, Children and Other Vulnerable Groups': Gender, Strategic Frames and the Protection of Civilians as a Transnational Issue." *International Studies Quarterly* 49, no. 2 (2005): 295–334.

Center for Civilians in Conflict. *"If I Leave . . . I Cannot Breathe": Climate Change and Civilian Protection in Iraq*. Washington, DC: CIVIC, July 2022.

Cetorelli, Victoria, and Sareta Ashraph. *A Demographic Documentation of ISIS's Attack on the Yazidi Village of Kocho*. London: London School of Economics, Middle East Centre, June 2019. https://www.un.org/sexualviolenceinconflict/wp-content/uploads/2019/08/report/a-demographic-documentation-of-isiss-attack-on-the-yazidi-village-of-kocho/Cetorelli_Demographic_documentation_ISIS_attack.pdf.

Cetorelli, Valeria, Isaac Sasson, Nazar Shabila, and Gilbert Burnham. "Mortality and Kidnapping Estimates for the Yazidi Population in the Area of Mount Sinjar, Iraq, in August 2014: A Retrospective Household Survey." *PLoS Medicine* 14, no. 5 (2017): 1–15.

Chandra, Kanchan. "What Is Ethnic Identity and Does It Matter?" *Annual Review Political Science* 9, no. 1 (2006): 397–424.

Checkel, Jeffrey T., ed. *Transnational Dynamics of Civil War*. New York: Cambridge University Press, 2013.

Chenoweth, Erika. *Civil Resistance: What Everyone Needs to Know*. New York: Oxford University Press, 2021.
Chivers, C.J. "Answering a Cleric's Call, Iraqi Shiites Take Up Arms." *New York Times*, June 9, 2014. https://www.nytimes.com/2014/06/22/world/middleeast/iraq-militia.html.
Christia, Fotini. *Alliance Formation in Civil Wars*. New York: Cambridge University Press, 2012.
Chulov, Martin, and Kareem Shaheen. "Destroying Great Mosque of al-Nuri 'Is Isis Declaring Defeat.'" *The Guardian*, June 22, 2017. https://www.theguardian.com/world/2017/jun/21/mosuls-grand-al-nouri-mosque-blown-up-by-isis-fighters.
"Civil Society Statement on the Protection of Civilians in Urban Conflict." International Rescue Committee, May 17, 2022. https://www.rescue.org/press-release/civil-society-statement-protection-civilians-urban-conflict-2022.
Clarfield, A. Mark, Geoffrey Gill, Christian J. Leuner, Allon E. Moses, and Ora Paltiel. "An Appeal to World Leaders: Health Care for Ethiopians in Tigray." *The Lancet* 399 (January 2022): 433.
Clark, David, and Patrick Regan. "Mass Mobilization Protest Data," version 4.0 (1990–2019). Mass Mobilization Project, accessed November 3, 2023. https://massmobilization.github.io.
Coker, Margaret, and Falih Hassan. "Iraq Prime Minister Declares Victory Over ISIS." *New York Times*, December 9, 2017. https://www.nytimes.com/2017/12/09/world/middleeast/iraq-isis-haider-al-abadi.html.
Condra, Luke N., Joseph H. Felter, Radha K. Iyengar, and Jacob N. Shapiro. "The Effect of Civilian Casualties in Afghanistan and Iraq." Working Paper 16152, National Bureau of Economic Research, December 2011. https://www.nber.org/papers/w16152.
Condra, Luke N., and Jacob N. Shapiro. "Who Takes the Blame? The Strategic Effects of Collateral Damage." *American Journal of Political Science* 56, no. 1 (2012): 167–187.
"Conflict and Stabilization Monitoring Framework." United States Institute of Peace, accessed November 27, 2023. https://www.usip.org/programs/conflict-and-stabilization-monitoring-framework.
Conflict to Peace Lab. *Report: Exploring Obstacles to Social Cohesion in the Aftermath of Violent Conflict*. Columbus: Mershon Center for International Security Studies, Ohio State University, November 2019. https://mershoncenter.osu.edu/sites/default/files/2020-02/C2P%20Report_Interactive.pdf.
Coşar, Nevin, and Sevtap Demirci. "The Mosul Question and the Turkish Republic: Before and After the Frontier Treaty, 1926." *Middle Eastern Studies* 42, no. 1 (2006): 123–132.
Costantini, Irene. "The Iraqi Protest Movement: Social Mobilization Amidst Violence and Instability." *British Journal of Middle Eastern Studies* 48, no. 5 (2021): 832–849.
Cottam, Martha L., and Joe W. Huseby. *Confronting Al Qaeda: The Sunni Awakening and American Strategy in Al Anbar*. Lantham, MD: Rowman and Littlefield, 2016.
"Country Reports on Terrorism 2019: Iraq." Bureau of Counterterrorism, U.S. Department of State, accessed October 19, 2023. https://www.state.gov/reports/country-reports-on-terrorism-2019/iraq/#:~:text=2019%20Terrorist%20Incidents%3A%20According%20to,2019%20as%20of%20December%201.

Crawford, Neta C. "Blood and Treasure: United States Budgetary Costs and Human Costs of 20 Years of War in Iraq and Syria: 2003–2023." Costs of War Project, Watson Institute of International Affairs, Brown University, March 15, 2023. https://watson.brown.edu/costsofwar/papers/2023/IraqSyria20.

Cronin-Furman, Kate, and Milli Lake. "Ethics Abroad: Fieldwork in Fragile and Violent Contexts." *PS: Political Science & Politics* 51, no. 3 (2018): 607–614.

Dafoe, Allan, Baobao Zhang, and Devin Caughey. "Information Equivalence in Survey Experiments." *Political Analysis* 26, no. 4 (2018): 399–416.

Dagher, Munquith, and Karl Kaltenthaler. "A Striking Positive Shift in Sunni Opinion in Iraq Is Underway. Here's What It Means." *Washington Post*, September 14, 2017. https://www.washingtonpost.com/news/monkey-cage/wp/2017/09/14/iraqi-sunnis-are-impressed-by-the-defeat-of-isis-heres-what-that-could-mean.

Dagher, Munqith, Karl Kaltenthaler, Michele J. Gelfand, Arie Kruglanski, and Ian McCulloh. *ISIS in Iraq: The Social and Psychological Foundations of Terror*. New York: Oxford University Press, 2023.

Darwish, Mahmoud. *Unfortunately, It Was Paradise: Selected Poems*. Berkeley: University of California Press, 2013.

Davis, Justine M., and Martha Wilfahrt. "Enumerator Experiences in Violent Research Environments." *Comparative Political Studies*, online first, June 8, 2023. https://doi.org/10.1177/00104140231178735.

Dawod, Saman. "Neglected Yazidi Mass Graves Finally Exhumed in Iraq." *Al-Monitor*, October 30, 2020. https://www.al-monitor.com/originals/2020/10/iraq-sinjar-yazidis-mass-graves.html.

Day, Adam, Vanda Felbab-Brown, and Fanar Haddad. *Mastering the Gray Zone: Understanding a Changing Era of Conflict*. Carlisle, PA: Strategic Studies Institute, U.S. Army War College, December 2014.

De Bruin, Erica, Gabriella Levy, Livia Schubiger, and Weintraub Michael. "The Partisans: Civilian Support and Indirect Violence in Civil War." Unpublished manuscript, February 2023.

Derzsi-Horváth, András, Erica Gaston, and Bahra Saleh. *Who's Who: Quick Facts About Local and Sub-state Forces*. Berlin: Global Public Policy Institute, August 2017.

Devictor, Xavier. *Forcibly Displaced: Toward a Development Approach Supporting Refugees, the Internally Displaced, and Their Hosts*. Washington, DC: World Bank Group, 2017.

Diker, Eleni, Mohammad Khalaf, Michaella Vanore, and Soha Yousef. *Iraqi Minorities in Diaspora Mapping of Community Structures, Perceptions on Return, and Connections to the Homeland*. New York: United Nations International Organization for Migration, 2020.

"Displacement from Sinjar: 3–14 August." REACH Initiative, August 18, 2014. https://reliefweb.int/report/iraq/displacement-sinjar-3-14-august.

Dodge, Toby. "Can Iraq be saved?" *Survival* 56, no. 5 (2014): 7–20.

———. *Iraq: From War to a New Authoritarianism*. London: Routledge, 2013.

Dodge, Toby, and Renad Mansour. *Politically Sanctioned Corruption and Barriers to Reform in Iraq*. London: Middle East & North Africa Program, Chatham House, June 2021.

https://www.chathamhouse.org/sites/default/files/2021-06/2021-06-17-politically-sanctioned-corruption-iraq-dodge-mansour.pdf.

Doocy, Shannon, and Emily Lyles. "Humanitarian Needs in Government-Controlled Areas of Syria." *PLoS Currents* 10 (February 2018). https://currents.plos.org/disasters/article/humanitarian-needs-in-government-controlled-areas-of-syria.

Dorff, Cassy. "Violent and Nonviolent Resistance in Contexts of Prolonged Crisis: The Civilian Perspective." *Journal of Global Security Studies* 4, no. 2 (2019): 286–291.

Downes, Alexander B. *Catastrophic Success: Why Foreign-Imposed Regime Change Goes Wrong.* Ithaca, NY: Cornell University Press, 2021.

Downes, Alexander B., and Jonathan Monten. "Forced to Be Free? Why Foreign-Imposed Regime Change Rarely Leads to Democratization." *International Security* 37, no. 4 (2013): 90–131.

Downes, Alexander B., and Lindsey A. O'Rourke. "You Can't Always Get What You Want: Why Foreign-Imposed Regime Change Seldom Improves Interstate Relations." *International Security* 41, no. 2 (2016): 43–89.

Driscoll, Jesse. *Doing Global Fieldwork: A Social Scientist's Guide to Mixed-Methods Research Far from Home.* New York: Columbia University Press, 2021.

Dukhan, Haian. "Tribal Mobilisation Forces in Iraq: Subtleties of Formation and Consequential Power Dynamics." *British Journal of Middle Eastern Studies*, online first, June 14, 2022. https://doi.org/10.1080/13530194.2022.2087599.

Edelstein, David M. *Occupational Hazards: Success and Failure in Military Occupation.* Ithaca, NY: Cornell University Press, 2011.

Egami, Naoki, and Kosuke Imai. "Causal Interaction in Factorial Experiments: Application to Conjoint Analysis." *Journal of the American Statistical Association* 114, no. 526 (2019): 529–540.

Eriksson, Jacob, and Ahmed Khaleel. *Iraq After ISIS: The Challenges of Post-war Recovery.* Cham, CH: Palgrave Pivot, 2018.

Euro-Mediterranean Human Rights Monitor. *Exiled at Home: Internal Displacement Resulted from the Armed Conflict in Iraq and Its Humanitarian Consequences.* Geneva, CH: Euro-Mediterranean Human Rights Monitor, June 2021. https://euromedmonitor.org/uploads/reports/IraqReportEN.pdf https://reliefweb.int/report/iraq/exiled-home-internal-displacement-resulted-armed-conflict-iraq-and-its-humanitarian.

Fahim, Kareem, and Suadad Al-Salhy. "Exhausted and Bereft, Iraqi Soldiers Quit Fight." *New York Times*, June 11, 2014. https://www.nytimes.com/2014/06/11/world/middleeast/exhausted-and-bereft-iraqi-soldiers-quit-fight.html.

Fair, C. Christine, Rebecca Littman, Neil Malhotra, and Jacob N. Shapiro. "Relative Poverty, Perceived Violence, and Support for Militant Politics: Evidence from Pakistan." *Political Science Research and Methods* 6, no. 1 (2016): 1–25.

"Fallujah: Anti-ISIL Drive Displaces 30,000 More Iraqis." *Al Jazeera*, June 19, 2016. https://www.aljazeera.com/news/2016/6/19/fallujah-anti-isil-drive-displaces-30000-more-iraqis.

Feaver, Peter D. "The Right to Be Right: Civil-Military Relations and the Iraq Surge Decision." *International Security* 35, no. 4 (2011): 87–125.

Ferris, Elizabeth. "Remembering Iraq's Displaced." Brookings Institution, March 18, 2013. https://www.brookings.edu/articles/remembering-iraqs-displaced.
Finkel, Evgeny. *Ordinary Jews: Choice and Survival During the Holocaust*. Princeton, NJ: Princeton University Press, 2017.
"First Gender Based Violence Strategic Plan Launched in Iraq." United Nations Iraq Press Office, February 2, 2022. https://iraq.un.org/en/170563-first-gender-based-violence-strategic-plan-launched-iraq.
Fishbein, Emily, and Nu Nu Lusan. "Young, Rebellious and the Myanmar Military's 'Worst Enemy.'" *Al Jazeera*, October 5, 2022. https://www.aljazeera.com/news/2022/10/5/young-rebellious-and-the-myanmar-militarys-worst-enemy.
Flood, Derek Henry. "From Caliphate to Caves: The Islamic State's Asymmetric War in Northern Iraq." *CTC Sentinel* 11, no. 8 (September 2018): 30–34.
Foltyn, Simona. "Iraq: Anbar's Post-ISIL Reconstruction Spawns Autonomy Debate." *Al Jazeera*, January 27, 2021. https://www.aljazeera.com/economy/2021/1/27/iraq-anbars-post-isil-reconstruction-spawns-autonomy-debate.
Fouad, Ahmed. "Egypt's Copts Have No Plans to Arm Youth Groups." *Al Monitor*, July 3, 2017. https://www.al-monitor.com/originals/2017/07/egypt-scouts-christians-military-training-militias-security.html.
Foulkes Lucy, and Sarah-Jayne Blakemore. "Studying Individual Differences in Human Adolescent Brain Development." *Nature Neuroscience* 21, no. 3 (2018): 315–323.
Fraiman, Keren, Austin Long, and Caitlin Talmadge. "Why the Iraqi Army Collapsed (and What Can Be Done About It)." *Washington Post*, June 14, 2014. https://www.washingtonpost.com/news/monkey-cage/wp/2014/06/13/why-the-iraqi-army-collapsed-and-what-can-be-done-about-it.
Frank, Anne. *The Diary of a Young Girl*. Edited by Otto M. Frank and Mirjam Pressler. Translated by Susan Massotty. New York: Bantam Books, 1997.
Gannon, J. Andrés, Erik A. Gartzke, Jon R. Lindsay, and Peter Schram. "The Shadow of Deterrence: Why Capable Actors Engage in Contests Short of War." *Journal of Conflict Resolution*, online first, April 20, 2023. https://doi.org/10.1177/00220027231166345.
Gartenstein-Ross, Daveed, and Sterling Jensen. "The Role of Iraqi Tribes After the Islamic State's Ascendance." *Military Review*, July–August 2015, 102–110.
Gaston, Erica. *Iraq After ISIL: Qaraqosh, Hamdaniya District*. Berlin: Global Public Policy Institute, August 2017.
———. *Sunni Tribal Forces*. Berlin: Global Public Policy Institute, August 2017.
Gates, Scott, and Sukanya Podder. "Social Media, Recruitment, Allegiance and the Islamic State." *Perspectives on Terrorism* 9, no. 4 (2015): 107–116.
Gharizi, Osama, and Joshua Lebowitz. *Four Years After ISIS, Iraq's Tal Afar Remains Riven by Communal Divisions*. Washington, DC: United States Institute of Peace, August 2021.
Ghobashy, Tamer El-. "Iraq's Elite Special Forces Struggle to Regroup After Bloody Fight for Mosul." *Washington Post*, July 21, 2017. https://www.washingtonpost.com/news/worldviews/wp/2017/07/21/iraqs-elite-special-forces-struggle-to-regroup-after-bloody-fight-for-mosul.

Gigerenzer, Gerd. "Dread Risk, September 11, and Fatal Traffic Accidents." *Psychological Science* 15, no. 4 (2004): 286–287.

Gigerenzer, Gerd, and Wolfgang Gaissmaier. "Heuristic Decision Making." *Annual Review of Psychology* 62 (2011): 451–482.

Gigerenzer, Gerd, and Reinhard Selten. *Bounded Rationality: The Adaptive Toolbox*. Cambridge, MA: MIT Press, 2002.

Gigerenzer, Gerd, and Peter M. Todd. "Fast and Frugal heuristics: The Adaptive Toolbox." In *Simple Heuristics That Make Us Smart*, edited by Gerd Gigerenzer and Peter M. Todd, 3–34. New York: Oxford University Press, 1999.

Giustozzi, Antonio. "The Taliban's 'Military Courts.'" *Small Wars & Insurgencies* 25, no. 2 (2014): 284–296.

"Global Terrorism Database." National Consortium for the Study of Terrorism and Responses to Terrorism, University of Maryland. https://www.start.umd.edu/gtd.

Gluck, Caroline. "Thousands of Civilians Flee Raging Battle for Falluja." United Nations High Commissioner for Refugees. May 31, 2016. https://www.unhcr.org/news/stories/thousands-civilians-flee-raging-battle-falluja.

Gluck, Matt. "An Examination of U.S. Military Payments to Civilians Harmed During Conflict in Afghanistan and Iraq." *Lawfare*, October 8, 2020. https://www.lawfareblog.com/examination-us-military-payments-civilians-harmed-during-conflict-afghanistan-and-iraq.

Gómez, Ángel, Mercedes Martínez, Francois Alexi Martel, Lucía López-Rodríguez, Alexandra Vázquez, Juana Chinchilla, Borja Paredes, Mal Hettiarachchi, Nafees Hamid, and William B. Swann. "Why People Enter and Embrace Violent Groups." *Frontiers in Psychology* 11 (January 2021). https://doi.org/10.3389/fpsyg.2020.614657.

Gordon, Michael R. *Degrade and Destroy: The Inside Story of the War Against the Islamic State, from Barack Obama to Donald Trump*. New York: Macmillan, 2022.

Grasse, Donald, Renard Sexton, and Austin Wright. "The Logic and Impacts of Rebel Public Services Provision: Evidence from Taliban Courts in Afghanistan." Unpublished manuscript, 2022.

Gray, Jeffrey Alan. *The Psychology of Fear and Stress*. New York: Cambridge University Press, 1987.

Groh, Tyrone L. *Proxy War: The Least Bad Option*. Palo Alto, CA: Stanford University Press, 2019.

Gutiérrez-Sanín, Francisco, and Elisabeth Jean Wood. "What Should We Mean by 'Pattern of Political Violence?' Repertoire, Targeting, Frequency, and Technique." *Perspectives on Politics* 15, no. 1 (2017): 20–41.

Habyarimana, James, Macartan Humphreys, Daniel N. Posner, and Jeremy M. Weinstein. *Coethnicity: Diversity and the Dilemmas of Collective Action*. New York: Russell Sage Foundation, 2009.

Haddad, Fanar. *Sectarianism in Iraq: Antagonistic Visions of Unity*. New York: Oxford University Press, 2011.

———. "Sectarian relations in Arab Iraq: Contextualising the Civil War of 2006–2007." *British Journal of Middle Eastern Studies* 40, no. 2 (2013): 115–138.

———. "Turbulent Times for the 'New Iraq.'" *Current History* 121, no. 839 (2022): 331–337.
———. *Understanding Iraq's Hashd al-Sha'bi: State and Power in Post-2014 Iraq*. Washington, DC: Century Foundation, May 2018.
Hägerdal, Nils. "Ethnic Cleansing and the Politics of Restraint: Violence and Coexistence in the Lebanese Civil War." *Journal of Conflict Resolution* 63, no. 1 (2019): 59–84.
———. *Friend or Foe: Militia Intelligence and Ethnic Violence in the Lebanese Civil War*. New York: Columbia University Press, 2021.
Hainmueller, Jens, Dominik Hangartner, and Teppei Yamamoto. "Validating Vignette and Conjoint Survey Experiments Against Real-World Behavior." *Proceedings of the National Academy of Sciences* 112, no. 8 (2015): 2395–2400.
Hainmueller, Jens, Daniel J. Hopkins, and Teppei Yamamoto. "Causal Inference in Conjoint Analysis: Understanding Multidimensional Choices Via Stated Preference Experiments." *Political Analysis* 22, no. 1 (2014): 1–30.
Hanna, Reine, and Gregory J. Kruczek. *Contested Control: The Future of Security in Iraq's Nineveh Plain*. Chicago: Assyrian Policy Institute, June 2020.
Hasan al-Qarawee, Harith. *Iraq's Sectarian Crisis: A Legacy of Exclusion*. Washington, DC: Carnegie Endowment for International Peace, April 2014. https://carnegieendowment.org/files/iraq_sectarian_crisis.pdf.
Hashemi, Nader, and Danny Postel. *Sectarianization: Mapping the New Politics of the Middle East*. New York: Oxford University Press, 2017.
Hass, Jeffrey K. *Wartime Suffering and Survival: The Human Condition Under Siege in the Blockade of Leningrad, 1941–1944*. New York: Oxford University Press, 2021.
Hassan, Falih, Omar Al-Jawoshy, and Tim Arango. "Protesters Storm Baghdad's Green Zone to Denounce Corruption." *New York Times*, April 30 2016. https://www.nytimes.com/2016/05/01/world/middleeast/iraq-protesters-storm-parliament-demanding-end-to-corruption.html.
Hassan, Ghazwan. "Iraq Insurgents Take Saddam's Home Town in Lightning Advance." Reuters, June 11, 2014. https://www.reuters.com/article/us-iraq-security/iraq-insurgents-take-saddams-home-town-in-lightning-advance-idUKKBN0EM11U20140611.
Hassan, Hassan. "More Than ISIS, Iraq's Sunni Insurgency." *Sada* (blog). Carnegie Endowment for International Peace, June 17, 2014. https://carnegieendowment.org/sada/55930.
Hassan, Hassan, and Will McCants. "Experts Weigh in (Part 7): Is ISIS Good at Governing?" Brookings Institution, April 18, 2016. https://www.brookings.edu/blog/markaz/2016/04/18/experts-weigh-in-part-7-is-isis-good-at-governing.
Hassan, Mai, and Ahmed Kodouda. "Sudan's Uprising: The Fall of a Dictator." *Journal of Democracy* 30, no. 4 (2019): 89–103.
Hassin, Ahmed, and Mays Al-Juboori. *Humanitarian Challenges in Iraq's Displacement Crisis*. London: Ceasefire Centre for Civilian Rights and Minority Rights Group International, December 2016. https://minorityrights.org/wp-content/uploads/2016/12/MRG-report-A4_english-DECEMBER-2016_WEB-2.pdf.
Hechter, Michael. *Alien Rule*. New York: Cambridge University Press, 2013.

Helfont, Samuel. *Compulsion in Religion: Saddam Hussein, Islam, and the Roots of Insurgencies in Iraq.* New York: Oxford University Press, 2018.

Higel, Lahib. *Iraq's Displacement Crisis: Security and Protection.* London: Ceasefire Centre for Civilian Rights, March 2016.

Hill, Kent R. "On the Brink of Extinction Christians in Iraq and Syria." In *Under Caesar's Sword: How Christians Respond to Persecution,* edited by Daniel Philpott and Timothy Samuel Shah, 30–69. New York: Cambridge University Press, 2018.

Hirschman, Albert O. *Exit, Voice, and Loyalty: Responses to Decline in Firms, Organizations, and States.* Cambridge, MA: Harvard University Press, 1970.

Hoekstra, Quint. "How Mosul Fell: The Role of Coup-Proofing in the 2014 Partial Collapse of the Iraqi Security Forces." *International Politics* 57, no. 4 (2020): 684–703.

Hoffman, Bruce. *Anonymous Soldiers: The Struggle for Israel, 1917-1947.* New York: Vintage, 2016.

Horn, Rebecca, Eve S. Puffer, Elisabeth Roesch, and Heidi Lehmann. "Women's Perceptions of Effects of War on Intimate Partner Violence and Gender Roles in Two Post-conflict West African Countries: Consequences and Unexpected Opportunities." *Conflict and Health* 8, no. 1 (2014): 1–13.

Howe, Paul. "The Triple Nexus: A Potential Approach to Supporting the Achievement of the Sustainable Development Goals?" *World Development* 124 (2019): 104629. https://doi.org/10.1016/j.worlddev.2019.104629.

Hubbard, Benjamin, and Hwaida Saad. "More Than 7,000 People Evacuated From 4 Besieged Syrian Towns." *New York Times,* April 14, 2017. https://www.nytimes.com/2017/04/14/world/middleeast/syria-towns-sieges-population-transfers-assad.html.

Hyyppä, Tiina. "Council in War: Civilocracy, Order and Local Organisation in Daraya During the Syrian War." *Small Wars & Insurgencies* 34, no. 1 (2023): 52–80.

"Inflation, Consumer Prices (Annual %)." World Bank, accessed October 30, 2023. https://data.worldbank.org/indicator/FP.CPI.TOTL.ZG.

Ingram, Haroro J. *The Long Jihad: The Islamic State's Method of Insurgency: Control, Meaning, & the Occupation of Mosul in Context.* Washington, DC: Program on Extremism, George Washington University, September 2021. https://doi.org/10.4079/poe.05.2021.03.

———. "Three Traits of the Islamic State's Information Warfare." *RUSI Journal* 159, no. 6 (2014): 4–11.

Ingram, Haroro J., Craig Whiteside, and Charlie Winter. *The ISIS Reader: Milestone Texts of the Islamic State Movement.* New York: Oxford University Press, 2020.

International Committee of the Red Cross. *IHL Database: Customary IHL—Rule 5. The Definition of Civilians.* Geneva: ICRC, July 2022.

"Iraq—Food Prices." Humanitarian Data Exchange, World Food Programme, accessed October 30, 2023. https://data.humdata.org/dataset/wfp-food-prices-for-iraq.

"Iraq: Investigate Deadly Raid on Protest." Human Rights Watch, April 24, 2013. https://www.hrw.org/news/2013/04/24/iraq-investigate-deadly-raid-protest.

"Iraq: Marked for Life: Displaced Iraqis in Cycle of Abuse and Stigmatization." Amnesty International, November 24, 2020. https://www.amnesty.org/en/documents/mde14/3318/2020/en.

"Iraq: Sunni Women Tell of ISIS Detention, Torture." Human Rights Watch, February 20, 2017. https://www.hrw.org/news/2017/02/20/iraq-sunni-women-tell-isis-detention-torture.

"Iraq: UN Envoy Urges Political Leaders to Help End Bloodshed Following Latest Bombings." UN News. May 17, 2013. https://news.un.org/en/story/2013/05/439922.

"Iraq's Electricity Supply and Demand, 2018–2030." International Energy Association, last updated April 25, 2019. https:// www.iea.org/data-and-statistics/charts/iraqs-electricitysupply-and-demand-2018-2030.

"Iraq's Sadr Warns Will 'Shake the Ground' Against Militants." *Al Arabiya News*, June 26, 2014. https://english.alarabiya.net/News/middle-east/2014/06/26/Iraq-s-Sadr-warns-will-shake-the-ground-against-militants-.

"ISIS Urges Militants to March to Baghdad." *Al Arabiya News*, June 12, 2014. https://english.alarabiya.net/News/2014/06/12/ISIS-militants-plan-to-march-on-Baghdad#:~:text=The%20al%2DQaeda%2Dinspired%20militant,in%20the%20country%27s%20northern%20regions.

"Islamic State Group Claims Responsibility for Deadly Attack on Iraqi Police." *France 24*, December 18, 2022. https://www.france24.com/en/middle-east/20221218-islamic-state-group-claim-responsibility-for-deadly-attack-on-iraq-police.

"Islamic State 'Kills 322' from Single Sunni Tribe." *BBC News*, November 2, 2014. https://www.bbc.com/news/world-middle-east-29871068.

Jackson, Ashley. *Negotiating Survival: Civilian-Insurgent Relations in Afghanistan by Ashley Jackson*. London: Hurst, 2021.

Johansen, Henriette, Kamaran Palani, and Dlawer Ala'Aldeen. *Ninewa Plains and Western Ninewa: Barriers to Return and Community Resilience*. Washington, DC: United States Institute of Peace; Erbil, IQ: Middle East Research Institute, April 2020.

Johansson, Anna, and Stellan Vinthagen. *Conceptualizing "Everyday Resistance": A Transdisciplinary Approach*. London: Routledge, 2019.

Johnston, Patrick B., Jacob N. Shapiro, Howard J. Shatz, Benjamin Bahney, Danielle F. Jung, Patrick Ryan, and Jonathan Wallace. *Foundations of the Islamic State Management, Money, and Terror in Iraq, 2005-2010*. Santa Monica, CA: RAND Corporation, May 2016. https://www.rand.org/pubs/research_reports/RR1192.html.

Jolof, Linda, Patricia Rocca, Monir Mazaheri, Leah Okenwa Emegwa, and Tommy Carlsson. "Experiences of Armed Conflicts and Forced Migration Among Women from Countries in the Middle East, Balkans, and Africa: A Systematic Review of Qualitative Studies." *Conflict and Health* 16, no. 46 (2022): 1–16.

Jones, Seth G., James Dobbins, Daniel Byman, Christopher S. Chivvis, Ben Connable, Jeffrey Martini, Eric Robinson, and Nathan Chandler. *Rolling Back the Islamic State*. Santa Monica, CA: RAND Corporation, April 2017. https://www.rand.org/pubs/research_reports/RR1912.html

Jose, Betcy, and Peace A. Medie. "Civilian Self-Protection and Civilian Targeting in Armed Conflicts: Who Protects Civilians?" *Oxford Research Encyclopedia of Politics*, December 22, 2016. https://oxfordre.com/politics/display/10.1093/acrefore/9780190228637.001.0001/acrefore-9780190228637-e-216.

———. "Understanding Why and How Civilians Resort to Self-Protection in Armed Conflict." *International Studies Review* 17, no. 4 (2015): 515–535.

Kahan, Dan M. "Misconceptions, Misinformation, and the Logic of Identity-Protective Cognition." Cultural Cognition Project Working Paper Series No. 164, Yale Law School, May 24, 2017. https://papers.ssrn.com/sol3/papers.cfm?abstract_id=2973067.

Kahneman, Daniel. *Thinking, Fast and Slow.* New York: Farrar, Strauss and Giroux, 2011.

Kaldor, Mary. *New and Old Wars: Organised Violence in a Global Era.* Stanford, CA: Stanford University Press, 2006.

Kalin, Michael, and Nicholas Sambanis. "How to Think About Social Identity." *Annual Review of Political Science* 21 (2018): 239–257.

Kalin, Stephen. "Basic Infrastructure Repair in Mosul Will Cost Over $1 Billion: U.N." Reuters, July 5, 2017. https://www.reuters.com/article/us-mideast-crisis-iraq-aid/basic-infrastructure-repair-in-mosul-will-cost-over-1-billion-u-n-idUSKBN19Q28F.

Kaltenthaler, Karl C., Daniel M. Silverman, and Munqith M. Dagher. "Identity, Ideology, and Information: The Sources of Iraqi Public Support for the Islamic State." *Studies in Conflict & Terrorism* 41, no. 10 (2018): 801–824.

———. "Nationalism, Threat, and Support for External Intervention: Evidence from Iraq." *Security Studies* 29, no. 3 (2020): 1–25.

Kalyvas, Stathis N. "Ethnic Defection in Civil War." *Comparative Political Studies* 41, no. 8 (2008): 1043–1068.

———. *The Logic of Violence in Civil War.* New York: Cambridge University Press, 2006.

———. "The Ontology of 'Political Violence': Action and Identity in Civil Wars." *Perspectives on Politics* 1, no. 3 (2003): 475–494.

Kalyvas, Stathis N., and Laia Balcells. "International System and Technologies of Rebellion: How the End of the Cold War Shaped Internal Conflict." *American Political Science Review* 104, no. 3 (August 2010): 415–429.

Kalyvas, Stathis N., and Matthew Adam Kocher. "Ethnic Cleavages and Irregular War: Iraq and Vietnam." *Politics & Society* 35, no. 2 (2007): 183–223.

Kane, Sean. *Iraq's Disputed Territories: A View of Political Horizon and Implications for U.S. Policy.* Washington, DC: United States Institute of Peace, March 2011.

Kapiszewski, Diana, Lauren M. MacLean, and Benjamin L. Read. *Field Research in Political Science: Practices and Principles.* New York: Cambridge University Press, 2015.

Kaplan, Oliver. *Resisting War: How Communities Protect Themselves.* New York: Cambridge University Press, 2017.

Keck, Margaret E, and Kathryn Sikkink. *Activists Beyond Borders: Advocacy Networks in International Politics.* Ithaca, NY: Cornell University Press, 1998.

———. "Transnational Advocacy Networks in International and Regional Politics." *International Social Science Journal* 68, nos. 227–228 (2019): 65–76.

Keltner, Dacher, and Jennifer S. Lerner. "Emotion." In *Handbook of Social Psychology*, vol. 1, edited by Susan T Fiske, Daniel T Gilbert, and Gardner Lindzey, 317–352. New York: Wiley Online Library, 2010. https://doi.org/10.1002/9780470561119.socpsy001009.

Khan, Azmat. "The Civilian Casualty Files: Hidden Pentagon Records Reveal Patterns of Failure in Deadly Airstrikes." *New York Times*, December 18, 2021. https://www

.nytimes.com/interactive/2021/12/18/us/airstrikes-pentagon-records-civilian-deaths.html.
Khan, Azmat, and Anand Gopal. "The Uncounted." *New York Times*, November 17, 2017. https://www.nytimes.com/interactive/2017/11/16/magazine/uncounted-civilian-casualties-iraq-airstrikes.html.
Khan, Nadeem Elias, and Craig Whiteside. "State Accompli: The Political Consolidation of the Islamic State Prior to the Caliphate." *Studies in Conflict & Terrorism*, online first, December 16, 2021. https://doi.org/10.1080/1057610X.2021.2013755.
Khayyat, Munira. *A Landscape of War: Ecologies of Resistance and Survival in South Lebanon.* Berkeley: University of California Press, 2022.
Kibarova, Kateryna. "We Did Not Ask for 'Liberation': A Resident of Bucha Tells Her Story." *Persuasion*, May 4, 2022. https://www.persuasion.community/p/bucha-testimony.
Kikoler, Nicole. *Our Generation Is Gone: The Islamic State's Targeting of Iraqi Minorities in Ninewa.* Washington, DC: Simon-Skjodt Center for the Prevention of Genocide, United States Holocaust Museum, 2015.
King, Anthony. *Urban Warfare in the Twenty-First Century.* Cambridge: Polity, 2021.
Kittleson, Shelly. "Iraqi Army, Non-local PMUs at Cross-Purposes in Western Anbar." *Al-Monitor*, October 21, 2018. https://www.al-monitor.com/originals/2018/10/iraq-anbar-syria-shiite-militias-tufuf.html.
Knights, Michael. "Back Into the Shadows? The Future of Kata'ib Hezbollah and Iran's Other Proxies in Iraq." *CTC Sentinel* 13, no. 10 (October 2020): 1–22.
——. "Iraq Is Quietly Falling Apart: Iran's Proxies Have Seized Power in Baghdad—and Are Gutting the State." *Foreign Affairs*, June 5, 2023. https://www.foreignaffairs.com/iran/iraq-quietly-falling-apart.
Knights, Michael, and Alexander Mello. "Losing Mosul, Regenerating in Diyala: How the Islamic State Could Exploit Iraq's Sectarian Tinderbox." *CTC Sentinel* 9, no. 10. (October 2016): 1–7.
Knoll, Lisa J., Jovita T. Leung, Lucy Foulkes, and Sarah-Jayne Blakemore. "Age-Related Differences in Social Influence on Risk Perception Depend on the Direction of Influence." *Journal of Adolescence* 60 (2017): 53–63.
Knuppe, Austin J. "Blowback or Overblown? Why Civilians Under Threat Support Invasive Foreign Intervention." *Journal of Peace Research* 59, no. 4 (2022): 478–494.
——. "The Civilians' Dilemma: How Religious and Ethnic Minorities Survived the Islamic State Occupation of Northern Iraq." *Journal of the Middle East and Africa* 14, no. 1 (2023): 37–67.
Kocher, Matthew Adam, Adria K. Lawrence, and Nuno P. Monteiro. "Nationalism, Collaboration, and Resistance: France Under Nazi Occupation." *International Security* 43, no. 2 (2018): 117–150.
Koehler, Kevin, Isabell Schierenbeck, Ilyas Saliba, Ellen M. Lust, and Jannis J. Grimm. *Safer Field Research in the Social Sciences: A Guide to Human and Digital Security in Hostile Environments.* London: Sage, 2020.
Krause, Jana. *Resilient Communities: Non-violence and Civilian Agency in Communal War.* New York: Cambridge University Press, 2018.

Krause, Peter. "A State, an Insurgency, and a Revolution: Understanding and Defeating the Three Faces of ISIS." In *The Future of ISIS: Regional and International Implications*, edited by Feisal al-Istrabadi and Sumit Ganguly, 223–246. Washington, DC: Brookings Institution Press, 2018.

Krause, Peter, and Ora Szekely. *Stories from the Field: A Guide to Navigating Fieldwork in Political Science*. New York: Columbia University Press, 2020.

Kreft, Anne-Kathrin, and Mattias Agerberg. "Imperfect Victims? Civilian Men, Vulnerability, and Policy Preferences." *American Political Science Review*, online first, April 19, 2023. https://doi.org/10.1017/S0003055423000345.

Krieg, Andreas, and Jean-Marc Rickli. *Surrogate Warfare: The Transformation of War in the Twenty-First Century*. Washington, DC: Georgetown University Press, 2019.

Kruczek, Gregory J. "Christian (Second-Order) Minorities and the Struggle for the Homeland: The Assyrian Democratic Movement in Iraq and the Nineveh Plains Protection Units." *Journal of the Middle East and Africa* 12, no. 1 (2021): 1–29.

Kruglanski, Arie W., Jocelyn J. Bélanger, and Rohan Gunaratna. *The Three Pillars of Radicalization: Needs, Narratives, and Networks*. New York: Oxford University Press, 2019.

Kuriakose, Noble, and Michael Robbins. "Don't Get Duped: Fraud Through Duplication in Public Opinion Surveys." *Statistical Journal of the IAOS* 32, no. 3 (2016): 283–291.

Lacina, Bethany. *Rival Claims: Ethnic Violence and Territorial Autonomy Under Indian Federalism*. Ann Arbor: University of Michigan Press, 2017.

Lackner, Helen. *Yemen in Crisis: Road to War*. London: Verso, 2019.

———. *Yemen: Poverty and Conflict*. London: Routledge, 2022.

Lafta, Riyadh, Nesreen A. Aflouk, Saba Dhiaa, Emily Lyles, and Gilbert Burnham. "Needs of Internally Displaced Women and Children in Baghdad, Karbala, and Kirkuk, Iraq." *PLoS Currents* 8 (June 2016). https://doi.org/10.1371/currents.dis.fefc1fc62c02ecaedec2c25910442828.

Lake, David A. *The Statebuilder's Dilemma: On the Limits of Foreign Intervention*. Ithaca, NY: Cornell University Press, 2016.

Lamothe, Dan, and Louisa Loveluck. "U.S. and Coalition Troops Killed in Rocket Attack in Iraq, Potentially Spiking Tensions with Iran." *Washington Post*, November 3, 2020, https://www.washingtonpost.com/national-security/2020/03/11/us-coalition-troops-killed-rocket-attack-iraq-potentially-spiking-tensions-with-iran.

Landau-Wells, Marika. "Dealing with Danger: Threat Perception and Policy Preferences." Ph.D. diss., Massachusetts Institute of Technology, 2018.

Larson, Jennifer M. "Networks and Interethnic Cooperation." *Journal of Politics* 79, no. 2 (2017): 546–559.

Leeper, Thomas J. "Cregg: Simple Conjoint Tidying, Analysis, and Visualization," R package version 0.3.0 (2018). Comprehensive R Archive Network, accessed November 3, 2023. https://cran.r-project.org/web/packages/cregg/cregg.pdf.

Leeper, Thomas J., Sara B. Hobolt, and James Tilley. "Measuring Subgroup Preferences in Conjoint Experiments." *Political Analysis* 28, no. 2 (2020): 207–221.

Lerner, Jennifer S., Ye Li, Piercarlo Valdesolo, and Karim S. Kassam. "Emotion and Decision Making." *Annual Review of Psychology* 66 (January 2015): 799–823. https://doi.org/10.1146/annurev-psych-010213-115043.
Levitt, Matthew. *Terrorist Financing and the Islamic State*. Washington, DC: Washington Institute for Near East Policy, November 2014.
Lichtenheld, Adam G. "Explaining Population Displacement Strategies in Civil Wars: A Cross-National Analysis." *International Organization* 74, no. 2 (2020): 253–294.
Lichtenheld, Adam G., and Justin Schon. "The Consequences of Internal Displacement on Civil War Violence: Evidence from Syria." *Political Geography* 86 (April 2021): 102346. https://doi.org/10.1016/j.polgeo.2021.102346.
"Life Expectancy at Birth, Total (Years)." World Bank, accessed October 30, 2023. https://data.worldbank.org/indicator/SP.DYN.LE00.IN.
Lodge, Milton, and Charles S. Taber. *The Rationalizing Voter*. New York: Cambridge University Press, 2013.
Loewenstein, George, and Jennifer S. Lerner. "The Role of Affect in Decision Making." In *Oxford Handbook of Affective Sciences*, edited by K. R. Scherer, R. J. Davidson, and H. H. Goldsmith, 619–642. New York: Oxford University Press, 2003.
Loveluck, Louisa, and Mustafa Salim. "Turkish Strike Kills at Least 8 Iraqi Tourists in Northern Resort." *Washington Post*, July 20, 2022. https://www.washingtonpost.com/world/2022/07/20/iraq-turkey-strike-tourists/#.
Lyall, Jason. "Are Coethnics More Effective Counterinsurgents? Evidence from the Second Chechen War." *American Political Science Review* 104, no. 1 (2010): 1–20.
Lyall, Jason, Kosuke Imai, and Graeme Blair. "Explaining Support for Combatants in Wartime: A Survey Experiment in Afghanistan." *American Political Science Review* 107, no. 4 (2013): 679–705.
Lyall, Jason, Yuki Shiraito, and Kosuke Imai. "Coethnic Bias and Wartime Informing." *Journal of Politics* 77, no. 3 (2015): 833–848.
Lyall, Jason, Yang-Yang Zhou, and Kosuke Imai. "Can Economic Assistance Shape Combatant Support in Wartime? Experimental Evidence from Afghanistan." *American Political Science Review* 114, no. 1 (2020): 126–143.
Lynch, Hannah. "The Budding Kurdish-Iranian Alliance in Northern Iraq." *New Lines Magazine*, June 24, 2021. https://newlinesmag.com/reportage/the-budding-kurdish-iranian-alliance-in-northern-iraq.
Lynch, Marc. *The Arab Uprising: The Unfinished Revolutions of the New Middle East*. New York: PublicAffairs, 2013.
———. "The End of the Middle East: How an Old Map Distorts a New Reality." *Foreign Affairs* 101, no. 2 (April 2022): 58–67.
———. *The New Arab Wars: Uprisings and Anarchy in the Middle East*. New York: PublicAffairs, 2016.
Maack, Danielle J., Erin Buchanan, and John Young. "Development and Psychometric Investigation of an Inventory to Assess Fight, Flight, and Freeze Tendencies: The Fight, Flight, Freeze Questionnaire." *Cognitive Behaviour Therapy* 44, no. 2 (2015): 117–127.

Mac Ginty, Roger. *Everyday Peace: How So-Called Ordinary People Can Disrupt Violent Conflict.* New York: Oxford University Press, 2021.
Mac Ginty, Roger, Roddy Brett, and Birte Vogel. *The Companion to Peace and Conflict Fieldwork.* London: Springer, 2021.
Makiya, Kanan. *Republic of Fear: The Politics of Modern Iraq.* Berkeley: University of California Press, 1998.
Malkasian, Carter. *Illusions of Victory: The Anbar Awakening and the Rise of the Islamic State.* New York: Oxford University Press, 2017.
Manekin, Devorah. "Violence Against Civilians in the Second Intifada: The Moderating Effect of Armed Group Structure on Opportunistic Violence." *Comparative Political Studies* 46, no. 10 (2013): 1273–1300.
Mansoor, Peter R. *Surge: My Journey with General David Petraeus and the Remaking of the Iraq War.* New Haven, CT: Yale University Press, 2013.
Mansour, Renad. *Networks of Power: The Popular Mobilization Forces and the State in Iraq.* London: Chatham House, February 2021.
———. "Your Country Needs You: Iraq's Faltering Military Recruitment Campaign" *Diwan* (blog). Malcom H. Kerr Carnegie Middle East Center, July 22, 2015. https://carnegie-mec.org/diwan/60810.
Mansour, Renad, and Faleh A. Jabar. *The Popular Mobilization Forces and Iraq's Future.* Washington, DC: Carnegie Endowment for International Peace, 2017. https://carnegieendowment.org/files/CMEC_63_Mansour_PMF_Final_Web.pdf.
Mansour, Wale, and Bledi Celiku. *Breaking Out of Fragility: A Country Economic Memorandum for Diversification and Growth in Iraq.* Washington, DC: World Bank Group, September 2020.
Marantz, Andrew. "How to Stop a Power Grab." *New Yorker,* November 23, 2020. https://www.newyorker.com/magazine/2020/11/23/how-to-stop-a-power-grab.
Marashi, Ibrahim Al-. "Iraq and the Arab Spring: From Protests to the Rise of ISIS." In *The Arab Spring: The Hope and Reality of the Uprisings,* 2nd ed., edited by Mark L. Haas and David W. Lesch, 147–164. London: Routledge, 2016.
March, Andrew F., and Mara. Revkin. "Caliphate of Law: ISIS' Ground Rules." *Foreign Affairs,* April 15, 2015. https://www.foreignaffairs.com/articles/syria/2015-04-15/caliphate-law.
Martin, Michaela, and Hussein Solomon. "Islamic State: Understanding the Nature of the Beast and Its Funding." *Contemporary Review of the Middle East* 4, no. 1 (2017): 18–49.
Maslow, Abraham H. *Motivation and Personality.* New York: Harper and Row, 1954.
Mason, R. Chuck. *U.S.-Iraq Withdrawal/Status of Forces Agreement: Issues for Congressional Oversight.* CRS Report No. R40011. Washington, DC: Congressional Research Service, January 2011.
Mazur, Kevin. *Revolution in Syria: Identity, Networks, and Repression.* New York: Cambridge University Press, 2021.
Mazurana, Dyan, Karen Jacobsen, and Lacey Andrews Gale, eds. *Research Methods in Conflict Settings: A View from Below.* London: Cambridge University Press, 2013.

McDermott, Rose. *Risk-Taking in International Politics: Prospect Theory in American Foreign Policy*. Ann Arbor: University of Michigan Press, 2001.

McDoom, Omar Shahabudin. "The Psychology of Threat in Intergroup Conflict: Emotions, Rationality, and Opportunity in the Rwandan Genocide." *International Security* 37, no. 2 (2012): 119–155.

Milliff, Aidan. "Facts Shape Feelings: Information, Emotions, and the Political Consequences of Violence." *Political Behavior* 45, no. 3 (2022): 1169–1190.

———. "Making Sense, Making Choices: How Civilians Choose Survival Strategies During Violence." *American Political Science Review*, October 24, 2023. https://aidanmilliff.com/media/Milliff_JMP.pdf.

Milner, Alex. "Mosul Dam: Why the Battle for Water Matters in Iraq." *BBC News*, August 18, 2014. https://www.bbc.com/news/world-middle-east-28772478.

Milton, Daniel. "The Islamic State: An Adaptive Organization Facing Increasing Challenges." In *The Group That Calls Itself a State: Understanding the Evolution and Challenges of the Islamic State*, edited by Bryan Price, Daniel Milton, Muhammad al-Ubaydi, and Nelly Lahoud, 36–76. West Point, NY: Combating Terrorism Center, United States Military Academy, 2014.

Mintz, Alex, Nicholas A. Valentino, and Carly Wayne. *Beyond Rationality: Behavioral Political Science in the 21st Century*. New York: Cambridge University Press, 2021.

Mironova, Vera, and Sam Whitt. "Maintaining Nonviolent Self-Discipline in Hostile Protest Environments: Evidence from the 2019 Baghdad Protests." *Social Movement Studies*, May 4, 2022. https://doi.org/10.1080/14742837.2022.2070466.

Morris, Benny. *1948: A History of the First Arab-Israeli War*. New Haven, CT: Yale University Press, 2008.

———. *Righteous Victims: A History of the Zionist-Arab Conflict, 1881-1998*. New York: Vintage, 2001.

Mousa, Salma. "Building Social Cohesion Between Christians and Muslims Through Soccer in Post-ISIS Iraq." *Science* 369, no. 6505 (2020): 866–870.

Mueller, John. "The Banality of 'Ethnic War.'" *International Security* 25, no. 1 (2000): 42–70.

Muhammad, Omar, Haroro J. Imgram, and Andrew Mines. "Episode 4, Part 2: Never Again, Silence." In *Mosul and the Islamic State*. Podcast, MP3 audio, 39:00, September 21, 2021. https://extremism.gwu.edu/mosul-and-the-islamic-state.

Mumford, Andrew. *Proxy Warfare*. Cambridge: Policy Press, 2013.

———. *The West's War Against Islamic State: Operation Inherent Resolve in Syria and Iraq*. London: Bloomsbury, 2021.

Murad, Nadia, and Jenna Krajeski. *The Last Girl: My Story of Captivity, and My Fight Against the Islamic State*. New York: Tim Duggan Books, 2017.

Mustafa, Balsam. "All About Iraq: Re-modifying Older Slogans and Chants in Tishreen [October] Protests." *Journal of Asian and African Studies* 58, no. 3 (2022): 401–420.

———. "The Bigh Daddy Show: The Potentiality and Shortcomings of Countering Islamic State Through Animated Satire." *Digest of Middle East Studies* 31, no. 2 (2022): 113–130.

Nanes, Matthew J. *Policing for Peace: Institutions, Expectations, and Security in Divided Societies*. New York: Cambridge University Press, 2021.

Oakford, Samuel. "Counting the Dead in Mosul." *The Atlantic*, April 5, 2018. https://www.theatlantic.com/international/archive/2018/04/counting-the-dead-in-mosul/556466.

Ochayon, Sheryl Silver. "Armed Resistance in the Ghettos: The Dilemma of Revolt." Yad Vashem: The World Holocaust Remembrance Center, accessed October 30, 2023. https://www.yadvashem.org/articles/general/armed-resistance-dilemma-of-revolt.html.

"192 Internally Displaced Persons Disappeared from Infamous Al Razaza Checkpoint in Iraq in a Single Day." MENA Rights Group, May 10 2019. https://menarights.org/en/articles/192-internally-displaced-persons-disappeared-infamous-al-razaza-checkpoint-iraq-single-day.

Orme, Bryan K. *Getting Started with Conjoint Analysis: Strategies for Product Design and Pricing Research*. Madison, WI: Research Publishers, 2010.

Ostrom, Elinor. "A Behavioral Approach to the Rational Choice Theory of Collective Action: Presidential Address, American Political Science Association, 1997." *American Political Science Review* 92, no. 1 (1998): 1–22.

Pape, Robert A. *Dying to Win: The Strategic Logic of Suicide Terrorism*. New York: Random House, 2005.

Pardini, Dustin, Jordan Beardslee, Meagan Docherty, Carol Schubert, and Edward Mulvey. "Risk and Protective Factors for Gun Violence in Male Juvenile Offenders." *Journal of Clinical Child & Adolescent Psychology* 50, no. 3 (2021): 337–352.

Parkinson, Sarah E. *Beyond the Lines: Social Networks and Palestinian Militant Organizations in Wartime Lebanon*. Ithaca, NY: Cornell University Press, 2023.

———. "(Dis)Courtesy Bias: 'Methodological Cognates,' Data Validity, and Ethics in Violence-Adjacent Research." *Comparative Political Studies* 55, no. 3 (2022): 420–450.

Patel, David S. *Order Out of Chaos: Islam, Information, and the Rise and Fall of Social Orders in Iraq*. Ithaca, NY: Cornell University Press, 2022.

Pearlman, Wendy. "Emotions and the Microfoundations of the Arab Uprisings." *Perspectives on Politics* 11, no. 2 (2013): 387–409.

———. "Narratives of Fear in Syria." *Perspectives on Politics* 14, no. 1 (2016): 21–37.

Peters, Ellen, Daniel Västfjäll, Paul Slovic, C. K. Mertz, Ketti Mazzocco, and Stephan Dickert. "Numeracy and Decision Making." *Psychological Science* 17, no. 5 (2006): 407–413.

Petersen, Roger D. *Resistance and Rebellion: Lessons of Eastern Europe*. New York: Cambridge University Press, 2001.

Pickney, Jonathan, Michael Niconchuk, and Sarah Ryan. *Motives, Benefits, and Sacred Values: Examining the Psychology of Nonviolent Action and Violent Extremism*. Peaceworks Report No. 170. Washington, DC: United States Institute of Peace, November 2021.

Pictet, Jean. *The Geneva Conventions of 12 August 1949: Geneva Convention Relative to the Protection of Civilian Persons in Time of War*. Vol. 4. Geneva: International Committee of the Red Cross, 1958.

Pretus, Clara, Nafees Hamid, Hammad Sheikh, Jeremy Ginges, Adolf Tobeña, Richard Davis, Oscar Vilarroya, and Scott Atran. "Neural and Behavioral Correlates of Sacred

Values and Vulnerability to Violent Extremism." *Frontiers in Psychology* 9 (December 2018). https://doi.org/10.3389/fpsyg.2018.02462.

Quinlivan, James T. "Coup-Proofing: Its Practice and Consequences in the Middle East." *International Security* 24, no. 2 (1999): 131–165.

Rawi, Ahmed K. Al-. "Anti-ISIS Humor: Cultural Resistance of Radical Ideology." *Politics, Religion & Ideology* 17, no. 1 (2016): 52–68.

———. "The Arab Spring & Online Protests in Iraq." *International Journal of Communication* 8 (2014): 916–942.

Rayburn, Joel. *Iraq After America: Strongmen, Sectarians, Resistance*. Palo Alto, CA: Hoover Institution Press, 2014.

Rayburn, Joel D., and Frank K. Sobchak. *The U.S. Army in Iraq: Surge and Withdrawal (2007-2011*. Washington, DC: Operation Iraqi Freedom Study Group, Office of the Chief of Staff, U.S. Army, January 2019.

Redvers, Louise. "Old Fault Lines, New Flash Points in Iraq's Anbar." *New Humanitarian*, July 2, 2014. https://www.thenewhumanitarian.org/analysis/2014/02/07/old-fault-lines-new-flashpoints-iraq-s-anbar.

Reno, William. "Protectors and Predators: Why Is There a Difference Among West African Militias?" In *Fragile States and Insecure People?*, edited by Louise Anderson, Bjorn Moller, and Finn Stepputat, 99–121. London Springer, 2007.

Revkin, Mara, and Will McCants. "Experts Weigh in (Part 1): Is ISIS Good at Governing?" Brookings Institution, November 20, 2016. https://www.brookings.edu/blog/markaz/2015/11/20/experts-weigh-in-is-isis-good-at-governing.

Revkin, Mara Redlich. "Competitive Governance and Displacement Decisions Under Rebel Rule: Evidence from the Islamic State in Iraq." *Journal of Conflict Resolution* 65, no. 1 (2020): 46–80.

———. "How Does Subnational Variation in Repression Affect Attitudes Toward Police? Evidence from Iraq's 2019 Protests." *Violence: An International Journal* 3, no. 1 (2022): 85–99.

———. "What Explains Taxation by Resource-Rich Rebels? Evidence from the Islamic State in Syria." *Journal of Politics* 82, no. 2 (2020): 757–764.

———. "When Terrorists Govern: Protecting Civilians in Conflicts with State-Building Armed Groups." *Harvard National Security Journal* 9 (2018): 100.

Revkin, Mara Redlich, and Ariel I. Ahram. "Perspectives on the Rebel Social Contract: Exit, Voice, and Loyalty in the Islamic State in Iraq and Syria," *World Development* 132 (August 2020): 104981. https://doi.org/10.1016/j.worlddev.2020.104981.

Revkin, Mara Redlich, and Elisabeth Jean Wood. "The Islamic State's Pattern of Sexual Violence: Ideology and Institutions, Policies and Practices." *Journal of Global Security Studies* 6, no. 2 (2021): 1–20.

Rosen, Nir. "No Going Back: Little Relief in Sight for Millions of Displaced Iraqis." *Boston Review* 32, no. 5 (2007): 19–26.

Roux, Martin. "Securing Coptic Churches: The Necessary Role of the Scouts." *Mada*, August 8, 2018. https://www.madamasr.com/en/2018/04/08/feature/society/securing-coptic-churches-the-necessary-role-of-the-scouts/#:~:text=The%20role%20of%20the%20scouts,those%20who%20volunteer%20at%20St.

Rubenstein, Beth L., Lily Zhi Ning Lu, Matthew MacFarlane, and Lindsay Stark. "Predictors of Interpersonal Violence in the Household in Humanitarian Settings: A Systematic Review." *Trauma, Violence, & Abuse* 21, no. 1 (2020): 31–44.

Rubin, Alissa J. "Iraqis Rise Against a Reviled Occupier: Iran." *New York Times*, November 4, 2019. https://www.nytimes.com/2019/11/04/world/middleeast/iraq-protests-iran.html.

Rudolf, Inna. *The Sunnis of Iraq's "Shia" Paramilitary Powerhouse*. Washington, DC: Century Foundation, February 2020.

"Ruinous Aftermath: Militias Abuses Following Iraq's Recapture of Tikrit." Human Rights Watch, September 20, 2015. https://www.hrw.org/report/2015/09/20/ruinous-aftermath/militias-abuses-following-iraqs-recapture-tikrit.

Rwanduzy, Mohammed. "Iraqi PM Decrees Full Integration of PMF Into Iraqi Forces." *Rudaw*, January 7, 2019. https://www.rudaw.net/english/middleeast/iraq/01072019.

Ryan, Missy, Mustafta Salim, and Harry Stevens. "Behind the Tally, Names and Lives." *Washington Post*, November 18, 2020. https://www.washingtonpost.com/graphics/2020/world/coalition-airstrikes-isis-civilian-death-toll.

"Sadr Supporters Rally Over US Troops in Iraq." *Al Jazeera*, May 26, 2011. https://www.aljazeera.com/news/2011/5/26/sadr-supporters-rally-over-us-troops-in-iraq.

Salverda, Nynke. "Complex Conflicts: Causes and Consequences of Multiparty Civil Wars." PhD diss., Queensland University of Technology, 2017.

Sayej, Caroleen Marji. *Patriotic Ayatollahs: Nationalism in Post-Saddam Iraq*. Ithaca, NY: Cornell University Press, 2018.

Sayle, Timothy Andrews, Jeffrey A. Engel, Hal Brands, and William Inboden. *The Last Card: Inside George W. Bush's Decision to Surge in Iraq*. Ithaca, NY: Cornell University Press, 2019.

Schon, Justin. *Surviving the War in Syria*. New York: Cambridge University Press, 2020.

Schubiger, Livia Isabella. "State Violence and Wartime Civilian Agency: Evidence from Peru." *Journal of Politics* 83, no. 4 (2021): 1383–1398.

Schulhofer-Wohl, Jonah. *Quagmire in Civil War*. New York: Cambridge University Press, 2020.

Scott, James C. *The Art of Not Being Governed*. New Haven, CT: Yale University Press, 2010.

———. *Domination and the Arts of Resistance: Hidden Transcripts*. New Haven, CT: Yale University Press, 1990.

———. *Weapons of the Weak: Everyday Forms of Peasant Resistance*. New Haven, CT: Yale University Press, 1985.

Seff, Ilana, Melissa Meinhart, Arturo Harker Roa, Lindsay Stark, and Andrés Villaveces. "Predicting Adolescent Boys' and Young Men's Perpetration of Youth Violence in Colombia." *International Journal of Injury Control and Safety Promotion* 29, no. 1 (2022): 123–131.

Serrieh, Joanne. "Over 500 People Killed Since Protests Erupted in Iraq: Human Rights Commission." *Al Arabiya News*, May 20, 2020. https://english.alarabiya.net/en/News/middle-east/2020/ 02/03/Over-500-people-killed-since-protests-erupted-in-IraqI raqi-Human-Rights-Commission.

Shaver, Andrew C., and Jacob N. Shapiro. "The Effect of Civilian Casualties on Wartime Informing: Evidence from the Iraq War." *Journal of Conflict Resolution* 65, nos. 7–8 (March 2021): 1–41.

Shesterinina, Anastasia. "Ethics, Empathy, and Fear in Research on Violent Conflict." *Journal of Peace Research* 56, no. 2 (2019): 190–202.

———. *Mobilizing in Uncertainty: Collective Identities and War in Abkhazia.* Ithaca, NY: Cornell University Press, 2021.

Silverman, Daniel. "What Shapes Civilian Beliefs About Violent Events? Experimental Evidence from Pakistan." *Journal of Conflict Resolution* 63, no. 6 (2019): 1460–1487.

"Situation of Christians in Baghdad." United Nations High Commissioner for Refugees, January 15, 2018. https://www.refworld.org/docid/5a66f80e4.html.

"Situation Report: Anbar Humanitarian Crisis." Situation Report No. 6, United Nations High Commissioner for Refugees, February 4, 2014. https://reliefweb.int/report/iraq/anbar-humanitarian-crisis-situation-report-6.

Sky, Emma. *The Unraveling: High Hopes and Missed Opportunities in Iraq.* New York: PublicAffairs, 2015.

Slemrod, Annie. "The Failure in Fallujah: And How Lessons Must Be Learnt for Mosul." *New Humanitarian*, June 28, 2016. https://www.thenewhumanitarian.org/2016/06/28/failure-fallujah.

Slovic, Paul, Melissa L. Finucane, Ellen Peters, and Donald G. MacGregor. "Risk as Analysis and Risk as Feelings: Some Thoughts About Affect, Reason, Risk, and Rationality." *Risk Analysis: An International Journal* 24, no. 2 (2004): 311–322.

Snir, Reuvan, ed. *Baghdad: A City in Verse.* Cambridge, MA: Harvard University Press, 2013.

Southall, David P., Rhona MacDonald, Olena Kostiuk, Volodymyr Shcherbakov, and Aniko Deierl. "The UN Must Provide Secure Medical and Humanitarian Assistance in Ukraine." *The Lancet* 399, no. 10332 (2022): 1301–1302.

Speckhard, Anne, and Molly D. Ellenberg. "ISIS in Their Own Words: Recruitment History, Motivations for Joining, Travel, Experiences in ISIS, and Disillusionment Over Time-Analysis of 220 In-Depth Interviews of ISIS Returnees, Defectors and Prisoners." *Journal of Strategic Security* 13, no. 1 (2020): 82–127.

Steele, Abbey. "Civilian Resettlement Patterns in Civil War." *Journal of Peace Research* 56, no. 1 (2019): 28–41.

———. *Democracy and Displacement in Colombia's Civil War.* Ithaca, NY: Cornell University Press, 2017.

Stein, Rachel M. *Vengeful Citizens, Violent States: A Theory of War and Revenge.* New York: Cambridge University Press, 2019.

Suerbaum, Magdalena. *Masculinities and Displacement in the Middle East: Syrian Refugees in Egypt.* London: Bloomsbury, 2020.

Sundberg, Ralph, Kristine Eck, and Joakim Kreutz. "Introducing the UCDP Non-state Conflict Dataset." *Journal of Peace Research* 49, no. 2 (2012): 351–362.

Suzuki, Akisato, Djordje Stefanovic, and Neophytos Loizides. "Displacement and the Expectation of Political Violence: Evidence from Bosnia." *Conflict Management and Peace Science* 38, no. 5 (2020): 1–19.

Svensson, Isak, Daniel Finnbogason, Dino Krause, Lúis Martínez Lorenzo, and Nanar Hawach. *Confronting the Caliphate: Civil Resistance in Jihadist Proto-states*. New York: Oxford University Press, 2022.

Tajfel, Henri. "Experiments in Intergroup Discrimination." *Scientific American* 223, no. 5 (1970): 96–102.

Tamimi, Aymenn Jawad Al-. "Hashd Formations of Iraq: Interview with Harakat Ahrar al-Iraq." *Pundicity*, January 18, 2019. https://www.aymennjawad.org/2019/01/hashd-formations-of-iraq-interview-with-harakat.

———. "Sunni Opposition to the Islamic State." *Middle East Review of International Affairs* 18, no. 3 (2014): 1–13.

Tarrow, Sidney G., and Charles Tilly. "Contentious Politics and Social Movements." In *The Oxford Handbook of Comparative Politics*, edited by Carlos Boix and Susan Stokes, 435–460. New York: Oxford University Press, 2007.

Tetlock, Philip E. "Thinking the Unthinkable: Sacred Values and Taboo Cognitions." *Trends in Cognitive Sciences* 7, no. 7 (2003): 320–324.

Tetlock, Philip E., Randall S. Peterson, and Jennifer S. Lerner. "Revising the Value Pluralism Model: Incorporating Social Content and Context Postulates." In *The Psychology of Values: The Ontario Symposium*, vol. 8, edited by Clive Seligman, James M. Olson, and Mark P. Zanna, 25–52. Mahwah, NJ: Lawrence Erlbaum Associates, 1996.

Thaler, Richard H. *Misbehaving: The Making of Behavioral Economics*. New York: W. W. Norton, 2015.

Thomas, Jakana L. "Sisters Are Doing It for Themselves: How Female Combatants Help Generate Gender-Inclusive Peace Agreements in Civil Wars." *American Political Science Review*, online first, June 26, 2023. https://doi.org/10.1017/S0003055423000461.

"Three Killed as Iraq Protesters Attack Iran Consulate in Karbala." *Al Jazeera*. November 4, 2019. https://www.aljazeera.com/news/2019/11/4/three-killed-as-iraq-protesters-attack-iran-consulate-in-karbala.

Tichý, Lukáš. "The IS and Attacks on the Oil and Gas Sector in Iraq." *Central European Journal of International & Security Studies* 12, no. 3 (2018): 106–127.

Tilly, Charles. "Social Boundary Mechanisms." *Philosophy of the Social Sciences* 34, no. 2 (2004): 211–236.

———. "To Explain Political Processes." *American Journal of Sociology* 100, no. 6 (1995): 1594–1610.

Tilly, Charles, and Sidney G. Tarrow. *Contentious Politics*. 2nd ed. New York: Oxford University Press, 2015.

Turner, John C., Michael A. Hogg, Penelope J. Oakes, Stephen D. Reicher, and Margaret S. Wetherell. *Rediscovering the Social Group: A Self-Categorization Theory*. New York: Basil Blackwell, 1987.

"Turning a Blind Eye: The Arming of the Popular Mobilization Units." Amnesty International, January 5, 2017. https://www.amnesty.org/en/documents/mde14/5386/2017/en.

"UN: Mosul Repairs Will Cost $1bn." *Middle East Monitor*, July 7, 2017. https://www.middleeastmonitor.com/20170707-un-mosul-repairs-will-cost-1bn.

"Unemployment, Youth Total (% Of Total Labor Force Ages 15–24) (Modeled ILO Estimate)." World Bank, accessed October 30, 2023. https://data.worldbank.org/indicator/SL.UEM.1524.ZS.

United Nations High Commissioner for Refugees. *Humanitarian Evacuations in Violence and Armed Conflict*. Baghdad: United Nations, June 2016. https://www.refworld.org/pdfid/57fe09284.pdf.

———. *International Protection Considerations with Regard to People Fleeing the Republic of Iraq*. New York: United Nations, May 2019. https://www.refworld.org/pdfid/5cc9b20c4.pdf.

———. *"They Came to Destroy:" ISIS Crimes Against the Yazidis*. A/HRC/32/CRP.2. New York: United Nations, June 2016. https://digitallibrary.un.org/record/843515?ln=en.

United Nations International Organization for Migration(IOM). *Managing Return in Anbar: Community Responses to the Return of IDPs with Perceived Affiliation*. Baghdad: IOM Iraq, March 2020. https://reliefweb.int/report/iraq/managing-return-anbar-community-responses-return-idps-perceived-affiliation.

———. *Rural Areas in Ninewa: Legacies of Conflict on Rural Economies and Communities in Sinjar and the Ninewa Plains*. Baghdad: IOM Iraq, November 2019. https://iraqdtm.iom.int/files/DurableSolutions/20224113849859_IOM_Iraq_Rural_Areas_in_Ninewa_Legacies_of_Conflict_Rural_Economies_Communities_Sinjar_Ninewa_Plains.pdf.

United Nations Office for the Coordination of Humanitarian Affairs. *Iraq: January 2021 Humanitarian Bulletin*. Baghdad: United Nations, February 16, 2021. https://reliefweb.int/report/iraq/iraq-humanitarian-bulletin-january-2021.

United Nations University. *Hybrid Conflict, Hybrid Peace: How Militias and Paramilitary Groups Shape Post-Conflict Transitions Centre for Policy Research*. New York: United Nations Press, April 14, 2020. https://reliefweb.int/report/world/hybrid-conflict-hybrid-peace-how-militias-and-paramilitary-groups-shape-post-conflict.

———. *The Protection of Civilians in United Nations Peacekeeping Handbook*. New York: United Nations Press, November 2020. https://peacekeeping.un.org/sites/default/files/dpo_poc_handbook_final_as_printed.pdf.

United States Institute of Peace. *Conflict Sensitivity in Peacebuilding*. Washington, DC: United States Institute of Peace, 2021. https://www.usip.org/academy/catalog/conflict-sensitivity-peacebuilding.

U.S. Department of State, Office of International Religious Freedom. *2019 Report on International Religious Freedom: Iraq*. Washington, DC: United States Department of State, June 2019. https://www.state.gov/reports/2019-report-on-international-religious-freedom/iraq.

"US-Led Coalition Airstrikes in Iraq and Syria." *Airwars*, July 7, 2022. https://airwars.org/conflict/coalition-in-iraq-and-syria.

Van Baalen, Sebastian. "Civilian Protest in Civil War: Insights from Côte d'Ivoire." *American Political Science Review*, online first, June 14, 2023. https://doi.org/10.1017/S0003055423000564.

———. "Local Elites, Civil Resistance, and the Responsiveness of Rebel Governance in Côte d'Ivoire." *Journal of Peace Research* 58, no. 5 (2021): 930–944.

Verini, James. *They Will Have to Die Now: Mosul and the Fall of the Caliphate*. New York: Simon and Schuster, 2019.
Voller, Yaniv. "Rethinking Armed Groups and Order: Syria and the Rise of Militiatocracies." *International Affairs* 98, no. 3 (2022): 853–871.
Voors, Maarten J., Eleonora E. M. Nillesen, Philip Verwimp, Erwin H. Bulte, Robert Lensink, and Daan P. Van Soest. "Violent Conflict and Behavior: A Field Experiment in Burundi." *American Economic Review* 102, no. 2 (2012): 941–964.
Walter, Barbara F. "The New New Civil Wars." *Annual Review of Political Science* 20 (2017): 469–486.
Walzer, Michael. *Just and Unjust Wars: A Moral Argument with Historical Illustrations*. 5th ed. New York: Basic Books, 2015.
Weber, Sigrid. "Controlling a Moving World: Territorial Control, Displacement and the Spread of Civilian Targeting in Iraq." Unpublished manuscript. 2023.
Weber, Sigrid, and Alexandra Hartman. "Property Rights and Post-conflict Recovery: Theory and Evidence from IDP Return Movements in Iraq." Unpublished manuscript. 2023.
Webster, Jamie. *U.S. Senate Committee on Energy and Natural Resources: Hearing on Terrorism and Global Oil Markets*, 114th Cong., 1st Sess. (December 10, 2015). https://www.energy.senate.gov/services/files/B392F59D-E85B-4678-BB51-6CE07B33FC19.
Wedeen, Lisa. *Ambiguities of Domination: Politics, Rhetoric, and Symbols in Contemporary Syria*. Chicago: University of Chicago Press, 1999.
———. *Authoritarian Apprehensions: Ideology, Judgment, and Mourning in Syria*. Chicago: University of Chicago Press, 2019.
Weidmann, Nils B., and Idean Salehyan. "Violence and Ethnic Segregation: A Computational Model Applied to Baghdad." *International Studies Quarterly* 57, no. 1 (2013): 52–64.
Weigand, Florian. "Afghanistan's Taliban—Legitimate Jihadists or Coercive Extremists?" *Journal of Intervention and Statebuilding* 11, no. 3 (2017): 359–381.
Weiss, Michael, and Hassan Hassan. *ISIS: Inside the Army of Terror*. 2nd ed. New York: Simon and Schuster, 2016.
Wenger, Andreas, and Simon J. A. Mason. "The Civilianization of Armed Conflict: Trends and Implications." *International Review of the Red Cross* 90, no. 872 (2008): 835–852.
"West Bank Anger Boils as Jenin Becomes Hotbed of Resistance." *Al Jazeera*, September 1, 2021. https://www.aljazeera.com/news/2021/9/1/west-bank-anger-boils-as-jenin-becomes-hotbed-of-resistance.
Weyland, Kurt. "The Arab Spring: Why the Surprising Similarities with The Revolutionary Wave of 1848?" *Perspectives on Politics* 10, no. 4 (2012): 917–934.
Whiteside, Craig. "Lying to Win: The Islamic State Media Department's Role in Deception Efforts." *RUSI Journal* 165, no. 1 (2020): 130–141.
Whiteside, Craig, and Anas Elallame. "Accidental Ethnographers: The Islamic State's Tribal Engagement Experiment." *Small Wars & Insurgencies* 31, no. 2 (2020): 219–240.
Wimpelmann, Torunn. *The Pitfalls of Protection: Gender, Violence, and Power in Afghanistan*. Berkeley: University of California Press, 2017.

Wood, Elisabeth Jean. *Insurgent Collective Action and Civil War in El Salvador.* New York: Cambridge University Press, 2003.
——. "The Social Processes of Civil War: The Wartime Transformation of Social Networks." *Annual Review of Political Science* 11 (2008): 539–561.
Yadav, Stacey Philbrick. *Yemen in the Shadow of Transition: Pursuing Justice Amid War.* New York: Oxford University Press, 2022.
Zelin, Aaron Y. *The Islamic State's Territorial Methodology.* Research Notes 29. Washington, D.C.: Washington Institute for Near East Policy, January 2016.
Zoonen, Dave van, and Khogir Wirya. *The Shabaks: Perceptions of Reconciliation and Conflict.* Erbil, IQ: Middle East Research Institute, July 2017.
——. *Turkmen in Tal Afar: Perceptions of Reconciliation and Conflict.* Erbil, IQ: Middle East Research Institute, July 2017.
——. *The Yazidis: Perceptions of Reconciliation and Conflict.* Erbil, IQ: Middle East Research Institute, July 2017.
Zubrzycki, Geneviève, and Anna Woźny. "The Comparative Politics of Collective Memory." *Annual Review of Sociology* 46 (2020): 175–194.
Zürcher, Christopher. "Nonviolent Communal Strategies in Insurgencies: Case Study on Afghanistan." In *Civil Action and the Dynamics of Violence*, edited by Deborah Avant, Marie Berry, Erica Chenoweth, Rachel Epstein, Cullen Hendrix, Oliver Kaplan, and Timothy Sisk, 203–228. New York: Oxford University Press, 2019.

Index

9 Nissan (Baghdad district), 188
1920 Revolution Brigades, 113
ʿabdat al-Shaytan (worshippers of Satan), 2, 205
Abadi, Haider al-: 17, 67, 73, 76, 87, 98, 100, 105, 166, 221, 224; and appointment of Daʿwa Party, 74; declaring victory over IS, 70, 86, 104, 163; militias into direct chain of command, 99; new Iraqi government, 86, 98
Abdul-Mahdi, Adil, 78, 169, 170
Abdul Mohsen al-Kadhimi Square (Baghdad), 72
Aboosh, Behnam, 151–52
Abu Ghraib, 54, 75, 79, 80–82, 111, 112, 221
Abu Risha, Abdul Sattar, 124
Adhim, 75
Adnani, Abu Muhammad al-, 72
Adhamiya (Baghdad district), 72, 75, 77–79, 82, 83, 91, 188, 227
adventure, motivation for joining IS, 132–33
Aethawi, Sheikh Wissam Hardan al-, 124

Afghanistan: 29, 38, 167, 205, 206, 207, 211, 213, 214, 217, 228, 241; Taliban operations in, 29, 39, 41, 167, 213, 214, 236; U.S. war in, 29, 213
Ahl al-Kitab (People of the Book), 2, 59
airpower, 63, 68, 76, 94, 95, 97, 143, 176, 184, 198, 200
Akre: 140; IDP arrival and resettlement in, 145, 148
Albu Aetha (Hardan), 124
Albu Fahad, 124, 127–128
Albu Faraj, 124, 131
Albu Mahal, 124
Albu Nimr, 112, 124, 128, 132, 220
Albu Risha, 124, 132
Albu Thiyab, 124
Allawi, Ayad, 20, 51–52, 87, 209
Alliance Toward Reforms coalition, 86
Al Abba, 120
Al Hayy (Baghdad subdistrict), 72
Al-Mustakella for Research. *See* Independent Institute for Administration and Civil Society Studies (IIACSS)

272 INDEX

Al-Nuri, Grand Mosque of, 56, 68, 162–163, 236, 246, 248
Al-Qaʿida, 13, 22, 37, 41, 45, 49, 53, 54, 87, 107, 109, 111, 121, 220
Al-Qaʿida in Iraq (AQI). See Al-Qaʿida
Al Qaʾim, 69, 118, 119, 124
Aleppo, 56, 141, 176
alienation. See *mazlumiyya* (alienation)
Alwani, Ahmed al-, 124, 132; arrest of, 53–54
Amiriya (Baghdad subdistrict), 78, 117
Anbar: 7, 18, 54, 66, 107, 109–116, 133, 140, 171; fieldwork in, 15, 200–202; IDP population of, 79–80, 117–120, 122, 143; IS occupation of, 66–67, 75; liberation of, 70; resistance against IS, 124, 128, 131–132; and support for IS; survival repertoires of local residents, 12, 15; war in, 37, 55–56, 64, 69–70
Anbar Awakening (*sahwa*), 37, 56, 72, 87, 111, 113, 127, 131–32, 203. See also Tribal Mobilization Force (TMF); Sons of Iraq (*Abnaʾ al-ʿIraq*)
Anfal Campaign, 137, 140–41
Arabization (*al-taʿrib*), 137, 141
Arab Barometer project, 101, 220, 227, 238, 244
Arab Uprisings, 16, 20, 22, 45, 49–52, 54, 100, 107, 109, 127, 140, 165, 174
arrests, 53–54, 107, 109, 110, 134, 151
Asaʾib Ahl al-Haq (League of the Righteous), 62, 63, 99
Assad, Bashir al-, 22, 51, 67–68, 81, 89, 176
Assafi, Thamer Ibrahim Tahir al-, 124
Assyrian: 2, 3, 18, 58, 143, 203, 232; diaspora activism of, 154–155; displacement of, 145–148; IS war against, 67, 78; persecution of, 158–159, 172, 175; resistance against IS, 151–152; survival repertoires of, 98, 136–138. See also sects (Sunnis, Shiʿa, Kurds)
Assyrian Democratic Movement (ADM): 138, 151, 233, 235, 258; political alignment of, 152–155
autonomy: 3, 4, 10, 12, 17, 18, 63, 166–68, 178, 215; as a survival repertoire, 31, 37–41; as a survival repertoire in Baghdad, 70, 79, 98–101, 105; as a survival repertoire in Anbar, 127–128; as a survival repertoire in Ninewa, 137, 153–155, 158; past research on, 9–11. See also survival repertoires
Azza (Sunni tribe), 124
Azzawi, Muzhir al-, 124

Babil governorate, 79, 117
Babylon Brigades: 152; and alignment with PMF, 151–152
Bahaism, 136, 138
Baʿthism: 51, 143; Baʿthist loyalists, 54; Baʿthist regime of Saddam Hussein, 13, 107, 140–141
Badr Brigade, 63–64, 87, 99, 124–25, 150, 151
Baghdad: 7, 19, 49, 50, 71, 107, 109, 143, 165–167, 171; central government located in, 2, 3, 52, 53, 69, 121, 127, 150, 154–155, 158, 175; counter-IS campaign in, 62–64; displacement of local residents, 78–82, 112, 116–118; IS at gates of, 56, 112, 141; protests in, 100–05, 110; public opinion of local residents, 86–98; residents living in, 4, 11, 12, 23, 32, 41, 48; survival repertoires of local residents, 17, 18, 98–100; survey in, 14, 83–86, 181–190; U.S. occupation of, 125; war in, 72–77
Baghdadi, Abu Bakr al-, 53, 56, 131, 141, 163
Balad, 72, 115, 119
Baiji, 72, 115, 119, 124
bayʿah (oath of allegiance), 42, 58, 61
beliefs: 25, 28, 73, 82, 175; of civilian collaborators, 25–28; of insurgents, 25, 153, 164

INDEX 273

Bilawi, Abu Abdulrahman al-, 55
Bosnia-Herzegovina, 26, 176
British Empire: 162, 227, 232; control over Mandatory Palestine, 44

Chaldean (Chaldean Catholic Church), 155, 232, 235
Chaldean Syriac Assyrian Popular Council, 151–152
charity (provided to civilians by IS), 61, 131, 157
caliphate (IS): 34; establishment of, 1, 55–56; demise of, 70; governance of, 56–62, 107; local opposition to, 34
checkpoint: controlled by insurgents, 5, 135; controlled by the anti-IS coalition, 77, 123, 135–136; controlled by IS, 34, 60, 117–118; controlled by state security forces; navigation as a civilian, 38, 80, 117; navigation as a IDP or refugee, 117, 146
children, 6, 23, 63, 106, 118, 120, 129, 130
Christianity, in Iraq, 136, 138
Christians: 2, 78, 98, 137–138, 144–145, 151, 154–155, 175, 205, 235, 236; and persecution by IS, 58–60, 172
church, 40, 151, 155, 232, 235
civil disobedience, 36, 100, 105, 170
civil resistance: 34–35; past research on, 9–11
civilian victimization: 2, 5, 7, 10, 18, 23–24, 154, 164, 174, 176; as a motivation for collaboration, 43–45, 129, 133; as a motivation for resistance, 137; as tactic of Iraqi Security Forces, 69; as tactic of insurgents, 54, 137, 149; and experience of Sunni Arabs, 54, 127
civil war: 12, 43, 176; academic literature on, 12; evolution of, 57; in Anbar governorate, 112, 121, 129; in Baghdad governorate, 75, 78; in Iraq, 41, 48–53, 55, 112, 129, 149, 160, 171, 186; in Ninewa governorate, 140, 144; past research on, 9–11; typologies of, 21–24, 47, 206
coethnicity bias, 4, 27, 43, 45
collaboration: 3, 10, 11, 23, 118, 130, 164; as a survival repertoire, 31–32, 42–46, 177–178; with the anti-IS coalition, 123, 127, 150, 151–152; with IS, 4, 24, 120, 122, 132, 158–160, 166. See also survival repertoires
collective punishment, 27, 129
conjoint experiment, 93–94, 184–186, 196–200
contention: 4, 6–7, 9, 16–17, 165–166, 168; as survival repertoire, 21, 27, 30, 31–37; as a survival repertoire in Baghdad, 72, 73, 86–98; as a survival repertoire in the Sunni Triangle, 109, 121–125; as a survival repertoire in Ninewa, 138, 148–153; past research on, 9–11. See also survival repertoires
cooperation: 2, 4, 6, 7, 9, 16, 165–66, 168, 178; as survival repertoire, 17, 21, 27–29, 31, 41–46; as a survival repertoire in Baghdad, 73, 89–90, 99, 100–105; as a survival repertoire in Sunni Triangle, 107, 109, 123, 129–134; as a survival repertoire in Ninewa, 137–138, 140, 155–161; past research on, 9–11. See also survival repertoires
corruption: 48–49, 60, 109, 150, 166, 169–170; of governing elites, 2, 17, 51, 55, 76, 100, 102–105; of IS, 3, 150
counterinsurgency: doctrine of, 16, 49, 165; in Israel, 36, 45; in urban warfare, 66; research on, 11; tactics, 8, 93
Council of Representatives (Iraq), 51, 74, 87, 101, 169
Counter Terrorism Service (CTS), 88, 94–95, 197, 200; role in liberating Mosul, 67–70, 143
Covid-19 pandemic, 15, 169, 171

Daʿesh. *See* Islamic State
Daʿwa Party, 74, 86, 101, 220n12
dawlah (state), 34, 215
ad-Dawlah al-Islamiyah (Islamic State). *See* Islamic State
defection, 10, 35, 43
Dhuluiya (subdistrict), 72
dignity, 179; questioning daily life before IS
disobedience, (as resistance repertoire), 4, 36, 60, 130
diwans, creation of under IS, 58–62, 131, 157
Diyala: IDP population of, 117, 143; liberation of, 67; resistance against IS, 124; protests against central government, 109–110; war in, 55–56, 63, 66, 70, 75, 141
Dahuk: 140, 168; IDP population of, 144–45
Dwek Nawsha, 152

economy: and political reform, 49; economic insecurity, 29, 46, 48, 54–55, 78, 99, 169; development, 14, 15, 18, 43, 160–161, 168; Iraqi public opinion on, 103, 134, 159; service provision, 23, 27; stagnation (lack of economic growth), 74, 80, 100; socioeconomic status, 41, 44, 83, 164
education: 6, 15; lack of educational opportunities, 53, 98, 120, 132, 134, 140; system under IS, 59–62; of survey respondents, 84–85, 184, 187–188, 194, 196, 198, 201–203
elections, 49–53, 74, 78, 86–87, 109, 111, 141, 170, 178
Erbil: 3, 175; fieldwork in, 15, 201–203; IDP population of, 116–117, 136–37, 140–141, 144–145; relationship with central government, 150, 153, 158, 167; resistance against IS, 66
ethnoreligious minorities, 2, 17, 39, 78, 136–137, 142–144, 148, 153–55, 166, 206

everyday resistance: as a survival repertoire, 6, 18, 31–35, 40, 46, 178; in Anbar governorate, 121–122, 125, 128, 130; in Ninewa governorate, 149, 164–166; past research on, 5. *See also* survival repertoires
extremism, (as motivation for collaborating with IS), 63, 156
Êzîdi Freedom and Democracy Party (PADE), 152
Êzîdihan Protection Units (HPE), 150, 152

Fahadawi, Mohammed Mahmoud Latif al-, 124
Fahadawi, Rafi al-, 124
Fallujah: 12, 15, 17, 54, 166, 171, 173; collaboration with IS, 129–133; fieldwork in, 201–203; IDP population of, 144–145, 114–120; IS occupation of; 76, 79; liberation of, 76, 79; protests against central government, 107, 109; public opinion in, 106–107; resistance against IS, 123–125; survival repertoires of local residents, 121–134; war in, 55, 63–67, 109–113
families: 24, 43, 69; displacement of, 146, 148; of IS victims, 70, 116, 118, 120, 131, 150, 157; and prominent elites, 98
Faraji, Sheikh Abdullah Jallal Mukhlif al-, 124
Fatah Alliance, 78, 169, 237
fatwa (religious edict), 62
Federal Police (Iraq): civilian informing to, 121; civilian support for, 169; deployed for political repression, 53, 110; Iraqi public opinion on, 76, 87–88, 94–95, 110, 127, 184, 197, 198, 200; local collaboration with, 121, 124; participation in anti-IS coalition, 55, 62–64, 66–67, 69, 143, 168–169; role in the liberation of Mosul, 67, 69, 143; retreat of, 1; support from foreign

coalition members, 113; Sunni confidence in, 127, 168; victimizing civilians, 53, 113. *See also* Iraqi Security Forces
forced marriage, 2, 18, 42, 43, 45, 119, 129–130, 137, 158, 171
France: 214; Iraqi public opinion on, 94–95, 184, 198

gender: and gender roles, 32; and public opinion, 84–86, 187; and survival repertoires, 6, 15, 21, 23–24, 26, 31–32, 60, 164, 172; and wartime victimization, 153, 172–173
genocide, 153, 155, 212, 235, 257, 261; of Yazidi communities in Sinjar governorate, 63–64
Ghazaliya (Baghdad subdistrict), 78
Golani, Abu Muhammad al-, 53
Golden Division. *See* Iraqi Counter-Terrorism Service (CTS)
Grand Mosque of al-Nuri. *See* Al-Nuri, Grand Mosque of
Gulf War (1990–91), 13, 63

hadd/hudud (form of corporal punishment), 58, 60
Hakari, Romeo, 151–152
Hama, 22, 45, 176
Hamdaniya: 136, 171; collaboration with IS, 158–159; IDP population of, 140, 144–145; IS occupation of, 138; liberation of, 147, 151; resistance against IS, 150; survival repertoires of local residents, 153; war in, 138–143
Hamrin Mountains, 70, 124, 168
Hardan, Sheikh Ibrahim Nayef Mshhan al-, 124
Hatra, 139; IDP arrival and resettlement in, 145, 148
Hawija: 139; survival repertoires of local residents, 120; war in, 54, 69, 110
health services, 53, 59, 70, 117, 120, 171

"hearts and minds," winning of, 22, 56, 111. *See also* population-centric counterinsurgency warfare (COIN)
Heiss, Hamid Farhan al-, 124
heuristic: 87, 90, 91, 98, 123, 126, 127, 136, 150, 211, 252; and influencing survival repertoires, 25–28; limits of, 30, 160
hiding: 2, 4–6; as a survival repertoire, 31, 37–39, 46, 125, 127–128, 153, 165
Hezbollah: operations in Iraq, 62–64, 99, 117, 239, 257; war against Israel, 22, 36
hisbah (religious police), 56, 59–60, 126
Hit: IDP population of, 115–117, 144–145; resistance against IS, 124, 128; war in, 63, 66, 112 "home-team discount" (public support during insurgency), 29. *See also* counterinsurgency
Homs, 176
human trafficking, 42, 60–61, 159, 215
Hussein, Saddam, 13, 48–50, 78, 140, 158

ideology, 25; of IS, 57, 61, 133, 156–159
IIACSS. *See* Independent Institute for Administration and Civil Society Studies (IIACSS)
Independent Institute for Administration and Civil Society Studies (IIACSS), 14–15, 209
in-group identity, 4, 11–12, 27, 43, 45, 140
in-group favoritism, 12, 95, 182
insurgency: and building public support, 22, 29; and internal displacement, 144; and resistance against insurgents, 17; and urban warfare, 66; civilian survival in, 70, 76, 79; evolution of, 49, 56, 112; in Ethiopia, 22; in Iraq, 48, 53, 69, 114; in Yemen, 45; inadvertent killing of civilians; resistance against, 131, 141; studies of, 12
internally displaced persons (IDPs), 6, 16; in Baghdad, 78–82; in Ninewa, 143–148; in the Sunni Triangle, 113–20; resulting from the IS insurgency, 20

innuendo, 33, 120, 171
International Stabilization and Assistance Force (ISAF), 29, 213
interviews, 45, 109, 137, 159, 175, 190; design of, 13–16, 84, 186, 201–203; ethics of, 13–14
Iran: in survey experiment vignettes, 183–186, 191–193, 197–198, 200; involvement in anti-IS coalition, 12, 62, 63, 64, 73, 99, 125; Islamic Revolutionary Guard Corps (IRGC), 99; Iraqi public opinion on, 12, 73, 89–90, 92, 93, 95, 99, 103, 125, 167–168; participation in anti-IS coalition, 12, 62, 63, 64, 73, 99, 125; relations with Iraqi central government, 78, 99, 100; role of, and proxies in Iraq, 22, 39, 62, 63, 64, 99; support for Assad regime in Syria, 23
Iraq: analysis of public opinion, 101; attitudes toward politics, 50, 51, 54, 73, 74, 76, 78, 86, 99, 100–102, 104, 158, 169, 170; attitudes towards stability of, 51–52; capacity of Iraqi Security Forces (ISF), 55, 56, 79, 146; dealing with legacy of IS, 116, 120, 126, 134, 156, 170–172; distrust in the military, 3, 17, 64, 78, 88, 98, 99, 107, 125, 151, 159, 168, 169, 172, 173; future of IS in, 70, 168; human rights in, 172–174; internally displaced persons (IDPs), 79–82, 105, 114–120, 123, 137, 138, 144–148, 173; after the IS caliphate, 126; intra-Shi'a split, 51, 74, 86, 101; Iraqis on control over lives, 2, 4, 9, 12, 20, 34, 57, 60, 62, 109, 121–123, 125, 126, 128–130, 133, 147, 165, 166, 177; Iraqis on disbanding of armed forces, 78, 99; Iraqis on presence of coalition forces, 3, 11, 87–88, 90–99, 104, 125, 133, 137, 144, 151, 155, 159, 166, 167; IS and, 1–4, 7, 11–13, 15, 16, 34, 35, 48, 49, 53–70, 72–79, 81–83, 86, 88–91, 98–100, 102–109, 111–134, 135–138, 140–151, 153–163, 165–168, 170–178; judicial system, 51; new political state in, 2, 29, 49, 55–60, 62, 98, 107, 112, 126, 130, 156, 164, 166, 167, 178; Sunni views of Iraqi state, 4, 17, 53, 54, 73, 76, 78, 107; perceptions of the national economy in, 49, 55, 74, 78, 80, 100, 103–105, 134, 160, 169; political change after IS occupation, 150, 155; possibility of IS rising again in, 70, 168; pro-Iranian forces in politics, 62–63, 78, 169; purge of Sunni politicians, 49, 51, 53–54, 74, 107, 109, 111, 132, 141; regional context of IS, 1–3, 7, 11, 12, 15, 34, 35, 53–70, 72–79, 81–83, 86, 88–91, 98–100, 102–109, 111–134, 135–138, 140–151, 153–163, 165–66, 168, 170–73, 175–78; role of Iran in, 12, 62–64, 73, 99, 125, 167–168; society of post-IS, 116, 120, 126, 134, 156, 170–172; Sunni-Kurdish relations in, 54, 109, 116, 138; survey data, 14, 17, 51, 73, 78, 84, 86, 88, 89, 91–94, 96, 97, 102–104, 170–172; Tishreen (October) protest movement, 166, 168, 170, 173; addressing the trauma of IS, 81–82, 116, 119, 120, 144, 146, 147, 148, 160, 161, 163, 172, 175; U.S. invasion of, 11, 13, 17, 46, 48, 49, 99, 109, 159, 168; U.S. war in, 11, 13, 46, 48, 49, 52, 62, 99, 109, 121, 125, 168; views of Iraqis, 2–4, 9, 11, 12, 17, 20, 34, 49, 50–55, 57, 60, 62, 64, 73, 74, 76, 78, 80, 86–88, 91, 92, 94–96, 98–105, 107, 109, 121–123, 125, 126, 128–130, 133, 134, 137, 144, 147, 151, 155, 158–160, 165–170, 172, 173, 177
Iraqi Army: and internal competition within the anti-IS coalition, 69; civilian collaboration with, 121, 124; civilian informing to, 122–123; civilian neutrality toward, 126, 135; collaboration with local militias and

self-defense groups, 124, 128, 152; confronting IS insurgents, 68; deployed to engage in political repression, 53, 54; engaged in coup proofing, 74; Iraqi public opinion on, 76, 87–88, 94–95, 109, 110, 127; participation in anti-IS coalition, 55, 62–64, 66–67, 69, 112, 113, 118, 143, 149, 168–69; retreat of, 1, 72, 126, 135; Sunni confidence in, 107, 118, 168; victimizing civilians, 53, 107, 110–111, 113. *See also* Iraqi Security Forces

Iraq Body Count (IBC), 16, 52, 84, 112, 142, 188, 226

Iraqi Federal Police. *See* Federal Police (Iraq)

Iraqi Commission for Human Rights, 173

Iraqi Security Forces (ISF): Iraqi public opinion on, 76, 87–88, 94–95, 110, 127; local collaboration with, 121, 124; participation in anti-IS coalition, 55, 62–64, 66–67, 69, 143, 168–169; victimizing civilians, 53, 113. *See also* Iraqi Army; Federal Police (Iraq)

Iraqiyya Coalition, 51

IRGC. *See* Iranian Islamic Revolutionary Guard Corps (IGRC)

IS. *See* Islamic State (IS)

Islamic State in Iraq (ISI). *See* Islamic State (IS)

Islamic State in Iraq and al-Sham (ISIS). *See* Islamic State (IS)

Islamic State: accountability for participating in, 11, 156, 160; Baghdadi and, 53, 56, 131, 141, 163; Breaking the Walls campaign, 54, 111; beliefs of, 57, 59–60; caliphate establishment, 56, 62, 141, 163; collaboration with, 4, 11, 111, 129–130; data on civilian life under, 4, 12; dealing with legacy of, 69; education, 59, 62, 158; forced marriage practices, 2, 18, 42, 43, 45, 119, 130, 138, 172; governance in Iraq, 3, 4, 56, 57, 59–61; health services, 59, 117; human trafficking of girls and women, 60, 61, 159; ideological affinity with insurgents, 2, 55, 132–133, 156, 159; judicial governance, 60; leadership of, 59; life in Mosul under, 2, 9, 12, 34, 56, 68–69, 138, 144, 147, 149, 157, 163, 174; losing support of Sunni communities, 124, 156, 159; management of oil and gas revenue, 57, 58; map of activity, 65; participation in, 106, 129, 131, 156–157, 160; participation in sexual and gender-based violence, 24, 60, 61, 159, 165; police force, 56, 58–60; likelihood of reemergence in Iraq, 168; public services, 1, 59, 71, 130, 157; radicalization by ideology, 62, 157; rape of Iraqi civilians, 60, 61, 164; resistance to, 2–4, 9, 12, 16, 18, 54, 73, 77, 86, 105, 109, 113, 121–125, 127, 128, 137, 148–152, 154, 163–166, 202; rise of, 1, 2, 13, 16, 46–48, 53, 55, 56, 74, 76, 86, 89, 91, 103, 105, 107, 163, 165; security as motivation to join, 61, 131, 156; status or prestige as motivation to join, 129–130, 132, 157; size and composition of, 55; structure of, 56, 58–62; suicide bombing, 54, 68, 73, 75, 77, 111; Syria and, 7, 53, 57, 59, 70, 142, 174; service provision, 1, 58–59, 61, 82, 99, 100, 130, 157

Israel, 36, 39, 44–45, 103

Issawi, Rafi al-, 53, 54, 107, 111

Jabhat an-Nusrah (Victory Front), 53

Jabbara, Sheikh Jasim, 124

Jabbouri, Ashem Sabhan al-, 124

Jabbouri, Major Sattam al-, 124

Jabbouri, Yazan al-, 124

Jabbouri, Abu Abir al-, 124

Jaysh al-Mahdi (Mahdi Army), 98

Jaysh Rijal at-Tariqa an-Naqshabandiyah (Army of the Men of the Naqshbandi Order) (JRTN), 113
Jesus, 162
jizyah (tax), 60
Jordan, 44; in survey experiment vignettes, 183–85, 191–93, 197–98, 200; Iraqi public opinion on, 89–91, 169
judiciary (IS), 58, 60, 149
judiciary (Iraq), 51, 60

Kakaʿi, 136, 138, 140
Kadhamiya (Baghdad district), 72, 75, 77–80, 82, 91, 227
Kaoud, Sheikh Ghazi al-, 124
Kaoud, Sheikh Jalal al-, 124
Kaoud, Sheikh Naim al-, 124, 128
Karkh (Baghdad district), 79, 80, 82
Karrada (Baghdad district), 41, 76–78
Kataʾib Hezbollah (Hezbollah Battalions), 62–64, 99, 117, 239, 257
Kadhimi, Mustafa al-, 72, 170
Kafala system, 61
Khadra (Baghdad subdistrict), 78
Khali, Ali, 152
khalifa. *See* caliphate
Khamro, Safaa, 152
Khedar, Khiary, 152
kidnapping, 151, 223, 233, 247
Kildani, Rayan al-, 151–152
Kindi (Baghdad subdistrict), 78
Kirkuk: 2, 54, 168–170; IDP population of, 144–45, 114–120; liberation of, 76, 79; public opinion in, 106–107, 170–71; war in, 55, 63–67, 69–70, 109–113
kuffar (unbelievers), 59
Kurdification, 137, 141, 151
Kurdistan Democratic Party (KDP), 136, 150–153, 158, 164
Kurds: and the Anfal campaign, 140; demographics of, 18, 138, 147, 158; displacement of, 78, 144; engaging in separatism, 168; interviews with, 15, 170, 171, 201–203; Iraqi public opinion on, 88, 95, 111, 206n8; Maliki and the, 54, 74; opposition forces in Syria, 22; participation in anti-IS coalition, 7, 62–65, 67, 69, 70, 73, 146, 150; protesting the central government, 109; resistance against IS, 172; suicide terrorism against the, 141; survival repertoires of, 4, 39, 98, 155, 167. *See also* Kurdistan Region (KRI); Kurdistan Regional Government (KRG); Peshmerga; sects (Sunnis, Shiʿa, Kurds)

Lalish Battalion, 152, 154
Lebanon, 44, 83, 169, 170, 208, 216, 257; civil war in, 36
Libya, 22, 63
life under IS: charity, 61, 131, 157; data for studying, 130, 149, 159–60; education, 61–62; employment for local residents, 43, 46, 61, 130, 159; health services, 59; judiciary, 60; law enforcement, 58–59; loyalty oath (*bayʿah*), 58, 61; management of oil and gas revenue, 58–59; marriage to IS fighters, 129–130; religious observance, 60–62; religious police (*hisbah*), 59–60, 126; revenue generation, 57–58; security provision, 60, 68; sexual and gender-based violence, 24, 60, 61, 159, 165; taxation, 58; welfare provision, 51, 59. *See also* Islamic State; Mosul

Madhi Army. *See* Jaysh al-Mahdi
Mahalawi, Sheikh Sabah al-, 124
Mahmoudiya (Baghdad district), 79, 81–82
Maliki, Nouri al-, 2, 56–57, 72, 107, 158; and Abadi succession, 74; and authoritarian tendencies, 16, 49, 56,

75, 165; and electoral competition, 74, 86–87, 100–101; and protests against, 54, 109–111; and purge of Sunni politicians, 50–53, 107–109, 127, 132, 141; and leadership of State of Law Coalition, 51, 74, 86, 158. *See also* State of Law Coalition (I'tilaf Dawlat al-Qanun)
Mamendo, Sarkis Aghajan, 151–152
Mandaean (Sabian), 136, 138
Mansour (Baghdad district), 188
mazlumiyya (alienation), 54, 109
medicine, availability under IS, 6, 37, 61, 68
mental health, of IS victims, 11, 171
migration: and access to safe transit routes, 23, 117; as a survival repertoire, 23; trends across Iraq, 137–138; versus forced displacement, 137
military trainers: Iraqi public opinion on, 93–97, 184–185, 194–195, 197, 200
Mosul: battle for, 67–69, 143, 163; concern about reemergence of IS; control of, 1, 55, 67, 141; cost of liberating, 69, 143, 176; education in former IS areas, 153; factors for Moslawis to join IS, 147, 157–158; fall of, 1, 55, 72, 75, 136, 141, 147, 163; life better or worse in, 137, 147, 156, 157; life under IS in, 137, 147, 156, 157; mix of state and non-state forces, 67, 150; Moslawis on IS control, 147, 149; pace of reconstruction, 163; protests and violence, 54, 110, 111; protests in, 54, 110, 111; public services in, 1, 142, 171; resistance to IS, 9, 34, 35, 124, 149, 150; security of neighborhoods, 150; self-defense groups in, 3, 150–151; state of health care in post-IS areas; sustenance issues of residents, 68, 150, 157
Moslawi (Mosul resident), 3, 34, 55, 138, 147, 149, 150, 153, 156–58, 163

Mosul University, 203
Muhammad, Tariq Yusef, 124
munafiq (hypocrite), 33
Muqdadiya, 62, 124
murtadun (apostates), 2, 59
mushrikun (polytheists), 2, 59, 205

narrative, 13, 28, 48, 206
national identity, 4, 5, 11, 14, 20, 27, 80, 88, 90, 92, 187
nationalism, 12, 187, 208, 214, 218, 220; Iraqi sense of, 167
Najjar, Said Yilmaz an-, 152
nepotism (within Iraqi government), 51, 55, 60
neutrality, 3, 4, 6, 7, 9, 10, 16, 17, 166, 168, 178; as a general survival repertoire, 21, 27, 30–31, 36–41; as a survival repertoire in Baghdad, 98–100; as a survival repertoire in Anbar, 125–128; as a survival repertoire in Ninewa, 153–155
nifaq (hypocrisy), 33
Ninewa Governorate, 15, 32, 136–137, 172; cooperation with IS, 155–161; displacement of local residents, 143–148; IS occupation of, 138; neutral survival repertoires, 153–155; resistance to IS, 148–153; liberation of, 67; war in, 60–70
Ninewa Plains Forces (NPF), 150, 152
Ninewa Plains Guard Forces, 152
Ninewa Plains Protection Units (NPU), 151, 152

Obama, Barack, 52
Odisho, Yousef, 151, 152
oil, 4, 11, 169, 170, 222, 232; as a revenue source for IS, 57–58
Operation Inherent Resolve (OIR), 63, 225
ostracism, 24, 119, 120, 160, 164, 172
Ottoman Empire, 136, 162

Palestine, 22, 36, 39, 44, 45; British mandate in, 44
Peace Companies. *See* Saraya al-Salam (Peace Companies)
People's Defense Forces (Hêzên Parastina Gel); 66, 140
Peshmerga (Kurdish paramilitaries): Iraqi public opinion on, 76, 87–88, 94–95, 110, 127; local collaboration with, 121, 124; participation in anti-IS coalition, 55, 62–64, 66–67, 69, 143, 168–169; victimizing civilians, 53, 113. *See also* Kurds
police: 39, 40, 48, 77, 126, 127; civilian victimization, 29, 35; location collaboration with, 124; corruption, 49; enlisting in, 33; fleeing from IS, 1, 121; in Anbar, 109; in Baghdad, 83, 86, 87, 99; in the Kurdistan Region, 151; Iraqi public opinion on, 87–88, 94, 95; life under IS, 55, 58–60; participation in anti-IS coalition, 62–67, 76. *See also* Federal Police (Iraq); *shurta*
Popular Mobilization Forces (PMF): accusations of human rights violations against Iraqi civilians, 172–173; clashes with other anti-IS coalition members, 113, 136, 168–169; criticism from Muqtada al-Sadr, 99–100; interviews with, 201–203; Iraqi public opinion on, 87–88, 94–95, 133, 184–185; mobilization of local units, 62, 166; civilian motivation for joining, 123–125, 150–152; participation in anti-IS coalition, 63–67, 72, 75–78, 86, 113, 142, 152–154; political pressure to disarm, demobilize, or reintegrate PMF units, 169–170; support from Iran, 64, 100, 167–168. *See also* Iraqi Security Forces; pro-government militias; self-defense groups

population-centric counterinsurgency warfare (COIN), 16, 165
pro-government militias, 73, 9, 23, 33, 36, 39, 62, 73, 117, 178, 202
protest, 166; and the 2019 Tishreen Movement, 168, 170, 173; against Iraqi central government, 166; as a survival repertoire, 33, 34; during the Arab uprisings in Iraq, 51–54; in Baghdad, 73, 76, 99–101, 107; in the Syrian civil war, 40; in the West Bank, 36; of Sunnis in Anbar governorate, 109–111, 127, 132. *See also* contention; resistance; survival repertoires
public opinion, 101, 105; in Baghdad, 82–86
public support: 10, 22; and cosectarian bias, 90; for foreign interveners, 91; for opposition forces, 132, 178; for the anti-IS coalition, 86, 98; for the Iraqi central government, 75; for the Iraqi Security Forces, 95; for the Popular Mobilization Forces, 87; for the Sunni tribes, 88; for the United States, 89; past research on, 29

Qatar, 22, 59
Qurʿan, 33–34, 42, 60

radicalization, 44–45
rafidun (refusers), 2, 59
Ramadi: 12, 15, 17, 171; collaboration with IS, 129–134, 174; fieldwork in, 201–203; IDP population of, 79–80, 114–120, 144–145; IS occupation of, 64–66; liberation of, 76, 79; protests against central government; public opinion in, 106–107; resistance against IS, 121–125; survival repertoires of local residents, 105, 166; war in, 54–55, 63–67, 109–113
rape, 42, 60–61, 164
Rashid (Baghdad district), 77, 188

Rawah, 69
reconstruction, 18, 137, 160, 163, 168, 171, 238
referendum (Kurdish independence vote), 69
relative deprivation theory, 4, 164
religious beliefs, IS fighters, 43, 59–61, 133, 157
reputation: as a predictor of survival repertoires, 5, 11, 19, 27–29, 156, 164, 168; of foreign interveners, 98; of Nouri al-Maliki, 100
resistance: 2–7, 163–166, 178; as survival repertoire, 23, 31–37, 40, 46; as a survival repertoire in Baghdad, 77, 86, 99, 100; as a survival repertoire in Sunni Triangle, 54, 56, 60, 109, 113, 121–130; as a survival repertoire in Ninewa, 136, 141, 148–52; past research on, 9–12, 44. *See also* contention; survival repertoires
Revolution Brigades. *See* 1920 Revolution Brigades
Rusafa (Baghdad district), 77, 79–80, 188, 227
Russia, 63, 89–94, 98, 174; in survey experiment vignettes, 183–185, 191–193, 197–198, 200; support for Assad regime in Syria, 176

sabotage, 33, 35, 122, 123
Saddamism, 13, 48
Sadr City, 72, 75, 77, 79, 80, 82, 91, 188, 227
Sadr, Muqtada al-, 51, 62–63, 72, 75–76, 86, 91, 98–100
Sadrain Square (Baghdad), 72
Safavid Empire, 162
sahwa (awakening). *See* Anbar Awakening (*sahwa*)
Salafism, 206
Salah al-Din: collaboration with IS; IDP population in, 114–119, 143–144; interviews in, 15, 201–203; liberation of, 113; occupation by IS, 11, 141; protests in, 105, 110; war in, 7, 55–56, 63–64, 66–67, 69–70, 75, 133, 140. *See also* Sunni Triangle
Samarra: IDP population in, 115, 119; protests in, 72, 109, 110; war in, 76, 79
Saqlawiya, 173
Saraya al Salam (Peace Companies), 61, 73, 98–99, 100, 149
Saudi Arabia, 63, 89–94; in survey experiment vignettes, 183–185, 191–193, 197–198, 200
secessionism, 38–39, 215
sects (Sunnis, Shiʿa, Kurds): and co-sectarian bias, 4, 27, 43, 45; and resistance against IS, 4, 11, 72, 75, 127, 137, 152; and social identity, 10, 27, 98, 126, 156–57, 160; and sectarianism, 2–4, 48; and self-defense groups, 3–4, 39–40, 136, 142, 150–154, 166; on being Iraqi as primary identity, 172; on confidence in central government, 86, 102, 104; on corruption of Iraqi government, 48, 102, 103; on distrust in the Iraqi Security Forces, 87–88, 94–95, 97; on economic situation in Iraq, 103–105; on fair treatment, 4, 49, 78; on favorable view of the Popular Mobilization Forces, 78, 87–88, 94–95, 150; on feeling discriminated against, 4, 49, 78; on government treatment of all groups in Iraq, 4, 49, 78; on Iranian involvement in Iraq, 12, 89, 95, 125; on not feeling safe in neighborhood, 159; on presence of coalition forces in Iraq, 87–88, 90, 93–95, 97, 168; on security in neighborhood, 88, 98, 150; on support for Islamic government, 2, 11, 75–76; on support for protests, 52, 76, 101, 105; survival repertoires of, 11, 12, 73, 98, 99, 105, 121, 126, 133, 156. *See also* sectarianism; coethnic bias; in-group favoritism

sectarianism, 2–4, 48. *See also* sects (Sunnis, Shiʿa, Kurds)
security: after IS occupation, 168–169, 170, 171, 177; apparatus of the Iraqi central government, 17, 51–52, 74–75, 86, 100, 121; assistance to anti-IS coalition members, 22, 142; as motivation for collaborating with IS, 165; as motivation for survival repertoires, 17, 27, 40, 126, 156, 168; basic need of Iraqi civilians, 2, 10, 13; checkpoints, 114, 117–118, 123, 136, 144, 146; erosion of, 1, 72, 126, 135; future research on, 177; increase in, 53, 98; in the occupied, Palestinian territories, 36; in Ninewa governorate, 135, 137, 140; in the Sunni Triangle, 113, 115, 117, 121–123, 125, 132–134; provision by anti-IS coalition members, 64, 67, 83, 121–123, 151; public opinion on, 87–91, 94–95, 97, 102–105; under IS, 57–60, 63; U.S. occupation of Iraq, 48, 56; within IDP camps, 80
separatism, 38, 39, 45, 140, 143
Shabaks: collaboration with IS, 11, 137–138, 158–160, 166; displacement of, 144, 147, 172; liberation of, 67; Participation in anti-IS coalition, 150–152; persecution by IS, 2; resistance against IS, 3, 150–152
shabbiha (ghosts), 23
shariʿa (Islamic law), 58–59, 118, 121, 167, 213
Shaqala, 116
Shekhan (Ninewa district), 138, 140, 145, 148
Shesho, Qasim and Haydar, 150, 152
Shiʿa: and intercommunal violence, 111, 113, 141, 159; and life in Baghdad, 48, 72, 83; and mobilization of the Popular Mobilization forces, 3; and threat of suicide terrorism in Baghdad, 75–77; autonomy of, 88–89; confidence in Iraqi Security Forces, 11; displacement of, 78–79, 144, 147; interviews with, 201–203; intragroup relations, 111; on belief in Iran as reliable partner, 12, 168; opposition to Iraqi cooperation with U.S. government, 52; participation in the anti-IS coalition, 62; protesting the central government, 74; relationship to the Maliki regime, 49–51, 74; resisting U.S. occupation, 17, 41, 150, 168; support for Muqtada al-Sadr, 62, 73, 77, 98, 100; support for the central government, 4, 103; support for the Popular Mobilization Forces, 125, 167; survival repertoires of, 73, 104–105; views on politics, 84, 86–87, 90–91, 94–95, 98; survival repertoires of, 153, 155; under IS control, 2, 58–59, 173. *See also* sects (Sunnis, Shiʿa, Kurds)
shurta (non-religious police under IS control), 58, 60
Sinjar: basic needs of local residents, 171–172; demographics of, 15; displacement of local communities, 141, 145–148; interviews with local residents, 151, 201–203; IS genocide of Yazidi residents, 44, 63–65, 142–144, 176; operation of local resistance units, 3, 135, 166; liberation of, 66, 171; resistance to IS, 136–137, 152; survival repertoires of local residents, 135, 153–155; war in, 138–140
Sinjar Resistance Units (YBS), 137, 140, 154
Sistani, Ali al- (Grand Ayatollah), 60, 62
smuggling, 23, 33, 42, 57, 117, 147
socialization, 9, 20, 25, 77
social cohesion, 41, 119–120, 125, 134, 155, 160, 172
social identity: 3, 12, 44–145, 48, 160; as an influence on survival repertoires, 21, 26–28, 87–88, 98, 121, 126, 128, 155–158; research on, 10–12, 164, 167

INDEX   283

social networks, 9, 22–26, 140
Sons of Iraq (Abnaʾ al-ʿIraq): interview with, 17, 201–203; participation in anti-IS coalition, 72; repression by Maliki regime, 17, 49, 54, 111, 113, 127; protection of Sunni communities in Anbar governorate; resistance against IS, 54, 66, 127. *See also* Anbar Awakening (*sahwa*)
spying, 33, 42
State of Law Coalition (Iʾtilaf Dawlat al-Qanun), 51, 74, 86, 158
stigmatism, 24, 81, 120, 160
stipend, as motivation for joining IS, 43, 56, 61, 130, 157–159
Sudan, 22, 34–35, 216, 253
suicide (as survival repertoire), 33
suicide bombing, 54, 68, 70, 72, 73–79, 86, 111, 141, 168
Sumaidaʿie, Mahdi al-, 124, 229
Sunni insurgency, 141
Sunni Triangle: 7, 32; displacement in, 113–116, 120; geography of, 107–109; residents collaborating with IS, 118; residents resisting IS, 119, 125, 142; war in, 112–113
Sunni: accusations of IS support, 64; and formation of tribal militias, 66, 172; and intercommunal violence, 113; autonomy of, 125–128; cooperation with IS, 11, 64, 129–130, 132, 155–160; description of in-group attachments, 98, 147; discrimination against, 171; displacement of, 79, 80–81, 105, 115–117, 119–120, 144; communities in the Sunni Triangle, 7, 17, 142, 166; fear of insurgents, 133; in Syria, 43; interviews with, 201–203; intragroup relations, 12, 73, 88, 137; on threat of Popular Mobilization Units, 173; participation in the anti-IS coalition, 124; protesting the central government, 109–111; and exclusion or repression by the central government, 4, 49, 51, 53, 74, 107, 111, 141; resisting U.S. occupation, 11, 168; resistance to IS, 7, 34, 105, 121, 124–125; role in the Anbar Awakening, 37; support for IS, 2, 17, 54, 61, 114, 129–130, 132, 159; survival repertoires of, 73, 98, 166; under IS control, 55–56, 59, 72, 75, 106–109, 112–113, 118, 138, 141, 149, 177; views on politics, 73, 76, 78, 80–85, 87–91, 94–95, 98, 133. *See also* sects (Sunnis, Shiʿa, Kurds); sectarianism
Sunni Endowment Diwan, 124
surge (troops), 48–49, 72, 78, 93, 121, 124, 141
survival repertoires, 4, 6–7, 15, 16, 26, 30–34, 178; definition of, 5, 20–21; evolution of, 46, 163; in Baghdad, 72–73, 77, 105, 136–137; in Ninewa, 151, 156; research on, 11–13, 163–166
Syria, 1, 7, 56, 63, 70, 138, 140, 176; and the Assad regime, 22, 51, 67–68, 81, 89, 176; civil war in, 22, 35, 39–40, 43; IS occupation of, 34, 53, 57, 59, 141, 149, 154, 174; Russian intervention in, 98

Tal Afar: collaboration with IS, 159–160; IDP population in, 141–144, 147–148; resistance to IS, 152, 156; post-IS governance, 171, 173; survival repertoires of local residents, 137, 153, 166; war in, 138–140, 171
Tal Kaif (Ninewa subdistrict), 138, 140, 148
Taliban, 29, 39, 41, 167, 214
Tarmiya (Baghdad district), 72, 79–82
territorial control, 4, 8, 10, 12, 20, 54, 79, 113, 137, 140, 167, 178
terrorism: as IS tactic, 8, 17, 70, 72–78, 86, 98, 165; past research on, 9–11

Tikrit: collaboration with IS, 129–134, 174; fieldwork in, 201–203; IDP population of, 79–80, 144–145, 114–120; IS occupation of, 64–66; liberation of, 76, 79; protests against central government; public opinion in, 106–107; resistance against IS, 121–125; survival repertoires of local residents, 105, 166; war in, 54–55, 63–67, 109–113

Tishreen (October) protests, Iraq, 166–170, 173

threat perception, 9, 10, 25–27, 105

totalitarianism (IS governance), 4

transitional justice, 160, 172, 174–175

Tribal Mobilization Force (al-Hashd al-ʿAshaʾiri), 113, 132

troop surge. *See* surge (troops)

"true believer," 164

Turkey, 22, 39, 63, 138–140, 144, 183–185; Iraqi public opinion on, 89–92, 94, 95; in survey experiment vignettes, 183–85, 191–193, 197–198, 200; participation in the anti-IS coalition, 143, 154; relations with Iraqi central government, 168

Turkmen, 2, 136–138, 173; collaboration with IS, 11, 155–161; displacement of, 144, 147; participation in anti-IS coalition, 152; resistance against IS, 3, 141, 150; survival repertoires of, 166

Turkmen Brigades, 152

unfair governance (as motivation form joining IS), 129, 151

Ukraine, 174, 176

Upper Zab River, 136

United Arab Emirates (UAE), 22, 90

United Kingdom, 95, 184, 197–198

United Nations, 8, 13, 90, 108, 139, 182–183

United States: airstrikes degrading IS, 66, 142, 176; blamed for escalating violence, 103; and de-escalation from Iraq in 2009–2010, 165; and *ex gratia* payments to war victims, 177; and formation of the anti-IS coalition, 63; and NGO advocacy in Iraq, 175; and relations with Nouri al-Maliki, 49, 52, 103; and security assistance to the Peshmerga, 176; and security assistance to the Iraqi Security Forces, 113, 168; and the Syrian civil war, 176; and 2003 intervention in Iraq, 11, 13, 17, 46, 48, 56, 62, 99, 109, 121, 125, 159; and 2007–2008 troop surge, 48, 49, 78; counterinsurgency strategy of, 16; Iraqi public opinion on, 89, 93, 95, 100, 102–104; withdrawal from Iraq, 16, 53, 74, 107, 109, 144, 165, 168

vandalism, 33, 35

vehicle-borne improvised explosive device (VBIED) attacks, 75

Victory Alliance coalition, 86

vigilantism, 33, 35

women as payment, motivation for joining IS, 2, 18, 42, 130, 137

wasta (social influence), 136

White Helmets (Syria Civil Defense), 39

Yarmuk (Baghdad subdistrict), 78

Yazidis, 18, 136, 138, 140, 147; as victims of sexual and gender-based violence, 60, 159, 165; and relations with the KDP in Erbil, 153, 166; collaboration with anti-IS coalition, 63–65, 136; displacement of, 66, 142–147; genocide of, 63, 176; interviews with, 201–203; participation in anti-IS coalition, 172; persecution by IS, 2, 44, 59, 138, 144, 205n3; resistance against IS, 150–152, 154–155

Zafraniya (Baghdad district), 188

zakat (tithe), 42, 43, 58, 131, 157

Zarkawi, Abu Musab al-, 53–54

Zayuna (Baghdad subdistrict), 79

GPSR Authorized Representative: Easy Access System Europe, Mustamäe tee 50, 10621 Tallinn, Estonia, gpsr.requests@easproject.com